FireWire®
System
Architecture,

Second Edition

The PC System Architecture Series

MindShare, Inc.

Please see our web site (http://www.awprofessional.com/series/mindshare) for more information on these titles.

FireWire®
System Architecture,
Second Edition

IEEE 1394a
MindShare, Inc.

Don Anderson

ADDISON–WESLEY

Boston • San Francisco • New York • Toronto • Montreal
London • Munich • Paris • Madrid
Capetown • Sydney • Tokyo • Singapore • Mexico City

The publisher offers discounts on this book when ordered in quantity for special sales. For more information, please contact:

Pearson Education Corporate Sales Division
201 W. 103rd Street
Indianapolis, IN 46290
(800) 428-5331
corpsales@pearsoned.com

Visit AW on the Web: www.awprofessional.com

Library of Congress Cataloging-in-Publication Data

Anderson, Don, 1953-.
     FireWire systems architecture: IEEE 1394a / Mindshare, Inc.;
Don Anderson.–2nd ed.
  p. cm.
Includes bibliographical references and index.
ISBN 0-201-48535-4
1. IEEE 1394 (Standard) I. Mindshare, Inc. II. Title.
TK7895.B87 A52 1998
  621.39'81 —dc21   98-43465
                                                  CIP

ISBN: 0-201-48535-4

Sponsoring Editor: Karen Gettman
Production Coordinator: Jacquelyn Young
Set in 10 point Palatino by Mindshare, Inc.

Text printed on recycled and acid-free paper.
ISBN   0201485354
7 8 9 101112 MA   06 05 04 03

7th Printing   July 2003

For my sisters Debbie and DeAnn and my brothers Doug and David, and their families.

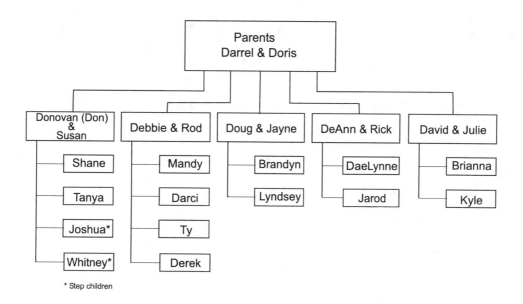

The PC System Architecture Series

The PC System Architecture Series is a crisply written and comprehensive set of guides to the most important PC hardware standards. Each title illustrates the relationship between the software and hardware, and thoroughly explains the architecture, features, and operation of systems built using one particular type of chip or hardware specification.

MindShare, Inc. is one of the leading technical training companies in the computer industry,

providing innovative courses for dozens of companies, including Intel, IBM, and Compaq.

> *"There is only one way to describe the series of PC hardware and architecture books written by Tom Shanley and Don Anderson: INVALUABLE."*
> —*PC Magazine*'s "Read Only" column

ISBN 0-201-40994-1

ISBN 0-201-70069-7

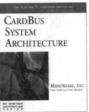

ISBN 0-201-40997-6

ISBN 0-201-40995-X

ISBN 0-201-48535-4

ISBN 0-201-40996-8

ISBN 0-201-30974-2

ISBN 0-201-72682-3

ISBN 0-201-40991-7

ISBN 0-201-30973-4

ISBN 0-201-40992-5

ISBN 0-201-41013-3

ISBN 0-201-40990-9

ISBN 0-201-55447-X

ISBN 0-201-30975-0

http://www.awl.com/cseng/series/mindshare/

✦ Addison-Wesley

Contents

About This Book

Contents

Part One
Introduction to FireWire
(IEEE 1394a)

Chapter 1: Why FireWire?

Chapter 2: Overview of the IEEE 1394 Architecture

Contents

Part Two
Serial Bus Communications

Chapter 3: Communications Model

Contents

Chapter 4: Communications Services

Contents

Chapter 5: Cables & Connectors

Chapter 6: The Electrical Interface

Contents

Chapter 7: Arbitration

Chapter 8: Asynchronous Packets

Contents

Contents

Contents

Contents

Chapter 15: Tree Identification

Chapter 16: Self Identification

Contents

Part Four
Serial Bus Management

Contents

Chapter 20: Bus Management Services

Part Five
Registers & ROM

Chapter 21: CSR Architecture

Contents

Chapter 22: PHY Registers

Chapter 23: Configuration ROM

Contents

Part Six
Power Management

Chapter 24: Introduction to Power Management

Chapter 25: Cable Power Distribution

Contents

Chapter 26: Suspend & Resume

Chapter 27: Power State Management

Contents

Figures

Figures

Figures

Figures

Figures

Figures

Tables

Tables

Tables

Acknowledgments

Thanks to the engineers at Compaq, Intel, and Jet Propulsion Laboratories who attended MindShare's FireWire pilot 1394 classes. Their suggestions and insight were invaluable.

Special thanks to the participants of the HP Ft. Collins class who found numerous errors and made very insightful suggestions and recommendations.

The technical reviews of this book have helped to make it a much better product than it otherwise would have been. Faced with deadlines and busy schedules of their own, the reviewers somehow found time to read the manuscript and provide many valuable corrections, clarifications, and comments. Special thanks to Lou Fasano of IBM microelectronics for reviewing portions of this book for technical accuracy on extremely short notice.

The Appendix: Example 1394 Chip Solutions, was written and supplied by Russell Crane of Texas Instruments.

Many suggestions and contributions were also made by Ravi Budruk, whose input has greatly improved the organization and flow of this book.

Finally, special thanks go to my daughter Tanya, who kept my other life in order while I was consumed by my book writing life.

About This Book

The MindShare Architecture Series

The MindShare Architecture book series includes: *ISA System Architecture, 80486 System Architecture, PCI System Architecture, Pentium System Architecture, PCM-CIA System Architecture, PowerPC System Architecture, Plug-and-Play System Architecture, CardBus System Architecture, Protected Mode Software Architecture, Pentium Pro and Pentium II System Architecture, USB System Architecture, FireWire (IEEE 1394) System Architecture, and AGP System Architecture.* The book series is published by Addison-Wesley.

Rather than duplicating common information in each book, the series uses the building-block approach. *ISA System Architecture* is the core book upon which the others build. The figure below illustrates the relationship of the books to each other.

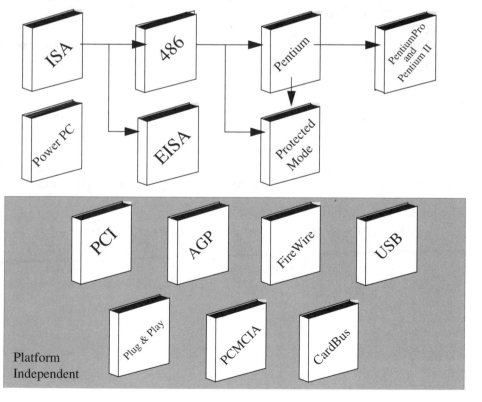

Cautionary Note

The reader should keep in mind that MindShare's book series often deals with rapidly-evolving technologies. With IEEE 1394, this is particularly true. This book is based in part on several incomplete specifications. This being the case, it should be recognized that the book is a "snapshot" of the state of 1394 technology at the time that the book was completed. We attempt to update each book on a timely basis to reflect changes in the targeted technology, but, due to various factors (waiting for the next version of the specification to be "frozen," the time necessary to make the changes, and the time to produce the books and get them out through the distribution channels), there will always be a delay.

Please check our web site for additions and errata on this and other MindShare books. As specifications and technologies change MindShare maintains errata, clarifications, and additions to the books to ensure that the reader has a way of keeping updated on recent developments (www.mindshare.com).

Organization of This Book

The book is divided into six parts and an appendix. Each part contains the chapters listed below and a brief description of the contents of each chapter.

Part One: Introduction to FireWire (IEEE 1394)

Chapter 1: Why FireWire?
This chapter describes background information regarding the development of the FireWire specification (1394-1995 and the 1394a Supplement) and discusses FireWire applications.

Chapter 2: Overview of the FireWire Architecture
This chapter describes the primary features of the FireWire serial bus implementation. The chapter also reviews the IEEE 1394 standards (IEEE 1394-1995 & IEEE 1394a) and IEEE ISO/IEC 13213 (ANSI/IEEE 1212) standard that the FireWire serial bus is based upon.

Part Two: Serial Bus Communications

Chapter 3: Communication Model

This chapter provides an overview of the serial bus communications model. It defines the basic transfer types and introduces the communication layers defined by the specification.

Chapter 4: Communications Services

This chapter describes the services defined by the specification that are used to pass parameters between layers during the execution of each transaction. The protocol layers and services for asynchronous and isochronous transactions are discussed. Asynchronous transactions exist in three forms: reads, writes, and locks, while isochronous transactions are performed only as writes.

Chapter 5: Cables & Connectors

This chapter discusses the cable characteristics and connectors used by the IEEE 1394 cable environment. It also mentions the Device Bay implementation being specified in PC environments.

Chapter 6: The Electrical Interface

This chapter details the serial bus signaling environment. This includes recognition of device attachment and removal, arbitration signaling, speed signaling, and data/strobe signaling.

Chapter 7: Arbitration

This chapter details the arbitration process. It defines the various types of arbitration including isochronous and asynchronous arbitration, as well as the newer arbitration types defined by the 1394a supplement.

Chapter 8: Asynchronous Packets

Asynchronous transactions exist in three basic forms: reads, writes, and locks. This chapter details the packets that are transmitted over the bus.

Chapter 9: Isochronous Packets

Isochronous transactions are scheduled so that they occur at 125µs intervals. This chapter discusses the format of the packet used during isochronous transactions.

Chapter 10: PHY Packet Format

This chapter discusses the various types of PHY packet. The role of each PHY packet is discussed, packet format is specified, and the fields within each packet are detailed.

Chapter 11: Link to PHY Interface

This chapter details the signaling interface between the link and PHY layer controller chips. The 1394a supplement makes this interface mandatory for implementations of separate PHY and link layer chips.

Chapter 12: Transaction Retry

This chapter discusses transaction retries that occur when the recipient of a packet is busy (e.g. has a buffer full condition). Two retry mechanisms are defined by the 1394 specification: single and dual phase. Each type of mechanism is discussed. Software may also initiate retries for transactions that fail.

Part Three: Serial Bus Configuration

Chapter 13: Configuration Process

This chapter overviews the configuration process comprising the initialization, tree ID, and self-ID phases. Once self-ID completes, additional configuration may optionally take place in the form of bus management activities that are also reviewed in this chapter.

Chapter 14: Bus Reset (Initialization)

This chapter details the bus reset phase of the cable configuration process. Initialization begins with the assertion of a bus reset by a given node on the bus. This chapter discusses the reset enhancements introduced by the 1394a supplement; debouncing the bias change detection, arbitration (short) bus reset, and new timing parameters.

Chapter 15: Tree Identification

Following bus initialization, the tree ID process begins to determine which node will become the root. This chapter details the protocol used in determining the topology of the serial bus.

Chapter 16: Self Identification

This chapter focuses on the self-ID process. During self-ID all nodes are assigned addresses and specify their capabilities by broadcasting self-ID packets.

Part Four: Serial Bus Management

Chapter 17: Cycle Master

This chapter describes the role of the cycle master node, and defines how the cycle master is identified and enabled.

Chapter 18: Isochronous Resource Manager

This chapter describes the role of the isochronous resource manager: how it is identified and enabled, and how other nodes interact with it.

Chapter 19: Bus Manager

In this chapter, the bus manager function is described including topology map and speed map generation and access, as well as power management.

Chapter 20: Bus Management Services

This chapter discusses the bus management services used by the bus manager and isochronous resource manager to perform their bus management roles.

Part Five: Registers and Configuration ROM

Chapter 21: CSR Architecture

This chapter discusses the CSR registers defined by the ISO 13213 specification with particular focus on the registers that are required by the 1394 specification.

Chapter 22: PHY Registers

This chapter introduces the PHY register map and port registers. Both the 1394-1995 and the 1394a PHY registers are detailed.

Chapter 23: Configuration ROM

This chapter details the contents of configuration ROM required by the ISO/IEC 13213 specification. The serial bus also defines ROM entries that are required by some nodes, depending on the capabilities.

Part Six: Power Management

Chapter 24: Introduction to Power Management
This chapter provides a brief introduction to the power management environment introduced by the 1394a specification. The chapter introduces the three documents that further define the power management specification: Cable Power Distribution, Suspend/Resume Mechanisms, and Power State Management.

Chapter 25: Cable Power Distribution
This chapter discusses power distribution in the cable environment. It discusses the four power types designations for nodes: power providers, alternate power providers, power consumers, and self-powered devices. Details regarding the power implementation of nodes in also included.

Chapter 26: Suspend & Resume
This chapter introduces the suspend and resume mechanisms. This capability allows the PHY layer within a node to enter a low power state under software control (either local node software or from another node). The mechanisms implemented for suspend and resume are detailed including: command and confirmation packets, suspend initiator actions, suspend target actions, and related suspend and resume signaling. The impact on PHY and port register definition is also discussed.

Chapter 27: Power State Management
This chapter describes the CSR registers and ROM entries that define power management capabilities and provide the mechanisms for controlling the power states of a node and of local units within a node.

Appendix

Example 1394 Chip Solutions
This chapter is provided by Texas Instruments and discusses a variety of 1394 component implementations.

Target Audience

This book is intended for use by hardware and software design and support personnel. Due to the clear, concise explanatory methods used to describe each subject, personnel outside of the design field may also find the text useful. This book is perhaps best used prior to reading the IEEE 1394-1995 specification and 1394a Supplement. It provides the important context, concepts, and relationships that are essential for understanding the specifications.

Prerequisite Knowledge

The reader should be familiar with computer architectures.

Documentation Conventions

This document contains conventions that are used in other MindShare books and in the IEEE 1394 documentation. Since this book is a companion to the specification, many of the standard documentation conventions are used here to ease the transition between the two documents.

Labels for Multi-byte Blocks

The CSR Architecture and the IEEE 1394 standards attempt to eliminate confusion of terminology relating to the terms: word as it applies to the size of an aligned block of bytes in address space. Depending on the manufacturer, a "word" may refer to 2 bytes or to 4 bytes. The IEEE standards chooses to define multibytes as follows:

- nibble (4-bits)
- byte (8-bits)
- doublet (two bytes)
- quadlet (four bytes)
- octlet (eight bytes)

Hexadecimal Notation

This section defines the typographical convention used throughout this book. Hex Notation. All hex numbers are followed by an "h." Examples:

```
9A4Eh
0100h
```

Binary Notation

All binary numbers are followed by a "b." Examples:

```
0001 0101b
01b
```

Decimal Notation

Numbers without any suffix are decimal. When required for clarity, decimal numbers are followed by a "d." The following examples each represent a decimal number:

```
16
255
256d
128d
```

Bit Versus Byte Notation

The Universal Serial Bus, as its name implies, transmits serial data, which results in numerous discussions of bit-related issues. This book employs the standard notation for differentiating bits versus bytes as follows.

All abbreviations for "bits" use lower case. For example:

1.5Mb/s
2Mb

All references to "bytes" are specified in upper case. For example:

10MB/s
1KB

Identification of Bit Fields (logical groups of bits or signals)

All bit fields are designated in big-endian bit ordering. Recognizing that the serial bus will be implemented in environments using both big-endian and little-endian, no bit position labels are specified. Groups of bits are shown with the most significant bit on the left and the least significant bit on the right without regard to bit position numbering; field size is specified by the number of bits rather than a range of bits as shown below:

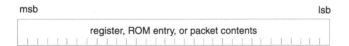

Visit Our Web Page

Our web site contains a listing of all of our courses and books. In addition, it contains errata for a number of the books, a hot link to our publisher's web site, as well as course outlines.

www.mindshare.com

Our publisher's web page contains a listing or our currently-available books and includes pricing and ordering information. Their home page is accessible at:

www.aw.com\cseng\mindshare

We Want Your Feedback

MindShare values your comments and suggestions. Please contact us via internet e-mail.

E-mail: don@mindshare.com

Please check our web site for phone, fax, and mailing address.

Part One

Introduction to FireWire
(IEEE 1394a)

1 *Why FireWire?*

This Chapter

This chapter provides a brief history of FireWire (IEEE 1394). It also discusses the need for FireWire and reviews the applications for which it is well suited.

The Next Chapter

The next chapter describes the primary features of the FireWire serial bus implementation. The chapter also reviews the IEEE 1394 standards (IEEE 1394-1995 & IEEE 1394.A) and IEEE ISO/IEC 13213 (ANSI/IEEE 1212) standard that the FireWire serial bus is based upon.

Overview

Development of FireWire began in the mid 1980s by Apple Computer. In fact, the term FireWire is a registered trademark of Apple Computer Corporation. As other manufacturers gained interest in FireWire, a working committee was formed to create a formal standard on the architecture. The resulting specification was submitted to IEEE and IEEE 1394-1995 was adopted.

Motivations Behind FireWire Development

FireWire provides a serial bus interconnect that allows a wide range of high performance devices to be attached. A variety of issues led to the development of FireWire. The primary characteristics of this serial bus include:

- Ease of use
- Low cost device implementations
- High speed application support
- Scalable performance
- Support for isochronous applications
- Huge amount of memory mapped address space supported (16 exabytes)
- Operation independent of host system

Inexpensive Alternate to Parallel Buses

The IEEE 1394 serial bus provides an alternative to more expensive parallel bus designs. Benefits of the serial bus over most parallel bus implementations are listed below.

- Reduced cost compared with many parallel bus implementations.
- Peripherals in current personal computer systems reside on a variety of buses (e.g. PCI and ISA buses). Communication between such devices can be problematic due to bus protocol and speed differences, thus slowing overall performance. FireWire provides an opportunity to locate a wide variety of peripheral devices that connect to the same serial bus, resulting in performance gains. Up to 63 nodes can be attached to a single serial bus.
- Many parallel buses are confined to a small physical area; however, serial bus has much greater flexibility (4.5 meters between devices).
- FireWire supports direct attachment of remote peripherals.
- The 1394 bus can be implemented in conjunction with the parallel bus to provide fault tolerance.

Plug and Play Support

Devices attached to the IEEE 1394 serial bus support automatic configuration. Unlike USB devices, each 1394 node that attaches to the bus automatically participates in the configuration process without intervention from the host system. Each time a new device is added to or removed from the bus, the 1394 bus is re-enumerated. This occurs whether or not the bus is attached to a host system.

Eliminate Host Processor/Memory Bottleneck

Like any bus that supports bus mastering, the 1394 bus has the ability to increase overall system performance. In a PC environment the 1394 bus can reduce traffic across PCI and reduce accesses to the memory subsystem. This can be accomplished by locating devices on the 1394 bus that communicate with each other frequently. This eliminates the need for the processor and memory subsystems to be involved in the transfer of data between devices.

High Speed Bus with Scalable Performance

Many peripheral devices such as hard drives and video cameras require high throughput. The 1394 bus accommodates these types of devices with a 400Mb/s transfer rate. This yields a theoretical throughput of 50MB/s in contrast to the throughput of ISA (8MB/s) and PCI (132MB/s). The 1394 serial bus provides scalable performance by supporting transfer rates of 400Mb/s, 200Mb/s, and 100Mb/s.

Support for Isochronous Applications

The serial bus supports isochronous transfers to support applications such as audio and video which require constant transfer rates. The isochronous transfer support reduces the amount of buffering required by isochronous applications, thereby reducing cost.

BackPlane and Cable Environments

1394 supports both a backplane and cable implementation, permitting flexibility of implementation. The backplane environment provides the ability of establishing a redundant serial bus communications channel in conjunction with a parallel bus implementation. The cable environment allows the remote attachment of peripheral devices with the possibility of supporting peripherals spread over a distance of greater than 250 meters. The capability makes the serial bus an attractive option for small network applications.

Bus Bridge

The huge amount of memory address space supported, high transfer rates, and low costs make the 1394 bus an attractive means of bridging between different host systems and between multiple serial bus implementations.

- Serial bus implementations can be used to bridge other buses together. The serial bus provides the ability to bridge between host systems of varying sizes and types, including PCs, mini-computers, and mainframes.
- A single serial bus supports 63 nodes but can supports up to 1024 serial buses, making the total number of nodes supported at nearly 64k.

1394 Applications

The scalable performance and support for both asynchronous and isochronous transfers makes FireWire an alternative for connecting a wide variety of peripherals including:

- Mass storage
- Video teleconferencing
- Video production
- Small networks
- High speed printers
- Entertainment equipment
- Set top box

IEEE 1394 Refinements

Early implementations based on different interpretations of the 1995 release of the specification resulted in some interoperability problems between different vendor parts. A supplement to the 1394-1995 specification is referred to as the 1394a supplement, and is designed to eliminate these problems. In addition to clarifying portions of the 1394-1995 specification, the 1394a supplement fixes problems, specifies enhancements that are designed to improve performance, and adds new functionality. This book covers the 1394a supplement (2.0 draft version) as it existed at the time of writing.

Power management support and a specification for designing 1394 bridges were also in development at the time of this writing. Portions of the preliminary Power Management specification are included in this text, while the state of the bridge specification was not mature enough to be included.

Yet another version of 1394 being developed is called the IEEE 1394.B specification. This specification defines even higher throughput including 800Mb/s, 1.6Gb/s, and 3.2Gb/s. This specification is being designed for backward compatibility to 1394-1995 and 1394a.

Primary Features

The primary features of FireWire's cable environment are summarized in Table 1-1 on page 17. The next chapter provides a more detailed overview of the FireWire architecture.

Table 1-1: FireWire Key Features

Scalable Performance	Speeds of 100, 200, and 400 Mb/s supported.
Hot Insertion & Removal	Devices can be attached or removed from the bus dynamically without powering the system down.
Plug and Play	Each time a device is attached or detached the bus is re-enumerated. Nodes on the bus are to a large degree self-configuring, and configuration does not require intervention from a host system (such as a PC).
Support for two types of transactions	Support for isochronous and asynchronous transfers.
Layered hardware and software model	Communications based on a transaction layer, link layer, and physical layer protocols.
Support for 64 nodes	Supports 64 node addresses (0-63) on a single serial bus implementation. Node address 63 is used as a broadcast address that all nodes recognize, permitting attachment of up to 63 physical nodes on the bus.
Address space of 16 petabytes per bus	Each of the 64 nodes has 256TB of address space, making the total address space of 16 petabytes.
Support for 1024 buses	The CSR architecture supports up to 1024 buses for a total address space of 16 exabytes.
Peer-to-Peer transfer support	Serial bus devices have the ability to perform transactions between themselves, without the intervention of a host CPU.

Table 1-1: FireWire Key Features (Continued)

Supports fair arbitration	Implements arbitration to ensure that isochronous applications are guaranteed a constant bus bandwidth, while asynchronous applications are permitted access to the bus based on a fairness algorithm.
Error detection and handling	CRC are performed to verify successful transmission of data across the serial bus. CRC errors are detected and transactions retried where possible.
Employs two twisted pairs for signaling.	Signaling is performed using two twisted pairs: one pair for data transmission and another for synchronization.
Cable power	Power available from the bus can be either sourced or sinked by a given node.
Expandable bus	The serial bus can be extended by connecting new serial devices to ports provided by serial bus nodes. Nodes that have two or more ports are termed branch nodes, which can daisy chain additional nodes to the bus. Nodes implementing a single port are termed leaf nodes, which represent the termination point of a given branch of the serial bus.

2 *Overview of the IEEE 1394 Architecture*

The Previous Chapter

The previous chapter discussed the need for FireWire and reviewed the applications for which it is well suited.

This Chapter

This chapter describes the primary features of the FireWire serial bus implementation. The chapter also overviews the IEEE 1394 standards (IEEE 1394-1995 & IEEE 1394a) and ISO/IEC 13213 (ANSI/IEEE 1212) standard that the FireWire serial bus is based upon.

The Next Chapter

The next chapter provides an overview of the IEEE 1394 communications model. It defines the basic transfer types and introduces the communication layers defined by the serial bus specification.

IEEE 1394 Overview

The IEEE 1394 specification defines the serial bus architecture known as FireWire. Originated by Apple Computer, FireWire is based on the internationally adopted ISO/IEC 13213 (ANSI/IEEE 1212) specification. This specification, formally named "Information technology—Microprocessor systems—Control and Status Registers (CSR) Architecture for microcomputer buses," defines a common set of core features that can be implemented by a variety of buses. IEEE 1394 defines serial bus specific extensions to the CSR Architecture.

IEEE 1394-1995 provides support for a backplane environment and a cable environment. This book focuses only on the cable environment.

Specifications and Related Documents

This book is based on a variety of specifications and documents, some of which are completed and approved, while others are in varying stages of completion and approval. To distinguish information based on approved specifications versus information based on pre-approved specifications and documents, a symbol is used to alert the reader to pre-approved references that might otherwise not be obvious. The following bulleted list includes the specifications and documents used as references when writing this book. The symbol previously mentioned is used to highlight those specifications and documents that are not approved at the time of this writing.

The following documents were used during the development of this book:

- CSR Architecture Specification — ISO/IEC 13213 (ANSI/IEEE 1212)
- IEEE 1394-1995 Serial Bus Specification
    - •IEEE 1394a Supplement
    - •Power Distribution Specification
    - •Power Management Specification
    - •Suspend/Resume Specification
    - •Open Host Controller Interface (OHCI) for 1394 Specification
    - •Device Bay Specification
    - •1394.1 Bridge Specification
    - •IEEE 1394.B Specification

The author strongly urges the reader to obtain the latest (and hopefully approved) versions of these specifications. Also please check MindShare's web site (www.mindshare.com) to check for errata, clarifications, and additions to this book. Due to the evolving nature of this topic, many changes are inevitable. Some of these specifications may be available on the IEEE 1394 Trade Association web site at: www.firewire.org.

IEEE 1394-1995 and the IEEE 1394a Supplement

The IEEE 1394 specification was released in 1995, hence the name IEEE 1394-1995. Different interpretations of the 1995 specification have led to interoperability problems. To clarify the specification a supplement to the 1995 specification has been developed, called 1394a. This supplement also adds additional features and makes improvements intended to increase performance or usability. This text incorporates the changes defined by 1394a. However, at the time of this writing 1394a was not an officially released document from IEEE.

IEEE 1394.B

A higher speed 1394 serial bus called the "B" version was also being developed, when this book was being written. This specification will define serial bus extensions for running the serial bus at speeds into the gigabit per second range. This specification is intended to be backwardly compatible with the 1394-1995 and 1394a implementations. Note that another solution has been proposed that also increases the serial bus speed, and is known as the 1394.2 version. This proposed solution, however, is not backwardly compatible with earlier 1394 versions, causing considerable opposition.

Unit Architecture Specifications

A wide variety of functional devices (e.g. hard drives, video cameras, and CD-ROMs) can be implemented as 1394 nodes. Functional devices are termed units by the 1394 specification. Certain types of devices may have related specifications called "unit architectures" that define implementation details such as protocols, ROM entries, control and status registers, etc. Two specifications of this type are:

- Serial Bus Protocol 2 (SBP2) Architecture — used for SCSI-based mass storage functions.
- A/V unit Architecture — used for audio/visual functions.

Check the 1394 Trade Association web site (www.firewire.org) for information regarding Unit Architecture documentation.

FireWire System Architecture

Figure 2-1: PC with IEEE 1394 Bus Attached to the PCI Bus.

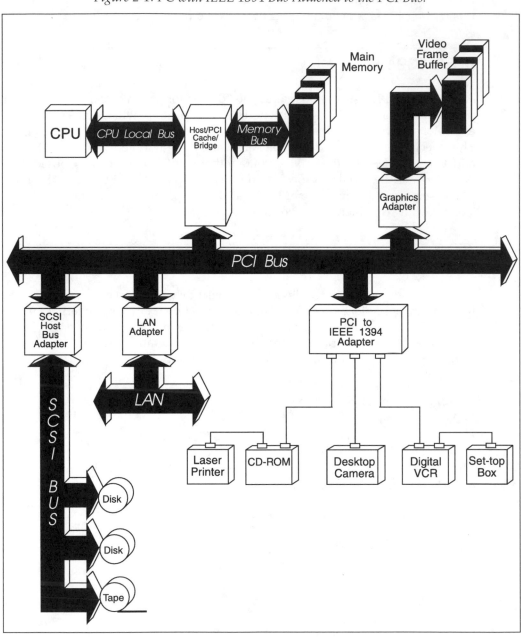

IEEE 1394 Topology

Figure 2-1 on page 22 represents a typical PC that incorporates an IEEE 1394 serial bus attached to the PCI bus. A PCI to 1394 bridge (Open Host Controller Interface, or OHCI) interfaces the computer to the serial bus. The serial bus allows attachment of high speed peripheral devices that would otherwise require a relatively expensive bus solution such as PCI or SCSI. As shown in Figure 2-1, a wide variety of peripheral devices can be attached and supported.

Multiport Nodes and Repeaters

1394 nodes may have one or more ports. A single port node discontinues the bus along a given branch of the bus, whereas nodes with two or more ports allow continuation of the bus, as illustrated in Figure 2-2 on page 23. Nodes with multiple ports permit the bus topology to be extended. Note that the signaling environment is point-to-point. That is, when a multiport node receives a packet, it is detected, received, resynchronized to the repeaters local clock and retransmitted over the other node ports.

Figure 2-2: IEEE 1394 Nodes May Extend the Bus Via Additional Ports

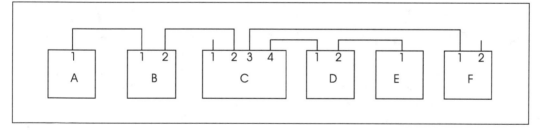

Configuration

Configuration is performed dynamically as new devices are attached and/or removed from the bus. The configuration process does not require intervention from the computer system.

Peer-To-Peer Transfers

Unlike most other serial buses designed to support peripheral devices (e.g. Universal Serial Bus) peer-to-peer transfers are supported so that serial bus nodes can transfer data between each other without intervention from a host system. This enables high throughput between devices without adversely affecting performance of the computer system. For example, a video camera can set up a transfer between itself and a video cassette recorder, when both reside on the same serial bus or bridged serial buses.

Device Bay

Device bay provides a standard mechanism for attaching serial bus devices into desktop systems. The device bay is designed specifically for PCs and allows attachment of serial bus devices (including Firewire and Universal Serial Bus (USB) devices) into a docking bay integrated into the computer system, rather than requiring a cable attachment. This is intended for devices such as hard drives, DVD drives, or modems that can be added to a desktop system without having to power the system down and load drivers. Specifications for Device Bay implementations can be found at: **www.device-bay.org**.

The ISO/IEC 13213 Specification

The ISO/IEC 13213 (ANSI/IEEE 1212) specification, formally named "Information technology—Microprocessor systems—Control and Status Registers (CSR) Architecture for microcomputer buses," defines a common set of core features that can be implemented by a variety of buses, including IEEE 1394. The primary goals of the ISO/IEC 13213 specification are to:

- Reduce the amount of customized software needed to support a given bus standard.
- Simplify and improve interoperability of bus nodes based on different platforms.
- Support bridging between different bus types.
- Improve software transparency between multi-bus implementations.

Chapter 2: Overview of the IEEE 1394 Architecture

Working groups involved in the development of IEEE 1394 (FireWire), IEEE 896 (Futurebus+), and IEEE 1596 (Scalable Coherent Interface) have helped define and have adopted the ISO/IEC 13213 specification. The specification defines the following features:

- Node Architectures
- Address space
- Common transaction types
- Control and Status Registers (CSRs)
- Configuration ROM format and content
- Message broadcast mechanism to all nodes or to units within a node
- Interrupt broadcast to all nodes.

The ISO/IEC 13213 specification also permits bus-dependent extensions and features that are defined by the IEEE 1394 serial bus specification. The following sections discuss the specific ISO/IEC 13213 features implemented by the IEEE 1394 specification.

ISO/IEC 13213 and IEEE 1394 are based on big endian memory addressing convention. Consequently, this book also follows the big endian convention to minimize the difficulty in translating between this book and the specifications.

Note: To simplify terminology the ISO/IEC 13213 specification is referred to as the "CSR architecture" in this text.

Node Architecture

The physical and logical organization of devices attached to a compliant bus is represented by particular terminology:

- Module — represents a physical device attached to the bus, which contains one or more nodes.
- Node — represents a logical entity within a module. Nodes are visible to the initialization software and contain CSRs and ROM entries that are mapped into the initial node address space. After the system has been initialized, most of the node's CSRs and ROM entries are no longer needed. Some of the node registers are shared between units within the node.
- Unit — represents the functional subcomponents of a node that may identify either processing, memory, or I/O functionality. Units within a node typically operate independently and are controlled by their own software drivers. Registers defined by a given unit are mapped into the node address space and are accessed by a unit specific software driver.

FireWire System Architecture

Figure 2-3 on page 26 illustrates the node architecture and reflects the units that can be implemented within a node. The number of units within a node is design dependent. As an example, a module might be a video tape deck with separate nodes for audio, video, and controls. Each node might define a unit architecture that specifies high level protocols needed for transferring data.

Figure 2-3: Module, Node, and Unit Architecture

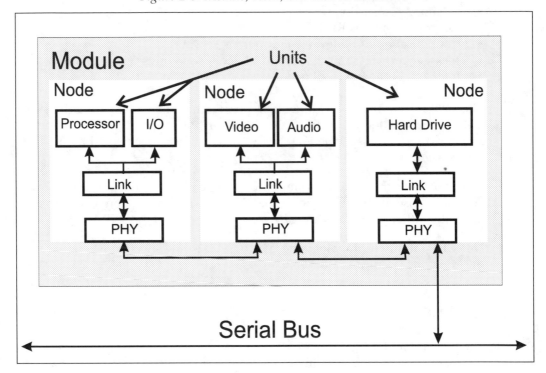

Figure 2-4: CSR Address Space with IEEE 1394 Extensions

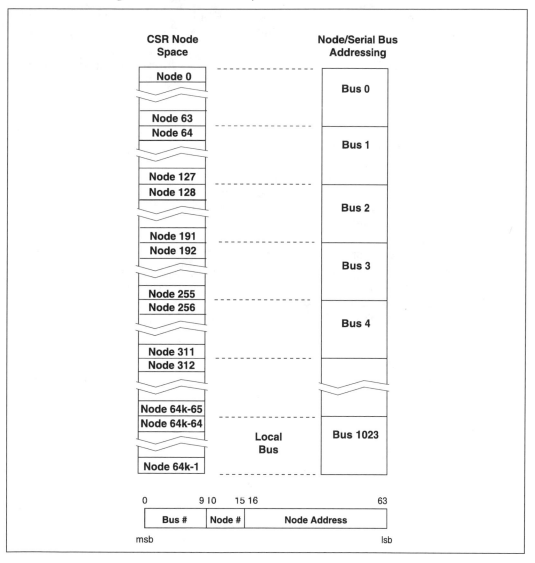

Address Space

The CSR architecture defines both 32- and 64-bit addressing models. The IEEE 1394 specification, however, supports only the 64-bit fixed addressing model. In this addressing scheme, the address space is divided into equal space for 64k nodes. The serial bus specification further assigns groups of 64 nodes as belonging to one of up to 1024 buses. Figure 2-4 on page 27 illustrates the 64-bit address space (16 exabytes) as defined by the CSR architecture and extended by the IEEE 1394 specification. Note that the high order address bits (0:9) define the target bus (one of 1024). Bits 10:15 identify the target node on the selected bus, and the 48 least significant address bits (16:63) define 256 terabytes (TB) of memory address space for each node.

Each node has 256 terabytes of address space allocated to it. This space is divided into blocks defined for specific purposes, with address ranges labeled as:

- Initial memory space
- Private space
- Initial register space
  - CSR architecture register space
  - Serial bus space
  - ROM (first 1KB)
- Initial units space

The Initial register space provides standardized locations used for serial bus configuration and management, while the private space is reserved for a node's local use. Figure 2-5 on page 29 represents the total 64-bit address space definition for the 1394 implementation.

Figure 2-5: Serial Bus Address Space

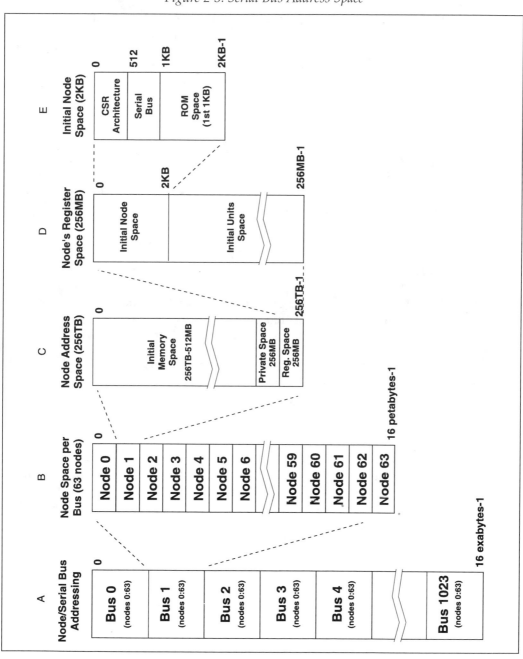

Transfers and Transactions

The nature of a given node application dictates the type of transfer(s) that it performs. Some applications may require periodic data transfer with guaranteed data delivery (asynchronous), while the rate of transfer may be crucial to other applications (isochronous). The serial bus supports both isochronous and asynchronous data transfer protocols.

The serial bus must share bus bandwidth among a variety of nodes residing on the bus. To accomplish bus bandwidth sharing, a given transfer is typically performed as a series of smaller transactions that occur over time. Isochronous transfers require transactions that occur at a constant rate, while asynchronous transactions may occur periodically.

Asynchronous Transfers

Some serial bus applications require data transfers to occur without any data corruption. Data transfers must be valid, otherwise the integrity of the application is compromised, or worse the entire system may fail. The serial bus provides verification of valid data delivery across the serial bus, as well as confirmation back to the initiator that the transfer was successfully received by the application. In the event that data is not received correctly, the failure is reported to the initiator of the transfer, which can retry the transfer.

The CSR architecture defines three basic transaction types that are used by the serial bus for asynchronous transfers:

- Reads
- Writes
- Locks

Due to the need to confirm data delivery, asynchronous transactions require a more complex bus protocol. An asynchronous bus transaction is initiated by a **requester** node and received by a **responder** node that returns a response. Thus, each **transaction** consists of two **subactions**:

1. request subaction — transfers the address, command, and data (writes and locks) from the requester to the responder.
2. response subaction — returns completion status (writes) back to the requester or returns data during read and lock transactions.

Figure 2-6 illustrates the transaction model. Note that the IEEE 1394 specification adds additional protocol layers that require read transactions to be split into two separate operations. Writes can be performed either as unified or split operations depending on the speed of the protocol layers. Various forms of transactions are discussed in the next chapter.

Figure 2-6: Transaction Model Consisting of Request and Response Subactions

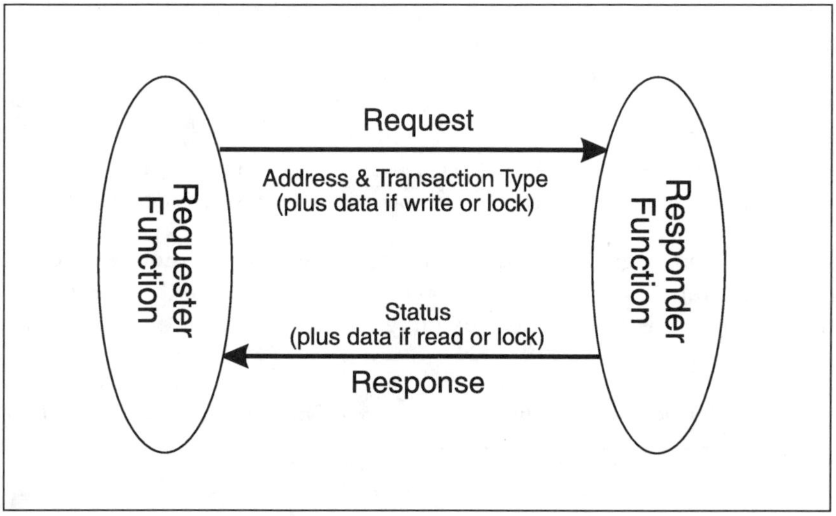

The locked transaction is a mechanism that permits read-modify-write operations without the implementation of a typical bus lock signal. Rather, the requester uses the locked transaction to notify the responder of its desire to perform an atomic operation. The responder is responsible for performing the test and set operation. See Chapter 8 for details regarding the implementation of locked operations.

The specification also defines error codes that are returned by the responder to the requester. Four standard code types are defined:

- type_error
- address_error
- conflict_error
- response_timeout

The error checking mechanism and the details regarding the implementation of these status codes are not defined by the specification. Details regarding the IEEE 1394 implementation of error handling are discussed in Chapter 12.

Isochronous Transfers

Isochronous applications, requiring that data be delivered at a constant rate across the bus, do not require confirmation of data delivery. For example, audio data being transferred from a music CD to a speaker via the serial bus must occur at a constant rate in order to reproduce the sound at the speaker without distortion. The audio data has a short life, therefore, if audio data is corrupted when transferred over the bus, there is no long-lasting effect. Furthermore, such applications do not need confirmation that the data has been received correctly.

Due to the nature of isochronous applications, the associated bus transactions are quite simple. An isochronous transaction sends data to a target device at regular intervals (every 125µs) and receives no feedback of any type from the receiving node. Consequently, a single isochronous transaction type is defined.

Figure 2-7 on page 32 illustrates the communications model used for isochronous transfers. Note that no response is returned. Note that the requester function is known as an isochronous talker and the responder function is called an isochronous listener.

Figure 2-7: Isochronous Transactions Consist Only of a Request Transaction

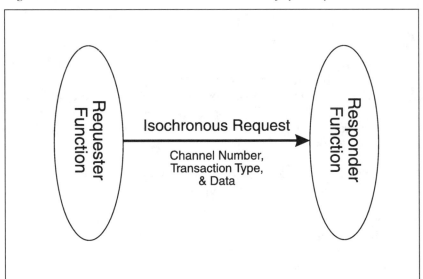

Control and Status Registers (CSRs)

All FireWire nodes must implement a group of core control and status registers (CSRs) defined by the CSR architecture. In addition to the core registers, the CSR architecture defines bus dependent space for registers that are defined by the FireWire specification. These registers provide a standard definition to permit easier implementation of software, interoperability between FireWire implementations that are based on different platforms, and bridging between different bus types that implement the CSR architecture. The CSR definition also supports the following design objectives:

- Power fail recovery by the operating system
- Error logging
- Fault-retry of bus transmission errors initiated by software
- Automatic configuration that is transparent to system software

All CSRs are 32-bits wide (referred to as a quadlet in the IEEE specification) and are aligned on even quadlet boundaries. Chapter 21, entitled "CSR Architecture," on page 361 details all CSRs defined for the FireWire environment.

Configuration ROM

The CSR architecture also defines a standard set of ROM entries that are intended to provide configuration information to be used during node initialization. Two ROM formats are defined:

- minimal—contains only a 24-bit vendor identifier
- general—contains the vendor ID, bus information block, root directory containing information entries and/or pointers to another directory or to a leaf (containing information entries)

ROM data structures provide information needed to associate an I/O software driver and diagnostic software with a particular module, node, or unit. ROM may also define additional parameters needed by software to access the device correctly, and to define the capabilities of the node regarding bus management activities.

Message Broadcast

The CSR architecture defines an optional broadcasting mechanism that permits a given node to broadcast a message over the bus that is intended to target multiple nodes. All broadcasts are accomplished by addressing node 63, which is reserved as a broadcast address. All nodes recognizing a transaction with address 63 know they are being targeted. As a result, broadcast transactions of all types prohibit the return of any response by the receiving nodes. Otherwise multiple nodes would be driving the bus simultaneously, causing contention on the bus.

Interrupt Broadcast

The serial bus also supports interrupt broadcasting to units within a given node or other nodes residing on the serial bus. See "Interrupt_Target and Interrupt_Mask Registers" on page 375 for a detailed discussion of interrupt broadcasting.

Automatic Configuration

Automatic configuration occurs during initial powerup of the system and when a node is attached or detached from the bus. Unlike most buses attached to PCs, the serial bus does not depend on a single processor (monarch processor) to execute configuration code. Instead, a deterministic configuration mechanism is defined that dictates the actions that nodes must take following a RESET broadcast to perform configuration. All nodes participate in the configuration process that is localized to the serial bus. Configuration results in a single node being assigned the responsibility for 1394 bus management. Chapter 13, entitled "Configuration Process," on page 265 details the configuration process.

Part Two

Serial Bus Communications

3 *Communications Model*

The Previous Chapter

The previous chapter described the primary features of the IEEE 1394 serial bus implementation. The chapter also reviewed the IEEE 1394 standards (IEEE 1394-1995 & IEEE 1394a) and the ISO/IEC 13213 (ANSI/IEEE 1212) standard that the FireWire serial bus is based upon.

This Chapter

This chapter provides an overview of the serial bus communications model. It defines the basic transfer types and introduces the communication layers defined by the specification.

The Next Chapter

The next chapter describes the services defined by the specification that are used to pass parameters between layers during the execution of each transaction.

Overview

Since the IEEE 1394 serial bus supports peer-to-peer transactions, arbitration must be performed to determine which node will obtain ownership of the serial bus. This arbitration mechanism supports a fairness algorithm that ensures that all transfers obtain fair access to the bus. Serial bus arbitration is discussed in detail in Chapter 7.

The serial bus supports two data transfer types:

- asynchronous transfers that do not require delivery at a constant data rate. Asynchronous transfers target a particular node based on a unique address. These transfers do not require a constant bus bandwidth and therefore do

not need regular use of the bus, but must get fair access over time.
- isochronous transfers that require data delivery at constant intervals. These transfers define a channel number rather than a unique address, permitting the isochronous data stream to be broadcast to one or more nodes responding to the channel number. These transfers require regular bus access and therefore have higher bus priority than asynchronous transfers.

Serial bus data transactions take place via a series of data and information packet transmissions. Each transaction is initiated by a "requester" and the request is received by a target device, called a "responder."

Asynchronous transactions require a response from the target node, which results in an additional transaction. The responding node either accepts or returns data as illustrated in Figure 3-1.

Figure 3-1: Request/Response Protocol

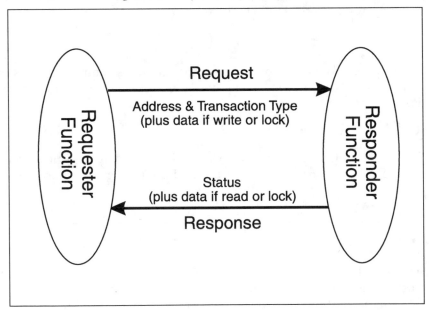

This basic communications model is defined by the CSR architecture. The serial bus provides further granularity in the transaction process, which includes verification of packet delivery, three protocol layers, and related services that perform specific functions during the process of transferring data between the requester and responder. These layers are described later in this chapter.

Isochronous transactions complete following the request as illustrated in Figure 3-2. Note that rather than an address, isochronous transactions use a channel number to identify target nodes. Additionally no response is returned from the target node.

Figure 3-2: Isochronous Transaction that Consists Only of a Request Transaction

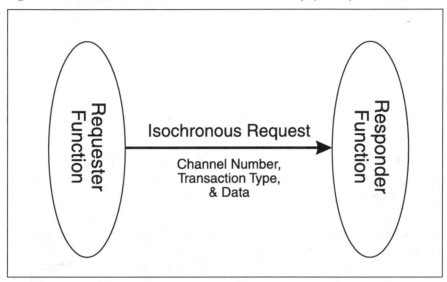

The actual transfer of data across the cable is done serially using data-strobe encoding (See page 122). Data can be transmitted at one of three speeds:

- 100 Mb/s (98.304 Mb/s)
- 200 Mb/s (196.608 Mb/s)
- 400 Mb/s (393.216 Mb/s)

Prior to transferring data, the transmitting node must obtain ownership of the 1394 bus via an arbitration mechanism. This ensures that only one node at a time is transmitting data over the wire.

Transfer Types

As illustrated in Figure 3-3, a mix of isochronous and asynchronous transactions may be performed across the serial bus by sharing the overall bus bandwidth. Notice that bus bandwidth allocation is based on 125µs intervals, called cycles. Details regarding these transaction types and their bandwidth allocation are discussed below.

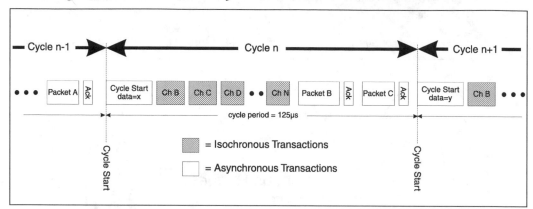

Figure 3-3: Isochronous and Asynchronous Transactions Share Bus Bandwidth

Asynchronous

Asynchronous transfers target a particular node by using an explicit 64-bit address. Asynchronous transfers (collectively) are guaranteed 20% (minimum) of the overall bus bandwidth. Thus, the amount of data transferred depends on the transmission speed. A given node is not guaranteed any particular bus bandwidth, but rather is guaranteed fair access to the bus via a fairness interval, in which each node wishing to perform an asynchronous transaction gets access to the bus exactly one time during a single fairness interval. Maximum packet size for asynchronous transfers is limited as specified in Table 3-1. Note that higher cable speeds have been specified by the 1394a supplement, but the maximum speed and maximum data payload supported remains at 400Mb/s.

Asynchronous transfers also verify data delivery via CRC checks and response codes, and in the event that errors occur during transmission, retries may be attempted under software control.

Table 3-1: Maximum Data Block Size for Asynchronous Transfers

	Cable Speed	Maximum Data Payload Size (Bytes)
	100Mb/s	512
	200Mb/s	1024
	400Mb/s	2048
☞	800Mb/s	4096
☞	1.6Gb/s	8192
☞	3.2Gb/s	16384

Isochronous

Isochronous transfers target one or more (multi-cast transactions) devices based on a 6-bit channel number associated with the transfer. Channel numbers are used by the isochronous listeners to access a memory buffer within the application layer. This memory buffer may or may not reside within the node's 256TB of address space.

Each isochronous application must also obtain the necessary bus bandwidth that it requires for its transfer. To ensure that sufficient bus bandwidth is available, applications wishing to perform isochronous transfers must request the needed bandwidth from the isochronous resource manager node. Bus bandwidth is allocated on a per cycle basis.

Once bus bandwidth has been acquired for an isochronous transfer, that channel receive a guaranteed time-slice during each 125µs cycle. Up to 80% (100µs) of each bus cycle can be allocated to isochronous transfers. The maximum packet size supported for a given isochronous transfer is limited to the available bus bandwidth, and must not exceed the maximum packet size specified in Table 3-2 on page 42. The maximum packet size limit for isochronous transactions has been added by the 1394a specification. The isochronous bus bandwidth available is maintained by the isochronous resource manager node. Each node wishing to perform isochronous transfers must request its desired bus bandwidth from the isochronous resource manager based of the number of desired allocation units. The maximum packet size may be limited by the amount of bandwidth available when the allocation request is made. (See "Bus Bandwidth Allocation" on page 339.)

Table 3-2: Maximum Data Block Size for Isochronous Transfers

	Cable Speed	Maximum Data Payload Size (Bytes)
	100Mb/s	1024
	200Mb/s	2048
	400Mb/s	4096
☞	800Mb/s	8192
☞	1.6Gb/s	16384
☞	3.2Gb/s	32768

The Protocol Layers

Four protocol layers are defined to simplify the implementation of hardware and software. Each layer has an associated set of services defined to support communications between the application and the 1394 protocol layers, and for configuration and bus management. Figure 3-4 on page 43 illustrates the relationships between these layers for a single node.

The protocol layers consist of the:

- Bus Management layer — supports bus configuration and management activities for each node.
- Transaction layer — supports the CSR architecture request-response protocol for read, write, and lock operations related to asynchronous transfers. Note that a transaction layer exists in both the requester and responder. Note also that the transaction layer does not provide any services for isochronous transfers. Instead, isochronous transfers are driven directly by the application.
- Link layer — provides the translation of a transaction layer request or response into a corresponding packet, or subaction, to be delivered over the serial bus. This layer also provides address and channel number decoding for incoming asynchronous or isochronous packets. CRC error checking is also performed here.
- Physical layer — provides the electrical and mechanical interface required

for transmission and reception of data bits (packets) transferred across the serial bus. The physical layer also implements an arbitration process to ensure that only one node at a time transfers data across the bus.

Each of the layers is described in more detail in the following sections.

Figure 3-4: Protocol Layers

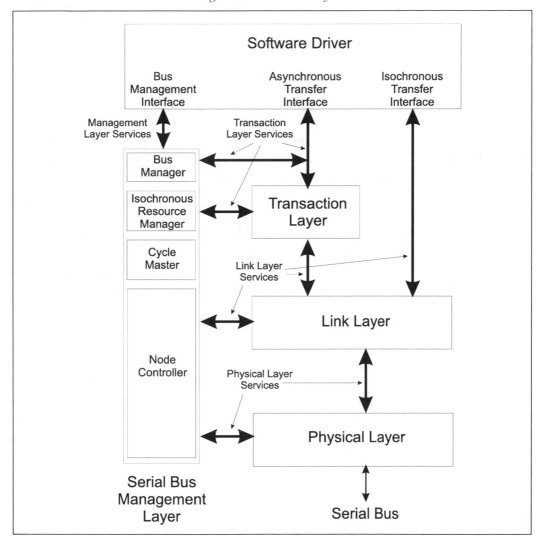

Bus Management Layer

Nodes implement the bus management layer to support a variety of functions including configuration and the application of power. The exact bus management support included depends on the capabilities of the node. All nodes must include support for automatic bus configuration, while other bus management functions are optional. For example, a given node may require power from the bus for its functional unit (e.g. video camera) and consequently will include bus management support for applying bus power.

Some nodes also participate in global bus management to ensure that the family of nodes residing on the bus live in harmony and can perform their functions efficiently. This global management consists of:

- Channel number and bus bandwidth allocation for isochronous transfers.
- Controlling the intervals at which isochronous transactions are performed.
- Verifying that all bus powered nodes have sufficient bus power.
- Tuning the bus to enhance performance (dependent on the bus topology).
- Providing services to other nodes (e.g. specifying the maximum speed at which two nodes can communicate with each other).

Bus management is discussed in detail in Chapter 17, Chapter 18, and Chapter 19. The 1394 specification identifies three global bus management roles that provide the support for a completely managed bus.

- Cycle Master
- Isochronous Resource Manager
- Bus Manager

Note that these roles may be performed by three separate nodes or one node may perform all three roles. Depending on the capabilities of the node residing on the bus, these roles may not be supported; thus, global bus management may be limited or may not occur at all.

Transaction Layer

The transaction layer supports only asynchronous transfers. As discussed in the previous chapter, the 1394 bus supports three basic asynchronous transaction types:

- Read
- Write
- Lock

The asynchronous transaction model is based on communication between a requester node and a response node. Each transaction consists of a request sub-action and a response subaction, with the link and physical layers operating between the requester and responder transaction layers.

1394 applications typically have little knowledge of the intermediate layers within the 1394 communications model. Rather, they simply issue data transfer requests to the transaction layer. This software layer translates a transfer request into one or more transaction requests that are needed to complete the transfer. The resulting transaction request indicates the transaction type (read, write, or lock), and if the transaction consists of a write or lock the transaction layer also supplies data to be transferred during the request. (Refer to Chapter 4, entitled "Communications Services," on page 65 for a detailed discussion of read, write, and lock transfers.)

Note that the transaction layer is not involved in isochronous transactions.

Transaction Layer Services

The transaction layer provides services related to transaction data flow. These service primitives are defined as:

- Request service — used by the requester to start a transaction (initiates the request subaction).
- Indication service — notifies the responder of the request (completes the request subaction).
- Response service — used by the responder to return status or data to the requester (starts the response subaction).
- Confirmation service — notifies the requester that the response has been received (completes the response subaction).

FireWire System Architecture

Figure 3-5 illustrates the transaction layer services, without regard to the intermediate layers. Note that the transaction layer provides the interface between the application (function) and the 1394 link layer.

Figure 3-5: Transaction Layer Communication

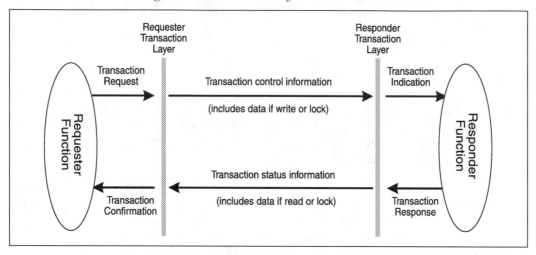

The 1394 specification adds verification of packet delivery to the transaction protocol, which is not part of the CSR architecture model. The transaction layer supplies an acknowledgment for each packet transferred. That is, most packets transferred across the bus require that a 1-byte acknowledgment packet be returned to the sender to verify successful delivery of the packet. In the event of a failed transfer, retries can then be performed. The term "most" is used because two types of packets require no acknowledgment:

1. broadcast packets — the serial bus supports the broadcast of packets that may target more than one node on the bus. In this case, an acknowledge packet is not returned to avoid bus contention from multiple nodes simultaneously returning the acknowledgment.
2. isochronous packets — delivery of isochronous packets require a guaranteed transmission rate, thus any failed packet transmission cannot be retried because it might result in desynchronized data transfers. Therefore no acknowledgment needs to be sent because no corrective action can be taken in the event of failed packet transfer.

Figure 3-6 illustrates the transaction layer actions, including the 1394-defined acknowledgment.

Figure 3-6: Acknowledge Packet is Added by the Transaction Layer

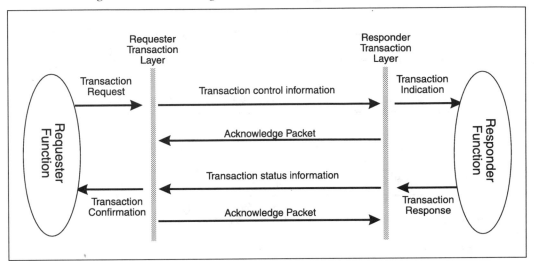

Link Layer

For asynchronous transactions, the link layer provides the interface between the transaction layer and the physical layer and provides services based on the same request/response model used by the transaction layer. The Requester's link layer translates transaction requests from the transaction layer into 1394 packets to be sent over the 1394 cable. When the packet is received by the responder, it is translated and forwarded on to its transaction layer. Figure 3-7 on page 48 illustrates the link layer actions and services.

For isochronous transactions the link layer provides the interface between the isochronous software driver and the physical layer. During transmission, the link layer creates the isochronous packet to be sent across the cable. The link layer also receives isochronous packets from the cable, decodes the packet's channel number and if the packet is destined for this node, the packet is forwarded to the software driver.

Figure 3-7: Link Layer Provides an Interface Between the Transaction and Physical Layers

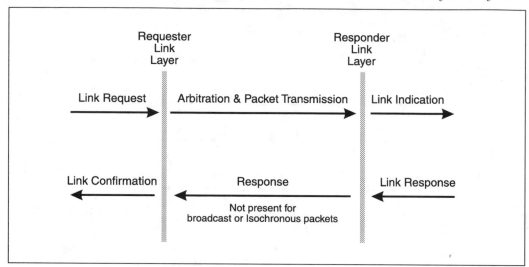

Figure 3-8 illustrates the link-layer services with the acknowledge layer added. The original owner of the bus during the request phase is the requesting node. However, when the acknowledge is returned by the response agent, it transmits the acknowledge packet without having to arbitrate for bus ownership. This is because the acknowledge packet must be returned quickly by the responding node before another arbitration can start. Bus ownership is implied in this case.

Figure 3-8: Request and Response with Acknowledge Packet Included

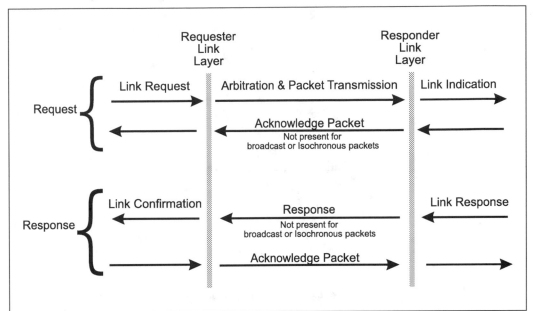

Split Transactions

Figure 3-9 on page 50 illustrates the link layer actions associated with a write transaction that results in a split transaction. The write transaction is initiated when the requester's transaction layer receives a write request from the application. The transaction layer translates the write request into a data packet request that is sent to the link layer. The link layer executes the request by arbitrating for control of the bus and generating a write-request packet. The responder's link layer detects the data packet and sends a data packet indication to the responder's transaction layer.

An acknowledgment must be returned to the requester to verify receipt of the request; however, the responding node is slow and cannot immediately verify that the write has been successful. As a result, the acknowledge returned to the requester confirms that the write-request has been received without error, but that the response confirming fulfillment of the request is still pending. Consequently, the responder must initiate a write-response packet targeting the requester. The transaction concludes with the requester returning an acknowledge packet to verify receipt of the write-response.

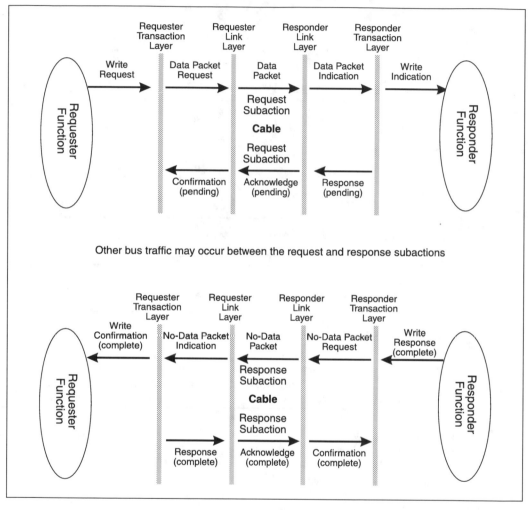

Figure 3-9: Link Layer Actions Taken During Split Write Transaction

Split transactions occur when the response subaction is slow, thereby permitting another node to perform subactions and/or transactions between the request and response subactions of this transaction. This provides a kind of transaction pipelining capability across the bus. In this regard transactions can be multi-threaded in nature, permitting a requester to start (or respond to) another transaction before the first ends.

Concatenated Transactions

The split transaction illustrated in Figure 3-9 can be performed more efficiently as a concatenated transaction. In the previous example, the responding node required time to complete the transaction request. That is, the responding node must successfully service the request before returning the response. While the responding node is servicing the request, other requests and responses may be transferred across the bus during the split transaction.

When the responding node is finally ready to complete the transaction, it must normally arbitrate for control of the bus again before transferring the response, which takes time. If, however, the responding node is fast, it could return the response immediately following the acknowledge packet by concatenating the response directly to the acknowledge packet. Concatenating the response to the request eliminates the need to arbitrate for bus control, which again results in a more efficient form of transaction. This concept is illustrated in Figure 3-10.

Figure 3-10: Conceptual Illustration of a Concatenated Transaction

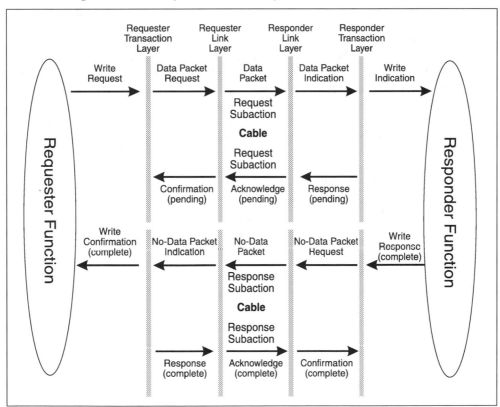

Unified Transactions

The previous examples show transactions that require separate request and response subactions, which may occur as split or concatenated transactions. Sometimes a write transaction can be speeded up if the request packet's response is returned from the application quickly. The quick response can result in the acknowledgment and response being combined to form a unified transaction. Consider the following example. A write request packet includes the data to be written to the target device. Receipt of the packet is acknowledged by the transaction layer. If the transaction layer receives the response from the application confirming that the data has been successfully written to the target device, the response completion code can be incorporated into the acknowledge packet.

Note that in the event of a read transaction, the 1-byte acknowledgment cannot serve as the response because the response must include the requested data as well as completion status. Thus, read as well as lock transactions can only be performed as split or concatenated transactions since both require that both data and status be returned during the response. Write transactions, however, can be performed as either split, concatenated, or unified transactions.

Figure 3-11 illustrates an example of a unified transaction. In summary, unified transactions take place when the request subaction and corresponding response subaction occur as a single unit (indivisibly) such that the response subaction is returned immediately following the request as part of the request acknowledgment packet. The acknowledgment packet specifies whether the response is complete or is pending. If complete, the request has been successfully processed, confirming the acknowledgment as a valid response. A unified transaction is only possible for write transactions because data has already been sent and the response only confirms that write data has been accepted by the application. Thus, if the application is fast enough the link can include the response within the acknowledge packet. Read and lock transactions are not candidates for unified operation because they must return data along with the response, which is clearly not suitable for the 1-byte acknowledge packet.

Figure 3-11: Unified Transaction Format

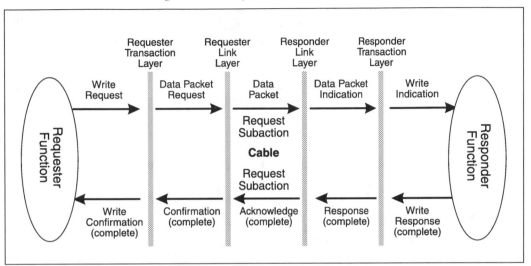

Physical Layer

The physical layer provides the actual interface to the serial bus. Figure 3-12 illustrates a physical layer (PHY) chip that provides the interface between the link layer and the cable. Figure 3-12 illustrates a PHY with two ports. Each port uses two twisted pairs (TPA/TPA* and TPB/TPB*) for signaling as discussed in the next section.

Figure 3-12: Example of PHY Chip in a Node

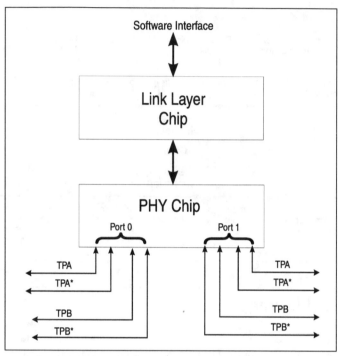

Twisted Pair Signaling

As illustrated in Figure 3-12 on page 54, the serial bus uses two twisted pairs (twisted pair A, or TPA and twisted pair B, or TPB) for signaling. These signal pairs are shared to support a variety of signaling events that are necessary to support the operation of the 1394 bus protocol, including:

- Bus configuration
- Arbitration
- Data transfer

The initial use of the twisted pair signals is to configure the bus. Once bus configuration has completed, all nodes can begin their participation in performing transactions across the bus. Since more than one node may have a transaction pending, bus arbitration must be performed before a data transfer can begin. In this way all multiple nodes share TPA and TPB during the arbitration phase of each transaction to determine which node gets bus ownership next. Once ownership of the bus has been determined, only the winner may use the bus to transfer data. Figure 3-13 illustrates the signaling phases of the bus and who participates. The following sections describe each phase.

Figure 3-13: Nodes Coordinate Use of the Serial Bus During Various Phases of Operation

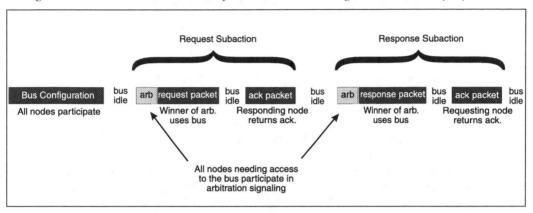

Bus Configuration. A major role of the physical layer is to participate in the configuration process. Configuration begins with power up or when a new device is added to the bus or when one is removed. Any of these events triggers the configuration process beginning with Reset and proceeding to the Tree ID, and Self ID stages as illustrated in Figure 3-14 on page 55. All nodes participate in bus configuration. "Part Four" of this book details the configuration process. Once bus configuration has completed, nodes arbitrate for access to the bus and begin normal bus transfers.

Figure 3-14: Stages Involved in Configuration Process

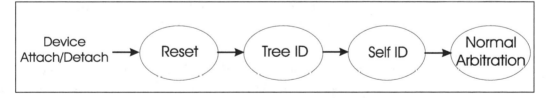

Arbitration. Nodes wishing to initiate a request over the bus or those that must send a response must first obtain ownership of the bus. This is also accomplished via TPA and TPB. Figure 3-13 on page 55 illustrates a split transaction that requires the requester and responder to arbitrate for bus ownership before beginning their data transmission. Note that the acknowledgment does not require arbitration and is treated as an atomic operation across the bus. Other nodes don't begin bus arbitration until the acknowledgment has been returned.

Data Transmission. Bi-directional data delivery occurs via Twisted Pair A and Twisted Pair B, using a combination of non-return to zero (NRZ) and data-strobe encoding. Data is transferred on TPB, while a strobe is delivered over TPA. Since the rate of data delivery can vary, speed information is also sent during packet transmission. Refer to Chapter 6 for details regarding the signaling environment.

Power Pair

A node may source power to the cable, sink power from the cable or neither. Cable voltage may range from 8.0 to 33vdc. Refer to Chapter 27 for details regarding power related issues.

Packet-Based Transactions

All transactions are transmitted across the bus in packetized form. Two groups of packets are defined: one for asynchronous transactions and one for isochronous transactions. Later chapters detail all packet types and describe isochronous and asynchronous transactions in all their forms. Below the basic forms of asynchronous and isochronous packets are described.

Asynchronous Packets. Most asynchronous transactions begin with delivery of a request packet and conclude with the return of a response packet from the target node. Following the transmission of each request and response packet, the recipient of these packets also acknowledges their receipt by returning an acknowledge packet. Asynchronous transactions may send data to the target node (asynchronous write) or request that data be returned from the target node (asynchronous read). Packet contents change depending on which form of asynchronous transaction is being performed. Packet content consists primarily of the following information. For complete contents and descriptions of the various asynchronous packet types, see "Asynchronous Packets" on page 165.

- Destinations Address — Sent by the requester to define the target bus (usually the local bus), node, and location within the node that is being accessed.
- Source ID — Sent by the node transmitting the packet to identify itself, and consists of the bus and node portion of the address.
- Transaction Type — Defines the type of packet being sent.
- Transaction Label — Allows a requesting node to match a response to one of two or more requests pending a response from the same target node.
- Response Code — Sent by the node in response to a previous request to specify completion status.

- Data — The actual information to be transferred. Depending on whether the packet is a write or read, the data resides within either the request or response packet.
- CRC — This cyclic redundancy check validates portions of the packet covered by the CRC.
- Acknowledge Code — Returned by the receiver of a packet to verify receipt.
- Acknowledge Parity — Used to verify that the acknowledge code is correct.

Figure 3-15 illustrates an asynchronous write operation consisting of the write request that includes data, and the acknowledge packet returned from the target device, followed by the response (containing completion status) and the acknowledge packet from the original requester. This is an example of a split write transaction, resulting in four packets being transferred to complete the write. Note that a unified write transaction includes the response notification within the request acknowledge packet, thus only two packets are required.

Figure 3-15: Packets Used During Asynchronous Split Write Transactions

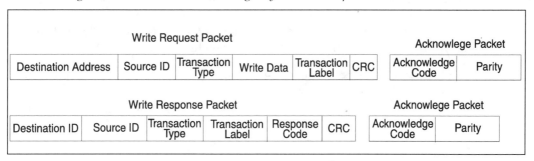

Asynchronous read transactions consist of the read request and acknowledge packets followed by the response and acknowledge packets as illustrated in Figure 3-16. During reads data is returned with the response.

Figure 3-16: Packets Used During Asynchronous Read Transactions

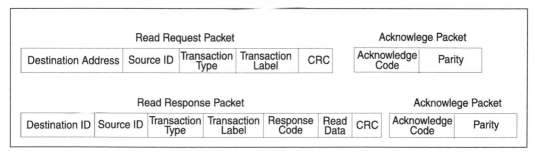

Asynchronous lock transactions consist of a request and a response packet, where each delivers data as illustrated in Figure 3-17. The extended transaction code define the type of lock operation to be performed.

Figure 3-17: Packets Used During Asynchronous Lock Transactions

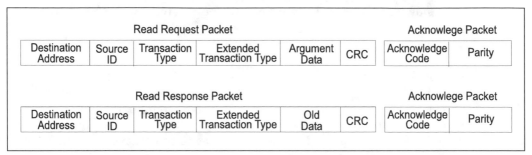

Isochronous Packet. Figure 3-18 on page 58 pictures an isochronous transaction. Unlike asynchronous transactions, these transactions are unidirectional in that data can only be sent by a requester. Furthermore, no acknowledge packet is returned by the target node, nor does it send a response to the requester. These packets are sent at regular intervals (~every 125µs). The primary components of an isochronous packet include:

- Channel Number — Nodes participating in isochronous transactions use a channel number as an address.
- Transaction Type — This field identifies this packet as an isochronous data packet.
- Data — The actual information to be transferred.
- CRC — This cyclic redundancy check validates portions of the packet covered by the CRC.

For complete details regarding the isochronous packet format and contents, see "Stream Data Packet" on page 199.

Figure 3-18: Packet Used During Isochronous Transactions

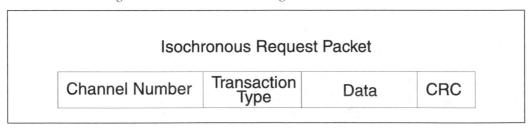

Port Repeater

Figure 3-19 illustrates the repeater functionality that must be implemented in all multiport nodes. Port interface receivers monitor the bus during the arbitration phase of a transaction to determine which port is receiving and which is transmitting a given packet. Arbitration control then enables the port interfaces that should transmit cable traffic. Three possible conditions may exist that affect the operation of the node's repeater.

- Packet originates at another node and targets another node — In this instance the node receives data on one of its ports and repeats it on all others (only one port in this example).
- Packet originates at another node and targets this node — In this case the decode circuitry detects that this node is being targeted and sends the packet to the link layer, and the repeater forwards the packet to all other ports.
- Packet originates at this node — In this case the packet is received from the link layer, encoded, and broadcast to all ports.

Note that the references to encoding and decoding refer to the NRZ and data/strobe encoding and decoding that is performed when sending and receiving packets. (See "NRZ Encoding" on page 123 and "Data-Strobe Encoding" on page 124.) The decode function also serves to determine if this node is a target of the isochronous channel or asynchronous node address.

Figure 3-19: Multiport Nodes Have Repeaters Used to Retransmit Cable Traffic

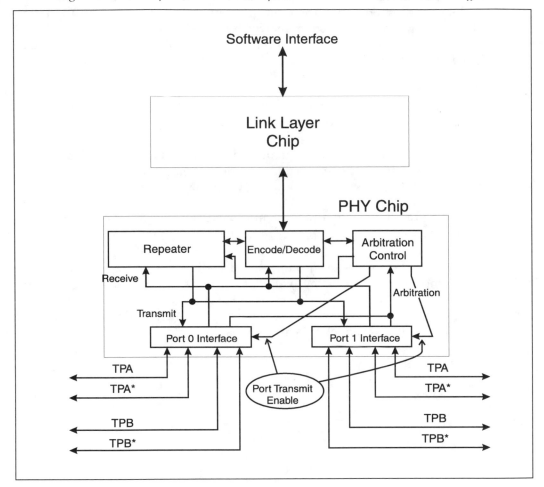

A Sample Asynchronous Transaction

The following example is provided to illustrate the principal aspects of the communication process and the role of each layer. In this example, a read transaction is being performed between two peer nodes as illustrated in Figure 3-20 on page 62. Node A, in this case, is the requester and node B is the responder. From the transaction layer perspective, the request is issued and an acknowledge is expected in return from the responder. The intermediate layers support serial bus-specific communication needs, and are detailed in the following sections. Figure 3-20 illustrates the communication flow between each layer in the protocol. Note that the solid lines represent the request subaction and dotted lines represent the response subaction.

The Request

Node A's link layer receives a transaction request and builds a read request packet that is transferred to the physical layer within the node. The physical node must arbitrate for control of the serial bus and then transmits the read request packet over the serial bus. The physical layer of all serial bus nodes on the serial bus receives the packet and decodes the address. The physical layer for node B recognizes that it is being addressed and sends the packet to the link layer. The link layer decodes the read request packet and sends an indication to the transaction layer, notifying the responder of the request.

The Response

The responder completes the transaction by returning the specified data to the requester. The transaction layer of the responder initiates the response by sending an acknowledgment request (including read data) to the link layer. The link layer translates the acknowledgment into a read response packet and forwards the packet to the physical layer for transmission over the serial bus. The responder's physical layer arbitrates for bus control and transmits the contents of the read response packet. The physical layer of the requester accepts the read response data and forwards it to the link layer where its packet is decoded. The read data is then sent to the transaction layer, thereby terminating the transaction.

Figure 3-20: Example Asynchronous Read Transaction

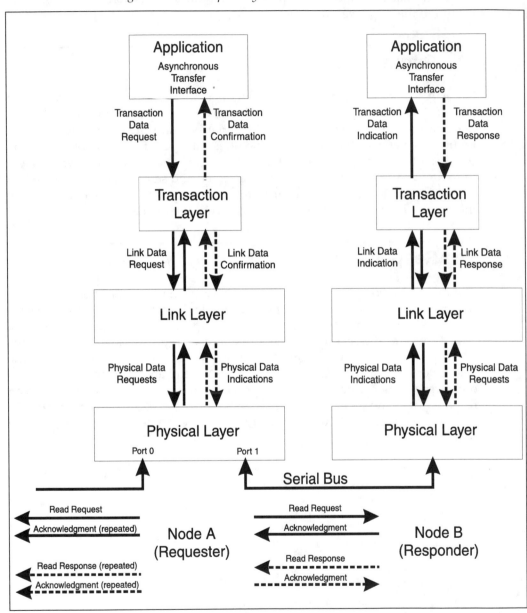

An Example Isochronous Transaction

This example describes and illustrates the communication process and the role of each protocol layer associated with an isochronous transaction. Refer to Figure 3-21 on page 63. Node A is the requester and node B is the responder. Notice that the 1394 specification defines the isochronous protocol with the application communicating directly with the link layer (i.e. bypassing the transaction layer).

Figure 3-21: Example Isochronous Transaction

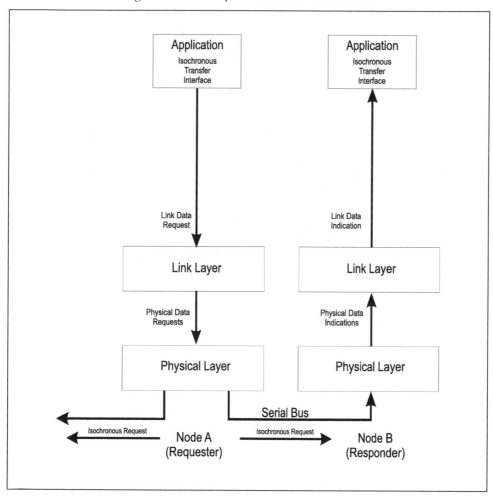

Isochronous transactions also use a channel number rather than a node address to target specific nodes. Thus, isochronous transactions are broadcast transactions where more than one node may be the recipient of the transaction. The other major difference between asynchronous and isochronous transactions is that there is no verification of packet delivery (i.e. no acknowledge packet returned) and no verification from the application that the data has been accepted. From the protocol layer perspective, the request is initiated via the link and PHY layers and received by the PHY and link layers as a request indication, thereby ending the transfer.

4 *Communications Services*

The Previous Chapter

The previous chapter provided an overview of the serial bus communications model. It defined the basic transfer types and introduced the communication layers defined by the specification.

This Chapter

This chapter describes the services defined by the specification that are used to pass parameters between layers during the execution of each transaction.

The Next Chapter

The next chapter discusses the cable characteristics and connectors used by the IEEE 1394 cable environment. It also discusses the Device Bay implementation being specified in PC environments.

Overview

The IEEE 1394 specification defines services that are used to pass parameters between each layer within the communications model. These services are used to initiate transactions or to respond to a transaction that has been received. The following sections describe the services used when performing asynchronous and isochronous transactions.

Anatomy of Asynchronous Transactions

Three primary types of asynchronous transactions are defined by the 1394 specification:

- reads
- writes
- lock

The following discussion reviews each of these transaction types and defines the protocol layers and services calls used to initiate and respond to asynchronous transactions. It also defines the packet types used and details the possible responses.

The following sections describe the steps involved in completing asynchronous transactions. The three basic asynchronous transaction types are described from initiation to response completion with the role of each layer in the protocol detailed.

The Request Subaction

The request subaction involves sending the request phase of an asynchronous transaction to a target node. Both the request and the response agent are involved in the request subaction as discussed below. The specification defines the protocol layers used during the request phase of an asynchronous transaction. The services used in performing a request subaction are listed in Table 4-1. These services are listed in order of reoccurrence during successful request subaction transmission. Note that the shaded entries indicate actions that take place within the responding node. These services are represented graphically in Figure 4-1 on page 68.

Table 4-1: Service Used During Asynchronous Request Subactions

Service Name	Direction of Communication	Purpose of Service
Transaction Data Request	From the Application	Causes transaction layer to initiate an asynchronous transaction.
Link Data Request	From Transaction Layer	Causes link layer to initiate an asynchronous transaction.

Chapter 4: Communications Services

Table 4-1: Service Used During Asynchronous Request Subactions (Continued)

Service Name	Direction of Communication	Purpose of Service
PHY Arbitration Request	From Link Layer	Causes the PHY to arbitrate for control of the serial bus.
PHY Arbitration Confirmation	From PHY	Reports results of arbitration request back to link.
PHY Clock Indication	From PHY	Following successful arbitration, the PHY notifies the link that it is ready to accept clocked data.
PHY Data Request	From Link Layer	Controls clocked transmission of the request packet onto the serial bus.
PHY Data Indication	To Link Layer	Notifies link of the receipt of data bits of the packet.
Link Data Indication	To Transaction Layer	Indicates the reception of a transaction request.
Transaction Data Indication	To Application	Indicates the reception of a transaction request.
Link Data Response	From Transaction Layer	Initiates return of acknowledge packet to the requesting node.
PHY Data Request	From Link Layer	Controls clocked transmission of the acknowledge packet onto the serial bus.
PHY Data Indication	To Link Layer	Notifies link of the receipt of the acknowledgment packet.
Link Data Confirmation	To Transaction Layer	Notifies transaction layer whether the request was successfully received.

FireWire System Architecture

Figure 4-1: Example Asynchronous Read Transaction

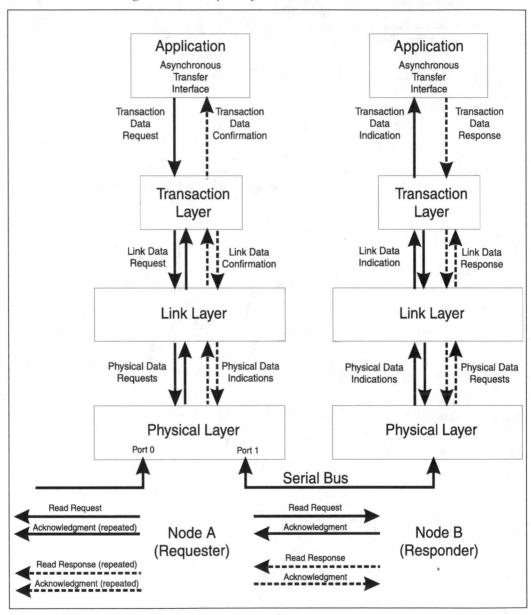

Initiating the Transaction (The Request)

Transaction Layer. Applications initiate asynchronous transactions via the "transaction data request" service. Transaction layer services can be thought of as calls to low level routines that insulate the application programmer from the programming interface associated with the link layer controller chip. The transaction layer also provides verification of packet delivery and initiates the acknowledge packet. The "transaction data request" service, communicates the following parameters:

- Transaction Type Code
  - Write
  - Read
  - Lock
- Extended transaction code (only defined for lock transaction)
- Destination Address
- Data Length
- Data (Data to be transferred during a write or lock transaction)
- Speed of transmission

The Link Layer. The transaction data request calls a link layer service routine that passes the transaction parameters specified by the application onto the link layer controller in the form that it understands. In addition, the retry code and transaction label parameters are added as the data request is passed onto the link layer controller. The actual mechanism for sending commands to the link layer controller is not defined by the specification. Parameters passed by the "link data request" service include:

- Destination Address
- Transaction Type Code
  - Write
  - Read
  - Lock
- Extended transaction code (only defined for lock transaction)
- Data Length
- Data (Data to be transferred during a write or lock transaction)
- Speed of transmission
- Retry code
- Transaction Label

The role of the link layer controller is to construct the necessary 1394 serial bus packets and pass them to the PHY for transmission over the serial bus. Format of the asynchronous packets is illustrated in Chapter 8, entitled "Asynchronous Packets," on page 165.

The PHY Layer. The interface between the Link and PHY is an informative part of the IEEE 1394-1995 specification (a suggested guideline, not a requirement), but it has been promoted to normative, or required status in the 1394a supplement.

The link layer controller first requests the PHY to arbitrate control of the bus using the "PHY arbitration request" service. This request communicates the following information to the PHY:

- Arbitration Class — Defines the type of arbitration that the PHY should use. Asynchronous transactions use either fair or priority (new to the 1394a supplement) arbitration.
- Speed Code — This parameter indicates which data rate that the upcoming packet will be transferred at (100, 200, or 400Mb/s).

The PHY reports the result of the arbitration back to the link via the "PHY arbitration confirmation" service. The status reported is either:

- Won — Arbitration was successful and the PHY will begin sending PHY clock indications to the link after speed and data_prefix has been signaled.
- Lost — Arbitration was not successful and the link must initiate the arbitration request again.

Upon receiving the PHY clock indication, the link can start clocked delivery of the packet via the "PHY data request" service. The values communicated to the PHY via this service include:

- DATA_ONE — a data bit with a value of one must be transmitted over the bus.
- DATA_ZERO — a data bit with a value of zero must be transmitted over the bus.
- DATA_END — signals the end of the data packet, thus PHY clock indications and PHY data requests are terminated.

Receiving the Request (The Indication)

The request is received by the addressed node that ultimately issues a response to the request. The following sections detail the actions taken by a node that is targeted by a request.

Physical Layer. As the responding node receives the data packet, its PHY initiates a "PHY data indication service" as data bits are received. The following parameters are communicated to the link via this service:

- Speed Code — indicates the data rate of the incoming data packet.
- DATA_START — indicates that a start of packet has been detected.
- DATA_ONE — a data bit with a value of one has been received from the bus.
- DATA_ZERO — a data bit with a value of zero has been received from the bus.
- DATA_END — the end of the data packet has been detected.

Link Layer. The link layer controller decodes the packet and passes it to the transaction layer via the "link data indication" service. The parameters passed via the "link data indication" service include:

- Source ID (node ID of transmitting node)
- Destination Address
- Transaction Type Code
  - Write
  - Read
  - Lock
- Extended transaction code (only defined for lock transaction)
- Data Length
- Data (Data to be transferred during a write or lock transaction)
- Speed of transmission
- Retry code
- Transaction Label
- Packet Status
  - GOOD — packet received without errors
  - BROADCAST — the bus and node address was FFFFh indicating a broadcast packet was received without error.
  - DATA_CRC_ERROR — a CRC error in the data block portion of the packet was detected.
  - FORMAT_ERROR — the packet contained an invalid value in one of its fields.

Transaction Layer. The transaction software layer notifies the application of the receipt of the packet using the "transaction data indication" service. The parameters passed to the application include:

- Transaction Type
  - Write
  - Broadcast
  - Read
  - Lock
- Extended transaction code (only defined for lock transaction)
- Destination Address
- Data Length
- Data (Data to be transferred during a write or lock transaction)
- Transaction Label
- Speed

The Acknowledgment. The transaction layer software not only notifies the application that a request has been received, but it also initiates the return of an acknowledgment to the requesting node. This acknowledgment verifies whether the request packet has been received. This acknowledgment is not the same as a response because the application has not yet responded to the request. The "link data response" service is used to initiate the return of the acknowledge code by communicating the following parameters to the link layer controller:

- Acknowledge Code (See Table 8-15 on page 192 for the possible code values and their definitions.)
- Bus Occupancy Control — this parameter specifies whether the link layer should release control of the bus once the acknowledgment is sent. Three possible parameters can be passed.
  - RELEASE is used if the response will follow at a later time. In this case, the responding node must arbitrate for control of the bus before returning the response.
  - HOLD specifies that control of the bus will not be relinquished following return of the acknowledgment because the application can respond quickly enough to concatenate the response to the acknowledge packet.
  - NO_OPERATION indicates that a broadcast address has been detected and that no acknowledgment should be returned.
- Speed of the packet transmission.

The PHY of the requesting node receives the acknowledge packet and sends it to the link controller via the "PHY data indication" service. The link layer controller forwards the acknowledgment to the transaction layer via a "link data confirmation" request to notify the local application whether the transaction request was successfully received by the target node.

Response Subaction

The application responds to the request by returning a response packet that ultimately confirms to the requesting application whether the request has been completed successfully or not. Table 4-2 on page 73 lists the protocol layer services that are employed during the response subaction. Note that the table lists the services in order of use as they typically would occur during a normal response. The shaded entries indicate services used by the original request agent.

Table 4-2: Service Used During Response Subaction

Service Name	Direction of Communication	Purpose of Service
Transaction Data Response	From Application	Initiates a response to the data request, thus confirming completion of the transaction.
Link Data Request	From Transaction Layer	This service initiates a packet transmission; in this case, a response packet.
PHY Arbitration Request	From Link Layer	Causes the PHY to (arbitration) for control of the serial bus.
PHY Arbitration Confirmation	From PHY	Reports result of arbitration request back to link.
PHY Clock Indication	From PHY	Following successful arbitration, the PHY notifies the link that it is ready to accept clocked data.
PHY Data Request	From Link Layer	Controls clocked transmission of the response packet onto the serial bus.

Table 4-2: Service Used During Response Subaction (Continued)

Service Name	Direction of Communication	Purpose of Service
PHY Data Indication	To Link Layer	Notifies link of the receipt of each data bit of the response packet.
Link Data Indication	To Transaction Layer	Notifies transaction layer that the response has been received.
Transaction Data Confirmation	To Application	Confirms the completion of the data request.
Link Data Response	From Transaction Layer	Transaction layer software initiates return of the acknowledge code.
PHY Data Request	From Link Layer	Controls clocked transmission of the acknowledge packet onto the serial bus.
PHY Data Indication	To Link Layer	Notifies link of the receipt of the acknowledgment packet.
Link Data Confirmation	To Transaction Layer	Notifies transaction layer whether the request was successfully received.

Reporting the Results (The Response)

The response is transferred from the target node back to the originator of the request as confirmation of whether the request was successfully serviced by the target device.

Transaction Layer Response. The target node's application uses the "transaction data response" service to initiate the response subaction. The parameters passed with this service include:

- Transaction type indication transaction type being completed.
  - write
  - broadcast write (no response expected, all other parameters are invalid)
  - read
  - lock
- Extended transaction code (lock transactions only)
- Response Code
- Transaction label

- Requester ID
- Data length (if data present)
- Data (read and lock transactions)
- Speed

Link Layer Response. Transaction layer software sends the response to the link layer controller using the "link data request" service, which causes the link controller to send the response packet that contains the response code. The parameters passed include:

- Destination Address
- Transaction Type Code
  - Write
  - Read
  - Lock
- Extended transaction code (only defined for lock transaction)
- Response Code
- Data Length
- Data (Data to be transferred during a read or lock transaction)
- Speed of transmission
- Retry code
- Transaction Label

PHY Layer Response. The same actions are taken by the link layer and PHY sending either a request or a response. The link layer controller must first request that the PHY arbitrate for control of the bus using the "PHY arbitration request" service. This request communicates the following information to the PHY:

- Arbitration Class — Defines the type of arbitration that the PHY should use. Asynchronous transactions use either fair or priority (new to the 1394a supplement) arbitration.
- Speed Code — This parameter indicates which data rate that the upcoming packet will be transferred at (100, 200, or 400Mb/s).

The PHY reports the result of the arbitration back to the link via the "PHY arbitration confirmation" service. The status reported is either:

- Won — Arbitration was successful and the PHY will begin sending PHY clock indications to the link after speed and data_prefix has been signaled.
- Lost — Arbitration was not successful and the link must initiate the arbitration request again.

Upon receiving the PHY clock indication, the link can start clocked delivery of the packet via the "PHY data request" service. The values communicated to the PHY via this service include:

- DATA_ONE — a data bit with a value of one must be transmitted over the bus.
- DATA_ZERO — a data bit with a value of zero must be transmitted over the bus.
- DATA_END — signals the end of the data packet, thus PHY clock indications and PHY data requests are terminated.

Response Reception

Physical Layer. As the responding node receives the data packet, its PHY initiates a "PHY data indication service" as data bits are received. The following parameters are communicated to the link via this service:

- Speed Code — indicates the data rate of the incoming data packet.
- DATA_START — indicates that a start of packet has been detected.
- DATA_ONE — a data bit with a value of one has been received from the bus.
- DATA_ZERO — a data bit with a value of zero has been received from the bus.
- DATA_END — the end of the data packet has been detected.

Link Layer. The link layer controller decodes the packet and passes it to the transaction layer via the "link data indication" service. The parameters passed via the "link data indication" service during a response include the response codes:

- Source ID (node ID of transmitting node)
- Destination Address
- Transaction Type Code
  - Write
  - Read
  - Lock
- Extended transaction code (only defined for lock transaction)
- Response Code
- Data Length
- Data (Data to be transferred during a write or lock transaction)
- Speed of transmission
- Retry code
- Transaction Label

- Packet Status
  - GOOD — packet received without errors
  - BROADCAST — the bus and node address was FFFFh indicating a broadcast packet was received without error.
  - DATA_CRC_ERROR — a CRC error in the data block portion of the packet was detected.
  - FORMAT_ERROR — the packet contained an invalid value in one of its fields.

Transaction Layer. The response is received by the requesting node as a confirmation of request completion. The "transaction data confirmation" service is used to pass the following parameters to the requesting application:

- Request status value:
  - complete (transaction completed successfully)
  - time-out (transaction response not received within time-out period)
  - acknowledge missing (no request acknowledge was received)
  - retry limit (retries exceeded the retry limit)
  - data error (data error detected in the data received)
- Response Code (complete or data error)
- Data (read and lock transactions)
- Data length (if data present)

The Acknowledgment. The transaction layer software not only notifies the application that response has been received, but it also initiates the return of an acknowledgment to the responding node. This acknowledgment verifies whether the response packet has been received without error. The "link data response" service is used to initiate the return of the acknowledge code by communicating the following parameters to the link layer controller:

- Acknowledge Code (See Table 8-15 on page 192 for the possible code values and their definitions.) Note that the response complete code must be used if the response packet was transmitted error free. This indicates the successful completion of the transaction.
- Bus Occupancy Control — this parameter specifies whether the link layer should release control of the bus once the acknowledgment is sent. Three possible parameters can be passed. However, in the case of a response packet the parameter will typically be RELEASE, because the transaction has completed.
  - RELEASE is used if the acknowledgment will follow at a later time. In this case, the responding node must arbitrate for control of the bus before returning the response.
  - HOLD specifies that control of the bus will not be relinquished following

return of the acknowledgment because the application can respond quickly enough to concatenate the response to the acknowledge packet.
- NO_OPERATION indicates that a broadcast address has been detected and that no acknowledgment should be returned.

- Speed of the packet transmission.

The PHY of the responding node receives the acknowledge packet and sends it to the link controller via the "PHY data indication" service. The link layer controller forwards the acknowledgment to the transaction layer software via a "link data confirmation" request to notify the software whether the transaction response was successfully received by the requesting node.

Transaction Label

The transaction label provides a unique identifier for each transaction that is issued by the requesting node. The transaction label value is produced by the transaction layer and sent with the request. This label must be returned along with the response to permit identification of this transaction in the event that another response is being returned by the same node. If a response is pending from a given node, then the requesting node cannot use the same label when starting another transaction targeting that same node.

During bus reset, all nodes must flush all queued asynchronous transactions, including requests and responses; thus, all labels can be reused without conflict.

Anatomy of Isochronous Transactions

Isochronous transfers are broadcast over the bus and target one or more devices based on the specified channel number associated with the transfer. Each isochronous transfer receives a guaranteed bus bandwidth. To ensure that sufficient bus bandwidth is available, nodes wishing to perform isochronous transfers must request the needed bandwidth from the node that performs the role of isochronous resource manager. Overall bus bandwidth is based on a total cycle time of 125µs.

Setting Up Isochronous Transactions

Before isochronous transactions can be initiated, an isochronous channel number and bus bandwidth must be obtained from the isochronous resource manager. Two registers located within the isochronous resource manager are defined for this purpose:

- CHANNELS_AVAILABLE
- BANDWIDTH_AVAILABLE

These registers must be accessed via a compare and swap lock transaction to ensure exclusive access when allocating these resources. Format of the channels available register and the procedure used to access it is described in "Channel Allocation" on page 337 and for the bus bandwidth register in "Bus Bandwidth Allocation" on page 339.

Once a channel number and sufficient bus bandwidth have been acquired, the target node or nodes must be configured so that they respond to the desired isochronous transactions. The application at the target node accomplishes this by assigning channel numbers associated with all isochronous transactions that it should accept. This is done via the "link isochronous control" request, which passes channel numbers that the link layer controller must recognize.

Maintaining Synchronization

Another aspect of initiating and receiving isochronous transactions is the ability to maintain synchronization with the isochronous clock intervals. The root node issues a cycle start packet at approximately 125µs intervals. The cycle start packet synchronizes all isochronous channels at the beginning of each isochronous interval and initiates isochronous transfers. When the PHY detects the cycle start packet, it sends an event notification to the link layer controller which, in turn, issues a "link cycle synch" indication to the application that includes the amount of delay between the cycle synchronization event and the actual start of the isochronous interval. Refer to "Cycle_Time & Bus_Time Registers" on page 377 for a detailed discussion of the cycle count generation. The "link cycle synch" service communicates the following parameters to the application:

- Current cycle count
- Current seconds count

Isochronous Transactions

The following sections describe the steps involved in completing isochronous transactions. Note that isochronous transactions do not participate in either the return of an acknowledgment packet or a response packet. This makes isochronous transactions simpler in terms of the protocol layers than the asynchronous forms. Isochronous transactions use a simplified form of address called a channel number. And isochronous transactions are broadcast, which makes it possible to target more than one node at a time.

Isochronous Transaction Initiation & Reception

Isochronous transactions do not use the transaction layer services. Instead, isochronous transactions directly use the link layer services to initiate transactions. Table 4-3 lists the protocol layer services used when performing an isochronous transaction. Note that the shaded table entries specify actions within the target nodes.

Table 4-3: Services Available for Isochronous Applications

Service Name	Direction of Communication	Purpose of Service
Link Isochronous Request	From Application	Causes the link layer to send one isochronous data packet.
PHY Arbitration Request	From Link Layer	Causes the PHY to arbitrate for control of the serial bus.
PHY Arbitration Confirmation	From PHY	Reports results of arbitration request back to link.
PHY Clock Indication	From PHY	Following successful arbitration, the PHY notifies the link that it is ready to accept clocked data.
PHY Data Request	From Link Layer	Controls clocked transmission of the request packet onto the serial bus.
PHY Data Indication	To Link Layer	Notifies link of the receipt of each data bit of the packet.

Table 4-3: Services Available for Isochronous Applications (Continued)

Service Name	Direction of Communication	Purpose of Service
Link Isochronous Indication	To Application	Indicates the reception of an isochronous packet for one of the channels identified by the Link Isoch Control Request.

Initiating the Transaction

Link Layer. The application uses the Link Isochronous Request to initiate an isochronous transaction by passing parameters to the link layer that it needs to initiate the transaction:

- Channel Number
- Data Length
- Data to be transferred
- Speed
- Tag
- Synchronization Code

Isochronous transfers are performed only as write transactions. For example, if two nodes are involved in transferring isochronous data to one another, each initiates data transfers when it has data to send. When a node transmits isochronous data, it is termed the talker and the receiver is termed a listener. In this way no isochronous read transfer is needed, nor is one supported. Also, more than one node may listen to an isochronous transmission, since no acknowledge packet is returned to the talker. Thus only one type of isochronous packet is defined.

The PHY Layer. The interface between the Link and PHY is an informative part of the IEEE 1394-1995 specification (a suggested guideline, not a requirement), but it has been promoted to normative (or required) status in the 1394a supplement.

The link layer controller first requests the PHY to arbitrate control of the bus using the "PHY arbitration request" service. This request communicates the following information to the PHY:

- Arbitration Class — Defines the type of arbitration that the PHY should use. In this case, isochronous arbitration is specified, informing the PHY to begin arbitration when it detects the next isochronous gap.
- Speed Code — This parameter indicates which data rate that the upcoming packet will be transferred at (100, 200, or 400Mb/s).

The PHY reports the result of the arbitration back to the link via the "PHY arbitration confirmation" service. The status reported is either:

- Won — Arbitration was successful and the PHY will begin sending PHY clock indications to the link after the speed and data_prefix has been signaled.
- Lost — Arbitration was not successful and the link must initiate the arbitration request again.

Upon receiving the PHY clock indication, the link can start clocked delivery of the packet via the "PHY data request" service. The values communicated to the PHY via this service include:

- DATA_ONE — a data bit with a value of one must be transmitted over the bus.
- DATA_ZERO — a data bit with a value of zero must be transmitted over the bus.
- DATA_END — signals the end of the data packet, thus PHY clock indications and PHY data requests are terminated.

Transaction Reception

The isochronous packet is received by the addressed node (based on a channel number) and is ultimately passed to the application. Note that the link layer has been previously configured for packet reception so that it knows which channels must recognize and generate a corresponding indication. This configuration is performed via the "Link Isochronous Control" Request, which communicates a channel list to the link layer controller. The following sections detail the actions taken by a node that is targeted by an isochronous request.

Physical Layer. As the responding node receives the data packet, its PHY initiates a "PHY data indication service" as data bits are received. The following parameters are communicated to the link via this service:

- Speed Code — indicates the data rate of the incoming data packet.
- DATA_START — indicates that a start of packet has been detected.
- DATA_ONE — PHY has received a data bit with a value of one.
- DATA_ZERO — a data bit with a value of zero has been received from the bus.
- DATA_END — the end of the data packet has been detected.

Link Layer. Once the packet is transferred to the link layer, it delivers the packet to the application via the "link isochronous indication" service. The parameters communicated to the application via this service are:

- Channel Number
- Data Length
- Data to be transferred
- Packet Status
- Speed
- Tag
- Synchronization Code

5 Cables & Connectors

The Previous Chapter

The previous chapter described the services defined by the specification that are used to pass parameters between layers during the execution of each transaction.

This Chapter

This chapter discusses the cable characteristics and connectors used by the IEEE 1394 cable environment. It also discusses the Device Bay implementation being specified in PC environments.

The Next Chapter

Next, the serial bus signaling environment is discussed. This includes recognition of device attachment and removal, arbitration signaling, speed signaling, and data/strobe signaling.

Cable and Connector Types

Two types of cables are supported by 1394. The original IEEE 1394-1995 specification defines a single 6-pin connector type and cable. The connectors are identical at both ends of the cable and can be plugged in either direction, between nodes.

The 1394a supplement defines an alternate 4-pin connector and cable that eliminates the power pins. Cables using this connector may have a 4-pin connector on one end of the cable and a 6-pin connector on the other end, or may have 4-pin connectors on each end. The specification places limits on the types of devices allowed to use 4-pin connectors.

6-pin Connector (1394-1995)

The original 1394-1995 specification defines a 6-pin plug and socket that is illustrated in Figure 5-1. The contact signal assignments are listed in Table 5-1 on page 87. Cable assemblies based on the 1995 version of the specification have mechanically-identical plugs at each end of the cable and all 1394 devices employed the standard 6-pin socket.

Figure 5-1: 6-Pin Plug and Socket

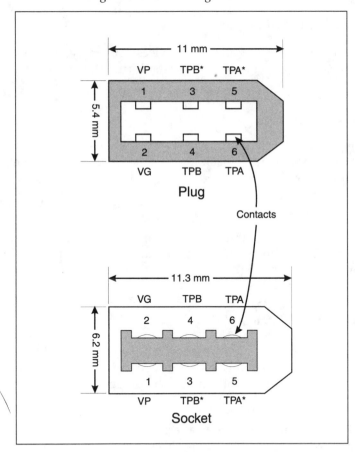

Chapter 5: Cables & Connectors

Table 5-1: Contact Signal Assignments and Numbers

Contact Number	Signal Name	Description
1	VP	Cable Power (voltage may range from 8 - 40 vdc).
2	VG	Cable Ground.
3	TPB*	Twisted pair B — differential data transmitted on TPB and differential strobe received on TPB.
4	TPB	
5	TPA*	Twisted pair A — differential strobe transmitted on TPA and differential data received on TPA.
6	TPA	

The socket dimensions are relatively small (11.3mm X 6.2mm) when compared to standard connectors used by many computer peripheral devices. The socket consists of a shell and contact wafer. The plug body fits into the socket shell and the contacts within the plug body slide over the socket's contact wafer as the plug is inserted.

Make First/Break Last Power Pins

The 6-pin socket has longer contact power and ground contact pins. This ensures that the power pins make contact prior to the data pair pins when the plug is inserted into the socket; and conversely, when a plug is removed the data pins break contact prior to the power pins. The separation between the power and data pins is specified to be a minimum of 0.8mm.

Optional 4-pin Connector (1394a supplement)

The 4-pin connector is defined by the 1394a supplement for use in 1394 applications where the standard 6-pin connector is too large. Figure 5-2 illustrates the 4-pin plug and socket. The connector was originally designed by Sony and included in their video cameras. The 1394a supplement adopted the Sony design. The specification defines two categories of 1394 devices that may benefit from a smaller connector:

- Battery operated devices — Since these nodes do not draw power from the cable, a less expensive cable and connector are possible and desirable. Furthermore, the power conductors can be a source of unwanted analog noise, which is a major concern for applications that include audio.

- Hand-held devices — The standard connector may be relatively bulky when implemented into small hand-held devices such as video camcorders.

Figure 5-2: 4-Pin Plug and Socket

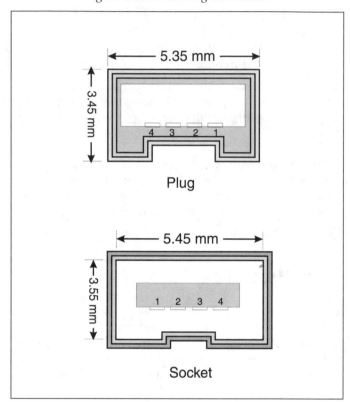

Positive Retention

Both connector types employ positive retention via a detent. Applying sufficient force releases the plug when removing the cable. The specification permits stronger retention features to be implemented. However, these additional retention features must not interfere with the ability to mate the plug or connector using the standard detent retention mechanism.

Chapter 5: Cables & Connectors

Cable Characteristics

Cable electrical characteristics are the same for the 4-conductor and 6-conductor cable, with the exception that the 4-conductor cable does not include the power wires. Standard electrical characteristics of the cables have the following parameters and characteristics. Test and measurement procedures are described in the specification.

- Suggested maximum cable length = 4.5 meters (with signal velocity = 5.05ns/meter)
- 110 ohms characteristic impedance — differential mode
- 33 ohms characteristic impedance — common mode
- Signal velocity equal to or less than 5.05ns/meter
- Signal pair attenuation:
  - 100MHz = <2.3dB
  - 200MHz = <3.2dB
  - 400MHz = <5.8dB
- Relative propagation skew ≤ 400ps @ 100MHz and ≤ 100ps @ 400MHz (the difference between the differential mode propagation delay of the two twisted pair conductors that must be measured in the frequency domain).
- TPA to TPB Crosstalk ≤ -26 dB (within 1MHz to 500MHz range).

6-Conductor Cables

Figure 5-3 illustrates the cross-section of a 6-conductor cable including the wires and insulation required.

Figure 5-3: Cross-section of 6-Conductor Cable

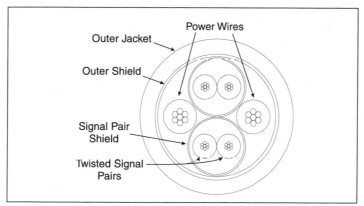

FireWire System Architecture

Figure 5-4 illustrates how the plug and cable are joined and shows the twisted pair cross-over between the plugs. Note that TPA (pins 5 and 6) on end A of the cable connects to TPB (pins 3 and 4) on end B and vice versa. Note also that the plug connectors at each end of the cable are identical. This means that it is possible for a user to connect 1394 nodes in such a way that a looped topology results, causing the system to fail during configuration. This condition is detectable by nodes residing on the bus and can be reported to software.

Figure 5-4: 6-Pin Connector Cable/Plug Assembly

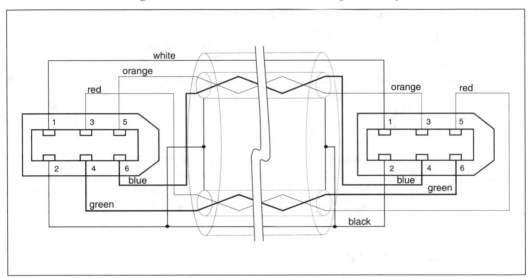

4-Conductor Cables

Figure 5-5 on page 91 illustrates the cross-section of a 4-conductor cable including the wires and insulation required. Two separate cable assemblies are possible with the 4-conductors plugs and cables:

1. Cable with identical 4-pins plugs at each end of the cable.
2. Cable with a 4-pin plug on one end and a 6-pin plug on the other end.

Figure 5-6 on page 91 illustrates how the plug and cable are joined and shows the twisted pair cross-over between the plugs with identical 4-pin plugs. Note that TPA (pins 3 and 4) on end A of the cable connects to TPB (pins 1 and 2) on end B and vice versa.

Figure 5-5: Cross-section of 4-Conductor Cable

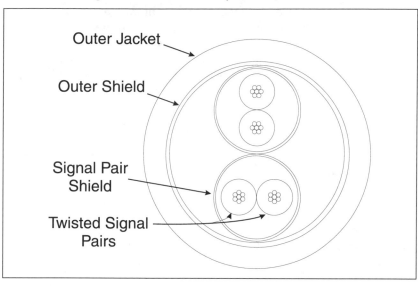

Figure 5-6: Cable/Plug Assembly with Identical 4-Pin Plugs

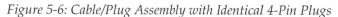
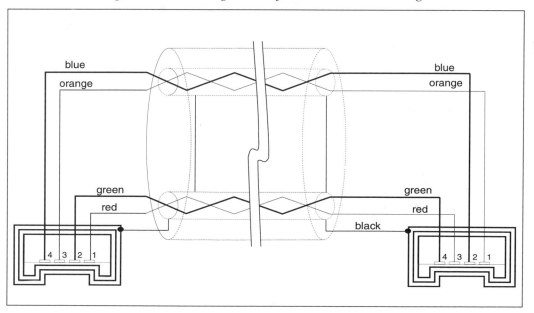

Figure 5-7 on page 92 illustrates how the plug and cable are joined when the cable has a 4-pin plug on one end of the cable and a 6-pin plug on the other. Note that TPA of the 6-pin plug (pins 3 and 4) connects to TPB of the 4-pin plug (pins 1 and 2) and vice versa. Since there are no power conductors in the cable, the voltage ground (VG) pin of the 6-pin plug is connected to the cable shielding.

Figure 5-7: Cable/Plug Assembly with a 4-Pin Plug and 6-Pin Plug

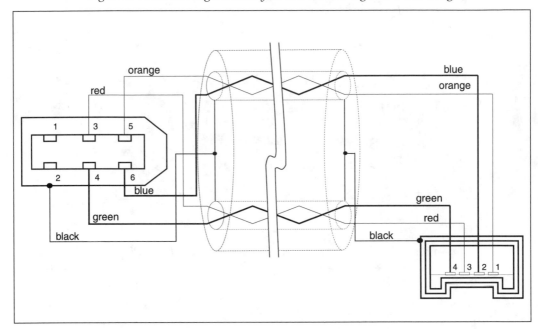

Device Bay

Some manufacturers support a docking bay into which 1394 and Universal Serial Bus (USB) devices can be inserted. The device bay specification was developed by Compaq, Intel, and Microsoft. Device bay is intended to provide an easy method of adding and upgrading peripheral devices without the need to open the computer chassis.

Since 1394 and USB both support hot insertion and removal, when a peripheral is inserted into or removed from the device bay, the event is automatically detected and the device is either installed or uninstalled without user intervention. In this way, devices can be added or replaced as easily as the insertion or the removal of a floppy disk. Three form factors, each with different heights, have been defined:

- Device Bay 13 — 13 mm in height
- Device Bay 20 — 20 mm in height
- Device Bay 32 — 32 mm in height

These different-sized bays are intended to accommodate different system requirements (e.g. portable, desktop, and server systems).

6 *The Electrical Interface*

The Previous Chapter

The previous chapter discussed the cable characteristics and connectors used by the IEEE 1394 cable environment. It also discussed the Device Bay implementation being specified in PC environments.

This Chapter

This chapter details the serial bus signaling environment. This includes recognition of device attachment and removal, arbitration signaling, speed signaling, and data/strobe signaling.

The Next Chapter

The next chapter discusses the arbitration process. It defines the various types of arbitration including isochronous and asynchronous arbitration, as well as the newer arbitration types defined by the 1394a supplement.

Overview

The IEEE 1394 serial bus employs two twisted pairs of signal wires (Twisted Pair A, or TPA and Twisted Pair B, or TPB). Additionally, a single pair of wires may be used to provide power for nodes. TPA and TPB provide both differential and common mode signaling to support the following functions.

- Recognition of device attachment/detachment
- Reset
- Arbitration
- Packet transmission
- Automatic configuration
- Speed signaling

The twisted pair signals are crosswired within the cable, such that TPA and TPB of one node connects respectively to TPB and TPA of the other. The individual twisted pair signals are referred to as TPA/TPA* and TPB/TPB*. Either node may initiate a transaction and therefore use identical signaling interfaces. The following sections discuss the functional aspects of the 1394 signaling environment.

Common Mode Signaling

Common mode signaling is used for the following functions:

- Device attachment/detachment detection
- Speed signaling
- Suspend/resume signaling

These signaling environments utilize DC signals to accomplish the required functionality. The characteristic impedance of the signal pairs is 33±6Ω. Since the signaling is based on DC signaling, there is no concern regarding unwanted reflections. Common mode values are specified as the average voltage on the twisted pair A or B (e.g. Average voltage of TPA and TPA*).

Differential Signaling

Differential signaling is used for the following functions:

- Reset
- Arbitration
- Configuration
- Packet transmission

Differential signaling can occur at speeds of 100, 200, or 400MHz. The goal of the 1394 differential signaling environment is to eliminate signal reflections from occurring over the cable. This is accomplished by terminating the differential pairs to obtain a reflection coefficient of zero. The characteristic impedance of each signal is 110±6Ω, therefore 110Ω termination resistors (two 55Ω resistors in series) are employed to eliminate reflections on each signal line. See "Differential Signal Specifications" on page 104 for details regarding the differential signaling environment.

Chapter 6: The Electrical Interface

Differential signaling has two major advantages that are used by the 1394 bus:

- Noise immunity
- Three signaling states: differential 1, differential 0, and Hi Z

The three signaling states are used to define a variety of bus conditions and are detailed later in this chapter.

Recognition of Device Attachment and Detachment

Recognition of whether a device is attached to a given port or not differs between the 1394-1995 specification and the 1394a supplement. Both mechanisms are described in the following sections.

IEEE 1394-1995 Device Attachment/Detachment

Each node provides an offset voltage on its TPA signal lines by driving a TpBias voltage in the range of 1.665v to 2.015v. This voltage is driven by a twisted pair bias voltage source driver as illustrated in Figure 6-1. On the other end of the cable, TpBias is detected by the attached node's port status receiver via TPB. Accounting for signal attenuation across the wire, the receiver senses a voltage between 1.165v and 2.015v.

Figure 6-1: Bias Voltage Applied to the Cable Permits Detection of Node Attachment/Detachment.

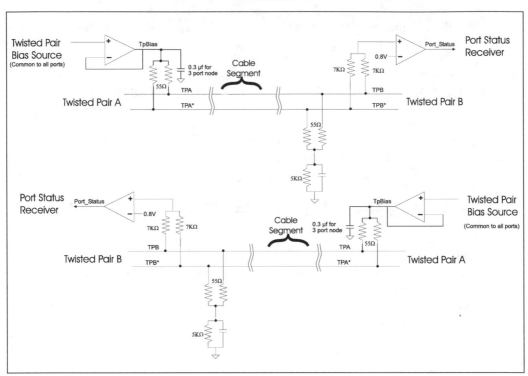

Note that both signaling pairs have the bias voltage permanently applied once another node is attached. Each node detects the bias voltage being applied by the node on the opposite end of the cable. A port status receiver continuously compares 0.8vdc reference voltage to the voltage on the cable. When a node is attached to a given port, the bias voltage causes the cable voltage to rise above 0.8vdc, thereby signifying the attachment of a node. Table 6-1 gives the threshold voltages for the port receiver. When a previously attached node is removed from the network, the bias voltage will be also removed, causing the port status receivers to detect node removal.

Table 6-1: Port Status Voltage States

Port_Status	Common Mode Input Signal State (vdc)
Node Detached	TPB input ≤ 0.6v
Indeterminate	0.6v < TPB input < 1.0v
Node Attached	TPB input ≥ 1.0v

IEEE 1394a Device Attachment/Detachment

The port suspend feature introduced by the 1394a supplement permits port circuitry to enter a low power state. In this state only TpBias and port connect status monitoring takes place. A suspended port is required to remove TpBias to confirm that it has entered the suspended state. A 1394-1995 node connected to the suspended port would detect the removal of TpBias and assume that the node had been detached, when in fact it is still connected but suspended. To differentiate between a suspended port and a detached node, new circuitry has been added to 1394a compliant nodes.

When a port enters the suspend state it must activate its port connection detect circuit (new to 1394a). This circuit monitors the physical connection between suspended ports. Figure 6-2 illustrates the connection detect circuitry. In the absence of TpBias, the connect_detect receiver will recognize detachment of a node. The current source I_{CD} must not exceed 76µA to ensure that the Port_Status receiver of the attached node does not exceed 0.4 vdc. If the attached node is removed, the input voltage at the connection detect circuit will rise above 0.4 vdc because the current path to ground will have been removed. This permits the port to recognize that the previously attached node has been disconnected.

Note that the connection_detect receiver is only valid when TpBias has been disabled. TpBias is removed when a port is either suspended, disabled, or disconnected.

Figure 6-2: Port Connection Detect Circuitry

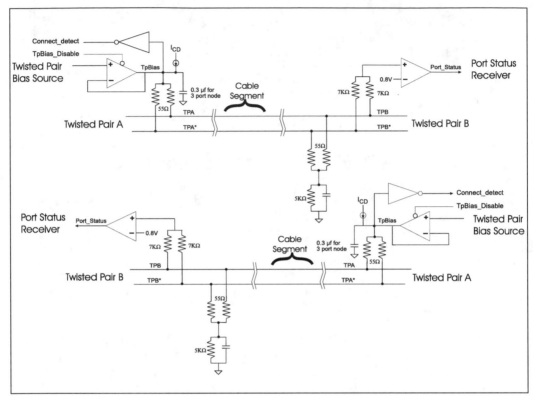

Bus Idle State

Once a node is attached to an active port, the bias voltage remains applied to both TPA and TPB of each node interface, unless the port is suspended. This offset voltage results in an idle condition on the bus until either the strobe or the data drivers are enabled and subsequently drive a differential value onto the bus. The idle condition is detected by the arbitration comparators as discussed later in this chapter.

The Port Interface

Figure 6-3 on page 102 illustrates the port interface between two attached IEEE 1394-1995 nodes and Figure 6-4 on page 103 illustrates the port interface between two 1394a nodes. The port interface for 1394-1995 and for 1394a are identical except that modifications to 1394a have been made to support two additional port states:

- disabled
- suspended

Note that the twisted pair signals are crosswired within the cable, such that TPA of one node connects to TPB and TPB connects to TPA. The individual twisted pair signals are referred to as TPA/TPA* and TPB/TPB*. Either node may initiate a transaction and therefore use identical signaling interfaces. The following sections discuss the functional aspects of the 1394 signaling environment.

Figure 6-3: The IEEE 1394-1995 Signal Interface

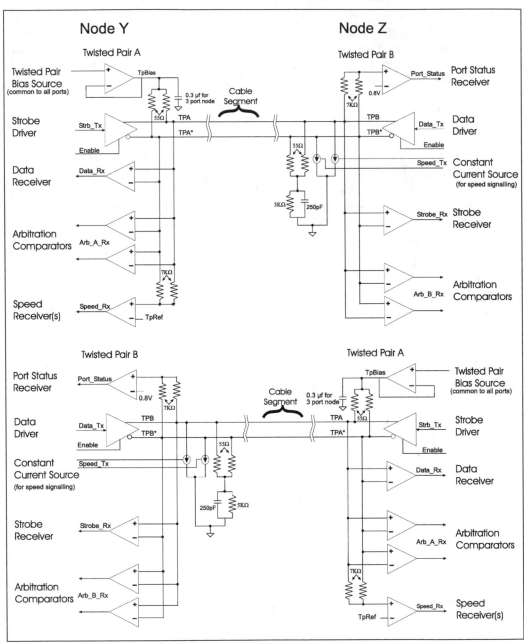

Figure 6-4: 1394a Port Interface

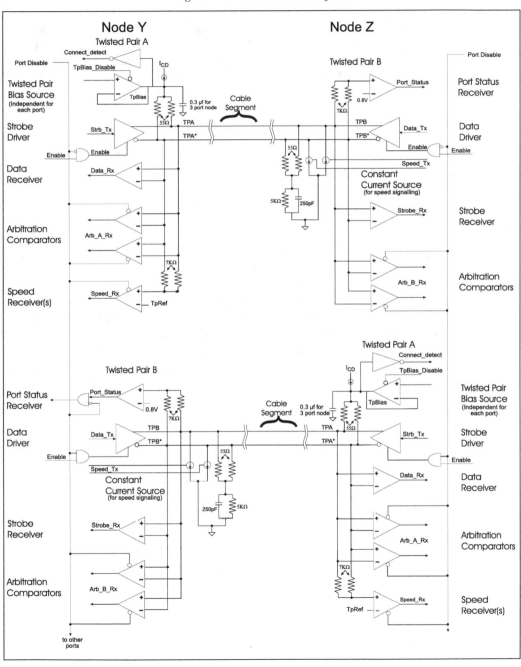

Differential Signal Specifications

The minimum and maximum differential output voltages are given in Table 6-2. The differential output voltage is measured between TPA/TPB and TPA*/TPB* respectively. A logical one is signaled differentially when the TPA/TPB voltage is greater than the TPA*/TPB* voltage respectively, while a zero is signaled when the TPA*/TPB* voltage is greater than the TPA/TPB voltage. When both the strobe and data drivers connected to the signal pair are disabled, a High impedance (Hi Z) state exists on the bus and no potential difference is detected between TPA and TPA* or TPB and TPB*.

Table 6-2: Differential Output Signal Amplitude

Maximum	Minimum
265 mV	172 mV

The sensitivity of the differential receivers must be designed based on worst case signal amplitudes that might be observed at the receiving port. The signal amplitude that is output at the driver is shown in Table 6-2. However, the cable will attenuate the signal as it is transmitted across the cable. This attenuation, caused by conductor skin effects, is a function of frequency and cable length as shown below. Note that cable length is assumed to be 4.5 meters.

* 100MHz = <2.3dB
* 200MHz = <3.2dB
* 400MHz = <5.8dB

As the frequency increases the signal loss increases; thus, the input receiver must be able to tolerate the lesser signal strength. Table 6-3 lists the minimum and maximum input voltage ranges for packets speeds of 100Mb/s, 200Mb/s, and 400Mb/s.

Table 6-3: Differential Receive Signal Amplitude

Signal	S100 (mV) (speed signaling off)		S200 (mV)		S400 (mV)	
	Min	Max	Min	Max	Min	Max
During Arbitration	173	260	171	262	168	265
During Clocked Data Reception	142	260	132	260	118	260

Arbitration Signaling

Arbitration signaling supports five distinct functions:

- Bus Reset
- Tree Identification
- Self Identification
- Normal Arbitration
- Starting and Ending Packets
- Port State Control (1394a only)

Each of the arbitration signaling environments is discussed later; however, in each case the actual signaling mechanism is the same. Only the signal states change to specify the event being signaled. The signaling mechanism is discussed in the following two sections.

Line State Signaling (1, 0, and Z)

Arbitration employs bi-directional signaling and uses three logical line states:

- Z (driver disabled)
- 1 (NRZ one being driven)
- 0 (NRZ zero being driven)

The strobe and data drivers may be disabled leaving the line undriven (Z) or may be enabled and driving either a logical 1 or 0 onto the line. Arbitration signaling transmitted via TPA is termed Arb_A_Tx and is delivered via the strobe driver, while arbitration B is delivered via the data driver as illustrated in Figure 6-5 on page 106. Arb_A_Tx is detected, or received, by arbitration comparators at the opposite end of the cable and is termed Arb_B_Rx due to the crossover in the cable. Similarly Arb_B_Tx is detected as Arb_A_Rx.

Note that arbitration signaling does not involve clocked data, but rather a steady state signaling across TPA and TPB. The specification defines the rules for driving the three arbitration line states as listed in Table 6-4 on page 107.

The pair of arbitration comparators on each strobe or data receiver can detect a logical Z, 1, or 0. Note that when a logical Z persists on the cable, both arbitration comparators in the pair will be reverse biased. When a logical 1 persists on the cable, one arbitration comparator will be forward biased and the other will be reverse biased. The opposite scenario is when a logical 0 persists on the cable, causing the inverse conditions from logical 1.

Figure 6-5: Arbitration Signaling

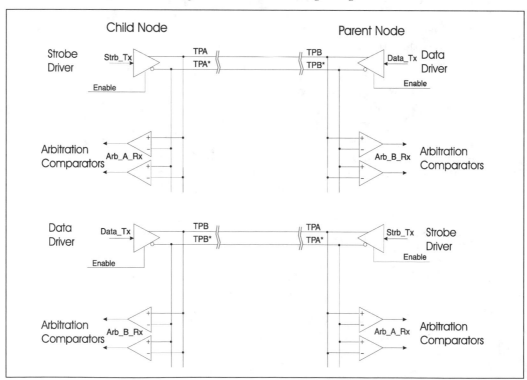

Table 6-4: Arbitration Signal Generation Rules

Arbitration Signal	Strobe Driver		Data Driver	
	Strb_Enable	Strb_Data State	Data_Enable	Data_Tx State
Z	0	NA	0	NA
0	1	0	1	0
1	1	1	1	1

Line State Detection

The arbitration receivers detect the line state driven on TPA and TPB and must decode the information that is received to determine if a Z, 0, or 1 is being signaled. Figure 6-6 on page 108 pictures the arbitration receivers and a decode block. The line states define a variety of events or conditions and are involved in 1394 bus configuration, bus reset, and of course arbitration.

Refer to Table 6-5 on page 109, which describes the decoding rules for the arbitration comparator outputs. In most instances the decoding is straight forward. However, two inconclusive conditions exist that leave the interpretation of the line state in question. Column one of Table 6-5 lists the arbitration value being driven over the strobe or data drivers during arbitration time (called Arb_A_TX and Arb_B_TX), while the second column lists the value being received by the transmitting node at its arbitration receivers. Column three lists the decoded value.

The first three rows present no problem in interpreting what the decoded value should be. The node has its driver off; therefore, the value detected by the arbitration receivers is the state driven by the node at the other end of the cable, which becomes the decoded value.

Figure 6-6: Arbitration Comparator Outputs Must Be Decoded by Associated Arbitration Logic

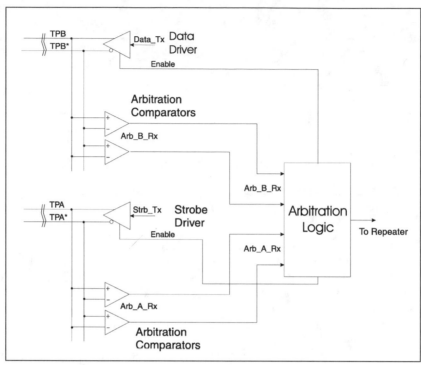

Row three in the table indicates that this node is driving a zero line state, but is detecting a Z at its arbitration receivers. This means that the node on the other end of the cable is driving a one that counters the zero being driven by this node. The line states being driven disagree, which leaves the interpretation of the line state in question. The specification defines the decoded state as a one, and is referred to as the dominance rule for one. This particular condition is specified as the first half of the dominance rule for one. The second half of the dominance rule for one occurs when this node drives a one but detects Z. In this case the node at the opposite end of the cable is driving a zero, which also results in a decoded value of one.

Table 6-5: Arbitration Comparator Signal Decoding Rules

Arb_A/B_Tx Value	Arb_A/B_Rx Value	Decoded Arb Value	Explanation
Z	Z	Z	If this port driver is disabled, then the received signal is the same as that driven by the port on the other end of the cable.
Z	0	0	
Z	1	1	
0	Z	1	If this port is driving a zero but a Z is detected, then the other port must be driving a one. (First half of the dominance rule for one.)
0	0	0	If this port is driving a zero and its arb. comparators detect a zero, then the other port driver is either sending a zero or is disabled.
1	Z	1	If this port is sending a one, but is receiving a Z, then the other port must be sending a zero. (Second half of the dominance rule for one.)
1	1	1	If this port is sending a one and receiving a one, the other port is either sending a one or its driver is disabled.

Note that the convention used by the specification to specify the line states is in the form: $S_{TPA}S_{TPB}$, where S is the state of either twisted pair A or B that is being either transmitted or received. The documentation convention in the specification lists line states A first and line state B second. For example, a TX_REQUEST is defined as "Z0" where "Z" is signaled by the strobe driver on TPA (i.e. strobe driver is disabled) and "0" is signaled by the data driver on TPB. When the TX_REQUEST is detected by the node on the other end of the cable (RX_REQUEST), the cross-wired cable results in a "0Z" designation, since "0" is received via TPA and "Z" is received via TPB.

Reset Signaling

When bus reset is signaled by a node, the repeaters in all other nodes propagate the reset across all cable segments. Each node detects reset via its arbitration comparators. A single node may initiate reset signaling due to a variety of events including recognition of device attachment or detachment (See Chapter 14 for details). Table 6-6 lists the transmitted and received line states for reset.

Reset can be signaled at any time and is independent of any traffic on the bus. During normal transfer of packets, data/strobe signaling is performed and the strobe and data receivers are active. The arbitration comparators and the arbitration decode logic monitors the bus in order to detect the end of packet (Data End). Once packet end is detected, arbitration decode logic then monitors the line state to detect the next arbitration signaling event. If reset is being signalled, it will override any other arbitration signaling event due to 1's dominant decoding.

Table 6-6: Bus Reset Signaling

Line State Name Transmitted	Line State Transmitted		Line State Name Received	Line State Received/decoded	
	Arb_A	Arb_B		Arb_A	Arb_B
Bus_Reset	1	1	Bus_Reset	1	1

Line States During Configuration

The automatic configuration process also uses the arbitration mechanism. Arbitration signaling is used during both the tree-identification and self-identification processes. Table 6-7 on page 111 lists the signaling names and states used during tree identification and Table 6-8 on page 111 lists the signal name and state used during self identification. See Chapter 13, entitled "Configuration Process," on page 265 for more detail on the configuration process.

Table 6-7: Signaling States Used During Tree Identification

Line State Name Transmitted	Line State Transmitted		Line State Name Received	Line State Received/decoded	
	Arb_A	Arb_B		Arb_A	Arb_B
TX_PARENT_NOTIFY (probable child node)	0	Z	RX_PARENT_NOTIFY (probable parent node)	Z	0
TX_CHILD_NOTIFY (parent node)	1	Z	RX_PARENT_HANDSHAKE (child node)	0	1
TX_PARENT_NOTIFY is removed by child node	Z	Z	RX_CHILD_HANDSHAKE (parent node sees its own TX_CHILD_NOTIFY)	1	Z
TX_PARENT_NOTIFY (both nodes)	0	Z	RX_ROOT_CONTENTION (both nodes)	0	0

Table 6-8: Signaling States Used During Self-Identification

Line State Name Transmitted	Line State Transmitted		Line State Name Received	Line State Received/decoded	
	Arb_A	Arb_B		Arb_A	Arb_B
TX_IDENT_DONE (child node)	1	Z	RX_IDENT_DONE (parent node)	Z	1
TX_SELF_ID_GRANT (parent node)	Z	0	RX_SELF_ID_GRANT (child node)	0	0

Line States During Normal Arbitration

Arbitration signaling determines which node will gain ownership of the bus and initiate the next transaction. When a node wishes to use the bus, it must transmit a arbitration bus request (TX_REQUEST) to its parent node (the node toward the root node). Nodes use their strobe and data drivers to send a bus request, which is detected by arbitration comparators within the parent node. This chapter discusses the signaling conventions used during arbitration but does not detail the arbitration process. See Chapter 7 for a detailed discussion of the arbitration process.

The arbitration process employs six line states as listed in Table 6-9 and includes both the transmitted and associated line states that are received. The following paragraphs illustrate the bi-directional use of the lines during a bus request and grant handshake between a child node and its parent.

Table 6-9: Arbitration Line States During Normal Arbitration

Line State Name Transmitted	Line State Transmitted		Line State Name Received	Line State Received/decoded	
	Arb_A	Arb_B		Arb_A	Arb_B
TX_REQUEST (child node)	Z	0	RX_REQUEST (parent node)	0	Z
TX_GRANT (parent node)	Z	0	RX_GRANT (child node)	0	0
TX_REQUEST removed by child node	Z	Z	RX_REQUEST_CANCEL (parent node detects its own TX_GRANT)	Z	0
TX_DATA_PREFIX (parent node)	0	1	RX_DATA_PREFIX (child node)	1	0

Arbitration signaling begins with a node requesting use of the serial bus by sending a bus request (TX_REQUEST) to its parent node. This occurs after a period of idle time on the bus during which all drivers are disabled, resulting in the "ZZ" state on all cable segments. Figure 6-7 illustrates a child node sending TX_REQUEST (Z0) and its parent node receiving RX_REQUEST (0Z). Figure 6-6 shows that logic associated with the arbitration comparators is used by the PHY to differentiate between the logical states and to decode the line states.

Figure 6-7: Child Node Sending Transmit Request to its Parent Node

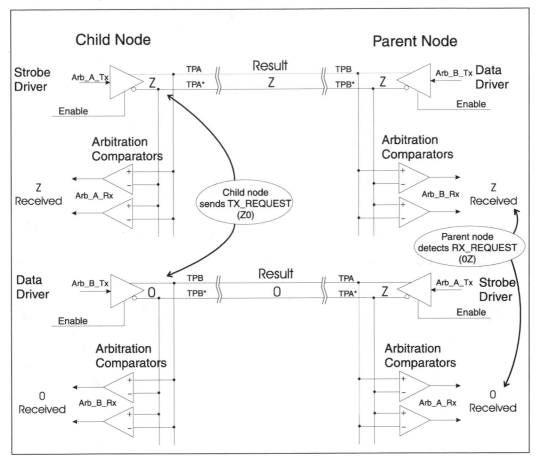

Assuming that the child node in this example has the highest priority, it will win ownership of the bus. The parent node sends a TX_GRANT (Z0) to the child node to inform it that it can start a transaction. Since the child continues to send TX_REQUEST, both the parent and child node will be driving the bus simultaneously. The line states driven by both the child and the parent are (Z0). However, due to the cross-wiring the received value will be "00" as illustrated in Figure 6-8.

Figure 6-8: Parent Node Sending Transmit Grant While Child Continues Driving Transmit Request

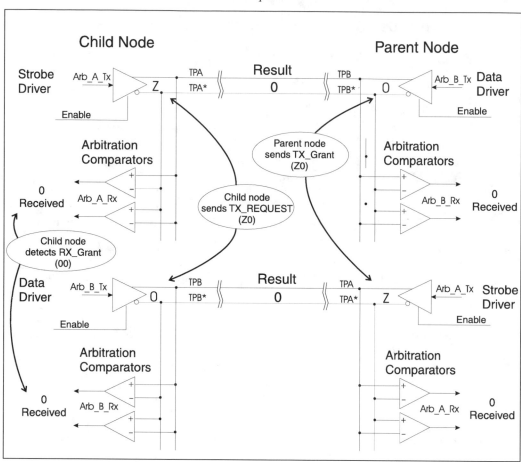

Starting and Ending Packet Transmission

Once arbitration completes the winning node can initiate a transaction. Packet transmission begins with "data prefix" signaling and typically ends with "data end" signaling. Figure 6-9 illustrates how a packet is framed by data prefix and data end.

Figure 6-9: Packet Framed By Data_Prefix and Data_End

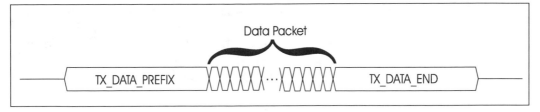

A packet may end with data prefix rather than data end signaling, when another packet is concatenated to the end of the current packet. Two concatenated packets are illustrated in Figure 6-10 with the first packet framed by two data prefix states followed immediately by the concatenated packet.

Figure 6-10: Packet Framed By Two Data_Prefixes During Concatenated Packet Transmission

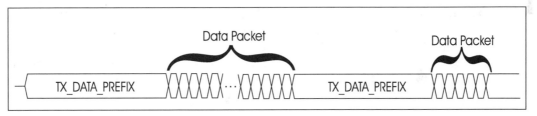

Data prefix and data end signaling is accomplished via the arbitration line states listed in Table 6-10.

Table 6-10: Data Prefix and Data End Signaling

Line State Name Transmitted	Line State Transmitted		Line State Name Received	Line State Received/decoded	
	Arb_A	Arb_B		Arb_A	Arb_B
TX_DATA_PREFIX	0	1	RX_DATA_PREFIX	1	0
TX_DATA_END	1	0	RX_DATA_END	0	1

Dribble Bits

Note that during packet transmission, the transmitting node must insert additional bits at the end of the packet to ensure that the last few bits of the packet are flushed through the receive circuitry. These additional bits are called dribble bits. Depending on the packet transmission speed either 1 (100Mb/s), 3 (200Mb/s), or 7 (400Mb/s) dribble bits are required.

The need for the dribble bits relates to clock generation during the reception of a packet. The receiving PHY uses the incoming data and strobe to recover the clock used by the transmitting PHY to send the data. When the packet ends so does clock generation, because the RX_DATA_END line state does not include any transitions. Since the receive clock stops when the last data bit is received, additional clocks are needed to flush the last bits of the packet through the receive circuitry.

Dribble bits are driven to a value such that the two signals TPA and TPB are put to the correct line states depending on whether the bus is being held (DATA_PREFIX) or not (DATA_END). The dribble bits are not contained in the packet that is delivered from the link to the PHY, but rather are inserted by the PHY before the PHY transmits the packet to the cable. Conversely, a packet received from the cable by a PHY is stripped of the dribble bits before the packet is sent to the link.

Port State Control

The 1394a supplement defines two new states that individual ports can be placed into. These states are:

- Disabled
- Suspended

Table 6-11 lists the line states used to disable and suspend ports. Both the transmitted and received line states are specified. Chapter 26, entitled "Suspend & Resume," on page 445 for more details regarding port disable and port suspend.

Table 6-11: Port Disable and Suspend Line State Signaling

Line State Name Transmitted	Line State Transmitted		Line State Name Received	Line State Received/ decoded	
	Arb_A	Arb_B		Arb_A	Arb_B
TX_DISABLE_NOTIFY	Z	1	RX_DISABLE_NOTIFY	1	Z
TX_SUSPEND	0	0	RX_SUSPEND	0	0

Speed Signaling

Since the rate of data delivery can vary, speed information is sent prior to packet transmission during data prefix time. The IEEE 1394 cable environment supports speeds of:

- 98.304Mb/s (aka 100Mb/s and S100)
- 196.608Mb/s (aka 200Mb/s and S200)
- 393.216Mb/s (aka 400Mb/s and S400)

All nodes are required to support 100Mb/s transfers, while some may also support one or both of the higher speeds. During the configuration process speed capabilities of each node are passed to other nodes residing on the bus. Most importantly, during configuration two nodes that attach to the same cable exchange speed capabilities information, and gives each node knowledge of the maximum speed at which the other can operate.

If a given packet is sent at a higher speed than is supported by the attached node, then that packet will not be transferred to the slower node. Consequently, a node must know the speed of a given packet so that it can determine whether to repeat it to other nodes attached to its ports. Figure 6-11 on page 119 illustrates an example topology with the maximum PHY speed supported by each node. The speed specified for each cable is governed by the slowest speed device attached to a cable. Consider the following examples.

High Speed Devices Slowed Due to Topology

Note that both nodes C and F in Figure 6-11 support speeds of 400Mb/s, but the maximum speed at which they can communicate is limited by the slowest node in the path between them. Consider the consequence of node F attempting to send a packet to node C at the 400Mb/s rate. Note that before sending a packet a node must first signal packet speed information to notify nodes of the transmission speed of the upcoming packet. Node F recognizes that the node it attaches to (i.e. node D) supports 400Mb/s operation and therefore the packet can be send to node D at the fast rate. When node D receives speed signaling from node C, it recognizes that the packet is being sent at 400Mb/s. Node D checks the speed of the node attached to each of its ports and determines that none are equipped to handle packet reception at 400Mb/s. Consequently, node D does not repeat the packet to any of its ports, causing the transaction to fail. In lieu of repeating the packet to other ports, data prefix is signaled by node D to the slower nodes to keep them quiet until packet transmission ends. Note that when packet transmission ends, DATA_PREFIX being signaled by node D to the slower nodes (A and E) is changed to the DATA_END line state prior to returning the bus to idle.

If node F chose to transmit the packet at 200Mb/s, node D would repeat the packet to node A but would block packet transmission to node E. Node A, however, would be unable to repeat the transaction to B because it only supports 100Mb/s traffic, and again the transaction would fail. This limits the maximum packet speed between C and F to 100Mb/s.

Notice that the user could increase the overall performance of the bus if nodes C and E were switched, thereby grouping all 400Mb/s nodes so that they connect to each other.

Devices of Like Speed Directly Connected

When two devices communicating with each other operate at the same speed they will obviously be successful. In some instances this communication may not be seen by any other nodes. For example, if node F initiates a 400Mb/s request that targets node D, speed signaling will notify D of packet speed, causing it to signal data prefix to its other ports. Thus nodes D and F complete the transaction while all other nodes are forced to wait.

Figure 6-11: Topology with Speed Information Included

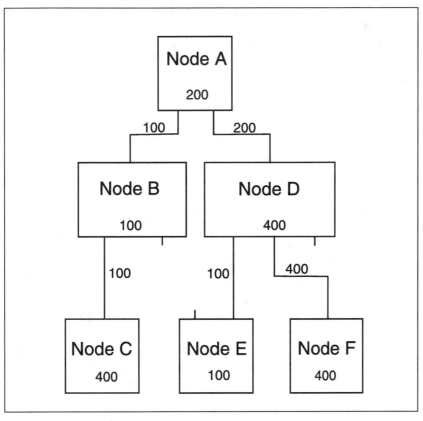

Speed Signaling Circuitry

Speed information is current encoded using common mode signaling as follows:

- 100Mb/s — No speed information is sent since all nodes support 100Mb/s traffic (i.e. common mode signaling is off). The absence of speed information is interpreted as 100Mb/s packet transmission.
- 200Mb/s — A current between 2.53ma and 4.84ma (~3.5ma) is sourced during 200Mb/s packet transmission.
- 400Mb/s — A current between 8.10ma and 12.40ma (~10ma) is sourced during 400Mb/s packet transmission.

Figure 6-12 illustrates the speed signaling circuitry. A constant current source is used to encode speed information during packet transmission. The current is drawn from the bias voltage source causing the line voltage to change as a result of the additional current being sourced. A comparator (called the speed receiver) detects the change in the average voltage on TPA and TPA* due to the additional current being drawn from the TpBias source through the 55Ω terminating resistors.

Figure 6-12: Speed Signaling Circuitry for S400 PHY

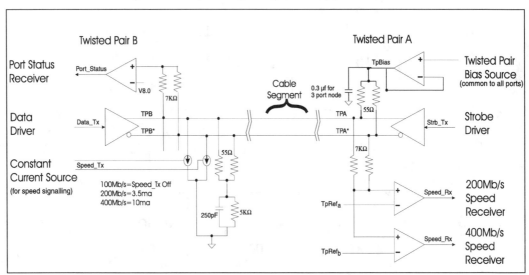

The current encoded speed signaling is performed during data prefix time, prior to the start of clocked data transmission. Speed signaling may occur up to 20ns prior to the start of the data prefix. Speed signaling must complete at least 40ns prior to the start of clocked data. Figure 6-13 on page 121 illustrates the timing relationship between speed signaling and data prefix signaling.

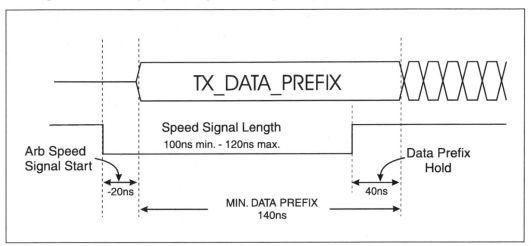

Note that a node that supports only 100Mb/s packet transmission need not implement a constant current source nor a speed receiver. Nodes that support 200Mb/s packet transmission must include a constant current source capable of delivering 3.5ma of current and must include one speed receiver. Nodes supporting 400Mb/s must be capable of sourcing 3.5ma and 10ma of current and must include speed receivers for both 200 and 400Mb/s transmission speeds.

Table 6-12 on page 122 shows the specified current for the different speeds. The common mode current speed signaling current is measured as one half of the algebraic total current flowing from the TPB pins.

Designers must detect the specified current by calculating the average voltage on TPA and TPA* (common mode voltage) that results from the additional speed-related current. The current specified in Table 6-12 is reflected as an offset voltage from the normal TpBias voltage. Note that the voltage on TPA goes down when the higher speeds (greater current) are being signaled. That is, the voltage on TPA decreases as the constant current source supplies more current. The additional current results when an FET within the constant current source is biased on, causing more current flow; through the 55W resistors on the TPA side. Consequently, the voltage at the non-inverting input of the speed receivers will be lower when speed signaling is on. Note also that the speed receivers must be biased differently to detect the voltage difference resulting from the 3.5ma versus the 10ma of current induced into the line.

The common mode output voltage at TPA (receiving port) will be detected between 1.438v and 1.665v during S200 packet transmission, and between 1.030v and 1.438v during S400 packet transmission. When no speed signaling is performed (S100 packet transmission), the common mode output voltage will be greater than 1.665v. The input voltage at the opposite end of the cable (TPB) can have up to a 0.5vdc drop due to line loss in the cable. The common mode input voltages at TPB (transmitting port) will be equal to or greater than 1.165v when no speed signaling is used. When S200 speed signaling is used the input voltage ranges from 0.935 to 1.165v and with S400 speed signaling the voltage ranges from 0.523 to 0.935v. Note that during S200 and S400 speed signaling the input voltage to the port status receiver drops below 0.8v. Unless some action is taken the PHY would detect node detachment. To prevent this from occurring, the PHY must ignore disconnect status during speed signaling.

Table 6-12: Common Mode Current for Speed Signaling

Signaling Active	Data Rate (mA)					
	Tx_Speed = 100		Tx_Speed = 200		Tx_Speed = 400	
	Max	Min	Max	Min	Max	Min
Common mode signaling off	0.44	-0.81	0.44	-0.81	0.44	-0.81
Common mode signaling on	0.44	-0.81	-2.53	-4.84	-8.10	-12.40

Data/Strobe Signaling

The actual packet is delivered via the data driver using a combination of NRZ and data-strobe encoding. Data is transferred across one signal pair while the strobe is delivered over the other pair. Single direction transfers require the use of both signal pairs, therefore bi-directional transfers are accomplished via a half-duplex implementation. During normal differential transmission of packets, the transmitter delivers the strobe via TPA and data via TPB as illustrated in Figure 6-14. Since the rate of data delivery can vary, speed information is also sent prior to packet transmission.

Figure 6-14: Data-Strobe Signaling During Packet Transmission

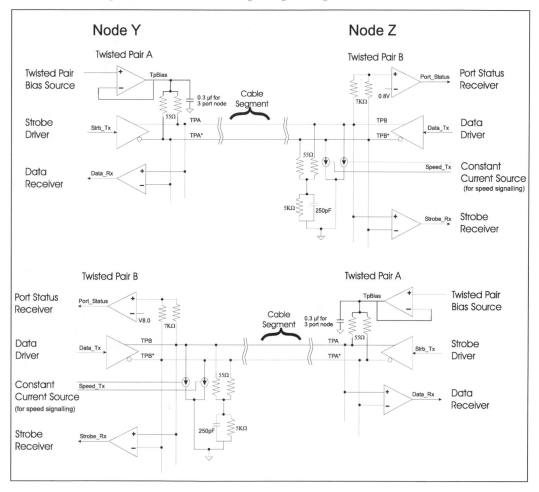

NRZ Encoding

Non-return to zero (NRZ) encoding is used to reduce the frequency component of a bipolar data stream comprised of ones and zeros. As its name implies, NRZ encoded data does not return to zero after signaling each state. Instead, it transitions only when a change from zero to one or one to zero occurs. Figure 6-15 illustrates a bipolar data stream that is not encoded followed by NRZ encoded data.

Data-Strobe Encoding

Figure 6-15: NRZ Data Stream

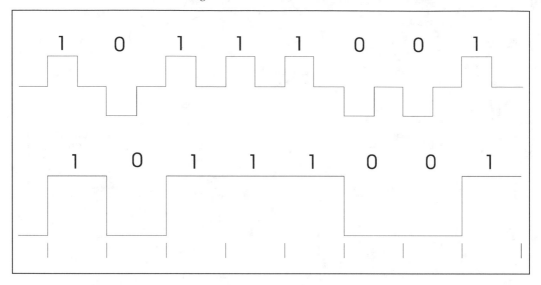

NRZ data is transmitted via TPB and detected by the differential data receiver on TPA. The data stream is accompanied by a strobe signal that provides a means of reconstructing a clock signal that can be used to synchronize the incoming data stream. Strobe is transmitted via TPA and received by the differential strobe receiver on TPB. The data-strobe encoding improves the transmission characteristics of data sent over the cable. Figure 6-16 illustrates an example data stream and the accompanying strobe. Note that a clock signal can be constructed by performing an exclusive OR on the data and strobe.

Figure 6-16: Data-Strobe Encoding/Decoding

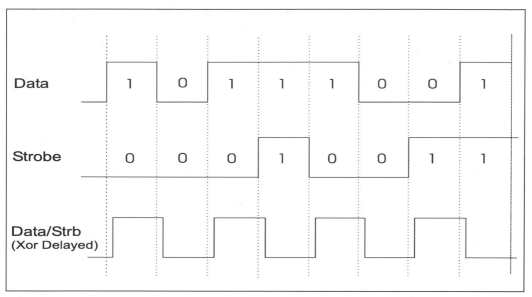

Gap Timing

Between packet transfers the bus returns to the idle state for a period of time, called an interpacket gap. For example, when a read transaction begins, a request packet is sent to the target device and the target node responds by returning data to the initiating node. Sufficient turn-around time must be given for the target node to return data. A variety of idle times (called gaps) are employed by the IEEE 1394 implementation. These gaps include:

- Acknowledge Gap—An acknowledge gap is the bus idle time that exists between the end of an asynchronous packet (request or response) and the start of the acknowledgment packet. Note that the request or response packet and the subsequent acknowledge packet are performed as atomic operations on the bus. No other bus activity is allowed to take place during this interval. This gap must be shorter than the subaction gap which is used to notify a node that it may begin arbitration for ownership of the bus.
- Isochronous Gap—The period of bus idle time before the start of arbitration for an isochronous channel subaction. This gap is also shorter than the subaction gap; thereby providing a higher arbitration priority for isochronous

transactions versus asynchronous transactions which must wait for a longer period of idle time before arbitrating.

- Subaction Gap—The bus idle time before the start of arbitration for an asynchronous subaction. The subaction gap is not present between the request and response subactions of a concatenated transaction. The width of this gap can be tuned depending on the maximum number of cable hops in the physical topology.
- Arbitration Reset Gap—The period of bus idle prior to the beginning of a fairness interval. The width of this gap can be tuned depending on the maximum number of cable hops in the physical topology.

Figure 6-17 illustrates the gaps associated with asynchronous transactions. In some cases subactions can be concatenated, thereby eliminating the subaction gap.

Figure 6-17: Split Asynchronous Transaction with Gaps Defined

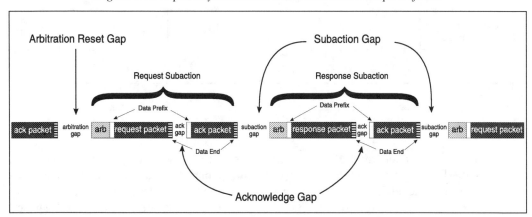

Isochronous gaps occur between isochronous transfers that are not concatenated as illustrated in Figure 6-18.

Figure 6-18: Isochronous Transaction with Gaps Defined

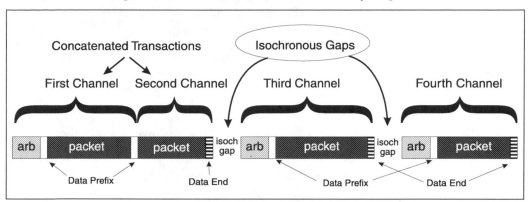

Note that the various gaps are of differing lengths as defined in Table 6-13. Gap count is related to the number of cable hops between nodes, and can be adjusted to reduce the amount of idle time on the bus. The maximum cable hop value is defined as the largest number of cables that must be traversed when any two nodes residing on the same 1394 bus communicate with one another. The default gap count value used to calculate the subaction and arbitration reset gap timing is 63 and is sufficient to accommodate 32 cable hops. This is a conservative gap count since the specification allows a maximum of 16 cable hops on a single 1394 bus.

Table 6-13: Gap Timing

Gap Type	Detection Time (measured at responding node)		Description
	Minimum	Maximum	
Acknowledge gap	0.04µs	0.05µs	~4/base rate—time between end of packet and return of acknowledgment (at port transmitting the Ack. packet)
Isochronous gap	0.04µs	0.05µs	~4/base rate—bus idle time between nonconcatenated isochronous transactions

Table 6-13: Gap Timing (Continued)

| Gap Type | Detection Time (measured at responding node) | | Description |
	Minimum	Maximum	
Subaction gap	27+(gap count * 16) /98.304Mb/s	29+(gap count * 16)/98.304Mb/s	~10µs—time between asynchronous transaction subactions
Arb. Reset gap	51+(gap count * 32)/98.304Mb/s	53+(gap count * 32)/98.304Mb/s	~20µs—the gap that occurs between fairness intervals

Cable Interface Timing Constants

Table 6-14: 1394-1995 Cable Interface Timing Constants

Timing Parameter	Min.	Max.	Description
ACK_RESPONSE_TIME	0.05µs	0.17µs	Time between reporting the end of a packet (DATA_END) and requiring that an acknowledging link layer respond with an arbitration request.
ARB_SPEED_SIGNAL_START	-0.02µs		Time delay between a transmitting port signalling TX_DATA_PREFIX and the same port transmitting a speed signal for either an unconcatenated packet or the first packet in a concatenated sequence.
BASE_RATE	98.294 Mbit/s	98.314 Mbit/s	Base bit rate (98.304 Mbit/s ± 100 ppm)
CONFIG_TIMEOUT	166.6µs	166.9µs	Loop detect time (~16384/ BASE_RATE)
DATA_END_TIME	0.24µs	0.26µs	End of packet signal time (~24/ BASE_RATE)

Table 6-14: 1394-1995 Cable Interface Timing Constants (Continued)

Timing Parameter	Min.	Max.	Description
DATA_PREFIX_TIME	0.04µs	0.16µs	Remaining time after speed sampling before clocked data starts. Also the time between the acknowledge and response data in a concatenated response. (~4/BASE_RATE and ~16/ BASE_RATE)
FORCE_ROOT_TIMEOUT	83.3µs	166.9µs	Time to wait in state T0: Tree-ID Start before acknowledging RX_PARENT_NOTIFY. (between ~8192/BASE_RATE and ~16384/ BASE_RATE) NOTE—Designers are encouraged to use 162.0 µs as the maximum; this value prevents false detection of a loop in cases where more than one node has its force_root variable set TRUE.
MAX_ARB_STATE_TIME		166.9µs	Maximum time in any state (before a bus reset shall be initiated) except A0: Idle, T0: Tree-ID Start or a state that exits after an explicit time-out.
MAX_BUS_HOLD		1.63µs	Maximum time an originating node may transmit TX_DATA_PREFIX between concatenated packets. The link shall ensure that this time is not exceeded.
MAX_BUS_OCCUPANCY		100µs	Maximum time a node may transmit
MAX_DATA_PREFIX_DELAY		PHY_ DELAY	Maximum delay between a RX_DATA_PREFIX signal arriving at a receive port and a TX_DATA_PREFIX being sent at a transmit port.
MIN_PACKET_SEPARATION	0.34µs		Minimum time between packets

Table 6-14: 1394-1995 Cable Interface Timing Constants (Continued)

Timing Parameter	Min.	Max.	Description
NOMINAL_CYCLE_TIME	124.988 μs	125.013 μs	Average time between the start of one isochronous period and the next (125 μs ± 100 ppm)
RESET_TIME	166.6μs	166.7μs	Reset hold time. (~16384/ BASE_RATE)
RESET_WAIT	166.8μs	166.9μs	Reset wait time. (~16400/ BASE_RATE)
ROOT_CONTEND_FAST	0.24μs	0.26μs	Time to wait in state T3: Root Contention if the random bit is zero. (~80/BASE_RATE)
ROOT_CONTEND_SLOW	0.57μs	0.60μs	Time to wait in state T3: Root Contention if the random bit is one (~160/BASE_RATE)
SID_SPEED_SIGNAL_START	-0.02μs	0.02μs	Time between a child port signalling TX_IDENT_DONE and the same port sending its speed capability signal.
SPEED_SIGNAL_LENGTH	0.10μs	0.12μs	Duration of a valid speed signal (~10/BASE_RATE)

Table 6-15: 1394a Cable Interface Timing Constants

Timing Parameter	Min.	Max.	Description
ARB_RESPONSE_DELAY	0.03 μs	PHY_ DELAY	Delay through a PHY from the start of arbitration line state reception to the start of transmission of the associated arbitration line state at all transmitting ports. Note that arbitration line states must be repeated by the at least as fast as clocked data.
ACK_RESPONSE_TIME	na	na	No longer defined - See MAX_RESPONSE_TIME.

Table 6-15: 1394a Cable Interface Timing Constants (Continued)

Timing Parameter	Min.	Max.	Description
ARB_SPEED_SIGNAL_START	-0.02µs		Time delay between a transmitting port signalling TX_DATA_PREFIX and the same port transmitting a speed signal for either an unconcatenated packet or the first packet in a concatenated sequence.
BASE_RATE	98.294 Mbit/s	98.314 Mbit/s	Base bit rate (98.304 Mbit/s ± 100 ppm)
BIAS_FILTER_TIME	41.6µs	52.0µs	Time to filter Bias_Detect upon detection of tpbias before updating the PHY register Bias bit (~4096/BASE_RATE)
BIAS_HANDSHAKE	5.3ms	10.7ms	Time to drive or detect TpBias low during the handshake between a suspended initiator and target; also the time permitted a resuming port to generate TpBias after detecting bias (~16384/BASE_RATE)
CONCATENATION_PREFIX_TIME	0.16µs		For concatenated packets, the time a transmitting port shall signal TX_DATA_PREFIX between the end of clocked data for one packet and the start of speed signaling time for the next.
CONFIG_TIMEOUT	166.6µs	166.9µs	Loop detect time (~16384/BASE_RATE)
CONNECT_TIMEOUT	330ms	350ms	Connection debounce time
DATA_END_TIME	0.24µs	0.26µs	End of packet signal time (~24/BASE_RATE)
DATA_PREFIX_HOLD	0.04µs		At a transmitting port, the time between the end of speed signalling (when present) and the start of clocked data.
DATA_PREFIX_TIME	na	na	This timing constant is no longer defined; see CONCATENATION_PREFIX_TIME, DATA_PREFIX_HOLD and MIN_DATA_PREFIX.
FORCE_ROOT_TIMEOUT	83.3µs	CONFIG_TIMEOUT	Time to wait in state T0: Tree-ID Start before acknowledging RX_PARENT_NOTIFY. (between ~8192/BASE_RATE and ~16384/BASE_RATE) NOTE—Designers are encouraged to use 162.0 µs as the maximum; this value prevents false detection of a loop in cases where more than one node has its force_root variable set TRUE.

Table 6-15: 1394a Cable Interface Timing Constants (Continued)

Timing Parameter	Min.	Max.	Description
MAX_ARB_STATE_TIME	200µs	400µs	Maximum time in any state (before a bus reset shall be initiated) except A0: Idle, T0: Tree-ID Start or a state that exits after an explicit time-out.
MAX_BUS_HOLD		1.63µs	Maximum time an originating node may transmit TX_DATA_PREFIX between concatenated packets. The link shall ensure that this time is not exceeded.
MAX_BUS_OCCUPANCY	na	na	This timing constant is no longer defined; see MAX_DATA_TIME.
MAX_DATA_PREFIX_DELAY	na	na	This timing constant is no longer defined; see ARB_RESPONSE_DELAY.
MAX_DATA_TIME		84.31µs	The maximum time that clocked data may be transmitted continuously. If this limit is exceeded, unpredictable behavior may result.
MAX_RESPONSE_TIME	0.04µs	PHY_DELAY +0.1µs	Idle time, measured at the cable connector, from the end of RX_DATA_END or TX_DATA_END that follows a PHY packet or primary packet to the start of the next arbitration line state: TX_DATA_PREFIX, TX_DISABLE_NOTIFY or TX_SUSPEND.
MIN_DATA_PREFIX	0.14µs (0.18µs)* page		The time a transmitting port must signal TX_DATA_PREFIX prior to clocked data for either an unconcatenated packet or the first packet in a concatenated sequence.
MIN_IDLE_TIME	0.04µs		Minimum idle time between packets at either an originating or repeating port. (~4/BASE_RATE)
MIN_PACKET_SEPARATION	0.34µs		Minimum time that TX_DATA_PREFIX must be signaled between concatenated packets. (~34/BASE_RATE)
NOMINAL_CYCLE_TIME	124.988µs	125.013µs	Average time between the start of one isochronous period and the next. (125 µs ± 100 ppm)
PHY_DELAY	0.06µs	PHY register	Best-case repeater data delay has a fixed minimum.
RESET_DETECT	80.0ms	85.3ms	Time for an active port to confirm a reset signal.
RESET_TIME	166.6µs	166.7µs	Reset hold time. (~16384/BASE_RATE)
RESET_WAIT	0.16µs		Reset wait delta time. (~16/BASE_RATE)

Table 6-15: 1394a Cable Interface Timing Constants (Continued)

Timing Parameter	Min.	Max.	Description
ROOT_CONTEND_FAST	0.76µs	0.80µs	Time to wait in state T3: Root Contention if the random bit is zero.
ROOT_CONTEND_SLOW	1.60µs	1.64µs	Time to wait in state T3: Root Contention if the random bit is one. (~160/BASE_RATE)
SHORT_RESET_TIME	1.30µs	1.40µs	Short reset hold time. (~128/BASE_RATE)
SID_SPEED_SIGNAL_START	-0.02µs	0.02µs	Time between a child port signalling TX_IDENT_DONE and the same port sending its speed capability signal.
SPEED_SIGNAL_LENGTH	0.10µs	0.12µs	Duration of a valid speed signal. (~10/BASE_RATE)

* MIN_DATA_PREFIX is recommended to be 0.18µs for 1394a nodes that originate a transaction. This is to improve interoperability with legacy devices.

Suspend/Resume

The 1394a supplement adds power conservation features to each node. See Chapter 26, entitled "Suspend & Resume," on page 445 for details regarding suspend and resume signaling.

Cable Power

A serial bus may be either powered or unpowered depending on the capabilities of the nodes attached. A node residing on the serial bus may source power to the bus, sink power, or neither. The following sections discuss power-related issues based on the IEEE 1394-1995 specification. Many enhancements have been made in the IEEE 1394a supplement. These enhancements are discussed in Chapter 27.

Cable Power Requirements

Table 6-16 lists the cable power requirements for nodes that source power for other nodes on the bus. Note that Table 6-16 identifies the maximum output voltage specified by the 1394-1995 specification. The output voltage can range from as little as 8vdc or as high as 40vdc.

Table 6-16: Cable Power Requirements — 1394-1995

Condition	Limit
Maximum output current per port	1.5 amps
Minimum output voltage	8 vdc
Maximum output voltage	40 vdc
Maximum output ripple (10 kHz to 400 MHz)	100 mv peak-to-peak
Maximum output ripple (below 10 kHz)	1 v peak-to-peak

The cable power requirements for 1394a nodes differ from the 1995 requirements as shown in Table 6-17. Note that the maximum voltage is reduced to 33vdc. Refer to Chapter 25, entitled "Cable Power Distribution," on page 431 for details regarding the 1394a cable power requirements.

Table 6-17: Cable Power Requirements — 1394a

Condition	Limit
Maximum output current per port	1.5 amps
Minimum output voltage	8 vdc
Maximum output voltage	33 vdc
Maximum output ripple (10 kHz to 400 MHz)	100 mv peak-to-peak
Maximum output ripple (below 10 kHz)	1 v peak-to-peak

All nodes that detect value cable voltage in the range of 7.5 to 33vdc of cable power must set the cable power status (PS) bit in their PHY register map. If the voltage falls below the 7.5vdc minimum, the PHY must clear the PS bit and notify software of the cable power failure.

Power Class

During configuration each node reports its ability to source cable power or its requirements for sinking cable power. Each node transmits a self-ID packet that contains power class information. Figure 6-19 illustrates the fields within self-ID packet zero and highlights the cable power class (pwr) field within the self-ID packet. Table 6-18 defines the contents of the power class field for 1394-1995 nodes, while Table 6-19 on page 136 lists the definition of the 1394a power classes.

Figure 6-19: Cable Power Class Reported Via Self-ID Packet

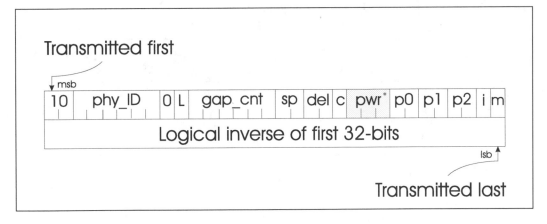

Table 6-18: Contents of the Power Field within the Self-ID Packet (1394-1995)

POWER_CLASS Code (binary)	Cable Power Consumption and Source Characteristics
000	Node does not need bus power and does not repeat power.
001	Self powered & provides 15W (minimum) to bus.
010	Self powered & provides 30W (minimum) to bus.
011	Self powered & provides 45W (minimum) to bus
100	May be powered by bus and uses up to 1W.
101	Powered by bus & uses 1W. Additional 2W needed to power link layer and higher layers.
110	Powered by bus & uses 1W. Additional 5W needed to power link layer and higher layers.
111	Powered by bus & uses 1W. Additional 9W needed to power link layer and higher layers.

Table 6-19: Definition of Power Class Values Within "Pwr" Field of Self-ID Packet—1394a

POWER_CLASS Code (binary)	Power Consumption and Source Characteristics
000	Node does not require bus power nor repeat bus power.
001	Node is self-powered and provides 15W (minimum) to the bus.
010	Node is self-powered and provides 30W (minimum) to the bus.
011	Node is self-powered and provides 45W (minimum) to the bus.
100	Node may sink power from the bus for the PHY only (3W max.), and may also provide power to the bus. The amount of bus power that it provides can be found in configuration ROM.

Table 6-19: Definition of Power Class Values Within "Pwr" Field
of Self-ID Packet—1394a (Continued)

POWER_CLASS Code (binary)	Power Consumption and Source Characteristics
101	Node is powered from the bus and consumes 3W maximum. An additional 2W maximum is needed to power the link and higher layers of the node.
110	Node is powered from the bus and consumes 3W maximum. An additional 5W maximum is needed to power the link and higher layers of the node.
111	Node is powered from the bus and consumes 3W maximum. An additional 9W maximum is needed to power the link and higher layers of the node.

Power Distribution

One or more nodes may source power to the bus. Since the specified output voltage has a relatively large range, each node that provides bus power may have different output voltages. As a result, power supplies must have diode protection so that if another node in the system is supplying a higher output voltage it will not cause current flow into the lower voltage source. Refer to Chapter 25, entitled "Cable Power Distribution," on page 431 for more information on power distribution issues defined by the 1394a supplement. Figure 6-20 illustrates the distribution of power across nodes that have multiple ports, and shows the location of the protection diodes.

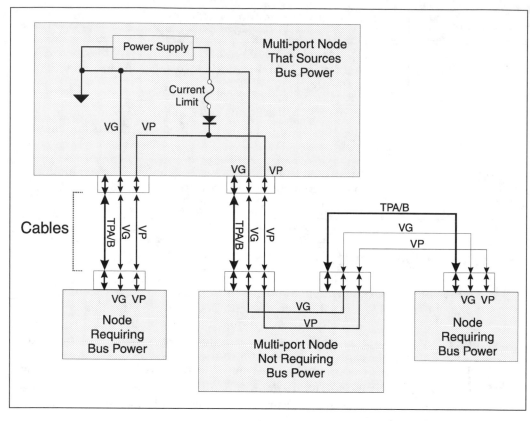

Figure 6-20: Serial Bus Power Distribution

Bus Powered Nodes

The bus may have no power available even though one or more nodes may require cable power. A device requiring power for the PHY chip and/or the Link chip will be non-functional in this unlikely circumstance.

Nodes that use cable power must satisfy the following requirements.

• When a node is initially attached to the bus or after a power reset, a node must not consume more than 1 watt of power from the cable. Only after receiving a link-on packet can the node consume power up to the limit declared when its self-ID packet was sent.

- In rush energy must not exceed 18mJoules in 3ms, and
- The node's current consumption must meet the following requirements, with I_{load} being the node's maximum current requirement:
- peak-to-peak ripple must be less than or equal to (I_{load}/1.5A) * 100mA).
- slew rate (change in load current) must be less that I_{load} in any 100µs period.

7 *Arbitration*

The Previous Chapter

In the previous chapter, the serial bus signaling environment was detailed. The chapter covered recognition of device attachment and removal, arbitration signaling, speed signaling, and data/strobe signaling.

This Chapter

This chapter details the arbitration process. It defines the various types of arbitration including isochronous and asynchronous arbitration, as well as the newer arbitration types defined by the 1394a supplement.

The Next Chapter

Asynchronous transactions exist in three basic forms: reads, writes, and locks. The next chapter details the asynchronous packets that are transmitted over the bus.

Overview

Arbitration is based on guaranteed bus bandwidth for isochronous channels and a fairness interval for asynchronous channels. Arbitration begins when a node recognizes a period of bus idle time, thereby indicating the end of the previous transmission. The period of bus idle time, or gap timing, varies between isochronous and asynchronous transactions as follows:

- isochronous gap — the period of bus idle time during isochronous data transmission that must be observed prior to the arbitration for the next isochronous transaction. The isochronous gap detection must be between 0.04μs and 0.05μs.

- subaction gap — the period of bus idle time during asynchronous data transmission that must be observed prior to arbitration starting for the next asynchronous transaction. This gap can be tuned so that arbitration can begin as early as possible without interfering with the normal completion of a subaction and its subsequent acknowledgment.

The first discussion in this chapter focuses on arbitration signaling because the arbitration signaling protocol is identical for both isochronous and asynchronous transactions. Next, the arbitration services are reviewed that are used by the link layer to request ownership of the bus via the physical layer. Since the arbitration process for asynchronous transactions is distinctly different from the arbitration process used for isochronous transactions, each topic is discussed separately. Finally, the two arbitration processes are discusses in light of the effect each has on the other. This occurs when a mix of isochronous and asynchronous transactions are being performed at the same time.

Arbitration Signaling

When any node on the bus wishes to perform a transaction it must arbitrate for use of the bus. Arbitration priority is based on which node requesting bus ownership receives grant from the root node. All nodes wishing to obtain bus ownership signal TX_REQUEST toward the root node. Any node that detects the arbitration request on one of its ports must forward the request on toward the root unless it is already signaling request either for itself or another node. Ultimately an arbitration request will reach the root node. The root then signals TX_GRANT to the first port on which it detects a RX_REQUEST. When RX_REQUEST from two nodes vying for control of the bus happen to reach the root at the same time, the root signals TX_GRANT on the requesting port that is designated with the lower port number.

Table 7-1 reviews the arbitration line states used during arbitration.

Table 7-1: Arbitration Line States During Normal Arbitration

Line State Name Transmitted	Line State Transmitted		Line State Name Received	Line State Received/decoded	
	Arb_A	Arb_B		Arb_A	Arb_B
TX_REQUEST (child node)	Z	0	RX_REQUEST (parent node)	0	Z
TX_GRANT (parent node)	Z	0	RX_GRANT (child node)	0	0
TX_REQUEST removed by child node	Z	Z	RX_REQUEST_CANCEL (parent node detects its own TX_GRANT)	Z	0
TX_DATA_PREFIX (parent node)	0	1	RX_DATA_PREFIX (child node)	1	0

Figure 7-1 illustrates a community of nodes residing on the serial bus with two nodes attempting to win use of the bus. Nodes A and E both signal an arbitration request (TX_REQUEST) to their parent nodes. Node A's TX_REQUEST is detected by node B, whose job it is to forward the request on to its parent. At the same time node E also signals TX_REQUEST to its parent (the root). Since Node E connects directly to the root node, its request reaches the root before Node E's request. When the root detects the request, it recognizes that a node is requesting use of the bus.

This example highlights the natural priority that exists due to the topology of the serial bus. Since the root is the source of the arbitration grant, it has the highest priority, followed by the nodes that connect directly to the root (lowest numbered ports first), etc. Natural arbitration priority for a given node then is based on the distance from the root node relative to other nodes. Note however, that nodes may not send TX_REQUEST at the same time; thus, natural priority does not guarantee that a node closer to the root will necessarily win arbitration over one further away from the root.

Figure 7-1: Two Nodes Start Arbitration by Signaling an Arbitration Request

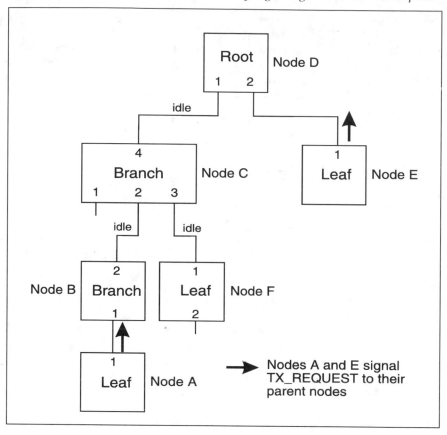

Upon detecting a request on its port number two, the root immediately returns TX_GRANT (to node E). The root also signals a DATA_PREFIX to all other ports (just port 1 in this case) to notify all nodes downstream from the root that it has granted the buses to a node and that a packet can be expected (See Figure 7-2).

When node E recognizes the TX_GRANT, it removes its request and begins packet transmission. Note that node C forwards the DATA_PREFIX that it receives from the root to all of its children. Node B detects this DATA_PREFIX from node C at the same time that it signals TX_REQUEST to node C. The DATA_PREFIX causes node B to stop signaling TX_REQUEST and to forward the DATA_PREFIX to its child port (node A). Node A detects the DATA_PREFIX and removes its TX_REQUEST, and recognizes that another node has won control of the bus.

Figure 7-2: Arbitration Signaling Reaches Root Node and TX_GRANT Returned

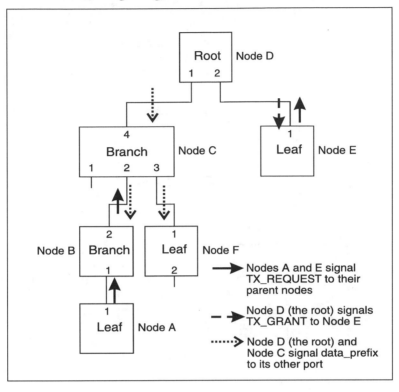

Figure 7-3 illustrates the state of the bus once the arbitration has been completely resolved. For a review of arbitration signaling line states, see "Line States During Normal Arbitration" on page 112.

Arbitration Services

When a link wishes to transmit a packet it must first request the PHY to obtain ownership of the bus. The type of packet to be transmitted determines the type of request that the LINK will make. The link layer must use one of four arbitration services when requesting bus ownership:

- Fair arbitration service (used when transmitting an asynchronous packet)
- Priority arbitration service (used when transmitting a cycle start packet or an asynchronous packet of high priority)

- Immediate arbitration service (used when transmitting an acknowledge packet)
- Isochronous arbitration service (used when transmitting an isochronous packet)

These services are described later in this chapter.

Figure 7-3: End of Arbitration / Beginning of Packet Delivery

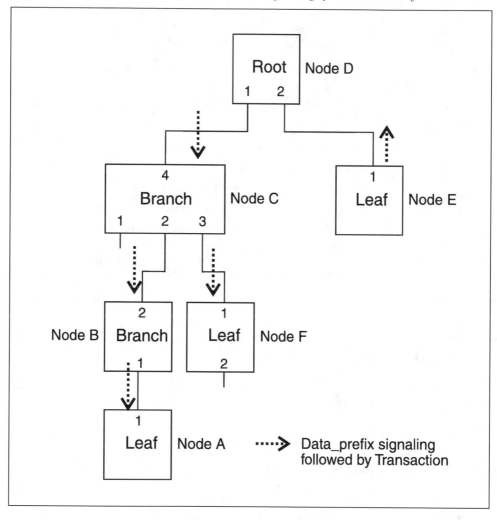

Asynchronous Arbitration

This section discusses asynchronous arbitration only and assumes that there are no isochronous transactions being performed on the bus. When the serial bus has only nodes capable of asynchronous transactions there is no requirement to assign bus bandwidth because asynchronous transactions operate based on a rotational priority scheme called the fairness interval. Furthermore, asynchronous nodes do not require a particular bus bandwidth.

Fairness Interval

The fairness interval ensures that each node wishing to initiate a transaction gets fair access to the bus. The principle of the fairness interval is that all nodes that have an asynchronous transaction pending are permitted to obtain bus ownership one time during each fairness interval. Once a node has performed one asynchronous subaction it must not request bus ownership to perform another asynchronous subaction until the next fairness interval begins. In this way, a rotational arbitration is achieved with the nodes with the highest natural priority gaining bus ownership first. The fairness interval then is the period of time that elapses during which all nodes that have an asynchronous subaction pending send one packet.

Arbitration Enable Bit

Following the self ID process all nodes can begin normal arbitration, because all nodes have their arbitration enable bits set as a result of the previous bus reset. Note that the arbitration enable bit resides within the PHY and is not a software visible bit.

Arbitration begins following the first subaction gap time (approximately 10μs by default). Immediately following the subaction gap all nodes wishing to obtain ownership of the bus can transmit an arbitration request. Arbitration requests propagate through parent nodes up to the root. As discussed in the previous section, when more than one node is requesting the bus, then the node closest to the root wins the arbitration due to it higher natural priority. However, once a node initiates a transaction it must clear its arbitration enable bit in the PHY. The PHY will not arbitrate for asynchronous arbitration requests until the next fairness interval begins. Consequently, no further asynchronous requests will be issued by any node until the arbitration reset gap is detected, which causes all PHYs to re-enable their arbitration enable bits.

Fair Arbitration Service

When the link layer is ready to transmit an asynchronous packet, it makes an arbitration request to the PHY using the "fair" arbitration service. The PHY confirms that the arbitration enable bit is set and determines when the bus is idle for the duration of the subaction gap (approximately 10μs by default). The PHY then signals an arbitration request (TX_REQUEST) towards the root. If the PHY detects RX_DATA_PREFIX, it knows that some other node has won ownership of the bus and discontinues TX_REQUEST signaling. If the PHY detects RX_GRANT, it recognizes that it has won ownership of the bus and informs the link layer. The link layer promptly starts clocking the packet to the PHY, which repeats the packet to its ports.

The PHY automatically clears the arbitration enable bit upon winning ownership of the bus. Clearing this bit prevents the PHY from transmitting any further fair arbitration requests until the arbitration enable bit is set again. The bit is set when the PHY detects bus idle time greater than the arbitration reset gap value (approximately 20μs by default).

Arbitration Reset Gap

Nodes continue arbitrating for control of the bus as long as their arbitration enable bits are set. Once all nodes wishing to initiate a transaction have gained access to the bus, they will be prevented from initiating another transaction because their arbitration enable bits will all be cleared. Thus, no more requests are issued and the bus remains idle beyond the subaction gap time. When idle time reaches approximately 20μs (based on default timing) all nodes recognize an arbitration reset gap, causing all nodes to set their arbitration enable bits. All nodes are now permitted to request bus ownership again. The fairness interval can be defined as the time that elapses between two arbitration reset gaps.

Figure 7-4 on page 149 illustrates a series of transactions and the concept of the fairness interval.

Figure 7-4: Asynchronous Arbitration and the Fairness Interval

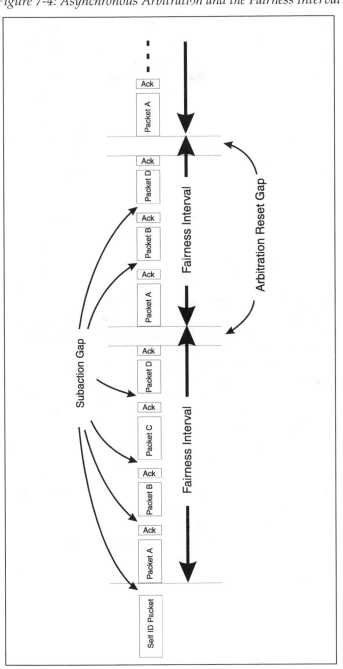

The Acknowledge Packet and Immediate Arbitration Service

Note that even though a node may have already initiated an asynchronous transaction, it may be the recipient of a transaction initiated by another node. In this case, the link layer may acknowledge receipt of a packet by returning an acknowledge packet. Access to the bus is obtained when the link layer uses the immediate arbitration service. When the PHY receives this service it recognizes that it need not arbitrate for use of the bus. Once the PHY detects an acknowledge gap (between 0.04 and 0.05µs) it indicates to the link layer that it is ready to send the packet. The link layer then clocks the packet to the cable via the PHY.

Isochronous Arbitration

This discussion assumes that all nodes residing on the bus are performing isochronous transactions only. Isochronous transactions begin immediately following broadcast of a cycle start packet. Specifically, isochronous arbitration begins when all nodes wishing to access the bus have observed approximately 0.04µs of bus idle time. Following arbitration, the winning node performs its isochronous transaction, after which the bus returns to the idle state. During isochronous transmission time this idle period is called an isochronous gap. Other nodes wishing to perform isochronous transactions begin arbitration again after detecting the 0.04µs isochronous gap. Note that this gap is the same width as the acknowledge gap that is defined for asynchronous transactions. Note that any node wishing to perform an asynchronous transaction would be prevented from arbitrating because the longer subaction gap will not occur until all isochronous transactions have completed.

Each isochronous channel requires a specific amount of bus bandwidth that it has previously obtained from the isochronous resource manager node. Bandwidth is allocated as a portion of each 125µs interval. Once each isochronous node has completed its transaction, the time remaining in the 125µs interval goes unused in the event that no asynchronous transactions are pending. Figure 7-5 on page 151 illustrates a group of isochronous transactions performing transactions at regular 125µs intervals.

Figure 7-5: Example of Isochronous Transaction Arbitration

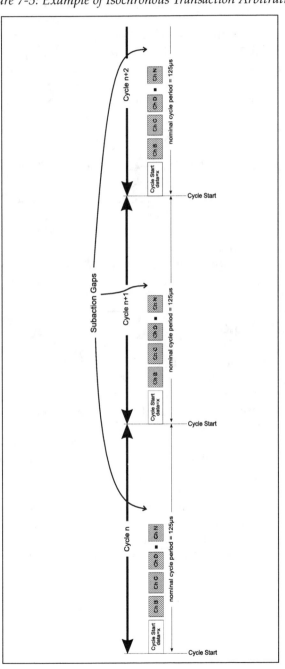

Cycle Start and Priority Arbitration

The root node fulfills the role of cycle master and delivers the cycle start packet at approximately 125µs intervals. The cycle start takes priority over other pending asynchronous transactions, thus permitting the start of isochronous transactions. Since the cycle master is by definition the root node, it will always win the asynchronous arbitration that occurs at the first subaction gap following the cycle synchronization event.

Combined Isochronous and Asynchronous Arbitration

Figure 7-6 on page 153 illustrates a collection of nodes performing both isochronous and asynchronous transactions. Note that up to 80% of the bus bandwidth may be allocated to isochronous transactions and the remaining 20% is left available for asynchronous transactions. This means that in the absence of isochronous traffic the throughput of asynchronous transactions may go up dramatically.

Cycle Start Skew

Another effect of combining isochronous and asynchronous transactions is the significant skew that can be encountered between the cycle start packets. Packet size for asynchronous transactions is limited to one half the isochronous bandwidth. At the base rate (100Mb/s) this equates to 512 bytes. This means that an asynchronous request that is issued near the end of a 125µs isochronous interval will prevent the cycle master from initiating the next isochronous transaction on time. This results in significant skew relative to the nominal start time for isochronous transactions. To deal with this problem, isochronous applications must provide sufficient data buffering to account for the delay of cycle start. In addition, the start of the cycle packet contains the contents of the cycle time register at the time that the cycle start packet was sent. Any node that receives the late cycle start packet can determine the amount of delay that has occurred from the actual cycle sync event to the delivery of the tardy cycle start packet.

Figure 7-6: Example of Fairness Interval Combined with Isochronous Transactions

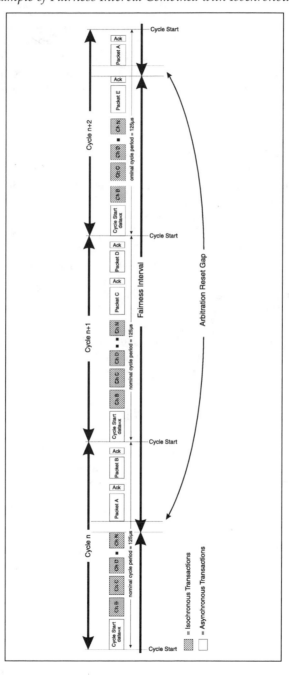

To illustrate this point, consider the example isochronous transactions in Figure 7-7 on page 155. Note that an asynchronous transaction started a lengthy packet transfer just prior to the first cycle sync, forcing a delay of 50μs. Once the asynchronous transaction ends, the cycle master sends the next cycle start packet (which encodes the 50μs delay). This leaves just approximately 75μs of time remaining before the next cycle sync event. If we presume that the maximum of 100μs (80%) of bus bandwidth has been allocated for isochronous transactions, once again by the time all isochronous transactions complete, the cycle sync will have already occurred. This time cycle start will be tardy by 25μs. Note that since the cycle sync occurs before the isochronous transactions end, the cycle master (the root) will immediately send another cycle start, thereby preventing the asynchronous transactions from starting. Since the isochronous transactions are 25μs tardy, the second cycle sync trigger will occur just after completion of the isochronous transactions. By the third isochronous interval the isochronous transactions will have caught up, leaving 25μs of bandwidth left over for asynchronous transactions prior to the next cycle sync event.

A more thorough illustration of cycle start jitter is shown in Figure 7-8 on page 156. Notice in Figure 7-8 that three complete cycles are illustrated. In the first row of transactions cycle n is performed, and the last asynchronous transaction of cycle n runs beyond the 125μs cycle sync time. This results in a significant delay in starting cycle n+1.

The next row illustrates cycle (n+1), which is short since only isochronous transactions are performed. The cycle master detects the cycle sync event while isochronous transactions are being performed and upon detecting the first subaction gap it broadcasts the next cycle start packet. This action prevents any asynchronous transaction from being performed during this cycle and ensures that the isochronous transactions will catch up.

The third cycle (n+2) is delayed from the normal 125μs interval but by only a small amount. However, once again the cycle sync event occurs just after a long asynchronous transaction has begun, which causes a significant delay in the start of cycle n+3.

Figure 7-7: Cycle Start Skew

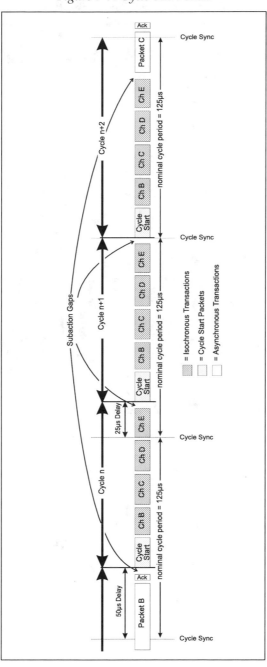

Figure 7-8: Cycle Start Packet Jitter

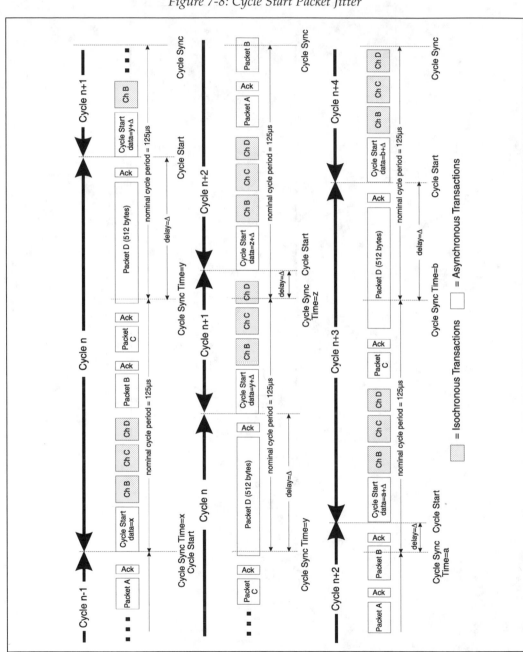

Chapter 7: Arbitration

1394a Arbitration Enhancements

Arbitration improvements results in better performance. Normally, asynchronous nodes must wait to observe the subaction gap prior to beginning asynchronous arbitration; however, two new arbitration enhancements reduce this delay, thereby increasing bus bandwidth:

- Acknowledge accelerated (ack-accelerated) arbitration
- Fly-by arbitration

Note that when these arbitration enhancements are used by nodes performing asynchronous transactions, any subaction that is performed (even if arbitration is not required) is still viewed as a fair arbitration event.

Acknowledge Accelerated Arbitration

During normal asynchronous arbitration, nodes must wait for the subaction gap before requesting use of the bus. That is, after detecting the end of packet (with data end) if bus idle time extends long enough the node recognizes that arbitration can begin. However, an intelligent node (one that implements ack-accelerated arbitration) can concatenate its own subaction to the acknowledge packet that it is returning, without having to arbitrate for the bus. This action eliminates the normal subaction gap that would otherwise be required so that the node can arbitrate for control of the bus. Figure 7-9 on page 158 illustrates the concept of acknowledge accelerated arbitration.

Ack-accelerated arbitration does not affect the fairness interval. Nodes are still permitted to perform a single asynchronous subaction during a fairness interval. However, the order in which transactions occur may be altered as a result of ack-accelerated arbitration. Recall that the normal arbitration mechanism ensures that a node residing closer to the root will win arbitration before nodes further from the root. When ack-accelerated arbitration is used, a node that is the target of a subaction may be located further from the root than another node that also has a subaction pending. When the target node returns the acknowledge packet it also concatenates it own subaction to the ack packet, thereby changing the order that transactions are performed during a fairness interval.

Another mode of acknowledge accelerated arbitration allows a PHY to begin arbitration immediately upon detecting an acknowledge packet; that is, without waiting for the subaction gap timing to elapse. This form of acknowledge accelerated arbitration is similar to isochronous arbitration mechanism which allows arbitration to begin after detecting 0.04µs of bus idle time.

Figure 7-9: Example of Acknowledge Accelerated Arbitration

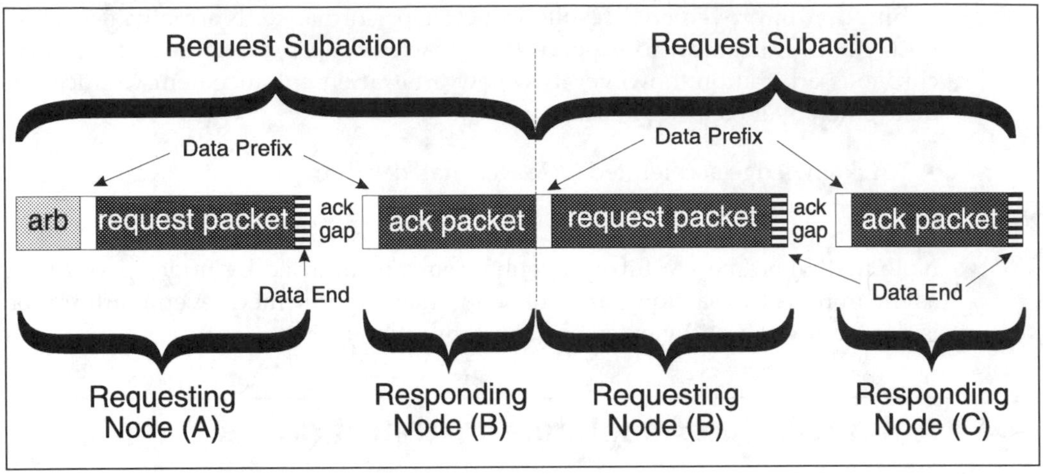

Fly-by Arbitration

Fly-by arbitration is another technique that can be used to eliminate delays during arbitration. When a transaction is being performed a multiport node must repeat the transaction on its other ports. If the packet being transmitted requires no acknowledge packet be returned from the target node, the repeating node can append (or concatenate) its packet to the end of the current packet. That is, rather than simply repeating the data end signaling to indicate end of the current packet, the repeating node could replace the data end with data prefix, followed by its own packet. This technique is termed fly-by arbitration. This action eliminates the need to arbitrate for the bus and eliminates the gap timing delays. The rules associated with performing fly-by arbitration are summarized below:

- Fly-by arbitration may only concatenate a new subaction to a packet that does not require an acknowledge packet in response. This restricts concatenation to acknowledge packets and isochronous packets.
- Fly-by arbitration can only be performed when the packet is moving toward the root (i.e., when the packet is received from a child port and is sent out on its parent port.
- Once a node has used fly-by arbitration to send an asynchronous subaction, the node must disable further asynchronous arbitration during this fairness interval.

- Packets to be sent at 100Mb/s must not be concatenated to packets being transmitted at a higher speed. This restriction ensures compatibility with 1394-1995 implementations. The 1995 specification does not require that speed information be sent when concatenating packets, thereby presuming that the packets are sent at the same speed. Since 100Mb/s packets do not signal speed information, nodes based on the 1995 version of the specification will presume that the concatenated 100Mb/s packet is being transmitted at the same speed as the previous packet.

Figure 7-10 on page 160 pictures the sequence of actions taken by a node when performing fly-by arbitration. The following descriptions pertain to each illustration in the sequence from top to bottom.

1. In the top illustration a packet is coming from a node downstream and heading toward the root. Note that a packet is preceded with a data prefix signal, followed by the actual packet, and concluded with a data end signal.
2. The second illustration shows the node performing its repeating function, where packet A is re-transmitted from all other ports.
3. In the third step, packet A has ended at the incoming port and that port has returned to the idle state. The other ports are still repeating packet A and are also nearing the end of packet. This repeating node also has a packet to transmit, although it is not yet visible.
4. The fourth step illustrates the packet B being concatenated to packet A by the repeating node as a result of fly-by arbitration. Note that the normal data end associated with packet A is stripped off and replaced with another data prefix, thereby signaling the start of another packet. Notice also that this packet must be repeated in the downstream direction, because the target node may reside downstream from this repeating node.

Acceleration Control

The arbitration enhancements increase the overall bus bandwidth by eliminating many of the long subaction gaps that would otherwise be required between asynchronous packets during the fairness interval. If either acknowledge-accelerated arbitration or fly-by arbitration is used after the cycle synchronization event has occurred, the elimination of the subaction gap that normally occurs after a transaction completes prevents the root node from acquiring the bus. Consequently, the root node cannot broadcast the cycle start packet, which causes a potential huge delay in the normal start of the isochronous interval.

Figure 7-10: Fly-By Arbitration Performed by Three-Port Node

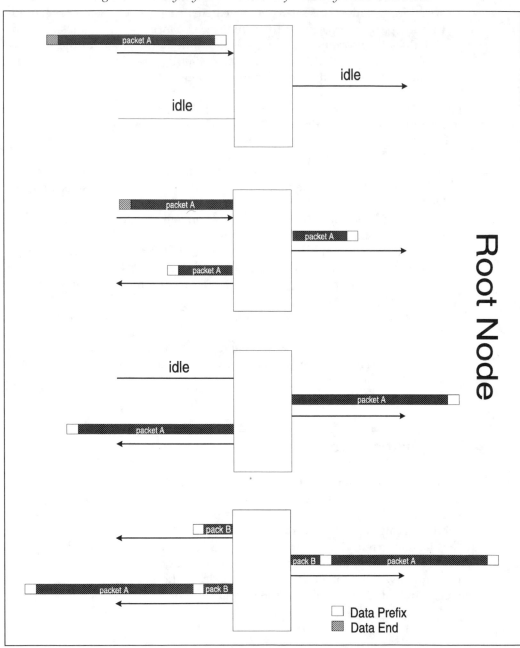

To prevent arbitration acceleration mechanisms from delaying the start of the isochronous interval, each node using these enhancements must implement a CYCLE_TIME register so that it recognizes when the cycle synchronization event occurs. Arbitration acceleration must be disabled when the cycle synchronization event occurs until the cycle start packet is delivered. This ensure that the root node will be able to win ownership of the bus at the end of the packet being transmitted at the time that the cycle synchronization occurs.

Each node is able to maintain synchronization with the root's cycle synchronization event because each node loads its CYCLE_TIME register with the data contained in the cycle start packet. The data contained within the cycle start packet is the contents of the root's CYCLE_TIME register at the time that the cycle start packet was broadcast. This represents the time that elapses between the cycle synchronization event within the root and the time that the root was able to send the cycle start packet.

Priority Arbitration Service

Priority arbitration allows a node that is transmitting asynchronous packets to cheat (within limits) by arbitrating for the bus more that once during a fairness interval. Previously only the cycle master could use the priority arbitration service to broadcast a cycle start packet. However, the 1394a specification allows other nodes to employ the priority arbitration service, but within the limits specified by the FAIRNESS_BUDGET register. This register is also referred to as the PRIORITY_BUDGET register (mapped at offset 218h in the CSR register space).

When the link layer makes a priority arbitration request to the PHY, the PHY ignores the arbitration enable bit value and begins to arbitrate for the bus, after detecting a subaction gap. The link layer can only make as many priority arbitration requests during a single fairness interval as specified by the Pri_req field in the FAIRNESS_BUDGET register.

The FAIRNESS_BUDGET register format is shown in Figure 7-11 and the field definitions are given in Table 7-2. This register controls the number of priority requests that a given node may perform within a given fairness interval.

Figure 7-11: FAIRNESS_BUDGET Register Format

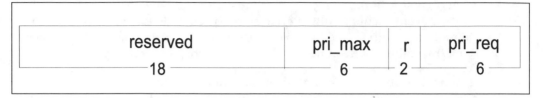

Table 7-2: Definition of FAIRNESS_BUDGET Register Fields

Name	Definition
Pri_max	This 6-bit field defines the highest value that can be specified in the pri_req field. This limits the maximum number of asynchronous priority requests that can be performed by this node during a fairness interval. Note that writes to this field are ignored.
Pri_req	This 6-bit field defines the current number of additional asynchronous priority requests that can be attempted by this node during a given fairness interval. The bus manager node reads the hardwired values in each node's Pri_max register and initializes each node's Pri_req field appropriately.

Priority requests can be made for the following transaction types:

- Write Request — Data Quadlet
- Write Request — Data Block
- Read Request — Data Quadlet
- Read Request — Data Block
- Lock Request
- Stream Data Block

Note that the bus manager must ensure that the sum of all pri_req values for nodes on the local bus is less than or equal to 63 minus the number of nodes.

Summary of Arbitration Types

When a node attempts to initiate a subaction (i.e. send a request or response) it must specify the type of transaction to be performed. The arbitration type is specified when the link layer signals the PHY layer to arbitrate for control of the bus. Several types of arbitration can be requested depending on the transaction type as follows:

- Fair arbitration - used to perform an asynchronous transfer (must follow fairness interval rules)
- Priority arbitration - used to perform an asynchronous transfer (circumvents the fairness interval)
- Immediate arbitration - used to return an acknowledge packet without actual bus arbitration occurring.
- Isochronous arbitration - used to perform an isochronous transaction

8 *Asynchronous Packets*

The Previous Chapter

The previous chapter detailed the arbitration process. It defined the various types of arbitration including isochronous and asynchronous arbitration, as well as the newer arbitration types defined by the 1394a supplement.

This Chapter

Asynchronous transactions exist in three basic forms: reads, writes, and locks. This chapter details the packets that are transmitted over the bus during asynchronous transfers.

The Next Chapter

The next chapter discusses isochronous transactions. These transactions are scheduled so that they occur at 125µs intervals. The chapter discusses the role of the application, link, and PHY in initiating and performing isochronous transactions. Format of the packet used during isochronous transactions is also detailed.

Asynchronous Packets

The link layer controller (Link) is responsible for constructing the 1394 packets required to transmit data over the 1394 serial bus. Packet contents vary depending upon the transaction type (See Table 8-1 on page 167 for transaction type codes). Data comprising the packet is transferred to the physical layer controller (PHY) via an interface defined by the specification. The link to physical layer interface is defined in Chapter 11.

FireWire System Architecture

Figure 8-1 on page 166 illustrates the basic construct of primary request packets that are used during asynchronous packet transactions. Primary packets have a standard header format and an optional data block, whose presence depends on the amount of data to be transferred.

Figure 8-1: Primary Asynchronous Packet Format

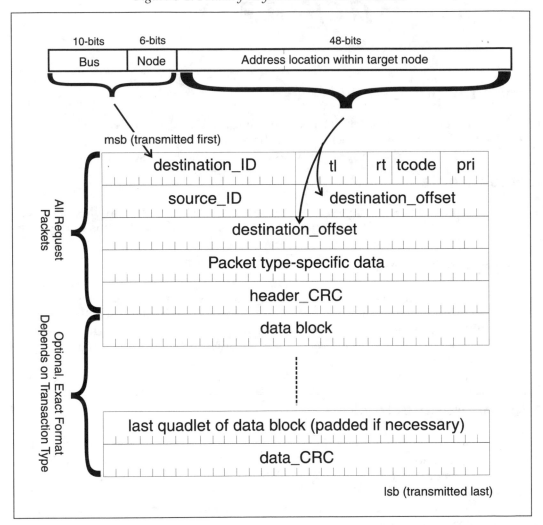

Table 8-1: Asynchronous Transaction Codes

Transaction Name	Code (Hex)
Write Request for data quadlet	0
Write Request for data block	1
Write Response	2
Reserved	3
Read request for data quadlet	4
Read request for data block	5
Read response for data quadlet	6
Read response for data block	7
Cycle start	8
Lock request	9
Asynchronous Streaming Packet	A
Lock response	B
Reserved	C
Reserved	D
Used internally by some link designs. Will not be standardized	E
Reserved	F

Data Size

The data payload of asynchronous packets is limited to minimize the possible overrun of asynchronous transaction time into the isochronous transaction time. Recall that during a 125µs cycle a mix of isochronous and asynchronous transactions may be performed. The data payload limit corresponds to transmission speed as listed in Table 8-2 on page 168.

Table 8-2: Maximum Data Payload for Asynchronous Packets

	Cable Speed	Maximum Data Payload Size (Bytes)
	100Mb/s	512
	200Mb/s	1024
	400Mb/s	2048
☞	800Mb/s	4096
☞	1.6Gb/s	8192
☞	3.2Gb/s	16384

Write Packets

Three packets are defined for performing write transactions, including two forms of write request packets. Each of the following packet types is illustrated in the following pages and each field within the packet is defined:

- Write Quadlet Request packet (Figure 8-2 on page 169 & Table 8-3 on page 169).
- Write Data Block Request packet (Figure 8-3 on page 171 & Table 8-4 on page 172).
- Write Response packet (Figure 8-4 on page 173 & Table 8-5 on page 173).

Figure 8-2: Write Request — Quadlet Format

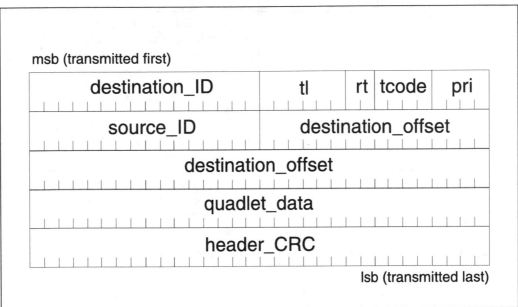

Table 8-3: Write Request — Quadlet Packet Components

Name	Abbrev.	Description
Destination Identifier	destination_ID	Combination of the bus address and physical ID of the node. Contains the address of the requesting node.
Transaction label	tl	A label specified by the requester that identifies this transaction. This value, if used, is returned in the response packet.
Retry code	rt	This code specifies whether this packet is an attempted retry and defines the retry protocol to be followed by the target node. 00 = Retry_1 (first attempt) 01 = Retry_X 10 = Retry_A 11 = Retry_B

Table 8-3: Write Request — Quadlet Packet Components (Continued)

Name	Abbrev.	Description
Transaction Code	tcode	A code value of zero defines write request for quadlet data, thereby defining the packet format illustrated in Figure 8-2 on page 169.
Priority	pri	Not used in cable environment.
Source Identifier	source_ID	Identifies the node that is sending this packet by specifying the bus that it resides on and its physical ID.
Destination Offset	destination_offset	Specifies the address location within the target node that is being accessed.
Quadlet Data	quadlet_data	Data being delivered to the target node.
Header CRC	header_CRC	CRC value for the header.

Figure 8-3: Write Request — Block Format

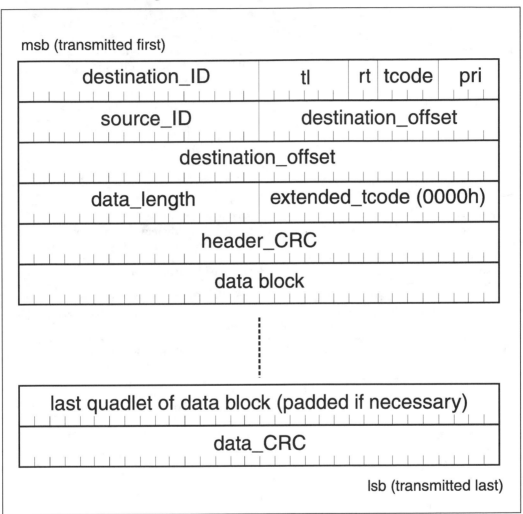

FireWire System Architecture

Table 8-4: Write Request — Block Packet Components

Name	Abbrev.	Description
Destination Identifier	destination_ID	Combination of the node address and physical ID of the node. Uniquely identifies a node. Contains the address of the requesting node.
Transaction label	tl	A label specified by the requester that identifies this transaction. This value, if used, is returned in the response packet.
Retry code	rt	This code specifies whether this packet is an attempted retry and defines the retry protocol to be followed by the target node.
Transaction Code	tcode	A code value of one defines write request for block of data, thereby defining the packet format illustrated in Figure 8-3 on page 171.
Priority	pri	Not used in cable environment.
Source Identifier	source_ID	Identifies the node that is sending this packet by specifying the bus that it resides on and its physical ID.
Destination Offset	destination_offset	Specifies the address location within the target node that is being accessed.
Data Length	destination_length	Specifies the amount of the data being sent in the data field of this packet. Maximum size in bytes is as follows: • 512 @ 100Mb/s • 1024 @ 200Mb/s • 2048 @ 400Mb/s
Extended Transaction code	extended_tcode	Reserved during write request packets.
Header CRC	header_CRC	CRC value for the header.
Data Field	data field	Contains the data being transferred to the target device. Data must be padded with zeros, if not an even 4 bytes. Amount of data is specified in the data_length field.
Data CRC	data_CRC	CRC value for the data field.

Figure 8-4: Write Response Packet Format

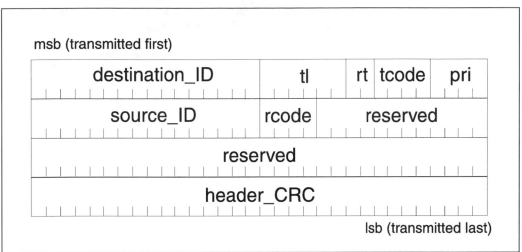

Table 8-5: Write Response Packet Components

Name	Abbrev.	Description
Destination Identifier	destination_ID	Combination of the bus address and physical ID of the node. Uniquely identifies a node. Contains the address of the node that is to receive the response packet.
Transaction label	tl	Contains the value sent by the requester for this transaction.
Retry code	rt	This code specifies whether this packet is an attempted retry and defines the retry protocol to be followed by the target node.
Transaction Code	tcode	A code value of two defines write response for either type of write request, and defines the packet format illustrated in Figure 8-4.

Table 8-5: Write Response Packet Components (Continued)

Name	Abbrev.	Description
Priority	pri	Not used in cable environment.
Source Identifier	source_ID	Identifies the node that is sending this response packet by specifying the bus that it resides on and its physical ID.
Response Code	rcode	Specifies the result of this transaction. Refer to Table 8-14 on page 191 for code definitions.
Header CRC	header_CRC	CRC value for the header.

Asynchronous Stream Packet

The 1394a supplement defines an asynchronous stream packet (tcode = A) that has the same format and characteristics as the isochronous packet, except that it occurs during a fairness interval and not during the isochronous bus interval. Format of this packet is illustrated in Figure 8-5 on page 175. The asynchronous stream packet is also referred to as a loose isochronous packets. This terminology derives from PHY implementations based on the 1995 specification. Some PHYs do not allow this packet to be transmitted during the asynchronous bus time (strict isochronous packets), while other implementations do allow the packet to be sent during the asynchronous time (loose isochronous packets).

The asynchronous stream transaction allows applications to perform data streaming when guaranteed latency is of little concern. This eliminates the requirement to allocate isochronous bus bandwidth (a limited resource) in order to perform their transaction. However, a channel number must be obtained in order to perform an asynchronous stream transaction. Maximum packet size is constrained to the values specified for all asynchronous packets as listed in Table 8-2 on page 168. This type of transaction could be used by devices that support broadcast and/or multicast operations, but do not require the transmission of real-time data.

Note that the link layer of a node wishing to transmit an asynchronous streaming packet uses a fair or priority arbitration service. When the PHY has obtained bus ownership, the link transmits the asynchronous streaming packet. Note that there is no acknowledge packet or response returned by the targeted node.

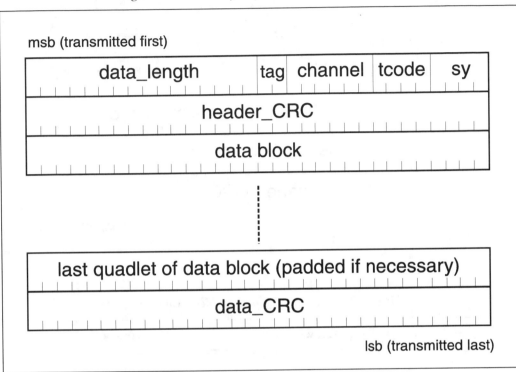

Figure 8-5: Format of Asynchronous Stream Packet

Read Packets

Four read packet formats are defined by the 1394 standard:

- Read Data Quadlet Request Packet
- Read Data Quadlet Response Packet
- Read Data Block Request Packet
- Read Data Block Response Packet

Each packet type is illustrated and described by the following figures and tables.

Figure 8-6: Read Request - Quadlet Packet Format

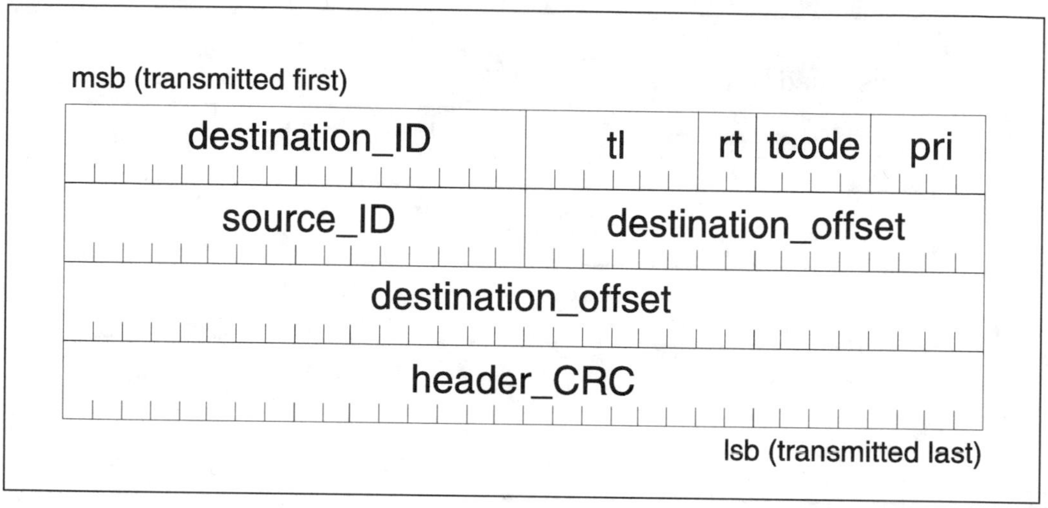

Table 8-6: Read Request — Quadlet Packet Components

Name	Abbrev.	Description
Destination Identifier	destination_ID	Combination of the bus address and physical ID of the node. Contains the address of the node that is to receive the request packet.
Transaction label	tl	A label specified by the requester that identifies this transaction. This value, if used, is returned in the response packet.
Retry code	rt	This code specifies whether this packet is an attempted retry and defines the retry protocol to be followed by the target node.
Transaction Code	tcode	A code value of four defines read request for quadlet data, thereby defining the packet format illustrated in Figure 8-6 on page 176.

Table 8-6: Read Request — Quadlet Packet Components (Continued)

Name	Abbrev.	Description
Priority	pri	Not used in cable environment.
Source Identifier	source_ID	Identifies the node that is sending this packet by specifying the bus that it resides on and its physical ID.
Destination Offset	destination_offset	Specifies the address location within the target node that is being accessed.
Header CRC	header_CRC	CRC value for the header.

Figure 8-7: Read Response — Quadlet Packet Format

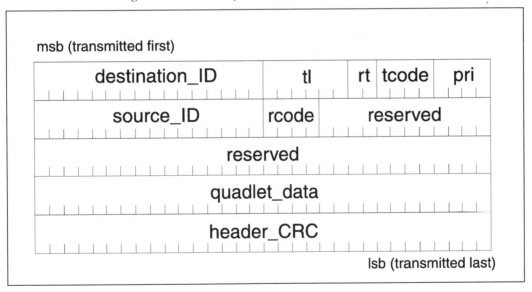

Table 8-7: Read Response — Quadlet Packet Components

Name	Abbrev.	Description
Destination Identifier	destination_ID	Combination of the bus address and physical ID of the node. Uniquely identifies a node. Contains the address of the node that is to receive the response packet.
Transaction label	tl	Contains the value sent by the requester for this transaction.
Retry code	rt	This code specifies whether this packet is an attempted retry and defines the retry protocol to be followed by the target node.
Transaction Code	tcode	A code value of six defines read response for read request for quadlet, and defines the packet format illustrated in Figure 8-7 on page 177.
Priority	pri	Not used in cable environment.
Source Identifier	source_ID	Identifies the node that is sending this response packet by specifying the bus that it resides on and its physical ID.
Response Code	rcode	Specifies the result of this transaction. Refer to Table 8-14 on page 191 for code definitions.
Quadlet Data	quadlet_data	Contains the requested read data.
Header CRC	header_CRC	CRC value for the header.

Figure 8-8: Read Request — Block Packet Format

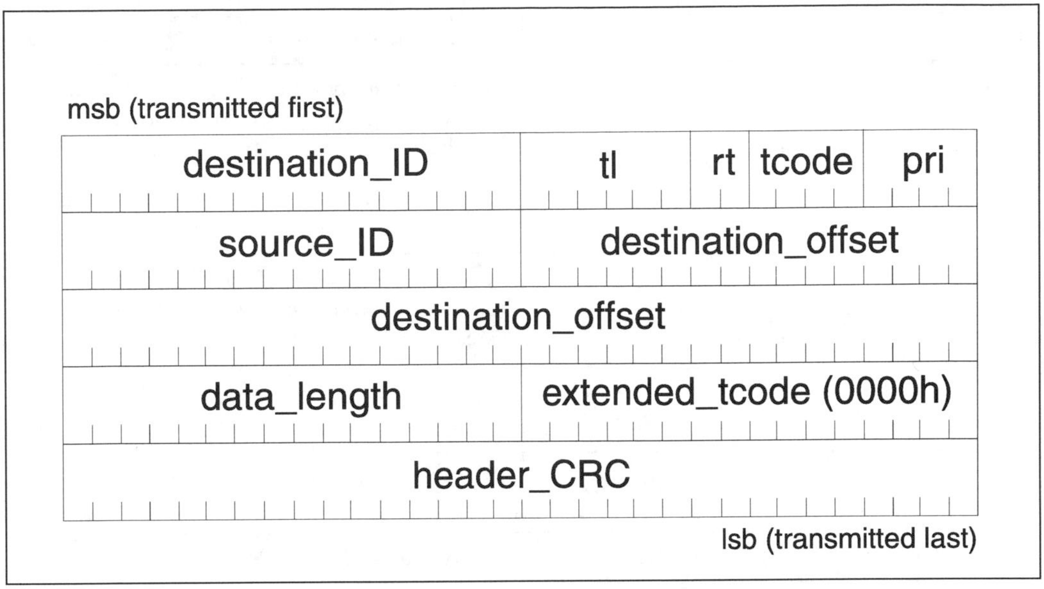

msb (transmitted first)

destination_ID	tl	rt	tcode	pri
source_ID		destination_offset		
destination_offset				
data_length		extended_tcode (0000h)		
header_CRC				

lsb (transmitted last)

Table 8-8: Read Request — Block Packet Components

Name	Abbrev.	Description
Destination Identifier	destination_ID	Combination of the bus address and physical ID of the node. Uniquely identifies a node. Contains the address of the node that is to receive the request packet.
Transaction label	tl	A label specified by the requester that identifies this transaction. This value, if used, is returned in the response packet.
Retry code	rt	This code specifies whether this packet is an attempted retry and defines the retry protocol to be followed by the target node.
Transaction Code	tcode	A code value of five defines read request for block of data, thereby defining the packet format illustrated in Figure 8-8 on page 179.

Table 8-8: Read Request — Block Packet Components (Continued)

Name	Abbrev.	Description
Priority	pri	Not used in cable environment.
Source Identifier	source_ID	Identifies the node that is sending this packet by specifying the bus that it resides on and its physical ID.
Destination Offset	destination_offset	Specifies the address location within the target node that is being accessed.
Data Length	destination_length	Specifies the amount of the data being requested from the target node. Maximum size in bytes is as follows: • 512 @ 100Mb/s • 1024 @ 200Mb/s • 2048 @ 400Mb/s
Extended Transaction code	extended_tcode	Reserved during read request packets.
Header CRC	header_CRC	CRC value for the header.

Figure 8-9: Read Response — Block Packet Format

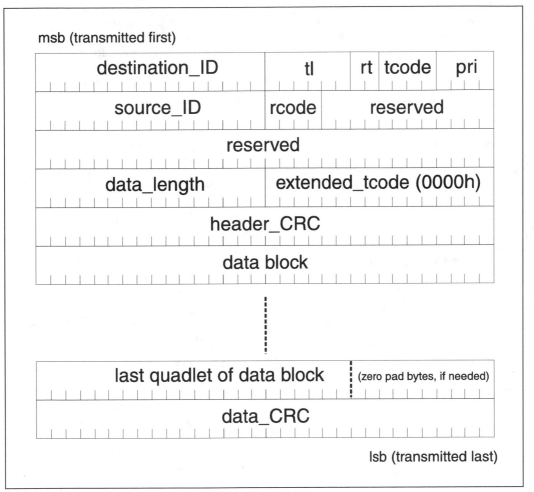

Table 8-9: Read Response — Block Packet Components

Name	Abbrev.	Description
Destination Identifier	destination_ID	Combination of the bus address and physical ID of the node. Uniquely identifies a node. Contains the address of the node that is to receive the response packet.
Transaction label	tl	Contains the value sent by the requester for this transaction.
Retry code	rt	This code specifies whether this packet is an attempted retry and defines the retry protocol to be followed by the target node.
Transaction Code	tcode	A code value of seven defines read response for block request, and defines the packet format illustrated in Figure 8-9 on page 181.
Priority	pri	Not used in cable environment.
Source Identifier	source_ID	Identifies the node that is sending this response packet by specifying the bus that it resides on and its physical ID.
Response Code	rcode	Specifies the result of this transaction.
Data Length	data_length	Specifies the size of the data being returned to the requesting node.
Extended Transaction Code	extended_tcode	Not used for read transactions.
Header CRC	header_CRC	CRC value for the header.
Data Field	data_field	Requested data being returned from the responding node.
Data CRC	data_CRC	CRC value for the data field.

Lock Operations

Lock transactions provide a mechanism to perform an atomic operation within the 1394 environment. The atomic nature of the operation is ensured by the responding node. A requesting node initiates a lock transfer by specifying the type of lock operation to be performed. The request packet passes argument and data values from the requesting node along with a description of the type of lock to be performed to the responding node. The responding node then performs the specified lock operation internally, by ensuring that no other access to the target location is permitted until the lock operation completes.

The responding node guarantees that the memory locations targeted by the lock transfer are not accessed by another node until the atomic operation has been completed. Between the request and response phases of the lock transaction other locations within the responding node can be accessed without concern. If any requesting node targets a locked memory location within a responding node, the responding node either retries the transaction or delays returning a response packet until the lock is released. The response packet confirms either success or failure of the lock operation and returns the contents (prior to any modification) of the target location.

Lock Request Packet

Figure 8-10 on page 184 illustrates the Lock packet format, which varies slightly depending on the type of lock operation being performed. Each field in the lock packet is defined in Table 8-10 on page 185. When a lock transfer is initiated the type of lock operation must be specified. The extended transaction code (extended_tcode) defines the type of lock operation to be performed. (See "Lock Transaction Types (Extended t_code Field)" on page 186.)

Figure 8-10: Lock Request Packets

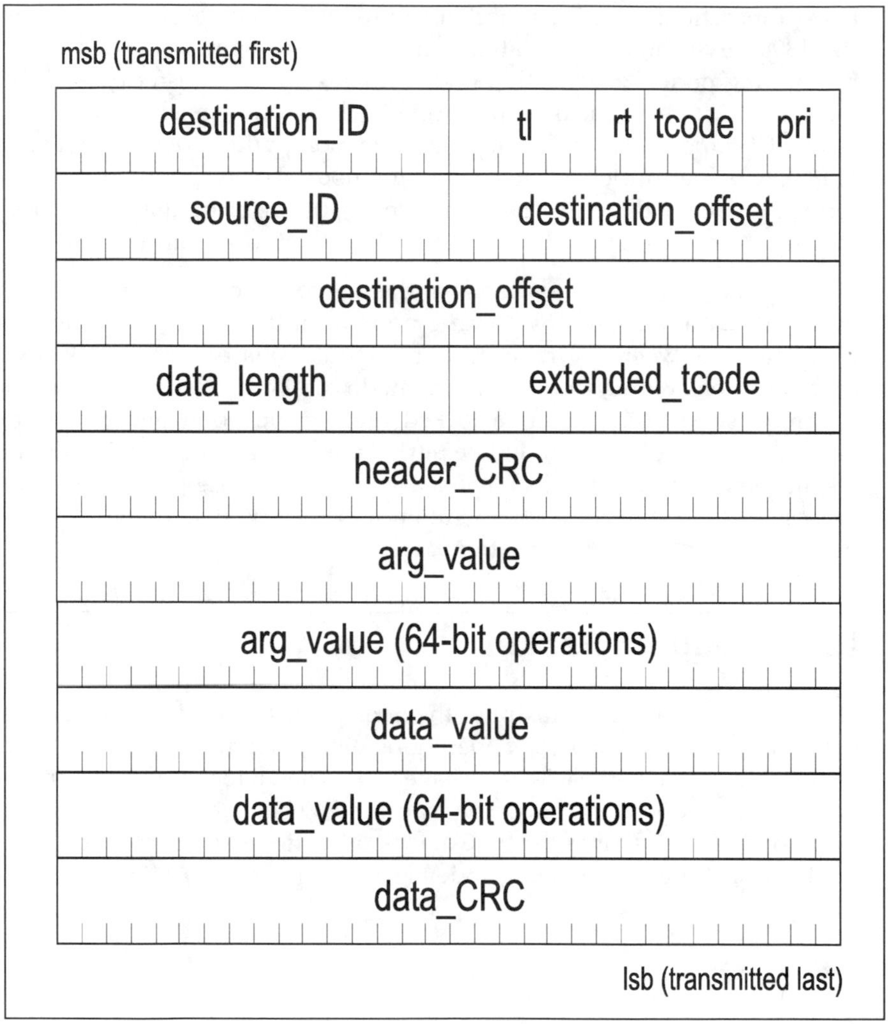

Table 8-10: Lock Request Packet Components

Name	Abbrev.	Description
Destination Identifier	destination_ID	Combination of the bus address and physical ID of the node. Uniquely identifies a node. Contains the address of the node that is to receive the request.
Transaction label	tl	A label specified by the requester that identifies this transaction. This value, if used, is returned in the response packet.
Retry code	rt	This code specifies whether this packet is an attempted retry and defines the retry protocol to be followed by the target node.
Transaction Code	tcode	A code value of nine defines a lock request packet, thereby defining the packet format illustrated in Figure 8-10 on page 184.
Priority	pri	Not used in cable environment.
Source Identifier	source_ID	Identifies the node that is sending this packet by specifying the bus that it resides on and its physical ID.
Destination Offset	destination_offset	Specifies the address location within the target node that is being accessed.
Data Length	data_length	Specifies the amount of the data being sent in the data field of this packet. Maximum size in bytes is encoded as shown in Table 8-12 on page 187.
Extended Transaction code	extended_tcode	Defines the type of lock transaction to be performed. See Table 8-11 on page 186 for definitions.
Header CRC	header_CRC	CRC value for the header.
Argument Value	arg_value	Contains the argument value for two argument lock functions, as specified by the encoded data_length field.
Data Value	data_value	Contains the data_value argument.

Table 8-10: Lock Request Packet Components (Continued)

Name	Abbrev.	Description
Data CRC	data_CRC	CRC value for the data field.

Lock Transaction Types (Extended t_code Field)

A variety of lock operations are defined by the specification. The type of lock operation is defined by the extended transaction code in the lock request packet. See "Lock Transaction Types (Extended t_code Field)" on page 186. Table 8-11 lists the extended code values, lock operation name, and description of the various forms of lock operation.

Table 8-11: Extended Transaction Code Field Definition for Lock Transactions

Code	Name	Description
0000h	reserved	NA
0001h	mask_swap	If bit values in target locations match bit values in arg_value, then those bit positions are updated with the corresponding values from the data_value field.
0002h	compare_swap	If value in target locations match arg_value, then update locations with data_value.
0003h	fetch_add	Contents of the target locations are added to the data_value and stored back into the target locations. The byte with the lowest address within the addressed integer is assumed to be the most significant bit.
0004h	little_add	Little Endian version of fetch_add. The byte with the lowest address within the addressed integer is assumed to be the least significant.
0005h	bounded_add	If value of target locations are not equal to the value of arg_data, then update the location with the sum of old_value plus data_value or else do not change the contents of target location.

Table 8-11: Extended Transaction Code Field Definition for Lock Transactions (Continued)

Code	Name	Description
0006h	wrap_add	If value of target locations are not equal to arg_value, then update the target location with sum of old_value plus data_value or else replace old value in the target location with the data_value.
0007h	vendor-dependent	NA
0008-FFFFh	reserved	NA

Data Block Length During Lock Request

The form of lock determines which fields within the data block will be present and defines their size. A lock request passes either one or two parameters to the responding node as listed in Table 8-12. For example, consider a fetch_add lock operation. A fetch_add can work on a 32- or 64-bit operand. The fetch_add lock operation adds the contents of the memory location specified in the destination offset to the contents of the data_value field within the data block. The result is written back to the memory location. Row one of Table 8-12 shows the data block length of the request packet when a 32-bit fetch_add is performed, while row three shows the 64-bit fetch_add data length.

Note that most lock operations require two arguments to be passed to the responding node. These arguments may also be either 32- or 64-bits wide as shown in Table 8-12.

Table 8-12: Data Length Field in Lock Request Packets

data_length	size of arg_value	size of data_value	Comment
4	0	4	Single argument 32-bit little_add/fetch_add
8	4	4	Two argument 32-bit function
8	0	8	Single argument 64-bit little_add/fetch_add
16	8	8	Two argument 64-bit function

Lock Response Packet

The response packet of a lock operation verifies whether the lock transaction completed successfully or not. Like other asynchronous responses, the response code (rcode) field contains the actual completion status. If the rcode field contains a value of zero then the transaction has completed normally (without errors or conflicts).

The application layer is responsible for verifying whether the lock operation completes successfully. In other words, a response code of zero does not necessarily indicate that the lock operation has been successful; rather, it indicates that the transaction has completed without errors. Verification of lock operation success must be verified when the response data block is returned to the application layer. By comparing the contents of the old_value field of the response packet to the argument_value sent in the request packet, the application can determine if the lock operation was successful or not.

For example, consider the lock compare_swap operation. The operation compares the contents of the address location specified by the destination_offset within the request packet to the contents of the request packet's argument_value. If the values match, the response agent will update the destination location with the contents of the data_value field of the request packet. The responding node will return the response packet containing the old value (value before modification) of the address location in the old_value field. If the old_value matches the argument value, then the comparison would have been true and the swap operation must have been performed. If however, the old_value and argument_value do not match, then the swap must not have taken place.

Figure 8-11: Lock Response Packet Format

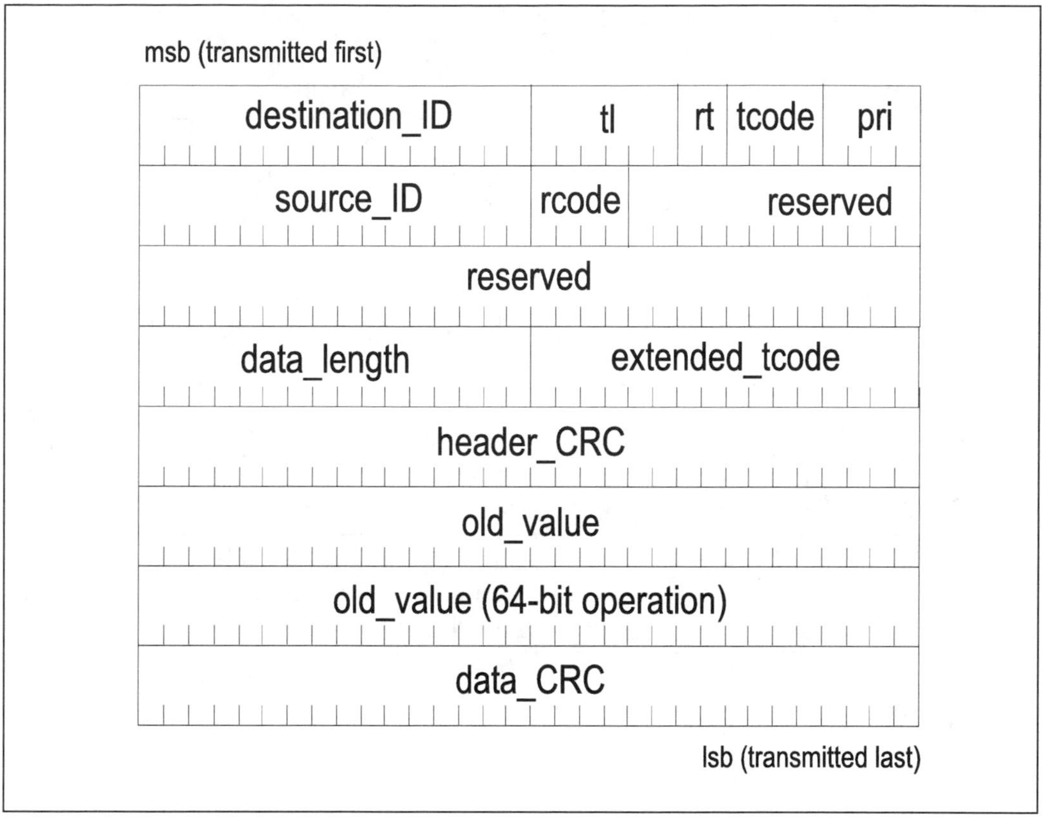

msb (transmitted first)

destination_ID	tl	rt	tcode	pri
source_ID	rcode		reserved	
reserved				
data_length	extended_tcode			
header_CRC				
old_value				
old_value (64-bit operation)				
data_CRC				

lsb (transmitted last)

Response Codes

Table 8-13: Lock Response Packet Components

Name	Abbrev.	Description
Destination Identifier	destination_ID	Combination of the bus address and physical ID of the node. Uniquely identifies a node. Contains the address of the node that is to receive the response packet.
Transaction label	tl	Contains the value sent by the requester for this transaction.
Retry code	rt	This code specifies whether this packet is an attempted retry and defines the retry protocol to be followed by the target node.
Transaction Code	tcode	A code value of Bh defines lock response, and defines the packet format illustrated in Figure 8-11 on page 189.
Priority	pri	Not used in cable environment.
Source Identifier	source_ID	Identifies the node that is sending this response packet by specifying the bus that it resides on and its physical ID.
Response Code	rcode	Specifies the result of this transaction.
Data Length	data_length	Specifies the size of the data being returned to the requesting node.
Extended Transaction Code	extended_tcode	See Table 8-11 on page 186.
Header CRC	header_CRC	CRC value for the header.
old_value	data_field	Contains the initial value read from the addressed location within the target node.
Data CRC	data_CRC	CRC value for the data field.

Table 8-14 lists the response codes that may be returned to the requesting agent.

Table 8-14: Definition of Response Code Values within Asynchronous Packets

Code	Name	Decription
0	resp_complete	Node successfully completed requested operation.
1-3	reserved	For future use.
4	resp_conflict_error	Resource conflict detected by responding agent. Request may be retried.
5	resp_data_error	Hardware error. Data not available.
6	resp_type_error	Field within request packet header contains unsupported or invalid value.
7	resp_address_error	Address location within specified node not accessible.
8-Fh	reserved	For future use.

Acknowledge Packet

The acknowledge packet consists of the acknowledge code and parity bit as illustrated in Figure 8-12. See Table 8-15 on page 192 for acknowledge codes and definitions. Note that three new codes are defined by the 1394a supplement. Some acknowledge codes provide the ability to retry transactions in the event that a node happens to be busy when the transaction is received. See Chapter 12 for details regarding transaction retry.

Figure 8-12: Acknowledge Packet

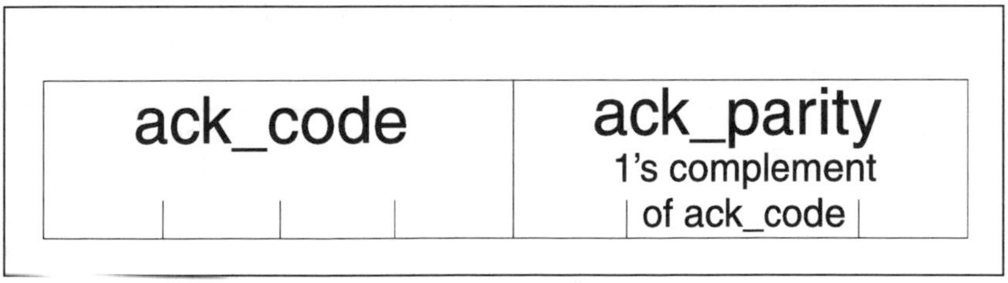

ack_code	ack_parity 1's complement | of ack_code |

Table 8-15: Acknowledge Code Values

1394a	Code	Name	Description
	0	reserved	
	1	ack_complete	Node successfully accepted the packet. If the packet was a request subaction, then the target node has completed the transactions and no response packet will follow (only occurs with write requests).
	2	ack_pending	Node successfully accepted the packet and a response packet will follow. This code will not be returned for a response packet.
	3	reserved	For future use
	4	ack_busy_x	The packet was not accepted by the target node, but may be accepted when retried.
	5	ack_busy_A	The packet was not accepted by the target node because it was busy. The node will accept the data when not busy during the next retry phase A.
	6	ack_busy_B	The packet was not accepted by the target node because it was busy. The target node will accept the packet when not busy during the next reoccurrence of a retry B.
	7-Ah	reserved	For future use
☞	Bh	ack_tardy	This code is supported only by 1394a devices that support the optional "standby" power conservation mode. This acknowledgment indicates that the packet was not accepted by the target node but that it can be retried in a subsequent fairness interval.
☞	Ch	ack_conflict_error	A resource conflict has prevented the packet from being accepted.
	Dh	ack_data_error	The packet was not accepted by the target node due to a data error within the data field. Error could be CRC error or data length error.
	Eh	ack_type_error	Packet not accepted due to error in the packet header, such as an illegal value in a field or an invalid transaction has been attempted (e.g. a write to a read-only address).
☞	Fh	ack_address_error	Packet not accepted because target address (specified by destination_offset field) is not accessible within the destination node.

Asynchronous Transaction Summary

Write Transactions

Write quadlet transactions may be performed in three forms:

- Split (illustrated in Figure 8-13)
- Concatenated (illustrated in Figure 8-14)
- Unified (illustrated in Figure 8-15 on page 194)

Figure 8-13: Split Write Transaction

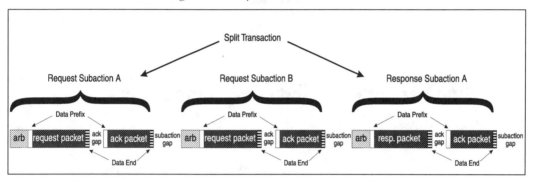

Figure 8-14: Concatenated Split Write Transaction

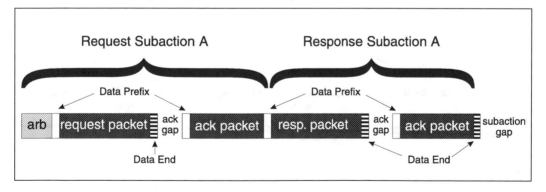

Figure 8-15: Unified Write Transaction

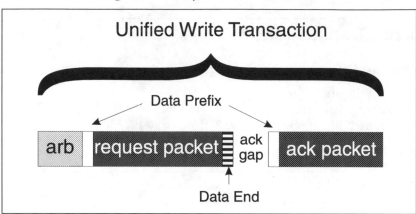

Summary of Read and Lock Transactions

The following section reviews the various forms of read and lock transactions, including:

- normal split transactions (illustrated in Figure 8-16 on page 194)
- concatenated transactions (illustrated in Figure 8-17 on page 195)

Figure 8-16: Normal Read or Lock Transaction

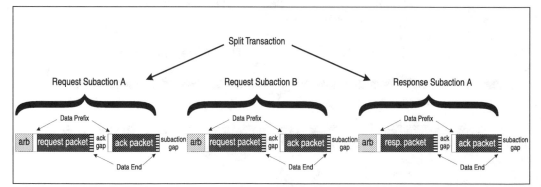

Figure 8-17: Concatenated Read or Lock Transaction

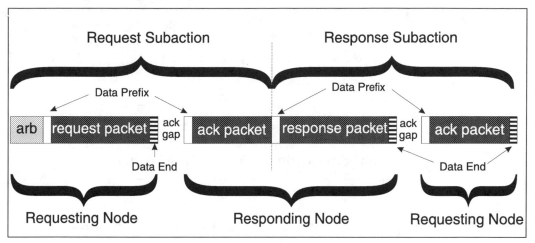

Cycle Start Packet

The cycle start packet is broadcast to all nodes periodically to signal the start of isochronous transactions at regular 125μs intervals. Since the cycle start packet is a broadcast packet, multiple nodes receive the packets, and therefore no acknowledgment or response is possible without contention. The node address of 63 (3Fh) is reserved as a broadcast address. When a target node decodes the address as 64, it knows not to send an acknowledgment packet. The cycle start packet format is illustrated in Figure 8-18 on page 196. Each field within the cycle start packet is defined in Table 8-16 on page 196.

Figure 8-18: Cycle Start Packet Format

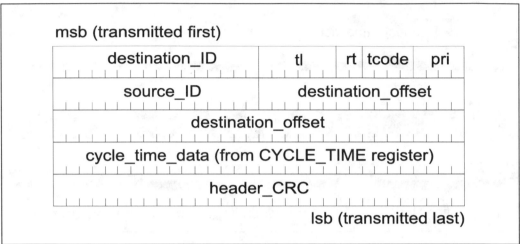

Table 8-16: Cycle Start Packet Contents

Name	Abbrev.	Description
Destination Identifier	destination_ID	For a cycle start packet the destination ID is all 1's to broadcast this packet to all nodes.
Transaction label	tl	This field is not used since no response is returned.
Retry code	rt	This packet will not be retried, since no acknowledge packet follows a broadcast packet.
Transaction Code	tcode	A code value of 8h defines a cycle start packet, thereby defining the packet format illustrated in Figure 8-18.
Priority	pri	Not used in cable environment.
Source Identifier	source_ID	Contains the bus number and phy_ID of the root node.

Table 8-16: Cycle Start Packet Contents (Continued)

Name	Abbrev.	Description
Destination Offset	destination_offset	Specifies the address location of the CYCLE_TIME register (offset 200h in CSR register space).
Cycle Time Data	cycle_time_data	Contents of the roots CYCLE_TIME register at the time that the cycle start packet was sent.
Header CRC	header_CRC	CRC value for the header.

9 *Isochronous Packet*

The Previous Chapter

Asynchronous transactions exist in three basic forms: reads, writes, and locks. The previous chapter discussed the asynchronous transaction types and related packets that are transmitted over the bus.

This Chapter

Isochronous transactions are scheduled so that they occur at 125μs intervals. This chapter discusses isochronous transaction issues and the format of the packet used during isochronous transactions.

The Next Chapter

Next, the various types of PHY packet are discussed. The role of each PHY packet is included, packet format is specified, and the fields within each packet are detailed.

Stream Data Packet

Isochronous transactions use a single data packet to perform a multicast or broadcast operation to one or more nodes. Target nodes are identified by a channel number rather than by a node ID and destination offset address. An isochronous transaction contains only a request phase with no acknowledgment and no response. An isochronous transaction uses a streaming data packet. The packet format is illustrated in Figure 9-1 on page 200 and each field is defined in Table 9-1 on page 201.

The stream data packet (know as the isochronous data block packet in the IEEE 1394-1995 specification) was supported solely for the isochronous bus period by the 1995 specification. The data stream packet has now been specified to occur during either the isochronous or asynchronous time by the 1394a supplement.

Prior to using an isochronous stream packet, the application must first obtain a channel number from the isochronous resource manager node. When a stream data packet is performed during the isochronous time, the application must all obtain the necessary bus bandwidth from the isochronous resource manager.

Figure 9-1: Format of an Isochronous Stream Packet

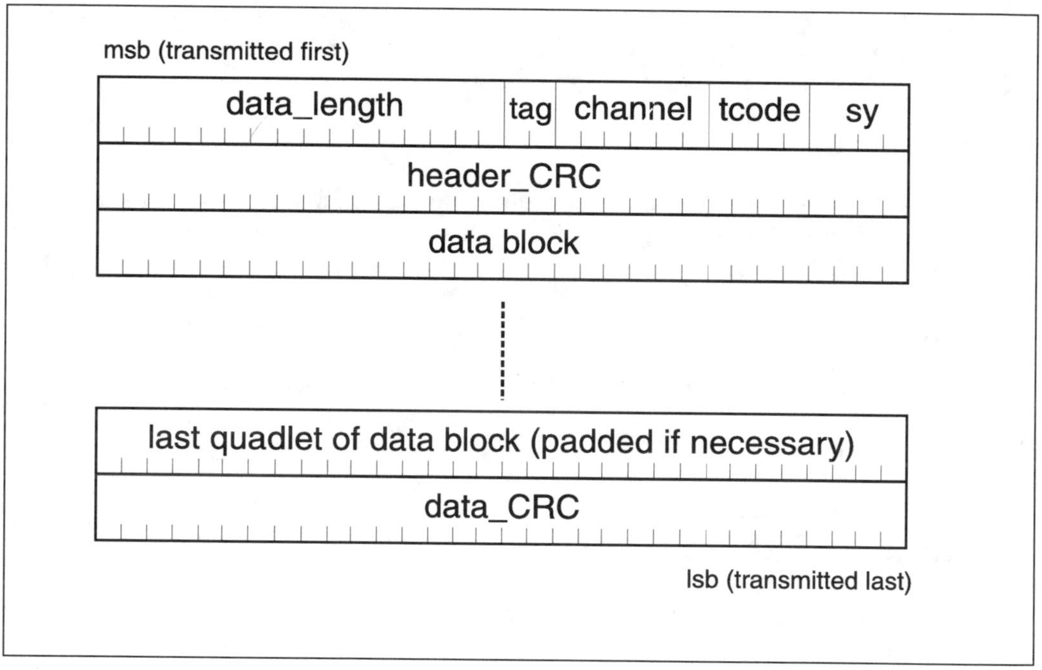

Table 9-1: Isochronous Stream Packet Components

Component Name	Abbreviation	Description
Data Length	data_length	Length can be any value from zero to all ones (FFFFh). When the data length is not a multiple of four bytes, then the talker must pad the last quadlet field with zeros.
Isoch Data Format Tag	tag	The value of 00b indicates that the isochronous data is unformatted. All other values are reserved.
Isoch Channel Number	Channel	Specifies the isochronous channel number assigned to this packet. Channel numbers are a simplified means of addressing. Channel numbers are assigned to a node for talking or listening.
Transaction code	tcode	The transaction code for an isochronous data block transaction is Ah.
Synchronization Code	sy	Application specific.
Header CRC	header_CRC	CRC value for header.
Data Block Payload	data_field	Data to be transferred by the talker. Last quadlet of data field must be padded with zeros if necessary.
Data Block CRC	data_CRC	CRC value for the data field.

Isochronous Data Packet Size

The maximum size of an isochronous transaction based on the 1394-1995 specification was limited to the maximum isochronous bus time, or 100µs. The 1394a supplement further constrains the maximum data block size to the values shown in Table 9-2 on page 202.

The specification describes a null isochronous stream packet. This packet has a data_length value of zero, making the size of this packet only 64-bit, or 2 quadlets. This is the only packet other than PHY packets with a length of 64-bits.

Table 9-2: Maximum Data Payload for Isochronous Packets

	Cable Speed	Maximum Data Payload Size (Bytes)
	100Mb/s	1024
	200Mb/s	2048
	400Mb/s	4096
☞	800Mb/s	8192
☞	1.6Gb/s	16384
☞	3.2Gb/s	32768

Isochronous Transaction Summary

The following illustrations summarize the standard and concatenated forms of isochronous transactions:

Figure 9-2: Non-Concatenated Isochronous Transactions

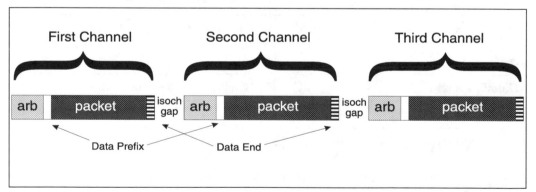

Figure 9-3: Concatenated Isochronous Transactions - If Sent by Same Node

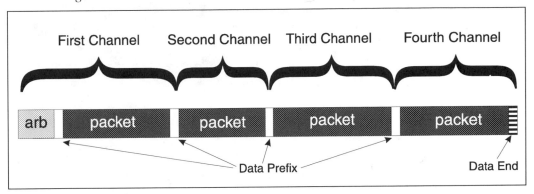

10 *PHY Packet Format*

The Previous Chapter

Isochronous transactions are scheduled so that they occur at 125μs intervals. The previous chapter discussed isochronous transaction issues and the format of the packet used during isochronous transactions.

This Chapter

This chapter discusses the various types of PHY packets. The role of each PHY packet is discussed, packet format is specified, the fields within each packet are detailed.

The Next Chapter

The next chapter details the signaling interface between the link and PHY layer controller chips.

Overview

Transactions discussed to this point target memory-mapped address locations within the node or access a memory buffer identified by a channel number. These address locations reside physically in the link layer, transaction layer, or application layer. The PHY contains no memory-mapped address locations. Some packets however, are designed to access registers within the PHY. These register locations are not mapped within the 256TB of address space allocation to each node and can only be accessed by the local application or via a PHY packet. The PHY packet types defined by the IEEE 1394-1995 specification include:

- Self Identification (Self-ID) packet
- Link-On packet
- PHY Configuration packet

The 1394a supplement defines extended PHY packet types that include:

- Ping packet
- Remote Access packet
- Remote Reply packet
- Remote Command packet
- Remote Confirmation packet
- Resume packet

All PHY packets are transmitted at the base rate of 100Mb/s. This is to ensure that all PHYs are able to receive PHY packet regardless of the maximum transmission speed that they support.

PHY packets are used for various bus management functions the following sections discuss each packet type and describes the bus management functions controlled or affected by each packet.

PHY Packet Format

The general format of a PHY packet is illustrated in Figure 10-1. A PHY packet is eight bytes in length (one octlet). The first four bytes (one quadlet) contain the PHY packet information. They are followed by four more bytes used for error checking. The second quadlet contains the 1's complement (logical inverse) of the first quadlet.

Figure 10-1: General Format of PHY Packet

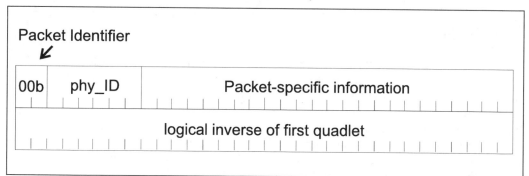

A PHY recognizes a PHY packet if the total packet length is 64-bits. No other packet has a size of 64-bits except for the possibility of a steam packet that contains no data. A PHY recognizes the difference between a null stream packet and a PHY packet because the stream packet uses a 32-bit CRC, whereas, a PHY packet uses a 32-bit 1's complement of the first quadlet.

The PHY packet types are differentiated by the first two bits of the packet as follows:

- 00 = PHY Configuration packet
- 01 = Link-on packet
- 10 = Self-ID packet

The extended packets are identified using the gap_count field of the PHY configuration packet format ("Extended PHY Packets" on page 214).

Self-ID Packets

During bus configuration each node must assign itself a node ID and notify other nodes of its serial bus capabilities. These actions take place during the self-identification process that occurs following a bus reset and tree identification. Each node broadcasts from one to three self-ID packets during the self-identification process. Note that this packet is created within the PHY layer.

Self-ID Packet Zero

Self-ID packet zero is illustrated in Figure 10-2. The format of self-ID packet zero is the same for 1394-1995 and the 1394a supplement. However power class fields within Self-ID packet zero are defined differently. Table 10-1 defines the fields for 1394-1995 and Table 10-2 on page 209 lists the new power class field definitions for 1394a. Note that self-ID packet zero permits identification of only three node ports (ports 0-2). If additional ports are implemented, then one or more self-ID packets is required.

The 1394a specification redefines the port status information within the self-ID packets. The four new states are defined as:

- 00b = port not present
- 01b = port not active (may be either suspended, disabled, or disconnected)
- 10b = port active and connected to parent node
- 11b = port active and connected to child node

Figure 10-2: Format of Self-ID Packet Zero

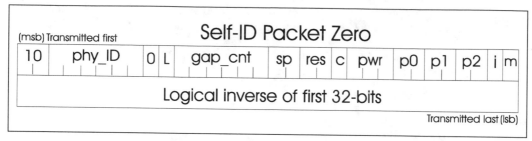

Table 10-1: Contents of the Self-ID Packet Zero — 1394-1995

Field Code	Field Name	Comments
10	Packet identifier	Transmitted at the beginning of the packet to identify this packet as a self-ID packet.
Phy_ID	Physical ID	Physical Identifier of the node sending this packet.
L	Link active	Set to indicate that Link and Transaction layers are active.
gap_cnt	Gap count	Current value of PHY_CONFIGURATION.gap_count field within the PHY register.
sp	PHY speed	Nodes speed capabilities: 00 = 98.304 Mb/s 01 = 98.304 Mb/s and 196.608 Mb/s 10 = 98.304 Mb/s, 196.608 Mb/s and 393.216Mb/s 11 = Reserved
del	PHY delay	Specifies the maximum repeater delay across this node. 00 = <= 144ns (~14/BASE_RATE) 01 = Reserved 10 = Reserved 11 = Reserved Note: This field is reserved in the 1394a specification. PHY delay is obtained by reading the PHY delay and PHY jitter fields within the 1394a PHY registers.
c	Contender	When set and Link active is set, this node is a contender for the role of bus or isochronous resource manager.

Table 10-1: Contents of the Self-ID Packet Zero — 1394-1995 (Continued)

Field Code	Field Name	Comments
pwr	Power class	Specifies power consumption and source characteristics: 000 = Node does need bus power and does not repeat power 001 = Self powered & provides 15W (minimum) to bus. 010 = Self powered & provides 30W (minimum to bus. 011 = Self powered & provides 45W (minimum to bus 100 = May be powered by bus and uses up to 1W. 101 = Powered by bus & uses 1W. Additional 2W needed to power link layer higher layers. 110 = Powered by bus & uses 1W. Additional 5W needed to power link layer higher layers. 111 = Powered by bus & uses 1W. Additional 9W needed to power link layer higher layers.
p0.. p2	Port number	Specifies port status: 00 = Port not present 01 = No connection to other node 10 = Connected to parent node 11 = Connected to child node
i	Initiated reset	This node initiated the current bus reset before receiving reset signaling. (Optional, if not used returns zero)
m	More packets	More packets follow this one to report additional port status.

Table 10-2: Definition of Power Class Values Within "Pwr" Field
of Self-ID Packet—1394a

POWER_CLASS Code (binary)	Power Consumption and Source Characteristics
000	Node does not require bus power nor repeat bus power.
001	Node is self-powered and provides 15W (minimum) to the bus.
010	Node is self-powered and provides 30W (minimum) to the bus.

Table 10-2: Definition of Power Class Values Within "Pwr" Field
of Self-ID Packet—1394a (Continued)

POWER_CLASS Code (binary)	Power Consumption and Source Characteristics
011	Node is self-powered and provides 45W (minimum) to the bus.
100	Node may be powered from the bus and is using up to 3W and no additional bus power is needed to enable the link.
101	Reserved for future implementations.
110	Node is powered from the bus and consumes 3W maximum. An additional 3W maximum is needed to enable the link.
111	Node is powered from the bus and consumes 3W maximum. An additional 7W maximum is needed to enable the link.

Self-ID Packets One, Two, and Three (1394-1995)

Each node sends one or more packets depending on the number of ports that it has:

- Leaf nodes (one port) or branch nodes with two or three ports send a single 32-bit self-ID packet (packet zero).
- Nodes with 4 to 11 ports (p3 - p10) send two self-ID packets
- Nodes with 12 to 19 ports (p11 - p18) send three self-ID packets
- Nodes with 20 to 27 ports (p19 - p26) send four self-ID packets

Twenty-seven nodes is the maximum number supported for a single node by the 1394-1995 specificaton. Figure 10-3 on page 211 pictures the format of the additional packets (packets one - three) and Table 10-3 on page 211 defines the contents of each field. Each 2-bit port field has the same definition as shown in Table 10-1 on page 208 for ports 0-2.

Figure 10-3: Format of Self-ID Packets One-Three

Transmitted first

0   31

| 10 | phy_ID | 1 | n | r | pa | pb | pc | pd | pe | pf | pg | ph | r | m |

Logical inverse of first 32-bits

R=reserved

Transmitted last

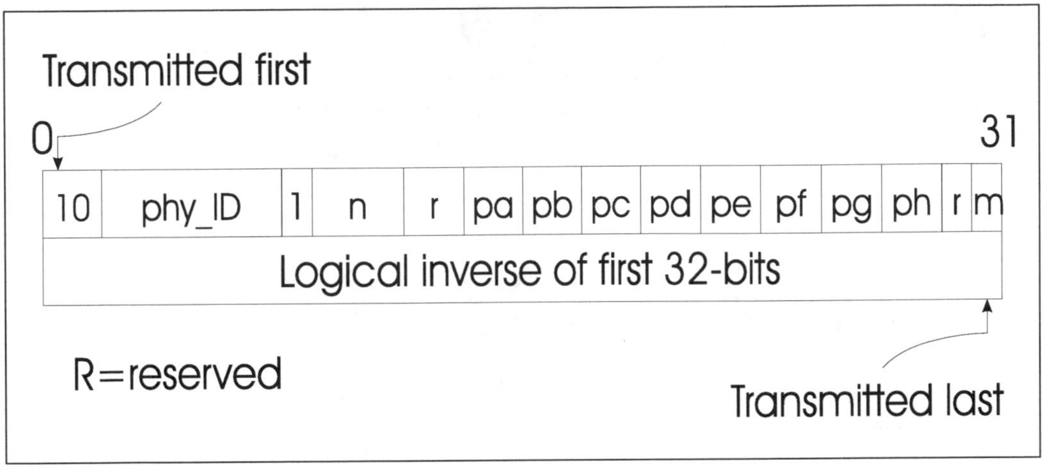

Table 10-3: Definition of Self-ID Packets One - Three (1394-1995)

Packet Number	Packet Field Name								
	n	pa	pb	pc	pd	pe	pf	pg	ph
Packet 1	0	port3	port4	port5	port6	port7	port8	port9	port10
Packet 2	1	port11	port12	port13	port14	port15	port16	port17	port18
Packet 3	2	port19	port20	port21	port22	port23	port24	port25	port26

Self-ID Packets One and Two (1394a)

The 1394a specification limits the number of ports on a single node to 16. Consequently, only two additional packets are needed to identify all ports. Figure 10-4 on page 212 illustrates the format of packets one and two. The format of the port fields is identical to the 1394-1995 self-ID packets.

Figure 10-4: Format of Self-ID Packets One and Two — 1394a

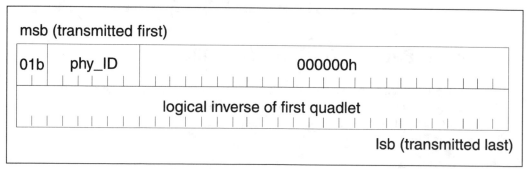

Self-ID Packet One

(msb) Transmitted first

| 10 | phy_ID | 1 | n (0) | r | p3 | p4 | p5 | p6 | p7 | p8 | p9 | p10 | r | m |

Logical inverse of first 32-bits

Transmitted last (lsb)

Self-ID Packet Two

(msb) Transmitted first

| 10 | phy_ID | 1 | n (1) | r | p11 | p12 | p13 | p14 | p15 | reserved |

Logical inverse of first 32-bits

Transmitted last (lsb)

r=reserved

Link-on Packet

The link-on packet is used to notify the target PHY to signal the node to apply power to the link. Figure 10-5 illustrates the format of the link-on packet. The two most significant bits of the packet (01b) identify this PHY packet as a link-on packet. The phy_ID field selects the target node, whose link should be powered.

Figure 10-5: Link-on Packet Format

msb (transmitted first)

| 01b | phy_ID | 000000h |

logical inverse of first quadlet

lsb (transmitted last)

PHY Configuration Packet

The PHY configuration packet is broadcast to all PHYs residing on the bus, allowing configuration of two 1394 bus functions:

- Selecting Root Node—software can force one node to become the root following the next bus reset.
- Optimizing Bus Gaps—software can update the gap count field within all nodes to improve bus efficiency by reducing idle time.

The PHY configuration packet contains fields used to select the root node and to update the gap count register within all nodes. Figure 10-6 illustrates the format of the PHY configuration packet.

Figure 10-6: PHY Configuration Packet Format

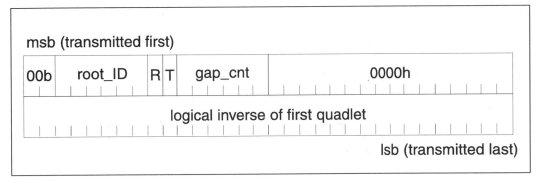

Force Root Node

When a PHY configuration packet is received with its "R" bit set the root_ID field contains a valid node ID. All PHYs will compare their node_ID field to the root_ID field from the packet. If the ID values match, the node will set its "Root Holdoff" bit located in an internal PHY register, and force this node to become the next root node. The node_ID values in all other nodes will of necessity not match the root_ID value, causing all of them to clear their Root Holdoff bits. ("Force Root Delay" on page 299 for a detailed description of how nodes are forced to become the root.)

Gap Count Optimization

The "T" bit within the PHY configuration packet verifies that a new gap count value is contained within the packet. All nodes must update the gap_cnt field within their PHY registers. The intent of this field is to allow software to determine the smallest gap timing possible. (See "Gap Count Optimization" on page 348 for details regarding bus optimization.)

Extended PHY Packets

The extended PHY packets are accessed via the PHY configuration packet format. The packet definition changes slightly to accommodate the extended packets as listed below:

- The "R" and "T" fields must be cleared, indicating that root_ID and Gap_cnt fields are not used.
- The gap_cnt field defines the extended PHY packet type.

Extended PHY packets include:

- Ping packet
- Remote access packet
- Remote reply packet
- Remote command packet
- Remote confirmation packet
- Resume packet

Each of the extended packet types are described in the following sections.

Ping Packet

The ping packet provides a means of measuring the two-way travel time of packets transmitted between two nodes on the bus that are farthest from one another in terms of cable hops. This value can be used to specify a gap count value that represents the greatest bus efficiency due to gap timing delay.

Figure 10-7 on page 215 illustrates the format of the ping packet. A "type" field value of 0000b designates the extended PHY packets as a ping packet, thus the PHY_ID field specifies the node that is to be "pinged." In response to a ping packet the target PHY broadcasts its self-packet(s). The requesting agent can measure the delay between sending the ping packet and the return of the self-ID packet, thereby measuring the two-way travel time between itself and the target node.

Figure 10-7: Ping Packet Format

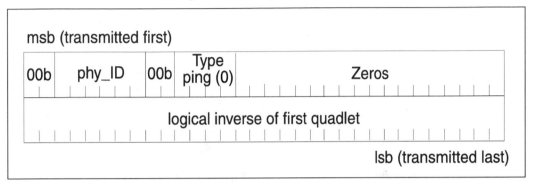

Remote Access Packet

The remote access packet provides a mechanism for accessing a PHY register within the target node. The section entitled "1394a PHY Register Map" on page 398 discusses the PHY registers, which are are all accessible by the remote access packet. Two type field values are supported for a remote access packet:

- type = 1 — One of the eight base PHY registers is to be read. The "reg" field specifies the target register.
- type = 5 — One of eight paged registers is to be read. The "page" field selects one of eight possible groups of paged registers to be read and the "reg" field specifies the target register within the selected page. If the page=0, then a group of PHY port registers is selected and the "port" field identifies the target port.

Table 10-4 summarizes the field code definitions within the remote access packet.

FireWire System Architecture

Figure 10-8: Remote Access Packet Format

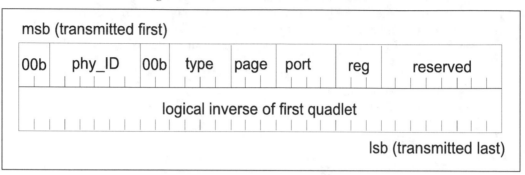

Table 10-4: Remote Access Packet Field Description Summary

Field Name	Description
phy_ID	Identifies target PHY whose registers are to be read.
type	1 = base register read 5 = paged register read
page	0 = one of 16 PHY register locations is selected (location selected depends on type field value and reg field designation)
port	0-7 = port whose registers are to be read when type =5 and page=0
reg	0-7 = identifies one of eight registers to be read

Remote Reply Packet

The remote reply packet returns the read data specified by the remote access packet. Format of the remote reply packet is illustrated in Figure 10-9 on page 217. Two forms of remote reply packets are defined:

- type 3 = read data from selected base register
- type 7 = read data from selected page register

The page, port, and register fields identify the selected page, port and register whose data is returned in the data field.

Figure 10-9: Remote Reply Packet Format

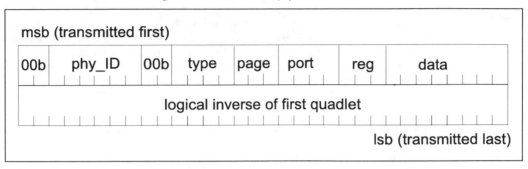

Remote Command Packet

The remote command packet provides the means to issue a variety of commands to the selected port within the target PHY. Figure 10-10 illustrates the packet format and Table 10-5 on page 218 defines each of the fields.

Figure 10-10: Remote Command Packet Format

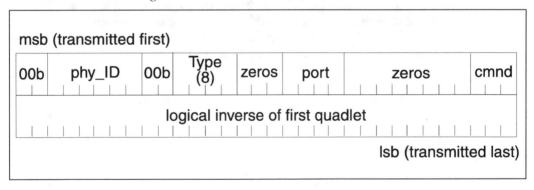

Table 10-5: Remote Command Packet Field Definitions

Field Name	Description
phy_ID	identifies phy being targeted by the remote command packet
type	8 = remote command packet
port	selects one of the phy's ports as the target of the command
command	defines the operation to be performed by the selected node and port. 0 = NOP 1 = Transmit TX_DISABLE_NOTIFY then disable port 2 = Initiate suspend (*i.e.*, become a suspend initiator) 4 = Clear the port's Fault bit to zero 5 = Enable port 6 = Resume port

Remote Confirmation Packet

The remote confirmation packet is returned by the node that was just targeted by a remote command packet to verify that the command has been successfully processed, or not. The confirmation packet also returns current status information for the selected port. Figure 10-11 illustrates the format of the remote confirmation packet.

Figure 10-11: Remote Confirmation Packet Format

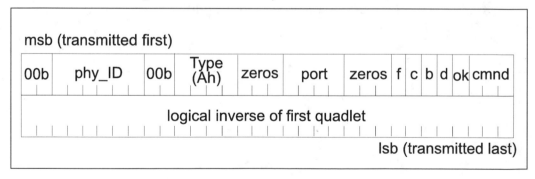

Table 10-6: Remote Confirmation Packet Field Description

Field Name	Description
phy_ID	Defines node that is the source of this packet.
type	Ah = Extended PHY packet is remote confirmation packet
port	Specifies the PHY port to which this packet pertains.
f (fault)	Abbreviated as f in the figure above, this bit is the current value of the Fault bit from PHY register 1001b for the addressed port.
c (connected)	current value of the Connected bit from PHY register 1000b for the selected port.
b (bias)	current value of the bias bit from PHY register 1000b for the selected port.
d (disabled)	current value of the disabled bit from PHY register 1000b for the selected port.
ok	0 = command was rejected by the PHY 1 = command was accepted by the PHY
cmnd	command value that this packet is confirming: 0 = NOP 1 = Transmit TX_DISABLE_NOTIFY then disable port 2 = Initiate suspend (*i.e.*, become a suspend initiator) 4 = Clear the port's Fault bit to zero 5 = Enable port 6 = Resume port

Resume Packet

The resume packet is broadcast to all PHYs to command that all suspended ports must resume normal operation. The phy_ID field contains the node ID of the node that initiated this packet. A type value of Fh indicates that the extended PHY packet is a resume packet. Figure 10-12 on page 220 illustrates the format of the resume packet.

Figure 10-12: Resume Packet Format

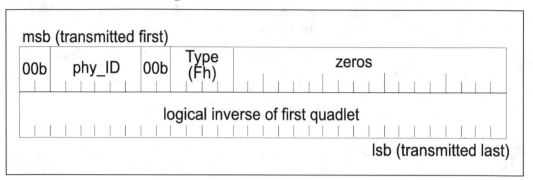

11 *Link to PHY Interface*

The Previous Chapter

The previous chapter discussed the various types of PHY packet. The role of each PHY packet was discussed, the PHY packet formats was specified, and the fields within each packet were detailed.

This Chapter

This chapter details the signaling interface between the link and PHY layer controller chips.

The Next Chapter

The next chapter discusses the transaction retries that can occur when the recipient of a packet is busy (e.g. has a buffer full condition). Two retry mechanisms are defined by the 1394 specification: single and dual phase. Each type of mechanism is discussed.

Overview

The IEEE 1394-1995 specification describes the interface between the Link and PHY chips. This interface definition is included in the 1394-1995 Appendix and is labeled as informative (not a required implementation). However, the 1394a supplement requires that this interface be used if the node is implemented with separate PHY and Link layer components. Note that there is no requirement that a node be designed with separate Link and PHY chips. These functions could be integrated within the same silicon, in which case the interface between these functions is implementation specific. The motivation for requiring the standard interface is to promote interoperability between PHY and Link layer chips from different manufacturers.

The Interface Signals

Figure 11-1 on page 222 illustrates the synchronous interface between the link and PHY. The interface is used by both the link and PHY. The link layer chip initiates transactions by sending requests to the PHY to send a packet, and the PHY forwards packets that it receives from the 1394 cable to the link via the interface. The function of each Link/PHY interface signal is defined in Table 11-1 on page 223.

Figure 11-1: Interface Between the Link and PHY

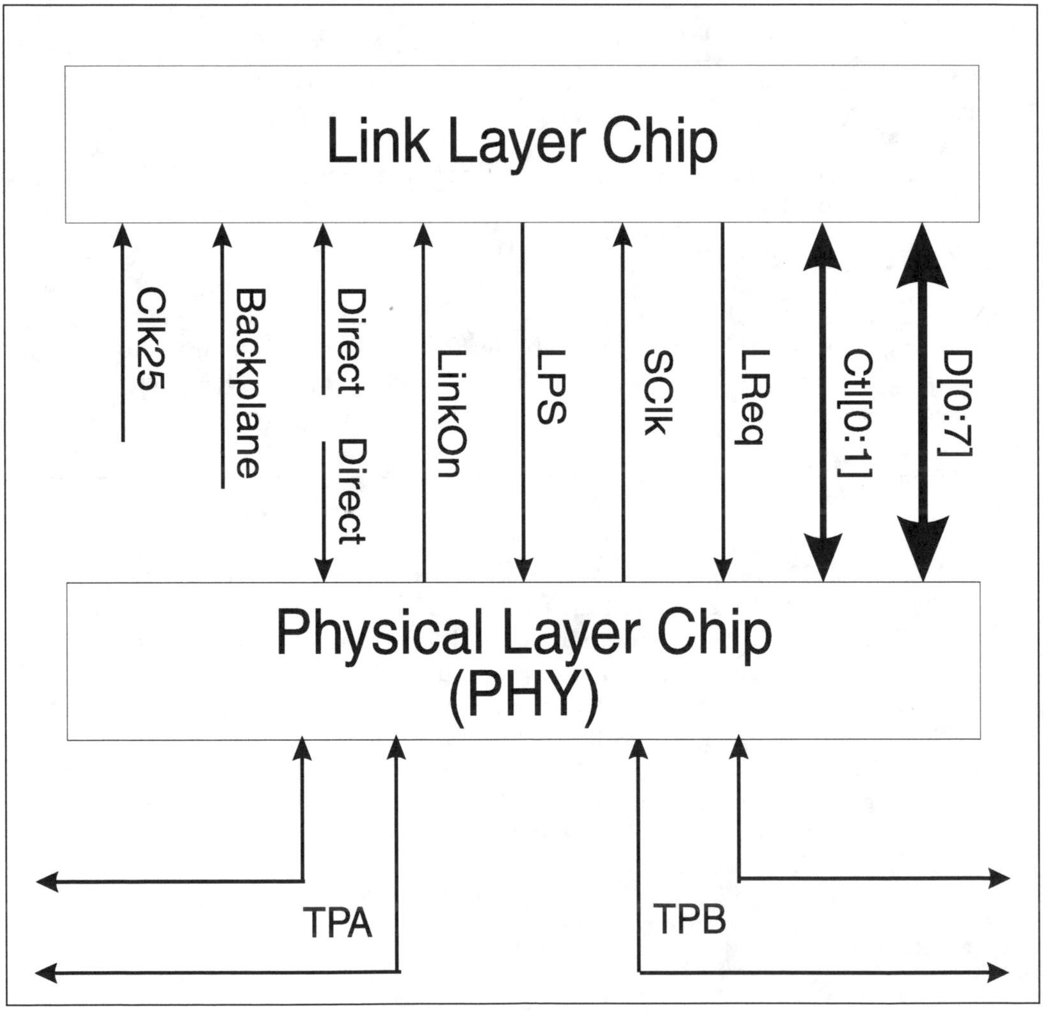

Chapter 11: Link to PHY Interface

Table 11-1: Link/PHY Signal Interface

Name	Driven by	Description
D[0:7]	Link or PHY	Data — packet data is delivered via the data lines. The number of data lines used depends on the speed supported as follows: D[0:1] = 100Mb/s D[0:3] = 200Mb/s D[0:7] = 400Mb/s
Ctl[0:1]	Link or PHY	Control — defines the state of the interface when being driven by the Link or PHY (e.g. idle, sending status, transmitting or receiving a packet).
LReq	Link	Link Request — this serial interface is used by the link to initiate a request. Is also used to request access to local PHY registers.
SClk	PHY	49.152MHz clock — the clock used to clock data between the PHY and Link.
LPS	Link	Link power status — indicates whether the link is powered or not.
Link On	PHY	Link has been powered-on via a link-on packet.
Direct	Neither	Direct connection between Link and PHY interface signals is implemented when this pin is asserted. When deasserted an isolation barrier is implemented.
Backplane	Neither	Pulled high for backplane PHY implementation.
Clk25	Neither	Pulled high if SClk is 24.576. (backplane environment only).

Sharing the Interface

The bi-directional control signals specify the type of transmission being made via the data lines. The type of transmission depends in part on whether the link or PHY is transmitting the data. The default owner of the PHY/link interface is the PHY. The link gains ownership of the interface via the LReq lines to transfer a packet to the PHY, which then transmits the packet over the cable. Ownership of the interface returns to the PHY after the link has completed sending the packet. The current state of the interface is defined by the control signals.

PHY Initiated Transfers

The PHY uses the interface to transfer information to the node's link layer controller. The information transferred includes:

- packets received from the serial bus that are forwarded to the link layer controller.
- contents of local PHY registers that have been requested by the link.
- status information which is reported to the link.

When the PHY owns the interface, one of four conditions may exist on the interface. The current state of the interface defines these conditions, which can be determined by monitoring the interface control lines (Ctl[0:1]. Table 11-2 lists the control signal definitions when the PHY owns the bus.

Table 11-2: Control Signal Definition with PHY Driving

Ctl[0:1]b	Type	Description
00	idle	No activity.
01	status	PHY is sending status information to link.
10	receive	Incoming packet is being transferred from PHY to link via data lines, or PHY generated data being sent to the cable and also to the link via the data lines (e.g. self-ID packets, remote command and reply packets).
11	grant	PHY is granting use of the bus to the link so that it can send a packet.

Idle State

Interface is idle indicating that neither the link nor the PHY currently have data to transfer.

Status State

When the PHY signals status via the control lines, it is sending status information across the data lines. Status transmission occurs when one of several PHY or cable events have occurred. These events include:

- An arbitration reset gap has been detected
- A subaction gap has been detected
- A cable reset has been detected
- Cable power failure
- Looped topology has been detected during the Bus ID procedure
- Arbitration state machine has timed out
- Bias change at a disabled port has been detected

Also, PHY register data is returned to the link in response to a PHY register read request.

Receive State

When the receive state is being signaled, the PHY is transferring an incoming data packet from the 1394 bus to the link for decoding, or is forwarding PHY generated packets to both the cable and the link. PHY packets include self-ID packets, configuration packet, link-on packet, and all extended PHY packets.

Grant State

Grant is signaled to the link to notify it that it can begin transmitting a packet. This is done only after the link has issued a packet request via the LReq line and the PHY has obtained ownership of the 1394 bus.

Link Initiated Transfers

The link uses the interface to request that the PHY chip perform one of the following actions:

- initiate an isochronous request.
- initiate a priority asynchronous request.
- initiate an immediate asynchronous request.
- initiate a fair asynchronous request.
- initiate a read from an internal PHY register.
- initiate a write to an internal PHY register.

Packet request includes the speed at which the packet should be sent. Once a link request has been made and the PHY has arbitrated for and won control of the 1394 bus, the PHY then grants use of the PHY/Link data lines to the link. After grant has been signaled to the link it knows that the PHY is ready to receive data. The link then uses the data lines to transmit the packet to the PHY.

The link identifies the state of the interface by driving the control lines to the appropriate state. Several conditions may exist on the bus and will be reflected on the control lines:

- the link may be transmitting data via the interface
- the link is retaining ownership of the interface while it prepares data to transmit.
- the link has just completed the transfer of data associated with a request, but wishes to send additional data without again arbitrating for control of the bus; thus, the link does not relinquish ownership of the interface.
- transmission has completed; thus, the link returns the interface to the idle state, and returns interface ownership to the PHY.

The current state of the interface can be determined by monitoring the interface control lines (Ctl[0:1]. Table 11-3 lists the interface states and the control signal definitions when the link owns the interface.

Table 11-3: Control Signal Definition with Link Driving

Ctl[0:1]b	Type	Description
00	idle	Transmission complete, bus is released by link.
01	hold	Link is holding the bus while preparing data to transmit, or it has completed the current data transfer and wishes to retain ownership without re-arbitrating before sending the next packet.
10	transmit	Link is sending a packet to the PHY via data lines.
11	NA	unused

Determining Transfer Rate Between Link and PHY

The data signals (D0:D7) are used by both the link and PHY for transferring data across the interface. The rate at which data is transferred in the cable environment is governed by the 49.152MHz SClk signal. Since the transmission rate is constant, the actual data rate is determined by the number of data lines used during the transfer:

- 2-bits = 100Mb/s
- 4-bits = 200Mb/s
- 8-bits = 400Mb/s

Note that the speed (i.e. the number of data lines used) of each data transfer between the link and PHY may change from one transmission to the next. This is because communication with one target node may require data transfer at a different speed than another. Consequently, the Link and PHY must notify each other of the transmission speed so the other knows how many data lines will be used during the current data transfer. The unused data lines are driven low. The mechanism used to specify the data rate is different for link to PHY and PHY to link transfers and is discussed later in this chapter.

Powering the Link

During bus configuration the link may be powered off. However, nodes that are capable of becoming bus managers or isochronous resource managers must have their link layer powered. The bus manager or isochronous resource manager (when the bus manager node is not present) must apply power to other nodes that have their link powered off during bus configuration.

Each node reports whether its link is powered during configuration when it sends its self-ID packet. The bus manager capable and resource manager capable nodes must save the self-ID packets so they can perform bus management functions in the event that they are chosen. Following bus configuration, the node performing power management must ensure that each node's link is powered by sending it a link-on packet.

Packet Transmission

When a functional device within a node wishes to perform a transaction, the associated application issues a transaction request to the link layer chip. The link layer then uses the PHY/link interface to forward the request to the PHY. The request is issued to the PHY chip via the LReq signal line. Once the request has been issued, the PHY must arbitrate for control of the IEEE 1394 bus and grant use of the PHY/Link interface so that the necessary packets can be sent to the PHY for transmission over the 1394 bus.

Generally, the request may be issued at any time to the PHY. However, to ensure proper operation of the link/PHY interface, certain rules of conduct are defined that limit when a link request can be issued. These rules depend on whether the link or PHY currently owns the interface and how the interface is currently being used.

Link Issues Request

The link requests access to the serial bus via the LReq line by sending a serial stream of bits to the PHY. These bits define the type of request being made and the speed at which the packet must be delivered. Note that the link always owns the unidirectional LReq line and can issue a request asynchronously to the PHY. However, certain requests can only be issued at particular times (discussed later in the section). When a transaction request is issued to the PHY it must arbitrate for control of the serial bus. Once ownership of the 1394 bus has been acquired, ownership of the interface can be turned over to the link controller. The PHY notifies the link that it owns the interface by driving grant on the control lines.

Format of the link request depends on the version of the 1394 specification that a particular link layer controller complies with. Specifically, the 1995 version of the specification and the 1394a supplement differ in the definition of packet speed information delivered to the PHY via the link request. The LReq format defined by the 1394-1995 specification includes three transfer speeds (100, 200, and 400Mb/s) and therefore requires only two bits for indicating the data rate (shown in Table 11-4).

Table 11-4: Bus Request Format for Cable Environment - 1394-1995 Standard

Bits(s)	Type	Description
0	start bit	Indicates start of request.
1-3	request type	Indicates type of bus request: • immediate (000b) • isochronous (001b) • priority (010b) • fair (011b) • register read request (100b) • register write request (101b) • acceleration control (110b)
4-5	speed	Speed at which the PHY will transmit the packet: • 100Mb/s (00b) • 200Mb/s (01b) • 400Mb/s (10b).
6	stop bit	Indicates end of transfer.

The 1394a supplement adds an additional speed bit to define faster data rates (although not yet supported). The 1394a link request is illustrated in Figure 11-2 on page 230 and the corresponding fields are defined in Table 11-5. Note that a PHY compliant with the 1394a standard must be able to handle both 1394-1995 and 1394a link request formats.

The following sections discuss the information that is transferred via the LReq line during a transaction.

Figure 11-2: The Link Request Specifies the Speed of the Upcoming Data Transmission

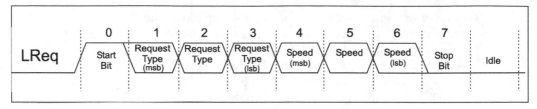

Table 11-5: Bus Request Format for Cable Environment - 1394a Standard

Bits(s)	Type	Description
0	start bit	Indicates start of request. Always driven to 1.
1-3	request type	Indicates type of bus request: • immediate (000b) • isochronous (001b) • priority (010b) • fair (011b) • register read request (100b) • register write request (101b) • acceleration control (110b)
4-6	speed	Speed at which the PHY will transmit the packet: • 100Mb/s (000b) • 200Mb/s (010b) • 400Mb/s (100b) • 800Mb/s (110b) • 1.6Gb/s (001b) • 3.2Gb/s (011b).
7	stop bit	Indicates end of transfer. Always driven to 0. If the speed is 100, 200, or 400Mb/s this stop bit may be omitted. This is because the last bit of the speed information is a 0 for these speeds, and must be interpreted by the PHY as a stop bit to maintain compatibility with the 1995 version of the standard.

Request Types

Note that the 1394 standards define four arbitration requests:

- isochronous
- fair
- priority
- immediate

When the link initiates a transaction or responds to a request that it receives from another node, it uses either the isochronous, fair, or priority request types, depending on the transfer type and the action pending. The immediate request is used by the link when it returns the acknowledgment to an asynchronous packet just received. These request types specify to the PHY the type of arbitration to perform.

Speed of Link to PHY Data Transmission

The link controller specifies the transmission speed of the packet to be sent via the LReq signal as specified in Table 11-6 on page 231. This request is sent serially to the PHY and includes the data rate at which the link will transfer the data. Notice that bits 4:6 specify the speed of the transfer. Table 11-6 on page 231 shows the encoding of the speed bits. Note that the 1394a supplement defines 800, 1600, and 3200 Mb/s transfer speeds in preparation for 1394.B implementations.

Table 11-6: Speed Signaling Link to PHY

LReq (4:6)	Data Rate (Mb/s)
000b	100
001b	1600
010b	200
011b	3200
100b	400
101b	Reserved
110b	800
111	Reserved

When Can the Link Issue a Request?

When a link controller receives a request from an application to send a packet, it uses the LReq signals to notify the PHY of the need to transfer a packet. The packet to be transferred could be one of several types:

- an isochronous request packet being sent to initiate an isochronous request packet.
- an asynchronous request packet being sent to initiate an asynchronous transaction.
- a response packet being returned to the requesting node to confirm completion of a previously received request.
- an acknowledge packet being returned by the packet recipient to verify receipt of an asynchronous request or response from another node. (Note that this packet originates within the link layer controller, not within the application.)

As soon as the link recognizes that it must transmit a packet, it generally is allowed to issue the request immediately via the LReq lines, regardless of the current activity on the Link/PHY interface. However, in some instances the LReq cannot be issued until the current interface activity completes. For example, if a request has just been issued by the link, another request must not be issued until the first has been completed. Table 11-7 lists the conditions under which the link may initiate requests to the PHY. Note that these rules depend on the type of request to be issued, the current owner of the interface, and the current state of the interface.

To help specify the conditions under which a request may be issued, the specification defines two labels (C_A and C_B) that are used in reference to the state of the control signals relative to the beginning of LReq signaling. Figure 11-3 illustrates the state of the bus before an LReq is signaled (C_A), while the Ctl state during and after the LReq is delivered is specified by C_B. Table 11-7 describes the control states that must be present immediately prior to starting an LReq (C_A).

Figure 11-3: LReq & Ctl Timing Relationship

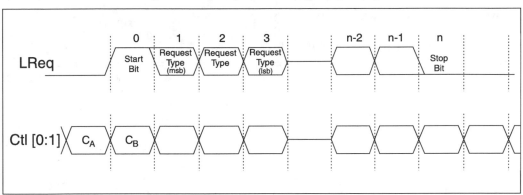

Table 11-7: Rules Governing When Link May Initiate a Request on LReq

Request Type	C$_A$ States that permit LReq When PHY Owns Ctl[0:1]	C$_A$ States that permit LReq When Link Owns Ctl[0:1]	Description
Fair	idle, status	None	Fair requests are not permitted until any outstanding bus requests complete. Thus, the Ctl[0:1] states of receive and grant prevent an LReq from being issued.
Priority	idle, status	None	Same as Fair Requests
Immediate	receive, idle	None	During asynchronous packet reception the link must decode the destination ID to determine if it is being targeted by the transaction. If targeted by the request packet, the link must return an acknowledge packet. The start bit of an immediate request (for transmitting an Acknowledge packet) must be sent no later than the 4th cycle after the interface has returned to the idle state.

Table 11-7: Rules Governing When Link May Initiate a Request on LReq (Continued)

Request Type	C_A States that permit LReq When PHY Owns Ctl[0:1]	C_A States that permit LReq When Link Owns Ctl[0:1]	Description
Isochronous	Any	Idle	These packets are sent during the isochronous arbitration period. When the link does not own the interface, the start bit of an isochronous packet request must be sent no later than the 4th cycle following the return of the interface to the idle state from the receive state. If the link owns the interface and has just transferred a packet, a pending isochronous request must be issued to the PHY no later than 8 Sclk cycles after the transmit to idle state transition on the interface. The link must not issue an Isochronous request when it intends to concatenate another isochronous request to the previous packet.

PHY Behavior When a Packet Request is Received

The PHY arbitrates for control of the bus after receiving a packet request from the link. If successful the PHY notifies the link of the successful arbitration by signaling "grant" via the control lines. This also serves to notify the link that the PHY is ready to receive the packet. In some situations the PHY may not be able to handle the request during some types of bus activity or due to some events, causing the PHY to discard the request. The link must continue to observe the control lines during and after LReq transmission until it detects grant. In this way, the link can detect conditions that it knows will cause the PHY to discard the request. If the request is discarded by the PHY, the link must re-issue the request. Table 11-8 defines how the PHY will handle a link request and how the link reacts to the various bus conditions.

Table 11-8: Link Requests and Corresponding PHY Behavior and Link Actions

Request Type	C_B States During or After LReq transmission	PHY Behavior	Link Action
Fair	Receive	Request is normally discarded when PHY enters the receive state. However, if arbitration acceleration is enabled the packet will be retained unless the received packet is no an acknowledge packet (8-bits).	Link monitors the Ctl lines to determine if the PHY will service or cancel the request based on known PHY behavior.
	Grant	1394 bus arbitration has been won for this node.	Link transmits the packet to the PHY.
	Idle, Status	Request is serviced unless a bus reset is reported during a status transfer.	Link monitors the Ctl lines until grant is signaled, unless a bus reset is sent.
Priority	Receive	Request is normally discarded when PHY enters the receive state. However, if arbitration acceleration is enabled the packet will be retained unless the received packet is no an acknowledge packet (8-bits).	Link monitors the Ctl lines to determine if the PHY will service or cancel the request.
	Grant	1394 bus arbitration has been won for this node.	Link transmits the packet to the PHY.
	Idle, Status	Request is serviced unless a bus reset is reported during a status transfer.	Link monitors the Ctl lines until grant is signalled, unless a bus reset is sent.
Immediate	Idle, Status	Request is serviced unless a bus reset is reported during a status transfer.	Link monitors the Ctl lines until grant is signaled, unless a bus reset is sent.
	Receive	PHY is repeating a packet. Request is retained for servicing once the current packet ends.	Link monitors Ctl lines.
	Grant	Wait for Packet.	Transmit Acknowledge Packet

Table 11-8: Link Requests and Corresponding PHY Behavior and Link Actions (Continued)

Request Type	C_B States During or After LReq transmission	PHY Behavior	Link Action
Isochronous	Idle		Monitor Ctl for the next change of state.
	Status	Request is serviced, unless status indicates a subaction gap event. This indicates that the isochronous bus time has expired, reflecting an error condition.	Link continues to monitor Ctl line, unless request is discarded.
	Receive	PHY retains the request.	Link monitors Ctl lines.
	Grant	The PHY has won arbitration and is ready to receive a packet.	Link transmits the packet.
	Transmit, Idle (interface driven by Link)	Request is retained by PHY.	Monitor Ctl lines after releasing control of interface to the PHY.

Receiving Packets

When a packet is being transmitted by another node the PHY detects the "Data-On" state. It then signals a receive condition on Ctl[0:1] and delivers all ones on the data lines. The PHY signals the beginning of the packet by sending the speed code over the data lines, which is immediately followed by packet contents. Note that the CRC check does not include the speed code information. Receive signaling is illustrated in Figure 11-4 on page 237.

Figure 11-4: Sequence and Format of Data Lines During Packet Receive State

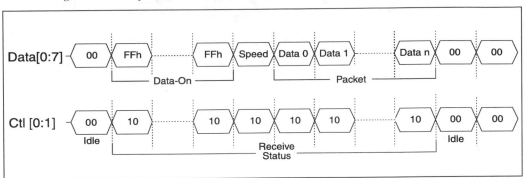

Speed of PHY to Link Data Transmission

When a packet is received by the PHY it must transfer the packet to the Link. The PHY transmits the packet to the link at the received speed. For example, if the packet is received at 100Mb/s only two of the data lines are used, whereas, if the packet is received at 400Mb/s all eight data lines are used. The PHY indicates the start of a receive packet by sending a speed code over the data lines. This serves to notify the link that a packet is being transmitted and the speed at which it will be sent (i.e. the number of data lines that will be used). Table 11-9 shows the speed code signaling used by the PHY when starting packet transfer over the PHY/Link data lines. Note that if packet speed is 100Mb/s only two bits are needed to define the speed (00b), while 200Mb/s transfers use four bits and 400Mb/s and greater use all eight lines.

A PHY may support a higher transfer rate than the link. In this case the link will recognize that it does not support the incoming packet when it detects the speed code and consequently will ignore the packet transmission. The link ignores all interface traffic until it detects the next idle state.

Table 11-9: Speed Signaling PHY to Link

D[0:7]	Data Rate (Mb/s)
00xxxxxxb	100
0100xxxxb	200
01010000b	400

Table 11-9: Speed Signaling PHY to Link (Continued)

D[0:7]	Data Rate (Mb/s)
01010001b	800
01010010b	1600
01010011b	3200
11111111b	"Data-On" indication

PHY Reports Status

The PHY returns status information to the link via the two least significant data bits and indicates the "status" state on the ctl[0:1] lines. Figure 11-5 illustrates the Data and Ctl signal format during status transfers. Four status bits are returned as shown in Table 11-10. Each status event that is reports is described in the following sections.

Figure 11-5: Format and Content of Data & Control Signals During Status Transfers

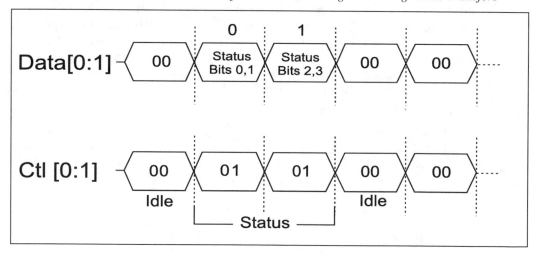

Table 11-10: Status Bits Returned Via D[0:1]

D[0:1]	Type	Description
0	ARB_RESET_GAP	PHY has detected an arbitration reset gap.
1	SUBACTION_GAP	Indicates that a subaction gap has been detected.
2	BUS_RESET_START	Indicates that the PHY has received or initiated a bus reset.
3	PHY_INTERRUPT	• Loop detect interrupt • Cable power fail interrupt • Arbitration state machine time-out • Bias change detect interrupt

ARB_RESET_GAP

When the PHY detects an arbitration reset gap it signals this event to the link. The link recognizes the start of the next fairness interval and knows that it can initiate the next fair request.

SUBACTION_GAP

Upon detecting a subaction gap the PHY sends status to the link, notifying the link that the next asynchronous arbitration can begin within the fairness interval. Once a cycle start packet is detected, the subaction gaps cease until all scheduled isochronous transactions have completed during this isochronous interval.

BUS_RESET_START

Bus reset start notifies the link that the PHY has detected a bus reset and has entered the reset state (i.e., the PHY has entered the initialize state).

PHY_INTERRUPT

When the PHY_INTERRUPT bit is set during a status transfer, the link recognizes that one or more of four interrupt conditions have been detected by the PHY.

- Loop detect interrupt
- Cable power fail interrupt
- Arbitration state machine time-out
- Bias change detect interrupt

To determine which interrupt condition has occurred, the link must perform a PHY register read (PHY register 0101b) to check related bit fields. See the bits labeled Loop, Pwr fail, and Time-out in Figure 11-6 on page 242. Once status has been read the status bits must be cleared by issuing a write register request to address 0101b with the related bit position set to one. Note that bias change must be read from the port registers to determine which port detected a change in bias or connection status.

Accelerated Arbitration Control

Arbitration acceleration employs techniques defined by the 1394a supplement that permits asynchronous packets to be concatenated by a node as it repeats another transaction being sent by another node, and to begin asynchronous arbitration without having to wait for the subaction gap to appear. This eliminates the normal subaction gap that normally appears between packets, which also eliminates the normal fair arbitration time. Thus, if arbitration acceleration were permitted to continue without restraint, the cycle master would not be able to arbitrate for bus ownership, and therefore would not be able to initiate the next cycle start packet. As a result, arbitration acceleration has the ability to suspend isochronous transactions indefinitely.

To prevent arbitration acceleration from disrupting isochronous transmissions the 1394a supplement defines rules to limit the duration of the arbitration enhancements. The specification defines a procedure that all nodes supporting these enhancements must implement, called acceleration control.

Arbitration acceleration must not be performed by any node during the interval between the beginning of the local cycle synchronization event (~ 125 μs intervals) until one of the following events has occurred:

- Cycle-Start Packet — This indicates that isochronous transactions have begun.
- Arbitration Reset Gap — This would occur prior to a Cycle-Start packet if no isochronous transactions were currently scheduled.
- Two subaction gaps — This would occur if no isochronous transactions are currently being performed and the current fairness interval has not yet ended.

During this period of time, a link must not send either a fair or priority request without first transmitting an acceleration control request with the accelerate bit cleared to zero. This defeats the PHYs ability to perform arbitration acceleration. Once one of the events listed in the previous bulleted list has occurred the link may re-enable fly-by arbitration by transmitting an acceleration control request with the accelerate bit set to one.

Table 11-11: Acceleration Control Request Format

Bits(s)	Type	Description
0	start bit	Indicates start of request.
1-3	request type	Indicates an acceleration control request (110b).
4	accelerate	0 = disable arbitration acceleration in PHY. 1 = enable arbitration acceleration.
5	stop bit	Indicates end of transfer.

Accessing the PHY Registers

A node application may read from or write to local PHY registers. PHY registers are identified by byte offsets within the PHY. These registers are not mapped into the node memory address space, and are accessible by a node's local application (read or write), or by a remote node via the remote access packet (read only). Figure 11-6 on page 242 pictures the PHY registers and offset locations. Note also that some of these registers are read only. The PHY registers are discussed in Chapter 22, entitled "PHY Registers," on page 393.

Figure 11-6: 1394a PHY Register Definition

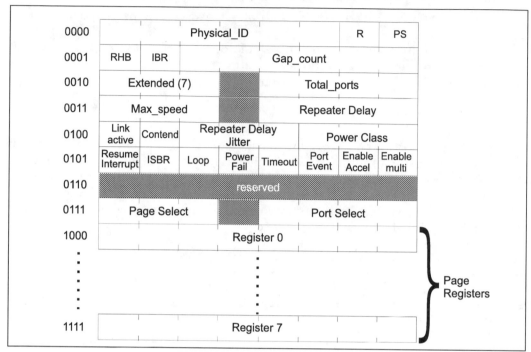

PHY Register Reads

The link controller uses the LReq line to request the contents of a PHY register be returned. Packet contents are returned by the PHY via the data lines. Table 11-12 shows the format of the register read request. A value of 110b on bits 1:3 indicates a PHY register read request, while bits 4:7 identify one of the 16 PHY registers to be read.

Table 11-12: Register Read Request Format

Bits(s)	Type	Description
0	start bit	Indicates start of request.
1-3	request type	Indicates a register read request (100b).
4-7	address	Internal PHY address to be read.
8	stop bit	Indicates end of transfer.

When Can a Register Read Request Be Issued?

Register read requests via LReq may be issued when either the Link or PHY currently own the interface. A register read request may be issued at any time except while another register read request is already pending completion.

PHY Behavior When a Register Read Request is Received

The PHY never discards a register read request from the link. However, depending on the current PHY activity the register read may be deferred. For example, if a packet is currently being received or if status is being reported to the link, the PHY will handle the current activity before servicing the register read request. Note that unlike all other link requests the PHY retains register read requests in the event of a bus reset.

Register Contents Returned by PHY

The PHY returns the contents of a register via a status transfer. The PHY drives the control lines to 01b (indicating status) and delivers the contents of the register across D[0:1]. The register read status transfer has a specific format used to return the contents of a register, and also reports the normal status bits (0:3) at the same time. Figure 11-7 on page 244 illustrates the contents of the control and data lines when register contents are being returned to the link. The relevant bits during a register read status transfer are bits 4:7 (specifying the register address) and bits 8:15 (containing the register contents).

Figure 11-7: Register Contents Returned During Status Transfer

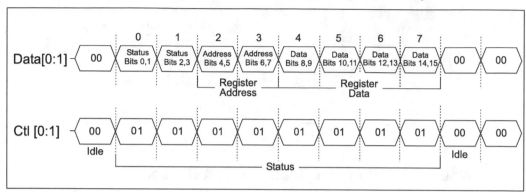

PHY Register Writes

Register writes differ from register reads in that the write data is included within the LReq rather than being transferred via the data lines. Table 11-13 shows the format of the LReq during a register write request.

Table 11-13: Register Write Request Format

Bits(s)	Type	Description
0	start bit	Indicates start of request.
1-3	request type	Indicates a register write request (101b).
4-7	address	Internal PHY address to be written.
8-15	data	Data to be written to the address specified.
16	stop bit	Indicates end of transfer.

When Can a PHY Register Write Request Be Issued?

Register writes may be issued at any time (with one exception) regardless of whether the PHY or Link currently controls the PHY/Link interface. The one exception is that a register access must never be issued until all previous register accesses have completed.

PHY Behavior When a Register Write Request is Received

The PHY never discards a register read request from the link and it is never deferred. PHY discards register write requests in the event of a bus reset.

Electrical Isolation Between PHY and Link

The specification defines two mechanisms for electrically isolating the Link and PHY chips. These are:

- Capacitive decoupling
- Transformer decoupling

For details please refer to the related 1394 specifications.

12 *Transaction Retry*

The Previous Chapter

The previous chapter detailed the signaling interface between the link and PHY layer controller chips. This interface is now required by 1394a implementations of a PHY or link controller chip.

This Chapter

This chapter discusses transaction retries that occur when the recipient of a packet is busy (e.g. has a buffer full condition). Two retry mechanisms are defined by the 1394 specification: single and dual phase. Each type of mechanism is discussed. Software may also initiate retries for transactions that fail.

The Next Chapter

The next chapter overviews the configuration process comprising the initialization, tree ID, and self-ID phases. Once self-ID completes, additional configuration may optionally take place in the form of bus management activities that are also reviewed in this chapter.

Overview

Asynchronous transaction retry is supported by 1394 and may occur under three circumstances:

- Node is Busy
- Failed Packet Transfer
- Node is Locked

The specification defines a retry protocol to be used when the recipient of a packet is temporarily busy (e.g. due to a buffer full condition or a locked transaction is being performed). This form of retry is handled by hardware. When packet transmission fails due to an error condition, the requesting node may re-initiate the transaction under software control.

Busy Retry

Serial bus nodes employ separate request and response queues. When a node has a queue full condition (busy), the link layer must return an acknowledge packet that specifies the status of the packet just transferred. The acknowledge codes returned indicate if the node was busy, and if so which type of retry that the target node supports. Table 12-1 lists the retry codes that can be returned in the acknowledge packet. Note that retries may be performed for both request and response packet transfers.

Table 12-1: Retry Codes Returned by Busy Node

Code	Name	Description
4	ack_busy_x	The packet was not accepted by the target node, but may be accepted when retried.
5	ack_busy_A	The packet was not accepted by the target node because the node was busy. The node will accept the data when not busy during the next retry phase A.
6	ack_busy_B	The packet was not accepted by the target node because the node was busy. The target node will accept the packet when not busy during the next occurrence of a retry B.

The First Packet Transmission Attempt

When the application wishes to initiate an asynchronous request or a response, it uses the "transaction data request" service or the "transaction data response" service, respectively. The transaction layer generates a "link data request" in response and specifies a retry code of retry_1 for the first attempt of sending a subaction. When the target node receives the packet, it may be able to accept the packet or it may initiate a retry in the event of a full queue. The retry behavior is described in the following sections.

Single Phase Retry

A node that receives a packet for the first time will detect a retry code of retry_1. If the node is busy, it returns an acknowledge code of ack_busy_x indicating that it supports single phase retries. The transmitting node will send the packet again but this time it will return the retry_x code that it received in the acknowledgment packet. Each time the transaction is retried a retry code of retry_x is used. The transaction is retried until it is successful or until the retry limit is exceeded. The retry limit is specified in the BUSY_TIMEOUT register (offset 210h in CSR space) illustrated in Figure 12-1. Note that the maximum number of single phase retries is limited to sixteen by the 4-bit retry_limit field.

Single phase retry provides no scheduling mechanism to handle older transactions that may have been retried many times prior to handling newer ones.

Figure 12-1: BUSY_TIMEOUT Register Showing Single Phase Retry Count

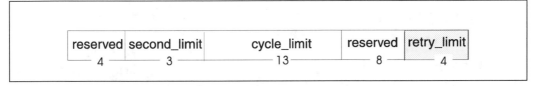

Sending-Node Retry Behavior (Outbound Retry)

The state machine diagram in Figure 12-2 illustrates the actions taken by the transaction layer of a node that is sending packets to a sometimes-busy node. Two states are defined in the state diagram Outbound Single Retry zero (OSR0): "Ready to Send" and Outbound Single Retry one (OSR1): "Pending Retry." The following list describes each of the state transitions.

- OSR0 — The initial entry into the Ready to Send state occurs when the link issues an initialization or reset control request to the transaction layer.
- OSR0 to OSR0 — This transition occurs when the subaction that has been just sent receives a normal acknowledgment (i.e. an acknowledgment other than any type of ack_busy).
- OSR0 to OSR1 — The subaction just sent receives an ack_busy acknowledgment of any type.
- OSR1 to OSR1 — The subaction that was just retried receives one of the three forms of ack_busy. The retry count has not been exceeded. And the transaction layer has not chosen to requeue the pending retry.

- OSR1 to OSR0 — This transition may be taken as a result of three separate conditions:
  1. The transaction layer receives an acknowledge code other than ack_busy. And the packet has been sent successfully.
  2. The retry count has been exceeded and the transaction layer terminates further retries of this packet. The failed transaction is reported to the application.
  3. The transaction layer receives one of the forms of ack_busy in response to the packet just retried. The retry count has not yet expired. And the transaction layer chooses to requeue to pending retry.

Figure 12-2: Outbound Retry State Machine — Single Phase

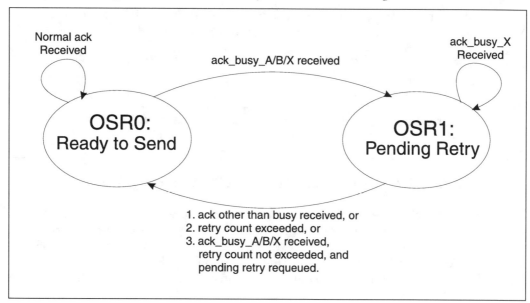

Receiving-Node Retry Behavior (Inbound Retry)

The state machine diagram in Figure 12-3 illustrates the actions taken by the transaction layer of a sometimes-busy node when it receives packets from other nodes. Two states are defined by the state diagram: Inbound Single Phase Retry zero (ISR0): Accept All and Inbound Single Phase Retry (ISR1): Busy All. The state transitions are described below.

- ISR0: This state is entered when the link layer sends an initialization or reset control request to the transaction layer. In this state the node is ready to accept primary packets from other nodes.

- ISR0 to ISR0 — This transition occurs when the node receives a primary packet and the transaction layer resources are available to accept this packet. The transaction layer returns a data response to the link and specifies the appropriate acknowledge code (not busy).
- ISR0 to ISR1 — The transaction layer resources are no longer available (i.e. the transaction layer is now busy).
- ISR1 to ISR1 — The transaction layer receives a primary packet and the resources are not available; thus, a link data response is issued to return an acknowledge packet set to ack_busy_X.
- ISR1 to ISR0 — The transaction resources have become available (i.e. the transaction layer is no longer busy).

Figure 12-3: Inbound Retry State Machine — Single Phase

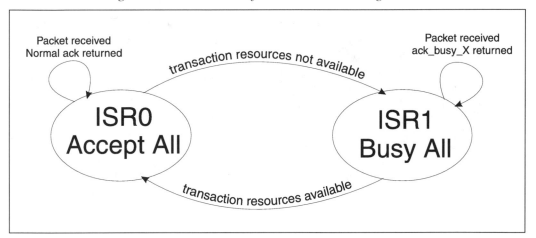

Dual Phase Retry

Just as with single phase retry, the initial access sends a retry code of retry_1. However, nodes that support dual phase retries return a retry acknowledge code of either ack_busy_A or ack_busy_B. When the initiator of the packet attempts packet transmission again, it specifies the same retry code as it received in the acknowledge packet.

To explain the actions of the target node, assume that it just received a packet that must be retried. The busy node returns an ack_busy_A code and waits for the retry to occur. However, if other packets target this same node with retry codes of retry_1, the target returns ack_busy_B retry codes. Since the A packet was sent first, the target node will service it first. When A completes success-fully and no other transactions with retry_busy_A are attempted after four fair-ness intervals, the target then begins to service the B group. While this group is being serviced, all new transactions (retry_1 code) will receive a retry_busy_A acknowledge code. After four consecutive fairness intervals during which no more retry_busy_B transactions occur, the target once again services transac-tions with retry_busy_A codes.

When all A packets have successfully completed, it starts accepting the B retries and issues ack_busy_A to other packet requests. When the B retries have all completed, it then services the As again. It ping pongs between A and B packet retries, thus serving earlier requests before later requests.

The retry limit for dual phase retries is based on the number of 125 microsecond intervals that pass before the retry is failed. Note that time counts from first transmission of the packet. Figure 12-4 below highlights the portion of the BUSY_TIMEOUT register used for dual phase retries. The cycle_limit (125µs granularity) and seconds_limit values are loaded with a count that specifies the maximum amount of time given for this node to complete a retried transaction when dual phase retry is used.

Figure 12-4: BUSY_TIMEOUT Register Showing Dual Phase Time-out Value

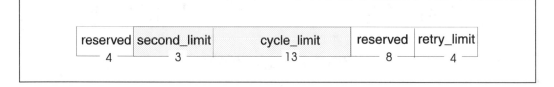

Sending-Node Retry Behavior (Outbound Retry)

The state machine diagram in Figure 12-5 on page 255 illustrates the transaction layer actions taken by a node that supports dual phase retries when it sends packets to a sometimes-busy node that also supports dual phase retries. The state transitions are described in the following list.

- ODR0: Ready to Send — The initial entry into the Ready to Send state occurs when the link issues an initialization or reset control request to the transaction layer.
- ODR0 to ODR0 — An acknowledge packet is received with a code other than ack_busy. The packet has been accepted by the target node and there is no need to perform a retry.
- ODR0 to ODR1 — An acknowledge packet is received with a code of

ack_busy_A indicating that the target node's transaction layer resources are not available and that it supports dual phase retries. This node transitions from the Ready to Send state to the Pending Retry Phase A state. In this state, retries will be issued with a retry code of retry_A.

- ODR1 to ODR1 — An acknowledge packet is received with a code of ack_busy_A, confirming that the target node is still busy; therefore, this retry is still pending.
- ODR1 to ODR0 — This transition is taken as a result of two possible conditions:
  1. An acknowledge packet is received with a normal code (something other than retry), confirming that this subaction is no longer pending retry.
  2. The retry time has been exceeded and the transaction layer discontinues retries for this subaction. The transaction layer notifies the application of the failed subaction.
- ODR1 to ODR2 — This transition is not expected to occur and represents an error condition. The target node has changed its mind regarding the acknowledge code for this subaction (from ack_busy_A to ack_busy_B). In this event, the specification defines the state transition from Pending Retry Phase A to Phase B.
- ODR0 to ODR2 — An acknowledge packet is received with a code of ack_busy_B, indicating that the target node's transaction layer resources are not available and it supports dual phase retries. This node transitions from the Ready to Send state to the Pending Retry Phase B state. In this state, retries will be issued with a retry code of retry_B.
- ODR2 to ODR2 — An acknowledge packet is received with a code of ack_busy_B, confirming that the target node is still busy and the retry time has not yet been exceeded; therefore, this retry is still pending.
- ODR2 to ODR0 — This transition is taken as a result of two possible conditions:
  1. An acknowledge packet is received with a normal code (something other than retry), confirming that this subaction is no longer pending retry.
  2. The retry time has been exceeded and the transaction layer discontinues retries for this subaction. The transaction layer notifies the application of the failed subaction.
- ODR2 to ODR1 — This transition is not expected to occur and represents an error condition. The target node has changed its mind regarding the acknowledge code for this subaction (from ack_busy_B to ack_busy_A). In this event, the specification defines the state transition from Pending Retry Phase B to Phase A.
- ODR0 to ODR3 — An acknowledge packet is received with a code of

ack_busy_X, indicating that the target node's transaction layer resources are not available and it supports only single phase retries. This node transitions from the Ready to Send state to the Pending Single Phase Retry state. In this state, retries will be issued with a retry code of retry_X.

- ODR3 to ODR3 — An acknowledge packet is received with a code of ack_busy_X, confirming that the target node is still busy and the retry time has not yet been exceeded; therefore, this retry is still pending.
- ODR3 to ODR0 — This transition is taken as a result of two possible conditions:

   1. The retry time has been exceeded and the transaction layer discontinues retries for this subaction. The transaction layer notifies the application of the failed subaction.
   2. An acknowledge packet is received with a normal code (something other than busy_retry_X), confirming that this subaction is no longer pending retry.

Note that the specification does not define the actions that should be taken by a sending node in the event that an acknowledge code returned by the busy node changes the busy code from dual to single phase retries or vice versa. Clearly, this behavior is not expected and would be an error condition.

Figure 12-5: Outbound Retry State Machine — Dual Phase

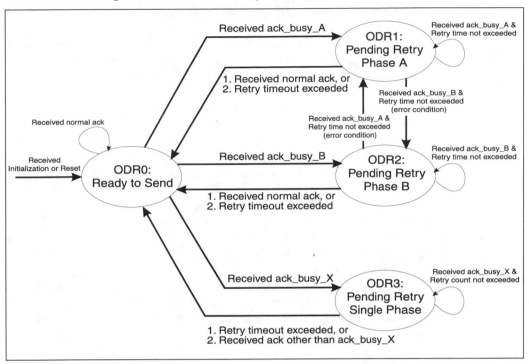

Receiving Node Retry Behavior (Inbound Retry)

The state machine diagram in Figure 12-6 illustrates the actions taken by a sometimes-busy node that supports dual phase retries as it receives packets from other nodes. The state diagram defines the transaction layer role in dual phase retries.

- IDR0 (Accept All Primary Packets Except retry_B) — This is the initial state that is entered upon a reset or initialization control request from the link layer.
- IDRO to IDR0 (a) — No state change occurs when a primary packet is received with a retry_X code and the transaction layer resources are busy. In this event the transactions layer issues a link data response with acknowledge set to retry_X.
- IDR0 to IDR0 (b) — No state change occurs when the resources are available and a packet is received with retry_1 (the first attempt), retry_X, or retry_A.

The transaction is serviced normally and the transaction layer returns the appropriate acknowledgment.

- IDR0 to IDR1 (Accept Retry_A Only) — The transition from the Accept All Primary Packets Except retry_B state to the Accept Retry_A Only state is made in two situations:
    1. The transaction layer has received a primary packet with a retry code of retry_1 or retry_A, and the transaction layer resources are busy. An acknowledge packet is returned with a code of ack_busy_A.
    2. A packet is received with a retry code of retry_B. This retry code is not expected in this state, since B phase transactions have not yet been issued (i.e. ack_busy_B has not been returned). If ack_busy_B has been issued previously, it should already have completed during the previous phase B retry time, or timed out.

- IDR1 to IDR1(a) — The transaction layer received a packet with retry_A and transaction layer resources are available. The packet is accepted normally and the appropriate acknowledge packet is returned.

- IDR1 to IDR1(b) — If a packet is received with retry_A but the transaction layer resources are busy, then the packet is rejected and a retry code of ack_busy_A is returned. This subaction will be retried until it completes or until the retry time expires.

- IDR1 to IDR1(c) — The transaction layer receives a packet with a retry code of retry_1 or retry_B. Whether resources are available or not, the packet is rejected and a busy code of ack_busy_B is returned in the acknowledge packet.

- IDR1 to IDR1(d) — If a packet is received with a retry_X code, the packet is rejected (because only retry_A packets are serviced in this state), and an acknowledge packet with a busy code of retry_X is returned.

- IDR1 to IDR2 (Accept All Primary Packets Except Retry_A) — Transitions from the Accept Retry_A Only state to the Accept All Primary Packets Except Retry_A state occur when all A phase packets have been serviced. In the previous state all new packets have been receiving an acknowledge code of busy_B and only retry_A packets have been serviced. If after four consecutive fairness intervals have occurred (four ARB_RESET_GAP indications) no retry_A packet has been received, a transition to IDR2 occurs and the transaction layer begins servicing retry_B and retry_X packets.

Note that the transaction layer may optionally keep track of the number of retry_1 packets that received ack_busy_A, and when that number of packets with retry_A has been serviced, the transition from IDR1 to IDR2 could take place without waiting for the four fairness interval time-out. Note also that the transaction layer must still be able to recognize the four fairness interval time-out conditions in the event that a given retry_A packet exceeds its retry time-out, which will cause the subaction to be cancelled. In this case, the number of retry_A packets serviced will never equal the number of retry_1 packets that received the busy_A acknowledgments.

- IDR2 to IDR2 (a) — No state change occurs when a primary packet is received with a retry_X code and the transaction layer resources are busy. In this event, the transactions layer issues a link data response with acknowledge set to retry_X.

- IDR2 to IDR2 (b) — No state change occurs when the resources are available and a packet is received with retry_1 (the first attempt), retry_X or retry_B. The transaction is serviced normally and the transaction layer returns the appropriate acknowledgment.

- IDR2 to IDR3 (Accept Retry_B Only) — The transition from the Accept All Primary Packets Except retry_A state to the Accept Retry_B Only state is made in two situations:

  1. The transaction layer has received a primary packet with a retry code of retry_1 or retry_B, and the transaction layer resources are busy. An acknowledge packet is returned with a code of ack_busy_B.

  2. A packet is received with a retry code of retry_A. This retry code is not expected in this state, since B phase transactions have not yet been issued (i.e. ack_busy_A has not been returned to any sender). If ack_busy_B has been issued previously, it should have already completed or timed out during the phase A retry time (IDR1).

- IDR3 to IDR3(a) — The transaction layer received a packet with retry_B and transaction layer resources are available. The packet is accepted normally and the appropriate acknowledge packet is returned.

- IDR3 to IDR3(b) — If a packet is received with retry_B but the transaction layer resources are busy, then the packet is rejected and a retry code of ack_busy_B is returned. This subaction will be retried until it completes or until the retry time expires.

- IDR3 to IDR3(c) — The transaction layer receives a packet with a retry code of retry_1 or retry_A. Whether resources are available or not, the packet is rejected and a busy code of ack_busy_A is returned in the acknowledge packet.

- IDR3 to IDR3(d) — If a packet is received with a retry_X code, the packet is rejected (because only retry_A packets are serviced in this state), and an acknowledge packet with a busy code of retry_X is returned.

- IDR3 to IDR0 — Transitions from the Accept Retry_B Only state to the Accept All Primary Packets Except Retry_B state occur when all B phase packets have been serviced. In the previous state, all new packets have been receiving an acknowledge code of busy_A and only retry_B packets have been serviced. If after four consecutive fairness intervals have occurred (four ARB_RESET_GAP indications) no retry_B packet has been received, the transaction layer transitions to the IDR0 state and begins servicing retry_A and retry_X packets.

Note that the transaction layer may optionally keep track of the number of retry_1 packets that received ack_busy_B, and when that number of packets with retry_B have been serviced the transition from IDR1 to IDR2 can take place without waiting for the four fairness interval time-out. Note also that the transaction layer must still be able to recognize the four fairness interval time-out condition. This is required in the event that a given retry_B packet exceeds its retry time-out causing the subaction to be cancelled. In this case, the number of retry_B packets serviced will never equal the number of retry_1 packets that received the busy_B acknowledgments.

Figure 12-6: Inbound Retry State Machine — Dual Phase

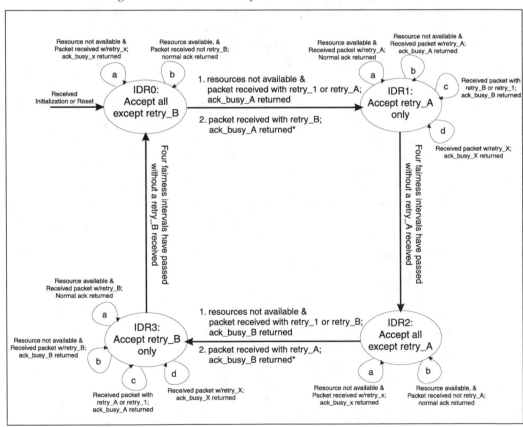

Transactions Errors

Transaction errors can result from a variety of conditions:

- Packet Transmission Errors (CRC or other packet errors)
- Acknowledge Packet Time-out (Ack not received in time)
- Response Transmission Error (CRC or other packet error)
- Response Packet Time-out (Response not received in time)
- Acknowledge Packet Corrupted

The layer responsible for handling a given error depends on the nature of the error. The following sections detail the types of errors that might occur and discuss which layer is responsible for handling the error condition.

Packet Transmission Errors

When a packet is transferred across the serial bus it may get corrupted in flight. This type of error is detectable via CRC checks that are performed when a packet is received. Depending on circumstances, a failed transaction may be initiated again by the application. Consider the following split transaction (see Figure 12-7) and possible errors that could occur. During this transaction, four packets are delivered and the possibility exists that an error could occur during transmission in any of the four, as discussed in the following enumerated list.

Figure 12-7: Split Transaction and Related Packets

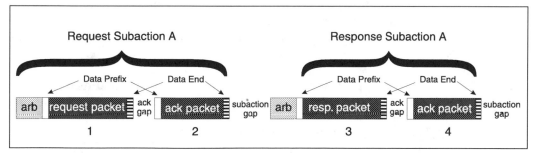

1. If a CRC error is detected by the responder when the request packet is transmitted, the acknowledge packet would return a code indicating that a CRC error was detected when the packet header or data block CRC was checked (either an ack_type_error or ack_data_error (write requests only) could be returned). Since the responding node recognizes that the request packet is

not valid, it ignores the request (i.e. the bad request is not forwarded by the transaction layer to the application). The requester, having been notified of the error, reports the error to the application, which may choose to re-issue the request. The specific actions taken by the request and response nodes are summarized below.

Responding node actions (incoming request packet) — The link layer of the responding node detects the CRC error and sends a "link data indication" to the transaction layer, indicating failed packet status. The transaction layer discards the packet, recognizing that it contains an erroneous request and returns a "link data response" to the link layer controller that contains an acknowledge code indicating the packet error. The link then sends an acknowledge packet to the requesting node.

Requesting node actions (outgoing request packet) — The link layer receives the acknowledge code and generates a "link data confirmation" to confirm to the transaction layer that the acknowledge packet has been received and to report the packet error. Having received an error condition, the transaction layer reports the packet transmission error to the application via the "transaction data confirmation," which passes the error parameter to the application. The actions taken to correct the error are application dependent.

2. Normally, an acknowledge packet will be received by the requesting node as a result of a non-broadcast asynchronous transaction request. In the absence of an acknowledgment, a time-out will occur causing the link layer to send a "link data confirmation" to the transaction layer with an acknowledge_missing confirmation code. The transaction layer passes this confirmation on to the application via a transaction data confirmation. Note that the state of the responding node is unknown. The corrective actions again are application dependent.

3. A CRC or other packet error may also occur when the responding node sends the response packet to the requesting node. In this instance, the requesting node recognizes that the response was corrupted in flight and therefore can't rely on its contents. Consequently, the requesting node ignores the response packet and returns an acknowledgment packet with the appropriate error code (ack_type_err or ack_data_err). The responding node recognizes the error condition and reports the error back to the application. The specification indicates that the error handling procedure is the province of the application. Specific actions taken by the responding and requesting nodes in the event of a response packet error are described in the following paragraphs.

Requesting node actions (incoming response packet) — When the response packet error is detected by the requesting node's link layer it sends a "link data indication" to the transaction layer, indicating the failed packet status. The transaction layer discards the packet, recognizing that it contains an erroneous response. The transaction layer also returns a "link data response" to the link layer controller, which contains an acknowledge code indicating the packet error. The link then sends an acknowledge packet to the requesting node via the PHY. Error handling in this instance is not reported to the application because the packet contents were corrupted in flight. Thus, the response is still pending for this transaction. The requesting node may receive the packet later, as a retry by the responding node, or may incur a time-out, which will be reported to the application.

Responding node actions (outgoing response packet) — The link layer receives the acknowledge code and generates a "link data confirmation" to notify the transaction layer that the acknowledge packet has been received and to report the packet error. Having received an error condition, the transaction layer reports the packet transmission error to the application via the "transaction data confirmation," which passes the error parameter to the application. The application can re-initiate the response in an attempt to complete the transaction successfully.

4. If the response packet is not returned in time, the requesting node will detect the response time-out and report the error to its application. In this case, the state of the responding node is unknown. The actions taken by the application may vary widely depending on the conditions. For example, the request may have been a read from a register location that is not prefetchable (i.e. once read the contents of the register may change and other side effects may occur within the node). If the transaction is re-initiated by the application, the results will likely be unpredictable. Once again the error handling is left to the application programmer who knows how best to handle a given error condition.

5. In the event that an acknowledge packet is corrupted, it is unknown whether or not the previous packet was received. For example, if the acknowledgment for a request packet was corrupted during flight, then the requesting node is uncertain whether or not the request was received correctly. The responding node may be servicing the request normally or it may not have received the request correctly. This type of error is handled in an application-specific manner. The application may wait for a normal response to be returned. If the response occurs without error, then the trans-

action completes normally. However, a response time-out may occur, indicating that the request may not have been received. In this event, the application may choose to re-initiate the request.

Packet Error Handling Summary

Error handling is performed by either the transaction software layer or the application as follows:

Incoming packet error handling — A node that receives a corrupted packet will detect the error within the link layer and notify the transaction layer software of the bad packet. Knowing that the packet is corrupted, the transaction layer will not pass the bad information on to the application, but will return an acknowledge packet to notify the sending node that the transmission failed.

Outgoing packet error handling — A node that sends a packet is normally apprised of the failed transaction when it receives an error code in the acknowledge packet. Since the packet was not received correctly, the application is responsible for retrying the transaction.

Part Three

Serial Bus Configuration

13 *Configuration Process*

The Previous Chapter

The previous chapter discussed transaction retries that occur when the recipient of a packet is busy (e.g. has a buffer full condition). Two retry mechanisms are defined by the 1394 specification: single and dual phase. Each type of mechanism is discussed.

This Chapter

This chapter overviews the configuration process comprising the initialization, tree ID, and self-ID phases. Once self-ID completes additional configuration may optionally take place in the form of bus management activities that are also reviewed in this chapter.

The Next Chapter

The next chapter details the bus reset phase of the cable configuration process.

Overview

1394 device configuration occurs locally on the serial bus without the intervention of a host processor. Each time a new device, or node, is attached or removed from the serial bus, the entire bus is reset and reconfigured. This chapter overviews the cable configuration process and subsequent chapters detail each step in the procedure.

Three primary procedures must be performed during cable configuration:

- Bus initialization
- Tree identification
- Self identification

Since cable configuration does not require interaction with the host processor, no single node can be identified as a root node based simply on the serial bus physical topology. Rather, a single node on the serial bus must be identified, via the Tree ID process, as the root node. The root node performs certain bus management functions for all devices residing on the bus. For example, the root node must take responsibility for establishing the intervals at which isochronous transactions are to be performed across the bus.

Since it is unknown at configuration time whether a given node supports 100, 200, or 400Mb/s transfers, all configuration transfers take place at the base rate of 100Mb/s.

During cable configuration the bus is reset and all 1394 bus traffic stops while the new topology is determined (during tree-ID) and while all nodes assign themselves a node ID (during Self-ID). All asynchronous transactions that are pending completion when cable configuration begins must be discarded and requeued by the local application once configuration completes. This is necessary because the node ID values used to target a given node may change due to a topology change. Consequently, all asynchronous transactions pending prior to reset may target the wrong node following a reset. Since isochronous transfers identify target(s) based on channel numbers (which are not affected by cable configuration), they can resume where they left off after configuration completes.

The speed at which the cable configuration process completes is obviously important since all pending transactions stopped during configuration. Figure 13-1 illustrates reset, tree-ID, and self-ID timing for the 1394-1995 environment. The following chapters detail each phase of the cable configuration process.

Figure 13-1: Overall Cable Configuration Time

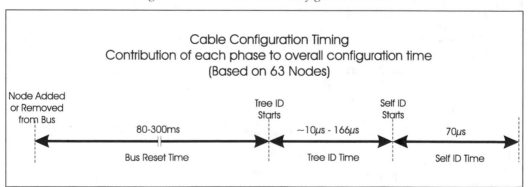

Bus Initialization (Bus Reset)

Reset occurs when power is applied to (e.g. initial power up) or removed from a node or when a node is attached to or removed from the 1394 bus. This forces all nodes to return to their initialized states. If the bus has been configured previously, then the topology will have been established. However, reset also clears all topology information from the nodes. Figure 13-2 illustrates a family of 1394 nodes with topology established and a subsequent view of the topology immediately following reset. Note that after reset all topology information is cleared, leaving each node at the same hierarchy in the topology. Reset initializes the bus and prepares each node to begin the tree identification process.

Figure 13-2 also illustrates that some nodes connect to only one other node, while others connect to one or more nodes. Nodes having a single port are termed leaf nodes (nodes A and E), and nodes with two or more ports are termed branches (nodes B, C, and D). The node labels A-E are provided for reference purposes only. Each node assigns a number to each of its ports, thereby providing a unique label for port identification. Port numbers are used during the self_ID process to determine the order (lowest to highest number) that ports are identified and also during normal arbitration as a tie breaker.

Reset signaling is sensed by the PHY layer of each node via the arbitration signal lines. Each node receiving RESET propagates reset signaling to the other nodes that it attaches to (if any), thereby ensuring that all nodes are reset. After each node is reset it enters the idle state and waits for a sufficient period of time to ensure all nodes have received a RESET and have entered their idle states. From the idle state all nodes begin the tree identification process.

Figure 13-2: Example of Bus Topology after Bus Reset

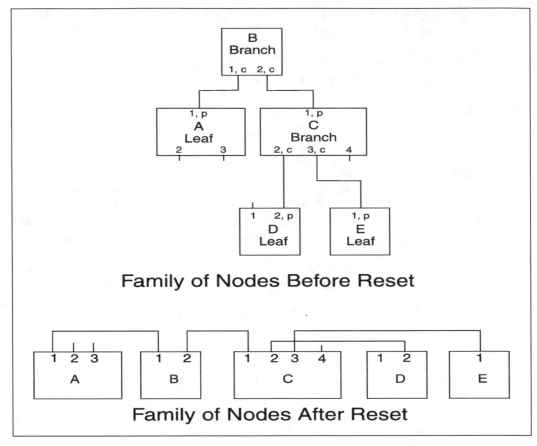

Tree Identification (The Family Tree)

The tree identification process defines the topology of the bus based on the new family of devices that now reside there. After tree identification, one node will have gained status as the root node. Prior to tree identification, each node knows whether it connects to a single 1394 node (when it is a single leaf on the bus) or more than one node (when it is a branch on the bus). Any node, a leaf or a branch, may become the root node. Figure 13-3 illustrates a series of nodes (branches and leaves) connected to the bus.

Figure 13-3: Example of Bus after New Device Is Attached and Bus Is Reset

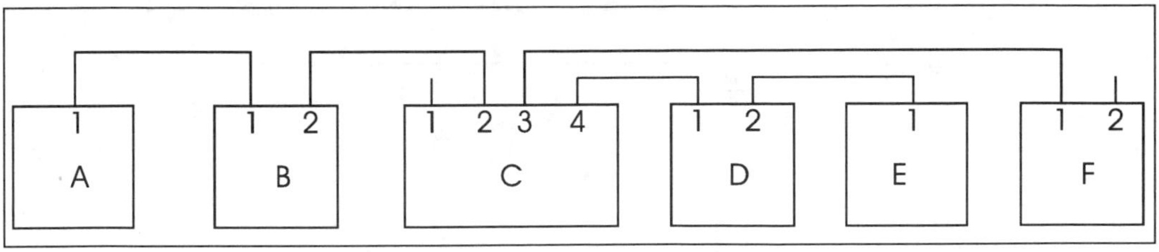

The tree identification process results in each port being identified as either a parent or a child. A node having a parent port designation means that the node at the other end of the cable is closer to the root, and that node will have identified its port as a child. A port identified as a child node points to a child node that is further away from the root. Any node having all of its ports identified as child ports becomes the root hub. A node can become the root node regardless of where it connects into the network of nodes.

Figure 13-4 illustrates the same family of nodes pictured in Figure 13-3, but after tree identification has completed. In this example, it is assumed that node D has been identified as the root node, thus both of its ports are identified as child ports. All other nodes have a least one of their ports identified as a parent port, meaning that there is another node higher in the topology hierarchy. Once tree identification has completed, the root node initiates the self-identification process.

Chapter 15 details the tree identification process and defines how the root node is selected.

Figure 13-4: Example Bus Following Tree Identification

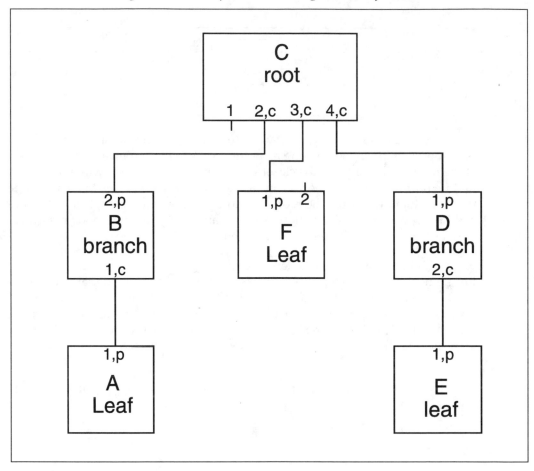

Self Identification

Once the Tree ID process has concluded, the self-ID process begins. During self-ID all nodes select a unique physical ID and return self-ID packets that identify themselves and specify parameters needed for the bus management function. Self-ID information is needed by serial bus nodes that perform certain bus management functions. The next section overviews the bus management process.

The root hub initiates the self-ID process by sending a self-ID grant (same as normal arbitration grant signaling) to all nodes beginning with its lowest numbered child (based on the port numbers defined by the root nodes). For example, node C in Figure 13-5 on page 271 would have observed the first self-ID grant. Node C and other branch nodes that receive a self-ID grant forward it to the child node attached to their lowest numbered port. This process continues until self-ID grant is received by a leaf node, which then returns a self-ID packet.

The first node to return a self-ID packet assigns itself as physical node 0. All other nodes monitor self-ID packet transmission and keep track of the self-ID packet count. When other nodes send their self-ID packets they assign themselves a physical node number based on the self-ID count. In this way each node identifies itself and a map of the bus topology can be built by the bus management node. Figure 13-5 illustrates the node IDs that would be assigned in our example. Chapter 16 details the self-identification procedure.

Figure 13-5: Example Bus Following Self-ID Process

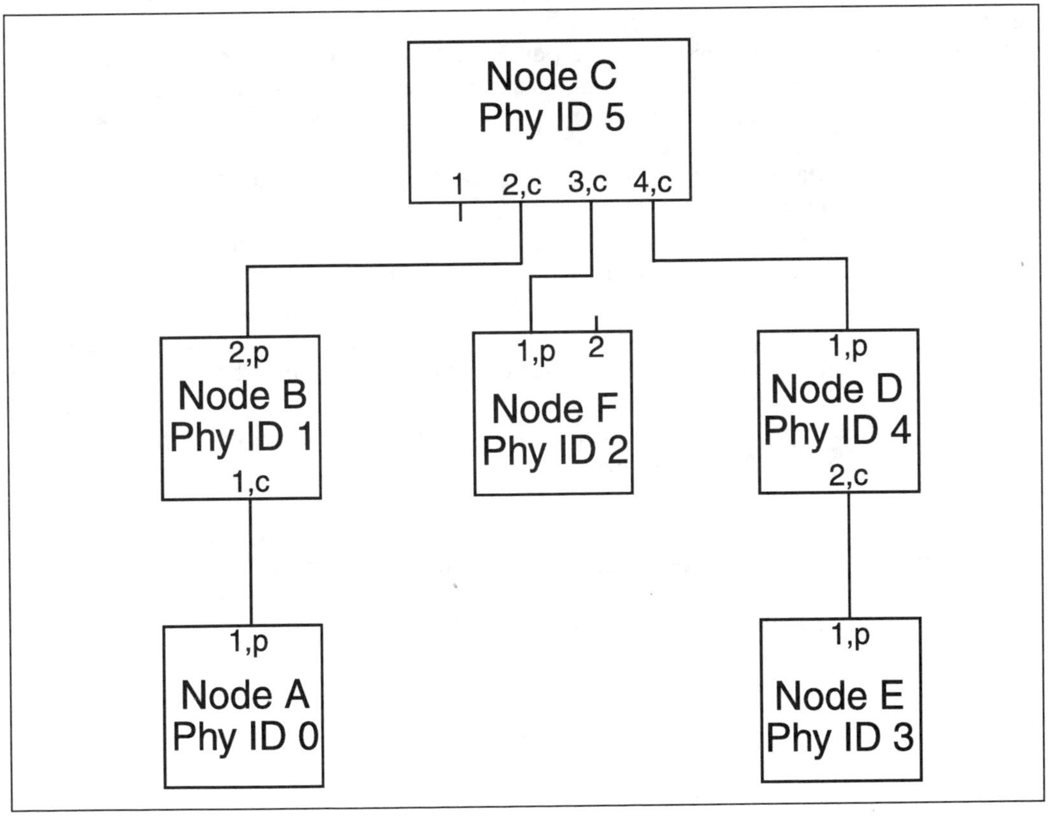

Bus Management

Once the self-ID process completes, a variety of actions must be taken to enable nodes on the bus to perform bus management activities. Many of these activities occur under software control via a set of services defined specifically for serial bus management. Bus management involves a wide range of activities used to support the family of nodes on the bus. Some bus management functions require knowledge of the bus topology and also the capabilities of individual family members and this is obtained from the self-ID packets broadcast by each node. The general categories of bus management include:

- Initiating the start of isochronous transactions.
- Tracking and allocating serial bus resources such as isochronous channel numbers and bus bandwidth.
- Tuning gap timing requirements to optimize overall bus bandwidth.
- Performing cable-power management activities.
- Supplying topology and speed information for other nodes to utilize.

Bus management activities are performed by one or more nodes that perform specific roles in the bus management process. Three separate roles are defined by the 1394 specification:

- Cycle Master—initiates the start of isochronous transactions on regular 125µs intervals
- Isochronous Resource Manager—tracks the number of isochronous channels available and the amount of isochronous bus bandwidth available and allocates these resources when requested by serial bus nodes.
- Bus Manager—publishes maps that specify the topology of the serial bus and that indicate the maximum packet speed support by each cable segment in the system. Also performs a variety of bus management functions associated with bus power, bandwidth reservation for asynchronous transactions, and bus optimization.

Given nodes that reside on the bus may be designed to fulfill the roles of cycle master, isochronous resource manager, and bus manager. Respective chapters follow that define each role and describe the process used to select the node or nodes that will assume the role of these bus management entities.

14 *Bus Reset (Initialization)*

The Previous Chapter

The previous chapter provided an overview of the configuration process. The process comprises Initialization, Tree ID, Self-ID phases, and bus management activities.

This Chapter

This chapter details the bus reset phase of the cable configuration process. Initialization begins with the assertion of a bus reset by a given node on the bus. This chapter discusses the reset enhancements introduced by the 1394a supplement; debouncing the bias change detection, arbitration (short) bus reset, and new timing parameters.

The Next Chapter

Following bus initialization, the tree ID process begins to determine which node will become the root. The next chapter details the protocol used in determining the topology of the nodes.

Overview

Bus reset forces all nodes into their initialization state, thereby initiating the configuration process. Bus reset is initiated under software control or as a result of hardware events as discussed below. Note that assertion of reset signaling by a node does not terminate a transaction currently being performed. When the transaction ends, all other nodes will have their drivers disabled, thus the reset signaling will be detected by all nodes.

When each node receives reset it clears all information related to the bus topology. However, the PHY of each port latches and saves connection status associated with each of its ports (i.e. whether a device is currently attached to each port or not). If a device is removed or attached to a port during reset, the change will be detected at the end of the initialization phase, thereby causing the node to signal reset again, forcing all nodes back into reset.

Sources of Bus Reset

Bus reset is initiated under the following circumstances:

- Bus reset is signaled when power status changes at the PHY.
- Bus reset signaled by an attached node.
- Node attachment or removal.
- PHY detects MAX_ARB_STATE time-out. That is, a PHY stays in any state (except Idle, Tree ID Start, or other state that has an explicit time-out defined) for longer than the MAX_ARB_STATE_TIME.
- PHY receives a bus reset request initiated by software.

The following sections describe each type of reset.

Power Status Change

When a locally powered PHY receives a power reset or detects a change in its power state, it must signal a bus reset. No bus reset is required if only the link layer power state changes.

Bus Reset Signaled by Attached Node

When a port detects reset signaled by an attached node it must repeat reset signaling to its other connected ports. This node may be in the process of repeating a packet when the reset is detected at one of its ports. Even if a packet is currently being repeated to that port, the arbitration comparators will detect reset signaling due to 1's dominance decoding of the arbitration comparator outputs.

Node Attachment or Removal

If a node's PHY recognizes that another node has been attached to or removed from one of its ports, it must signal reset to all of its active ports. The PHY must also signal the bus reset event to the link. Node attachment or detachment is detected by a port receiver when it detects a change in the bias voltage. A variety of conditions exist that determines the exact behavior of a node, after it has detected a bias change. These conditions and behaviors are discussed in "Effects of Bus Reset" on page 277.

MAX_ARB_STATE_TIME Expires

The MAX_ARB_STATE_TIME parameter applies to all states within the PHY with the exception of those listed below. When the PHY remains in a given state long enough for the MAX_ARB_STATE_TIME to be detected (200μs min. to 400μs max.), it must signal reset. The PHY states excluded from the MAX_ARB_STATE_TIME limit include:

- Bus Idle
- Tree ID Start
- Any state that has an explicit time-out value defined

Software Initiated Bus Reset

An application can initiate a bus reset by making a control_request to the node controller software, which in turn issues the request to the link and PHY. In response, the PHY sets its IBR (initiate bus reset) bit, causing the reset to be signaled. When reset signaling ends a reset_complete confirmation is returned to the link and forwarded on to the local application via the transaction layer application.

Bus Reset Signaling

When the PHY receives a reset request, it drives 1s on TPA and TPB for each of its ports. All other nodes receiving reset propagate, or repeat, reset signaling to their other ports. This action ensures that all nodes receive RESET. Figure 14-1 on page 276 illustrates reset being signaled and detected by two attached nodes. Note that even though a child node is currently signaling a TX_REQUEST in an attempt to gain bus ownership, the reset (1,1) prevails due to 1's dominate decoding of the received signals.

The duration of reset must be sufficiently long to permit a transaction being performed to complete. The longest reset timing requirement is a minimum reset duration of 167μs.

Figure 14-1: Reset Signaling and Detection

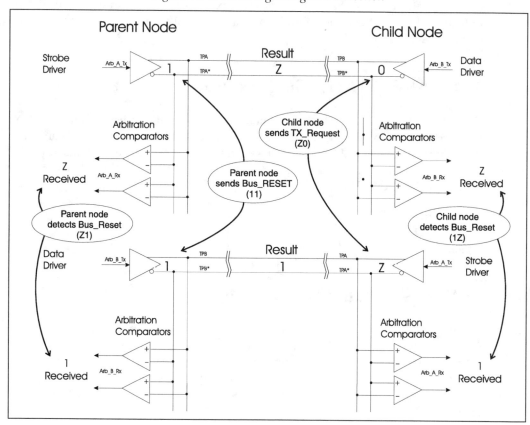

Chapter 14: Bus Reset (Initialization)

Effects of Bus Reset

Bus reset results in a variety of actions being taken within nodes. The primary effects include:

- Topology information is cleared at each port
- Some PHY register values return to defaults
- CSR register values affected

The effects of bus reset also depends on the source of the reset. For example, when power is cycled, a bus reset is performed and all register values within the PHY and link are cleared or returned to their initial values. Bus reset for any other reason has a less drastic effect, resulting in some register fields being preserved. The following discussion describes the effects of a bus reset not resulting from power being cycled.

Topology Information Cleared

Figure 14-2 illustrates how each node would view itself following RESET. Note that all nodes have the same peer relationship to each other. Following the completion of bus reset, all nodes enter their tree ID state and the topology is reestablished.

Figure 14-2: Nodes After Reset Have No Sense of Bus Topology

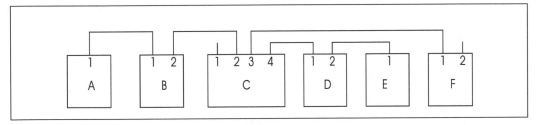

PHY Register Changes

Some fields within the port and PHY registers either lead to the generation of bus reset or are directly affected by a bus reset while others remain unaffected. Following is a description of the fields related to bus reset.

Port Bias and Connected Bits

If a port detects a connection change, that port will set bits indicating that a connection change has occurred. Specifically, if the port is not suspended, the bias bit will be cleared when a node is removed from the port. If a port is attached but suspended, bias is removed and the bias bit is cleared. When a node is disconnected from a suspended port the connected bit is cleared.

Port_Event Bit

When the Int_Enable bit in a port is set any change in the bias or connected bit causes the Port_event bit in the PHY to be set and a bus reset to be generated.

Initiate Bus Reset (IBR) and Initiate Short Bus Reset (ISBR)

When the local node application writes to the IBR bit, the PHY generates a long bus reset (~166µs). The bit is self-clearing once reset signaling has completed.

When the local node application writes to the ISBR bit, the PHY generates a short (or arbitrated) bus reset. The short bus reset is signaled for 1.3µs, but only after the PHY has arbitrated for and won ownership of the bus. This bit is self-clearing once reset signaling has completed.

Physical_ID Field

The Physical ID field within the PHY is cleared when a bus reset is detected. Following Self-ID the register is updated with the physical ID (or node ID) of this node.

Gap_Count

The only source of bus reset that indicates that the bus topology has changed is node attachment or detachment. In the 1394-1995 environment, this event is distinguishable from other forms of bus reset because multiple resets are guaranteed when a node is attached or detached from a port (due to the contacts making and breaking as a connector is plugged or removed). The other sources of bus reset result in a single bus reset event. This distinction is important since the contents of gap_count field should only change if the bus topology changes. Therefore, the PHY's gap count field is "sticky." The field is unaffected by a single bus reset, but a second bus reset forces the field to its default value (3Fh).

CSR Register Changes

Some of the registers within the CSR register space remained unaffected, while other registers return to their initial values. Chapter 21, entitled "CSR Architecture," on page 361 includes definitions of each required CSR register and defines which registers and specific fields are unaffected by bus reset and which return to their initial values.

1394-1995 and Reset Runaway

Reset time is extraordinarily long in the 1394-1995 environment. Reset is the greatest contributor to overall cable configuration (consisting of Reset, Tree-ID, and Self-ID). During cable configuration all bus traffic is suspended, including isochronous transactions. This causes a significant delay in the resumption of isochronous traffic, resulting in loss of isochronous data. It is important to shorten cable configuration as much as possible. The following sections discuss the long reset implemented by 1394-1995 nodes and methods of shortening reset time in the 1394a implementation. Several issues contribute to the long reset:

- Storm of resets occur due to contact scraping when node is attached or detached.
- Recognition of node attachment or detachment is not symmetric.
- Reset signaling must be prolonged in case a long packet is being sent when reset is signaled.

Each problem and the corresponding 1394a solution is discussed in the following sections. Note that the shortcomings of the 1394-1995 reset implementation are resolved by 1394a implementations; however, these solutions may not be effective in a mixed environment (1394-1995 and 1394a nodes combined on the same bus).

Problem One: The Reset Storm

When a node is attached to or removed from the bus, scraping of the contacts causes numerous connect/disconnect events. Specifically, the port status receivers of the adjacent nodes will report status change indications many times as a node is attached or detached. Each status change event (attachment or detachment) initiates another reset indication, thereby creating a "storm" of resets. The term "storm" is used in IEEE 1394a documents to describe this phenomenon.

The storm of resets is problematic because it extends the duration of reset signaling (perhaps on the order of hundreds of milliseconds), causing a significant delay in the resumption of isochronous traffic.

The 1394a Solution: Debounce Port Status Signal

The 1394a supplement addresses the reset storm problem by requiring the PHY to debounce the port status output resulting in a single reset event. The PHY must delay the start of reset signaling until the debounce time-out (connect_timeout) value has expired (330-350ms). Figure 14-3 on page 281 illustrates the reset timing parameters that contrast the 1394-1995 and 1394a implementations.

Note that the reset storm can persist if a 1394-1995 node residing on the bus detects another node has been attached or removed. The older nodes do not debounce the port status signal and will signal reset to other nodes on the bus for an extended period of time.

The problem can be lessened if a 1394a node detects a 1394-1995 node being remotely (i.e. away from the root) connected to the bus. Despite the storm of resets generated by the remote node, the 1394a node can delay propagation of the bus reset until the RESET_DETECT time (80.0ms min. to 85.3ms max.) elapses. Hopefully, the reset storm will have ended once RESET_DETECT has expired. If not, one or more additional resets will be signaled. Note that RESET_DETECT timing only applies to nodes that have detected a connection event and have received reset signaling on the port experiencing the connection event.

Figure 14-3: Timing Relationships Between 1394-1995 and 1394a Reset Detection & Signaling

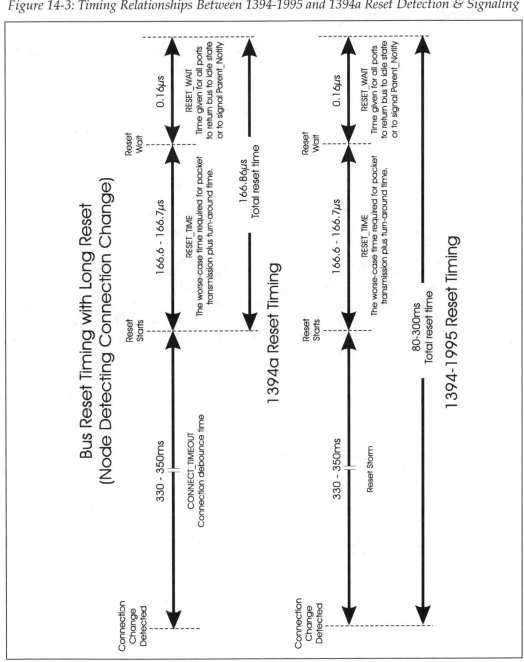

Problem Two: Recognition of Connection Change Not Symmetric

When two nodes are connected it would be remarkable if both nodes detected the connection change at the same time due to the contact scraping. The interval between two nodes detecting the bias change could be tens of milliseconds. When the first node detects the connection change it signals reset. If the other node much later than the first finally detects the connection change, it will also signal reset causing the first to start reset again. During the entire duration that reset is being signaled by both nodes, no other bus activity can be handled, which causes all bus traffic to cease.

The Solution: Slow Node Accepts Fast Node's Reset Signaling

The solution to the asymmetric connection change detection requires a port that is debouncing the connection change to ignore all arbitration signaling on that port except for reset signaling. Whichever node completes the debouncing first signals reset, which is detected by the node that continues the debouncing interval. Upon detecting reset, the slow node repeats reset signaling and discontinues its debounce timing.

Problem Three: Reset Signaled During Packet Transmission

When a node signals reset it may be that a packet transmission from another node has just begun. The node transmitting the packet will be unable to notify the link of the reset until packet transmission ends. Reset signaling will override the clocked data transmission in all other nodes. This is due to the dominance rule for 1's; thereby, allowing all nodes to detect and repeat the bus reset. For example, if a port is repeating a packet and the port at the opposite end of the cable is signaling reset, then reset will override the transmitted packet and the node will repeat reset to all of its other ports. (See Table 6-5 on page 109 for details regarding the dominance rule for 1). The repeating port upon detecting reset signaling also sends status information from the PHY to the link to notify the link of the bus reset. The link then conditions the CSR register in response to the bus reset.

The transmitting node like all other nodes recognizes the reset signaling at the PHY and repeats reset to all other ports. However, since the link is currently sending a packet to the PHY (even though the PHY is not repeating the packet) the PHY is unable to obtain control of the link/PHY interface to notify the link that a bus reset is in progress. Not until the link discontinues packet transmission and relinquishes control of the interface can the PHY report the bus reset.

The result of this problem is that the RESET_TIME parameter must be extended to ensure that reset signaling lasts beyond the longest packet transmission (100µs for a 1394-1995 isochronous data block packet). Solving this problem recovers 100µs of time from the total reset time.

1394a Solution: Arbitrated Bus Reset

Reset definition in the 1394-1995 environment assumes that the state of the bus is unknown when reset occurs and requires that reset be long enough to permit the longest transaction to finish and still complete reset (167µs). If a node that is performing a bus reset arbitrates for control of the bus prior to asserting reset, then reset duration can be shortened significantly (as little as 1.3µs). The new reset timing with arbitrated reset is illustrated in Figure 14-4 on page 284.

When implementing short (or arbitrated) bus reset, several cases must be considered:

- If a parent port detects a disconnect, there is no longer a connection with the root node, therefore arbitration will by definition never be successful. In this instance the node must generate a long reset in lieu of an arbitrated reset.
- If a node attempts an arbitrated reset, but the arbitration fails due to an arbitration state time-out (defined by the MAX_ARB_STATE_TIME parameter), a long bus reset must be initiated.
- If an isolated node with no connected ports detects a connection, it should delay generating a reset for one second. This action is in anticipation that the isolated node is being attached to a node that is connected to a network of operating nodes, and allows time for the connected node to generate a short bus reset. If a short bus reset is not detected within one second then the isolated node must generate a long bus reset.

Figure 14-4: Arbitrated Reset Timing

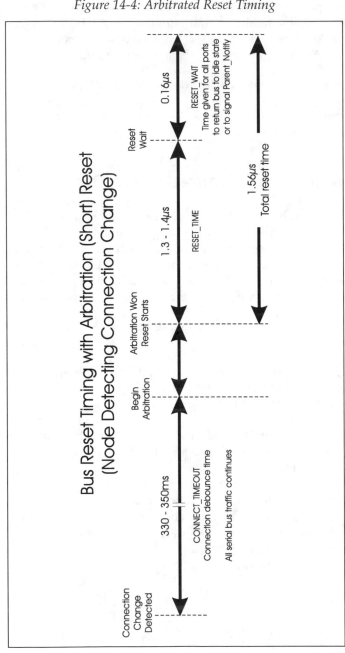

15 *Tree Identification*

The Previous Chapter

The previous chapter detailed the initialization phase of the configuration process. Initialization begins with the assertion of a bus reset by a given node on the bus.

This Chapter

Following bus initialization, the tree ID process begins to determine which node will become the root. This chapter details the protocol used in determining the topology of the serial bus.

The Next Chapter

The next chapter focuses on the self-ID process. During self-ID all nodes are assigned addresses and specify their capabilities by broadcasting self-ID packets.

Overview

Following bus initialization, nodes begin the tree identify phase to identify the root node and the topology of all attached nodes. The tree ID process results in all ports being designated as either child or parent ports. A child port connects to a node further away from the root, while a parent port connects to a node closer to the root.

Tree ID Signaling

Before discussing the tree ID process a review of the tree ID signaling may be helpful. All connected nodes perform Tree ID signaling via the strobe and data drivers and their respective arbitration comparators as illustrated in Figure 15-1. The strobe is delivered via TPA and is received by the attached node on TPB, while the state driven on the data is delivered via TPB and is received on TPA.

All nodes use the arbitration mechanism to communicate with other nodes that are attached directly to their ports. The tree ID process uses two of the arbitration line states defined as:

- Parent_Notify
- Child_Notify

These signal states are used to determine if a given node is closer to or further from the root node. The line states that are driven are listed in Table 15-1.

A Parent_Notify is signalled by driving a "0" onto the TPA, while leaving TPB in the idle or undriven state (Z). Child_Notify is signaled by driving a "1" on TPA and leaving TPB in the "Z" state. As illustrated in Figure 15-1 on page 287, the signals driven onto TPA are received and detected on TPB of the attached node's arbitration comparators, and signals driven on TPB are received and detected on TPA by the arbitration comparators. The following discussion details the Tree ID process.

Table 15-1: Line States that Signal Parent- and Child-Notify

	Parent_Notify	Child_Notify
TPA	0 (Strobe)	1 (Strobe)
TPB	Z (Data)	Z (Data)

The Tree ID Process

The Tree ID process begins with one or more nodes signaling Parent_Notify to their probable parents. Only those nodes that have received a Parent_Notify on all but one of their ports can signal a Parent_Notify. Immediately following reset this is true of only leaf nodes, since they have a single port. Thus, all leaf nodes immediately signal Parent_Notify to the attached nodes. Branch nodes that receive a Parent_Notify on one of their ports mark that port as a "child" port to signify that the attached node is further away from the root node. In response to the Parent_Notify, branch nodes also return a Child_Notify to the attached leaf node. However, a branch node will not signal the Child_Notify until all but one of its ports have received Parent_Notify. A leaf node that receives a Child_Notify marks its port as a parent port which signifies that the attached node is closer to the root node. Once all nodes have identified all other attached nodes as either children or parents, the Tree ID process is complete.

Figure 15-1: Strobe and Data Lines Used During Tree ID

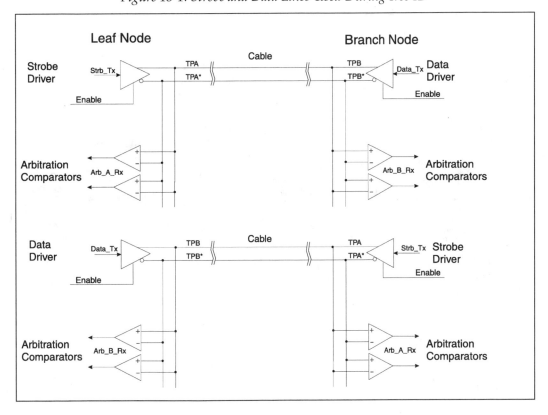

Leaf Nodes Try to Find Their Parents

The following discussion details the handshake performed between a pair of leaf and branch nodes during the Tree_ID process. Note that all leaf and branch nodes that connect to each other perform the same handshake. Immediately following Bus Initialization, all leaf nodes signal Parent_Notify via TPA=0 and

TPB=Z as pictured in Figure 15-2 on page 288. At this time, the branch node is not signaling any line state, thus its data and strobe drivers are in a high imped-ance (Z) state and the line states driven by the leaf node are unaffected by the branch node. Since the twisted pair signal lines are cross-wired between attached nodes, the branch node observes the Parent_Notify at its arbitration comparators as TPA=Z and TPB=0. At the same time, the leaf node's arbitration comparators observe the line states that its own drivers are signaling (TPA=0 and TPB=Z).

Figure 15-2: Leaf Node Signaling Parent_Notify

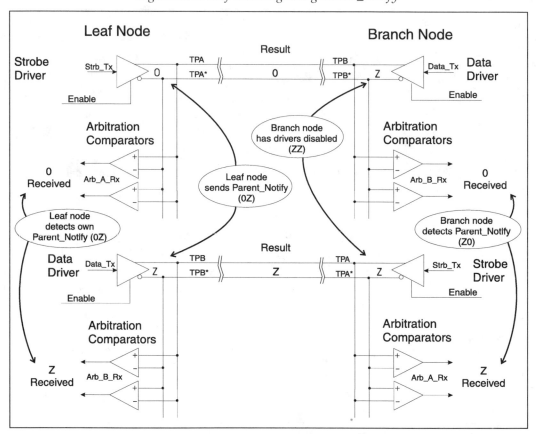

Parents Identify Their Children

The branch node, having received a Parent_Notify on one of its ports, recog-nizes that a leaf is attached to this port and marks the port as a child port. In response, the branch node signals a Child_Notify via TPA=1 and TPB=Z when it recognizes that all of its ports or all but one of its ports have received Parent_Notify. While the Child_Notify is being signaled by the branch node, the leaf continues to signal Parent_Notify. Figure 15-3 on page 289 illustrates the states driven by both nodes and the resulting line states. The resulting line states observed at the leaf's arbitration comparators are TPA=0 and TPB=1. The branch node also detects the Child_Notify as TPA=1 and TPB=0.

Upon detecting the Child_Notify, the leaf node marks its port as a parent port (i.e. it attaches to a node that is closer to the root). Having been identified as a child port, the node withdraws its Parent_Notify, which is viewed by the branch node as confirmation that the Child_Notify was received and accepted by the leaf node (i.e. the branch node observes the line state change from TPA=1 and TPB=0 to TPA=1 and TPB=Z). The leaf node's role in the Tree ID process is now finished and the first phase of the Tree ID process is complete.

Figure 15-3: Branch Node Signaling Child_Notify

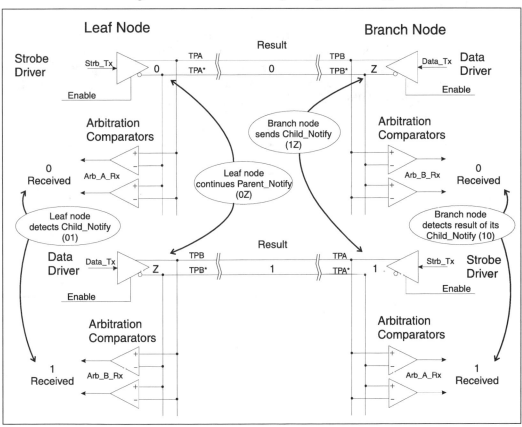

Three Example Scenarios

This chapter includes three example scenarios to describe the tree ID process. These scenarios each describe different conditions that can exist that will determine the outcome of the Tree ID process as follows:

- Scenario One provides an example of tree identification where no conflicts exist and where no action has been taken to force a particular node to become the root.
- Scenario Two illustrates node connections that result in two nodes contending for root node status during Tree ID.
- Scenario Three describes the Tree ID process when one node has its force_root bit set prior to reset, causing it to become the root.

Scenario One

Figure 15-4 illustrates a network of nodes and their relationship after reset and prior to Tree Identification. Tree ID signaling employs the arbitration signaling mechanism and defines a signaling sequence that permits one node to be identified as the root node. In this example node C will be identified as the root, as described in the following sections.

Figure 15-4: Example Node Network Following Bus Initialization

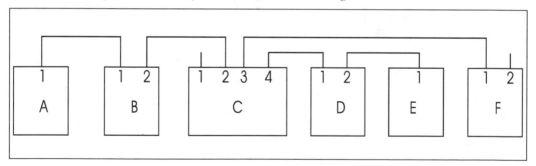

Leaf Nodes Signal Parent_Notify

Nodes A, E, and F in Figure 15-5 on page 291 all qualify to start signaling Parent_Notify since all are leaf nodes. When node B detects Parent_Notify on port 1 it recognizes that it now has only one other port that has not yet received

Parent_Notify, which makes it eligible to return Child_Notify to node A. Similarly, node D will detect Parent_Notify on port 2 and having only one port remaining that has not received Parent_Notify, it returns Child_Notify to node E. However, node C detects Parent_Notify on port 3 and recognizes that ports 2 and 3 have not yet received Parent_Notify, so it is not yet eligible to return Child_Notify to port F. (See Figure 15-6 on page 291.) Notice that the topology of the network has started to take shape.

Figure 15-5: Leaf Nodes Signal Parent_Notify

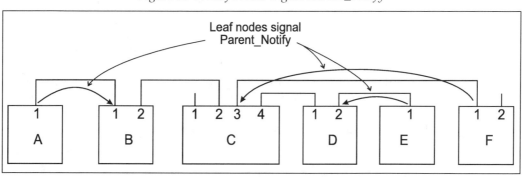

Figure 15-6: Node Network Following Leaf Node's A & E Having Identified Parents

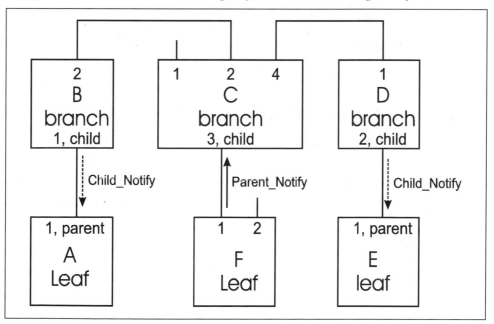

Branch Nodes Locate Their Parents

Since branch nodes B and D each have only two ports and since they have previously received Parent_Notify signaling from the attached leaf node, they meet the condition of having received a Parent_Notify on all but one of their ports. This means that nodes B and D can now signal Parent_Notify on their remaining ports in an attempt to find their probable parents. Notice that node C has received a Parent_Notify on port 3, but not on ports 2 and 4; thus, it must not signal Parent_Notify.

Nodes B and D begin signaling Parent_Notify immediately upon recognizing that they have only one remaining port that has not received a Parent_Notify. Although it wasn't mentioned in the previous section, Nodes B and D signal Parent_Notify to node C at the same time that they signal Child_Notify to their leaf nodes. Branch C detects a Parent_Notify on ports 2, 3, and 4 and performs a Child_Notify handshake with all three connected nodes as illustrated in Figure 15-7.

Figure 15-7: Branch Nodes Attempt to Locate Their Parents

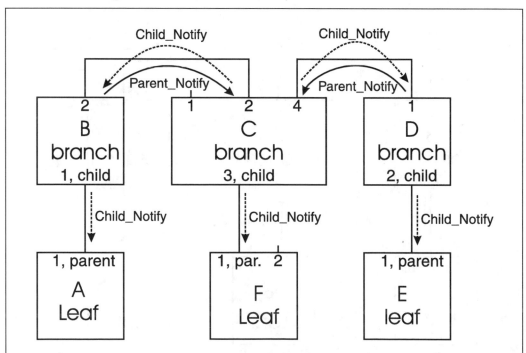

After completing the handshake, branch C will have marked its ports 2 and 4 as child ports, and nodes B and D will have marked port 2 and 1 respectively as parent ports. Nodes B and D, having now identified all of their ports, remove the Child_Notify signal from their child ports and leave the cable in the idle state. Since node C has all of its ports identified as children, it becomes the root node and also drops its Child_Notify signaling to ports B and D, which leaves those cable segments in the idle state. The final topology is illustrated in Figure 15-8.

Figure 15-8: Final Topology — Scenario 1

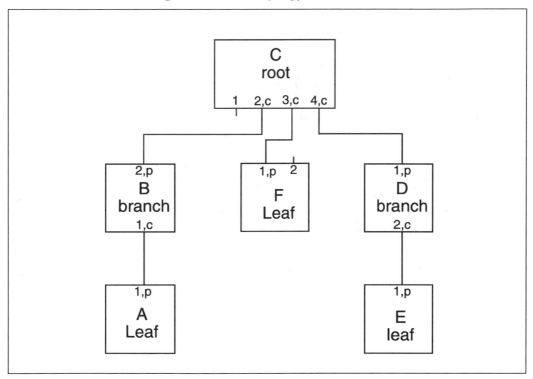

Scenario Two

This scenario illustrates serial bus nodes attached in a manner that results in contention as two nodes simultaneously signal Parent_Notify to each other. Figure 15-9 on page 294 illustrates a family of nodes after reset. The Tree ID process for these nodes is discussed in the following sections.

Figure 15-9: Example Node Network Following Reset — Scenario Two

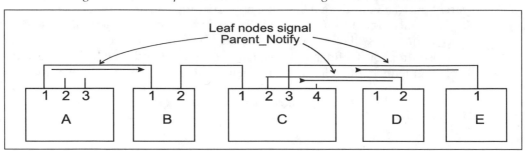

Leaf Nodes Locate Their Parents

Tree ID begins with leaf nodes A, D, and E all signaling Parent_Notify to their prospective parents. Node B detects the Parent_Notify from node A at the same time that Node C detects Parent_Notify from nodes D and E. Nodes B and C each respond by signaling Child_Notify to the attached leaf nodes. When leaf nodes A, D, and E detect the Child_Notify, they discontinue signaling Parent_Notify. Nodes B and C continue to signal the Child_Notify to the leaf nodes until all of their ports have been identified. Figure 15-10 illustrates the result of leaf node identification.

Figure 15-10: All Leaf Nodes Identified as Children

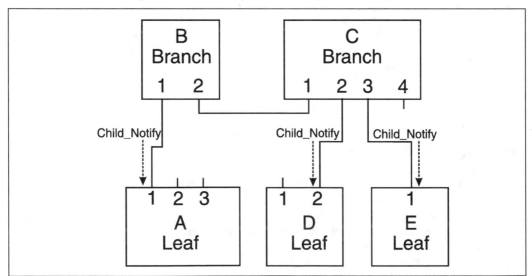

Root Contention

Upon detecting that all but one of their ports has received a Parent_Notify, nodes B and C each attempt to find their parent by signaling Parent_Notify. Node B signals Parent_Notify on its port 2 at the same time that Node C signals Parent_Notify on its port 1. As illustrated in Figure 15-10 on page 294, these two ports attach directly to each other, thus each node will signal Parent_Notify to the other. Consequently, both nodes drive the same cable with (TPA=0 and TPA=Z). In short, both nodes are attempting to find their probable parent by identifying themselves as children of the other, but of course two attached nodes cannot each be the parent of the other. The result is contention between the two nodes relative to which one is the child. The resulting line states are illustrated in Figure 15-11.

Each node expects to detect the Parent_Notify that it is signaling on its own arbitration comparators. However, since the attached node is also signaling a Parent_Notify, the resulting line states detected by each node's comparators is TPA=0 and TPB=0. This is interpreted as a root contention condition by each node. To resolve this condition each node will randomly select a time delay to determine how long it will wait before re-signaling a Parent_Notify. Each node has two choices:

- ROOT_CONTEND_FAST (0.24 - 0.26 microseconds)
- ROOT_CONTEND_SLOW (0.57 - 0.60 microseconds)

A node checks the line state with its arbitration comparators after its time delay expires. If it detects an idle condition, the node signals Parent_Notify and if the node is receiving Parent_Notify, it returns Child_Notify and completes the handshake. Four possible conditions may exist:

1. Node B may have chosen a slow timer value and node C a fast timer value. In this case, node C will time out first and signal Parent_Notify to node B. When node B's time delay expires, it detects the Parent_Notify being signaled by node C, marks its only remaining unidentified port as a child port, and it becomes the root.
2. Node C may have chosen a slow timer value and node B a fast timer value. In this case, node B will time out first and signal Parent_Notify to node C. After its time delay expires, node C detects the Parent Notify, marks its remaining unidentified port as a child port, and becomes the root.
3. In the event both nodes B and C happen to select fast timing, contention results again. They once again randomly select a time delay. Eventually one node will select slow timing while the other selects fast timing. The

node that successfully completes its Parent_Notify becomes the child port and the other will become the parent.

4. If both nodes B and C happen to select slow timing, contention also results and the same actions described in three above will ultimately occur.

In our example, let's assume that node C selects fast timing and node B selects slow timing. When B detects that a Parent_Notify has already been signaled by node C, it marks its port 2 as a child port and performs the handshake with C. Branch node C now marks its port 1 as a parent port since it has located its parent.

The tree ID process has now completed since each port has been identified as either a child or parent port. Refer to Figure 15-12 on page 297. The node that has all of it ports marked as child ports becomes the root node (node B in our example).

Figure 15-11: Root Contention — Two Attached Nodes Signaling Parent_Notify to the Other

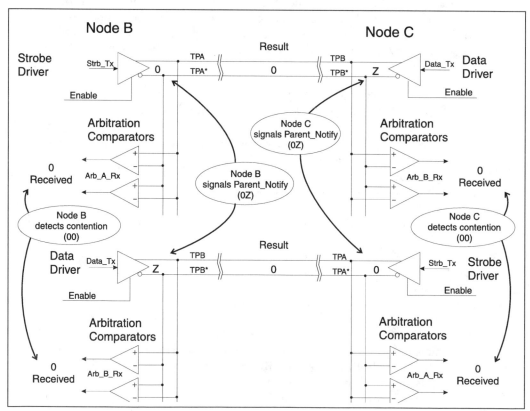

Figure 15-12: Example Topology after Completing Tree ID Process

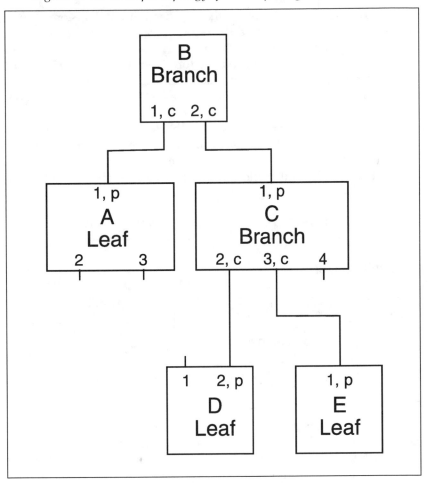

Scenario Three

Software has the ability to ensure that a given node will become the root node. This is done by broadcasting a PHY configuration packet over the serial bus. This packet contains two fields which specify that a particular node should set a bit within the PHY register called the force root bit. Figure 15-13 on page 298 illustrates the PHY configuration packet and identifies the node ID and force root fields. The force root field (R) specifies whether force root is enabled and the root_ID field identifies which node must set its force root bit. All nodes not identified by the root_ID field must clear their force root bits. Once the force root bit has been set, the next bus reset causes the bus to be configured again. This time during the Tree ID process the node that has its force root bit set will become the root. Note that the force root bit can also be set by local node software.

Figure 15-13: Format of PHY Configuration Packet

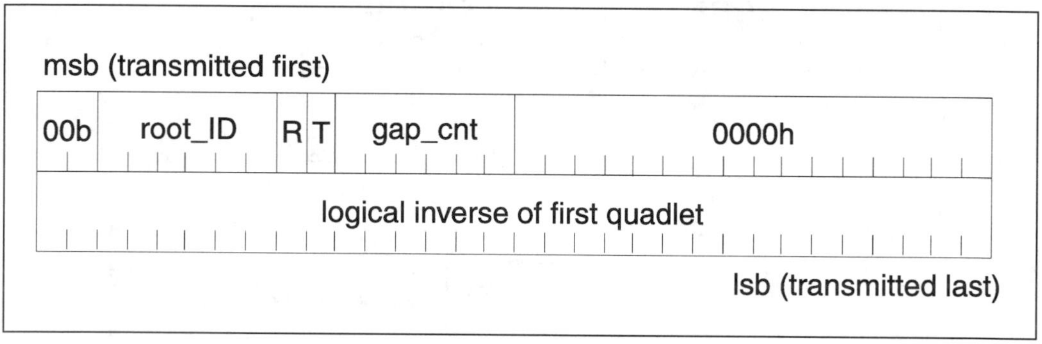

Figure 15-14 pictures the same family of nodes that was described in scenario one. The tree ID process in scenario one resulted in node C being designated as the root node as illustrated in Figure 15-8. In scenario one, no force root bit had been set; however, in this example let's assume that node E has its force root bit set. The following sections describe the Tree ID process for the same family of nodes used for scenario one, with node E having its force root bit set.

Figure 15-14: Family of Nodes after Reset with Node E's Force Root Bit Set

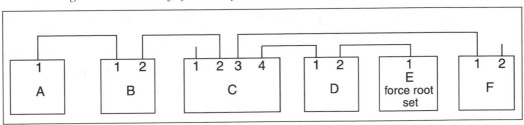

Force Root Delay

Root node determination described in the previous scenarios was determined by how the nodes were physically connected, with the node furthest away from the leaf nodes having the greatest chance of becoming the root. However, a software-aided node improves its chances of becoming the root node if it delays its participation in the tree ID process. This is called a force root delay. If the delay is long enough, all other nodes will have signaled Parent_Notify and identified their parents or are in the process of signaling Parent_Notify and are awaiting a response from the delayed node. When the node ends its delay it will detect Parent_Notify signaling at all of its ports. The delayed node then performs the Child_Notify on all ports, making all of its ports child ports, and it becomes the root.

As discussed previously, a force root bit can be set by software via a software initiated PHY configuration packet that will cause the node to delay its participation in tree ID signaling. The minimum force root delay is a minimum of 83.3μs and the maximum delay is equal to the CONFIG_TIMEOUT value of ~167μs.

In the event that two or more nodes have their Force_Root bit set, contention results and the root contention procedure discussed in scenario two resolves the conflict.

Leaf Nodes Attempt to Locate Their Parents

Leaf nodes begin the Tree ID process by signaling Parent_Notify just as described in scenario one, except that leaf node E has its force root bit set. Thus, it delays its participation in Tree ID signaling. Leaf nodes A and F signal Parent_Notify and Branch nodes B and C perform the Child_Notify handshake. Figure 15-15 illustrates the topology as it is known after leaf node identification.

Figure 15-15: Topology Following Leaf Identification

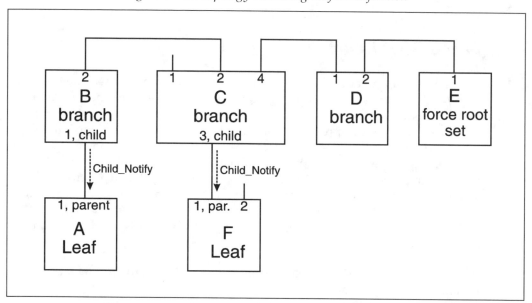

Branch Nodes Attempt to Locate Their Parents

Branch Node B is the only node that has received a Parent_Notify on all but one of its ports. Therefore, it signals Parent_Notify to branch node C. Nodes C and B complete the Child_Notify handshake, thereby completing stage one of the branch node identification process. Node C marks its port 2 as a child and node B marks its port 2 as a parent port as illustrated in Figure 15-16.

Figure 15-16: Topology Following Completion of Stage One of the Branch Identification Process

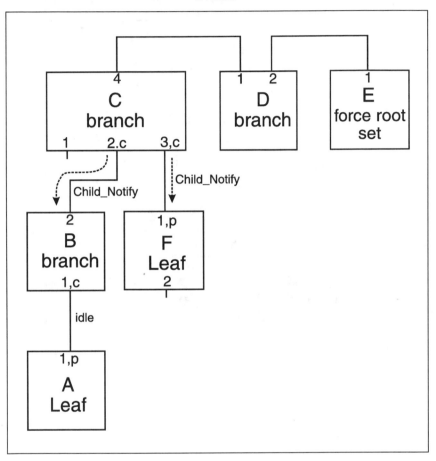

Branch node C now has received a Parent_Notify on all of its ports except port 4. Therefore, it signals a Parent_Notify to branch node D. Nodes C and D complete the Child_Notify handshake, and node C marks its remaining port as a parent port, while node D marks its port as a child port. Node C, having marked all of its ports, ceases to send Child_Notify to leaf node A. The topology now appears as shown in Figure 15-17.

Figure 15-17: Topology Following Stage Two of the Branch Identification Process

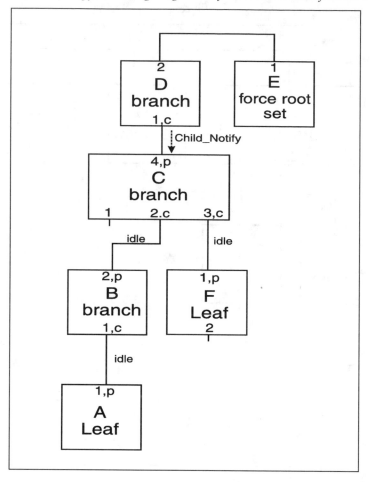

Node D is the only remaining branch node that has not identified all of its ports. Node D now signals Parent_Notify on its remaining port that attaches to node E. Note that Node E is still waiting for its force root time-out to occur. Node E will recognize the Parent_Notify when the time-out occurs, causing it to mark its only port as a child port and signal Child_Notify to branch node D. Node D will cease signaling the Parent_Notify and mark its port 2 as a parent port. Since Node E has its only port designated as a child port, it becomes the root node.

The final topology is illustrated in Figure 15-18.

Figure 15-18: Node with the Force Root Bit Set Becomes the Root Node

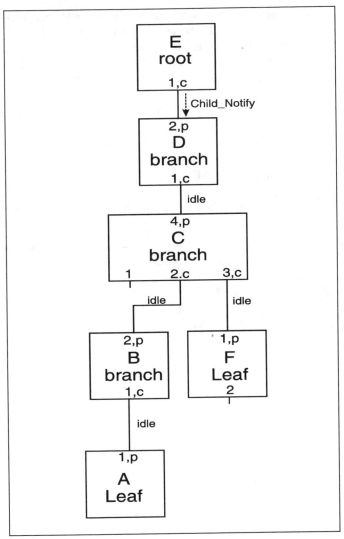

Looped Topology Detection

Nodes may inadvertently be connected in a loop. A looped topology will hang the bus during the tree ID process; therefore, looped topologies must be detected and reported. Consider the example node configuration pictured in Figure 15-19. In this example, the tree ID process has proceeded as far as it can. Leaf Nodes D and E have completed their Parent/Child handshake, but none of the remaining nodes (A, B, and C) can proceed with the tree ID process, because none have identified all but one of it ports. Thus, nodes A, B, and C hang in the state shown in Figure 15-19, with each waiting for a parent notify from the others. This problem is detected when the node arbitration timers time-out (approximately ~167μs). When the time-out is detected, the "loop" bit in the PHY register is set and the local application is notified.

Figure 15-19: Example of Looped Topology Resulting in a DeadLock During Tree ID

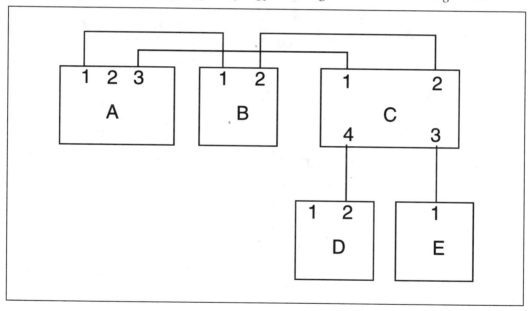

16 *Self Identification*

The Previous Chapter

Following bus initialization, the tree ID process begins to determine which node will become the root. The previous chapter detailed the protocol used in determining the topology of the serial bus.

This Chapter

This chapter focuses on the self-ID process. During self-ID all nodes are assigned addresses and specify their capabilities by broadcasting self-ID packets.

The Next Chapter

The next chapter describes the role of the cycle master node and defines how the cycle master is identified and enabled.

Overview

During the self-identification process configuration of the nodes begins. The following actions are performed during self-ID:

- Physical IDs are assigned to each node.
- Neighboring nodes exchange transmission speed capabilities.
- The topology defined during tree identification is broadcast.

During self-ID the root hub issues one self-ID grant signal for each node within the network. As each node receives its arbitration grant, it performs self-identification by assigning itself a physical ID and returning one or more self-identification packets. This process uses arbitrary port numbers that were assigned to each node during design time. These numbers are used to specify the order in which nodes attached to these ports will be assigned their physical IDs.

All signaling and packet transmission is done at the base rate (100Mb/s) since the speed capabilities of each node is unknown until the self-ID process has completed.

Self-Identification Signaling

Arbitration signaling states are used during the self-ID process. The signal states transmitted as listed in Table 16-1.

Table 16-1: Line States that Signal Parent- and Child-Notify

	SELF_ID_GRANT	DATA_PREFIX	IDENTIFICATION_DONE
TPA (Strobe)	Z	0	1
TPB (Data)	0	1	Z

Self-ID begins with the root signaling arbitration grant to its lowest numbered port and data prefix to its other ports. The following sections describe the entire self-ID process.

Physical ID Selection

At the start of the self-ID process, each node has identified whether each port points to a child or parent port as illustrated in Figure 16-1 on page 307. At this time no knowledge exists within any given node regarding the capabilities of its neighboring nodes or regarding the topology. The root node must determine how many nodes exist in the network and ensure that each is assigned a unique physical identifier. The following sections detail the process of assigning a physical ID to each node.

First Physical ID is Assigned

The self-ID process begins with the root port issuing an arbitration grant (TPA=Z and TPB=0) to its lowest numbered port and data prefix to its other ports. Arbitration grant is signaled by each branch node to its lowest numbered port until a leaf node is reached. Figure 16-2 illustrates the propagation of arbitration grant. In this example, when leaf node A receives the arbitration grant, it assigns itself a physical ID of zero (Phy 0). The physical ID assigned comes from the current self-ID count.

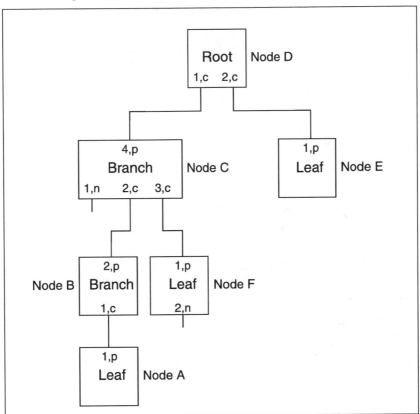

Figure 16-1: Example Node Network at Start of Self-ID

Self-ID Count

Each node tracks the number of self-ID packets that are broadcast during the self-ID process. The self-ID count within all nodes is initialized to zero after reset. Nodes increment their self-ID count after each self-ID packet is broadcast.

Figure 16-2: First Arbitration Grant Issued During Self-ID Process

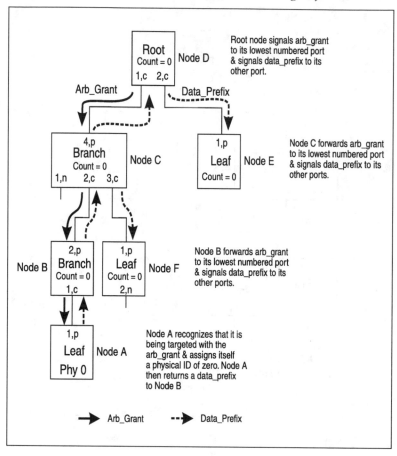

Branch Nodes Signal Arbitration Grant & Data Prefix

Refer to Figure 16-2 on page 308. Note that as each branch node receives the arbitration grant, it checks its ports to determine which have been identified, if any. Since the self-ID process has just begun none of the ports have been identified yet. Each branch node (nodes C and B in this example) signals arbitration grant to its lowest numbered unidentified port. Each branch node also signals data prefix to its other ports, including back upstream to the node signaling the arbitration grant.

When branch nodes signal data prefix upstream toward the root node, the upstream node continues to signal arbitration grant downstream. Consider the action taken by branch Node C when it receives arbitration grant from the root node. Figure 16-3 on page 309 illustrates the arbitration grant line state being signaled by the root node (TPA=Z and TPB=0) and the data prefix being signaled by node C (TPA=0 and TPB=1). The root node's arbitration comparators will detect the arbitration grant that it is signaling; thus, when the data prefix is driven at the opposite end of the cable, the root node detects a change in the line state. The resulting line state (TPA=1 and TPB=0) observed by the root, is interpreted as receipt of a data prefix (Rx_DATA_PREFIX). When the root node detects the data prefix it removes arbitration grant signaling and leaves only the data prefix being driven on the cable.

Figure 16-3: Identified Node Starts Self-ID Packet Transmission with Data Prefix

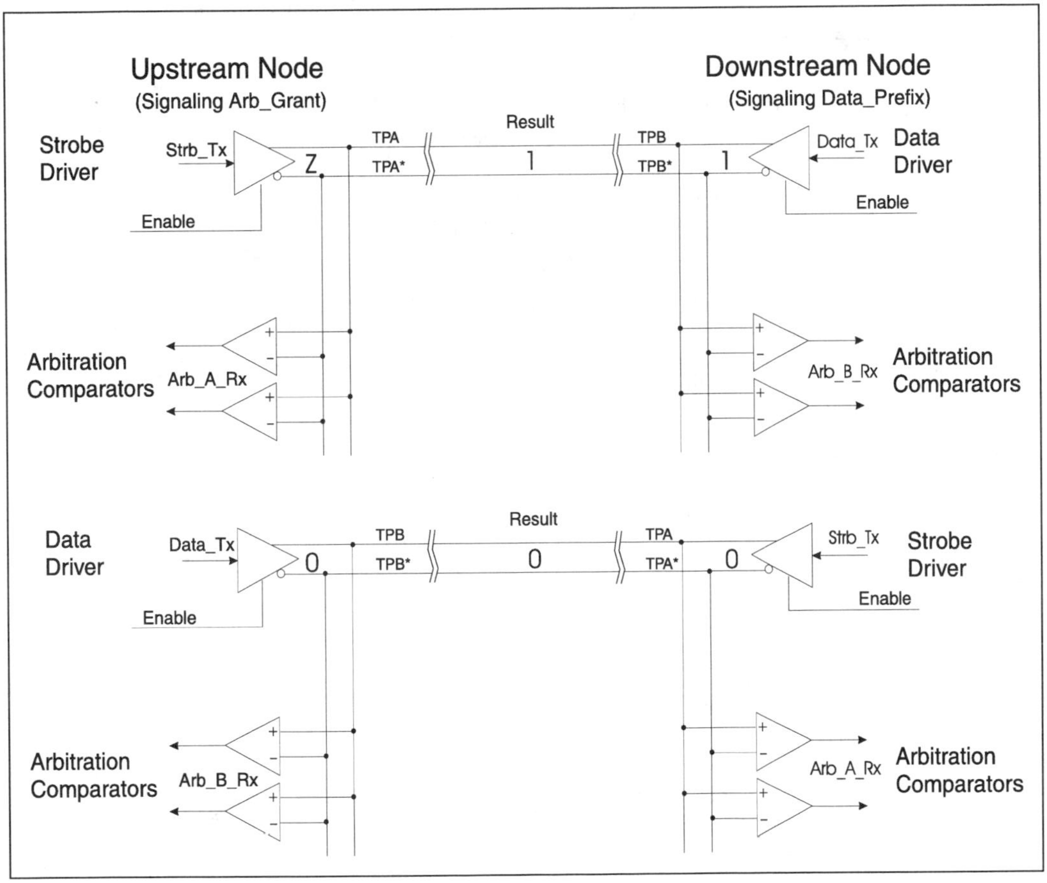

FireWire System Architecture

The same signaling convention described in the previous paragraph occurs between each branch node and the node attached to its lowest numbered unidentified port. When the arbitration grant signal finally reaches leaf node A, it returns data prefix to node B, resulting in data prefix being driven over every cable segment in the network.

Node A Broadcasts Its Self-ID Packet

Node A transmits its self-ID packet after it signals data prefix as pictured in Figure 16-4 on page 310. As each node detects the self-ID packet, it signals the packet to all of its other ports. The root hub also propagates the self-ID packet onto its higher numbered port. When other nodes detect this self-ID packet, they recognize that a node has assigned itself a physical ID of zero (the current self-ID count). The self-ID packet contains information that identifies the node and specifies its serial bus characteristics. The definition of the self-ID packets is discussed in "Self-ID Packets" on page 323.

Figure 16-4: Self-ID Packet Is Broadcast to All Nodes.

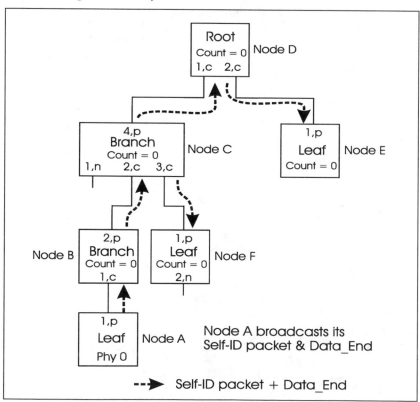

Node A signals data end (TPA=1 and TPB=0) after it has broadcast its self-ID packet. Data end notifies other nodes that the self-ID packet has ended. Upon detecting data end all nodes increment their self-ID counts to one.

Node A Signals Self-Identification Done

Refer to Figure 16-5 on page 311. Note that after Node A signals data end, the bus returns to the idle state since nothing is being signaled by any node in the network. Following data end, Node A completes its self-ID process by signaling identification done (IDENT_DONE) via TPA=1 and TPB=Z and Node B returns data prefix signaling (TPA=0 and TPB=1) to Node A as a handshake.

When Node A detects the data prefix being returned from Node B (resulting line state of TPA=1 and TPB=0), it ceases driving the cable and leaves data_prefix signaling from Node B. This completes the self-identification process for Node A and it no longer participates in the self-ID process.

Figure 16-5: Node A Signals Identification Done to End Its Self-Identification Process.

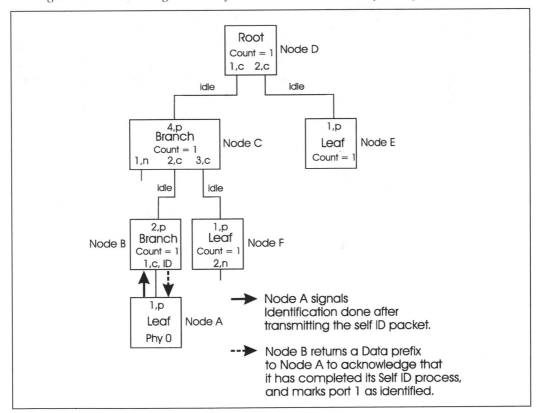

Nodes Exchange Speed Information

Note that during identification_done signaling each node also delivers its maximum speed capability. This is done using the normal current-encoded speed signaling mechanism. In this example, Node A signals its maximum speed as it signals ident_done, by current encoding its maximum speed capability. Node B will detect the speed capability of Node A and return its speed capability to Node A when it signals data_prefix back to Node A. In this way, all nodes connected to the same cable exchange speed information with each other.

Several possibilities may exist that affect the nature of the speed signaling exchange between two nodes as listed in Table 16-2. Only when both nodes support the 400Mb/s transfer rate will the fastest transfer rate be used across this cable segment.

Table 16-2: Possible Speed Signaling Combinations

Child Node's Maximum Speed	Parent Node's Maximum Speed	Maximum Cable Speed Supported
100	100	100
100	200	100
100	400	100
200	100	100
200	200	200
200	400	200
400	100	100
400	200	200
400	400	400

In our example, if Node A's PHY is only capable of transferring data at a 100Mb/s rate then it will not perform speed signaling during indent_done. Upon detecting no speed information Node B will not perform speed signaling despite the possibility that is may support 200 and 400Mb/s transmission rates. Since Node A only supports the 100Mb/s transfer speed the maximum transfer speed across this cable segment is limited to 100Mb/s. If however, Node A signals 200Mb/s support, Node B would also signal 200Mb/s support to the child node, even if it can support 400Mb/s transmission rates.

Second and Subsequent Physical ID Assignment

Following transmission of the first self-ID packet, the root node detects an idle condition on the cable, which it interprets as an indication that it can start the next self-ID process. See Figure 16-6 on page 313.

Figure 16-6: State of the Node Network Following the First Physical ID Assignment

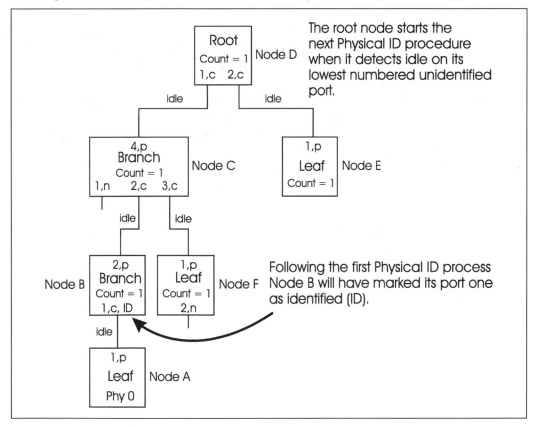

Second Self-ID Assignment

The root node initiates assignment of the second physical ID by issuing an arbitration grant to its lowest numbered unidentified port, along with data prefix to its other ports. Assignment of the second physical ID uses the same procedures described during the first physical ID assignment as enumerated below:

1. Node C detects the arbitration grant and forwards it to its lowest numbered unidentified port (port 2).
2. Node C signals data prefix to all other ports (ports 3 and 4).
3. The root node, upon detecting data prefix signaling, ceases to drive arbitration grant.
4. Node B receives the arbitration grant from Node C and recognizes that its only downstream port is identified. Consequently, Node B accepts the arbitration grant as a command to assign itself a physical ID of one (the current value of the self-ID count).
5. The newly identified node sends its self-ID packet upstream to identify itself. Self-ID packet transmission begins with data prefix followed by the self-ID packet and data end.
6. All nodes forward the self-ID packet to each node connected to their ports and increment their self-ID count to two upon detecting the data end.
7. After sending its self-ID packet, Node B signals identification done to Node C, and performs speed signaling.
8. In response, Node C signals data prefix back to Node B and marks its port 2 as identified, and signals its speed capability.
9. Detecting the data prefix prompts Node B to discontinue signaling identification done, thereby ending the self-ID process for Node B.
10. The root node detects idle on its ports when the self-ID packet transmission ends and signals arbitration grant to begin the next physical ID assignment procedure.

The state of the node network following the second physical ID process is illustrated in Figure 16-7 on page 315.

Figure 16-7: State of the Node Network Following the Second Physical ID Assignment

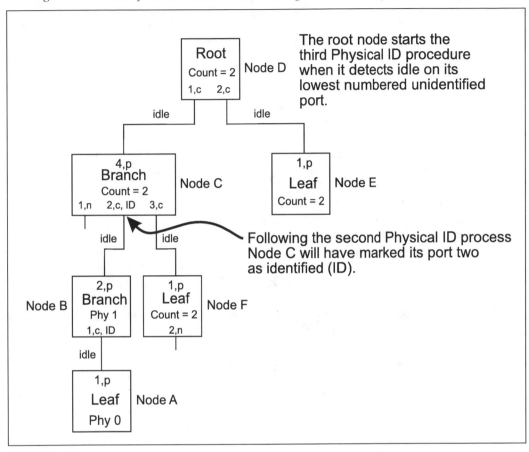

Third Physical ID Assignment

Assignment of the third physical ID proceeds as enumerated below:

1. The root node signals arbitration grant to its lowest numbered identified port (port 1) and data prefix to its other port.
2. Node C detects the arbitration grant and forwards it to its lowest numbered unidentified port (port 3).
3. Node C signals data prefix to port 4.
4. The root node, upon detecting data prefix signaling, ceases to drive arbitration grant.
5. Node F receives the arbitration grant from Node C and recognizes that its only downstream port is not connected. Consequently, Node F accepts the arbitration grant as a command to assign itself a physical ID of two (the current value of the self-ID count).
6. The newly identified node sends its self-ID packet upstream to identify itself. Self-ID packet transmission begins with data prefix followed by the self-ID packet and data end.
7. All nodes forward the self-ID packet to each node connected to their ports and increment their self-ID count to three upon detecting the data end.
8. After sending its self-ID packet, Node F signals identification done to Node C, and signals it speed capability.
9. In response, Node C signals data prefix (including speed info) back to Node B and marks its port 3 as identified.
10. Detecting the data prefix prompts Node F to discontinue signaling identification done, thereby ending its role in the self-ID.
11. The root node detects idle on its ports when the self-ID packet transmission ends and signals arbitration grant to its lowest numbered identified port, thus beginning the next physical ID assignment procedure.

Figure 16-8 on page 317 illustrates the state of the node network following assignment of the third physical ID.

Figure 16-8: State of the Node Network Following the Third Physical ID Assignment

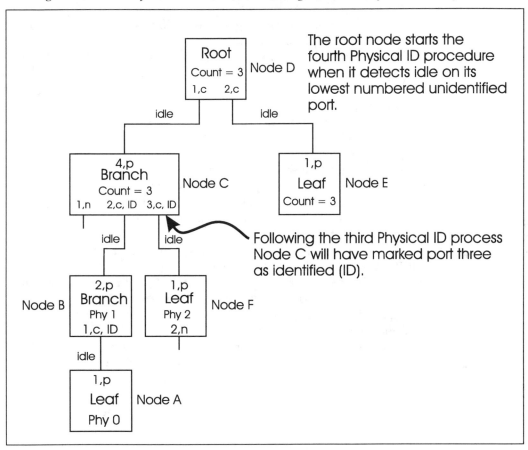

The root node starts the fourth Physical ID procedure when it detects idle on its lowest numbered unidentified port.

Following the third Physical ID process Node C will have marked port three as identified (ID).

Fourth Physical ID Assignment

Assignment of the fourth physical ID proceeds as enumerated below:

1. The root node signals arbitration grant to its lowest numbered identified port (port 1) and data prefix to its other port.
2. Node C detects the arbitration grant and recognizes that all of its downstream ports have been identified. Consequently, Node C accepts the arbitration grant as a command to assign itself a physical ID of three (the current value of the self-ID count).
3. The newly identified node sends its self-ID packet upstream to identify itself. Self-ID packet transmission begins with data prefix followed by the self-ID packet and data end.
4. The root node, upon detecting the data prefix at the beginning of self-ID packet transmission, ceases to signal arbitration grant.
5. The root node forwards the self-ID packet to Node E.
6. Both the root node and Node E increment their self-ID count to four upon detecting the end of the self-ID packet (data end).
7. After sending its self-ID packet, Node C signals identification done (and signals its maximum speed) to the root node.
8. In response, the root node signals data prefix (including speed signaling) back to Node C and marks its port 1 as identified.
9. Detecting the data prefix prompts Node C to discontinue signaling identification done, thereby ending its role in the self-ID.
10. The root node detects idle on its ports when the self-ID packet transmission ends and signals arbitration grant to its lowest numbered identified port (port 2), thus beginning the next physical ID assignment procedure.

Figure 16-9 on page 319 illustrates the state of the node network following assignment of the fourth physical ID.

Figure 16-9: State of the Node Network Following the Fourth Physical ID Assignment

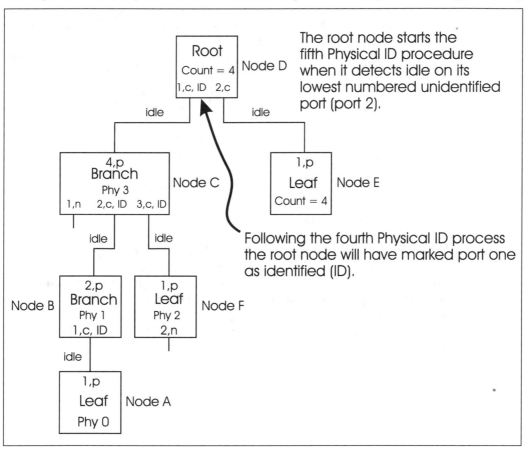

The root node starts the fifth Physical ID procedure when it detects idle on its lowest numbered unidentified port (port 2).

Following the fourth Physical ID process the root node will have marked port one as identified (ID).

Fifth Physical ID Assignment

Assignment of the fifth physical ID proceeds as enumerated below:

1. . The root node signals arbitration grant to its lowest numbered identified port (port 2) and data prefix to its other port.
2. Node E detects the arbitration grant and recognizes that it is being targeted to assign itself a physical ID of four (the current value of the self-ID count).
3. The newly identified node sends its self-ID packet upstream to identify itself.
4. The root node, upon detecting the data prefix at the beginning of self-ID packet transmission, ceases to signal arbitration grant.
5. The root node increments its self-ID count to five upon detecting the end of the self-ID packet (data end).
6. After sending its self-ID packet, Node E signals identification done (including speed signaling) to the root node.
7. In response, the root node signals data prefix (including speed signaling) back to Node E and marks its port 2 as identified.
8. Detecting the data prefix prompts Node E to discontinue signaling identification done, thereby ending its role in the self-ID process.
9. The root node detects idle on port 2 when the self-ID packet transmission ends and recognizes that all of its ports have been identified.

Figure 16-10 on page 321 illustrates the state of the node network following assignment of the fifth physical ID.

Figure 16-10: State of the Node Network Following the Fifth Physical ID Assignment

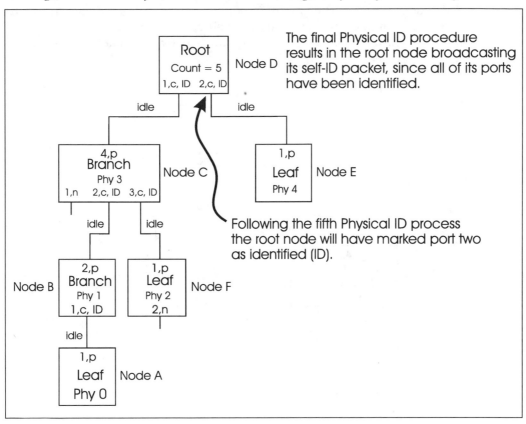

The final Physical ID procedure results in the root node broadcasting its self-ID packet, since all of its ports have been identified.

Following the fifth Physical ID process the root node will have marked port two as identified (ID).

Final Physical ID Always Belongs to Root Node

The root node is always the last node to assign itself a physical ID and transmit self-ID packets. This occurs after the root has flagged all of its ports as identified. In this example, the root node assigns itself a physical ID of 5 (the current self-ID count). Figure 16-11 pictures the node network after all physical IDs have been assigned.

Figure 16-11: State of the Node Network Following the Final Physical ID Assignment

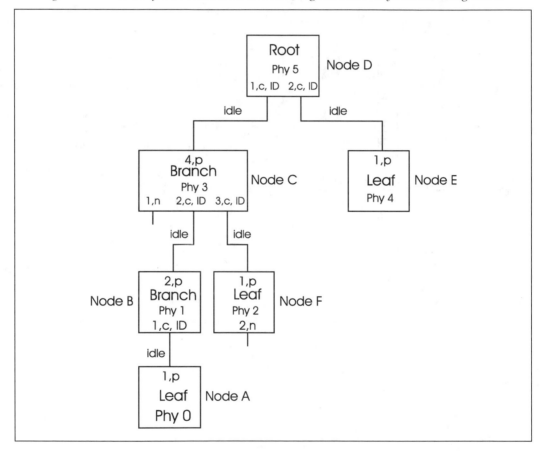

Self-ID Packets

Self-ID packets are broadcast by a node to identify itself to other nodes within the system. These packets contain information that specify their serial bus characteristics. All nodes transmit self-ID packet zero and if a branch node contains more than three ports, it must transmit additional packets.

Self-ID Packet Zero

Figure 16-12 on page 323 illustrates the self-ID packet zero format, while Table 16-3 defines each of the fields. Note that all self-ID packets are transmitted at the base cable rate and include the speed capabilities of each node.

Figure 16-12: Format for Self-ID Packet Zero

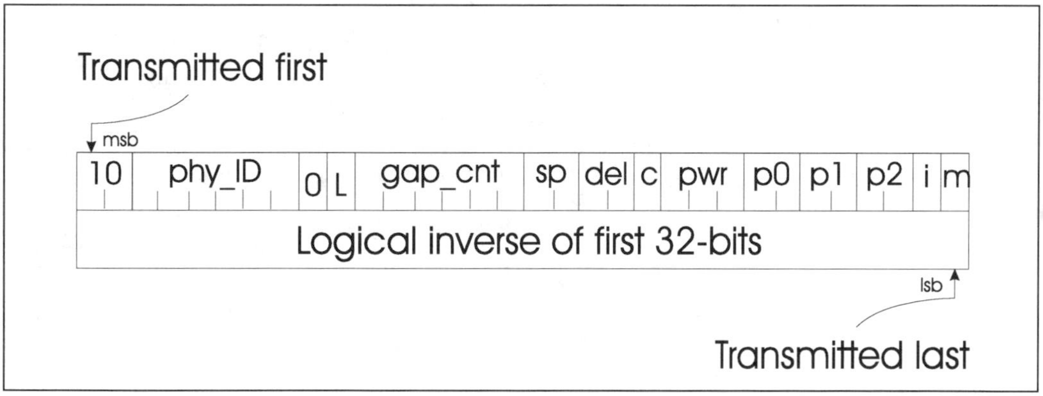

Table 16-3: Self-ID Packet Zero Field Definition

Field Code	Field Name	Comments
10	Packet identifier	Transmitted at the beginning of the packet to identify this packet as a self-ID packet.
Phy_ID	Physical ID	Physical Identifier of the node sending this packet.
L	Link active	Set to indicate that Link and Transaction layers are active.
gap_cnt	Gap count	Current value of PHY_CONFIGURATION.gap_count field.

Table 16-3: Self-ID Packet Zero Field Definition (Continued)

Field Code	Field Name	Comments
sp	PHY speed	Nodes speed capabilities: 00 = 98.304 Mb/s 01 = 98.304 Mb/s and 196.608 Mb/s 10 = 98.304 Mb/s,196.608 Mb/s and 393.216Mb/s 11 = Extended speed capabilities reported in PHY register 3.
del	PHY delay	Specifies the maximum repeater delay across this node. 00 = <= 144ns (~14/BASE_RATE) 01 = Reserved 10 = Reserved 11 = Reserved Note: This field is reserved for 1394a PHYs.
c	Contender	When set and Link active is set, this node is a contender for the role of bus or isochronous resource manager.
pwr	Power class	Specifies power consumption and source characteristics: 000 = Node does need bus power and does not repeat power 001 = Self powered & provides 15W (minimum) to bus. 010 = Self powered & provides 30W (minimum to bus. 011 = Self powered & provides 45W (minimum to bus 100 = Node may be powered from the bus and is using up to 3W and no additional bus power is needed to enable the link. 101 = Reserved for future implementations. 110 = Node is powered from the bus and consumes 3W maximum. An additional 3W maximum is needed to enable the link. 111 = Node is powered from the bus and consumes 3W maximum. An additional 7W maximum is needed to enable the link.
p0 .. p2	Port number	Specifies port status: 11 = Active and connected to child node 10 = Active and connected to parent node 01 = Not active (suspended, disabled, or disconnected) 00 = Port not present
i	Initiated reset	This node initiated the current bus reset before receiving reset signaling. (Optional, if not used returns zero)
m	More packets	More packets follow this one to report additional port status.

Chapter 16: Self Identification

Self-ID Packets One and Two (1394a)

Each node sends one or more packets depending on the number of ports that it has:

- Leaf nodes (one port) or branch nodes with two or three ports send a single 32-bit self-ID packet (packet zero).
- Nodes with 4 to 11 ports send two self-ID packets
- Nodes with 12 to 15 ports send three self-ID packets

Sixteen nodes is the maximum number supported for a single node. Figure 16-13 pictures the format of the additional packets (packets one and two). Each 2-bit port field has the same definition as shown in Table 16-3 on page 323 for ports zero through two. Note that the value "n" is the extended self ID packet sequence number.

Figure 16-13: Format of Self-ID Packets One and Two

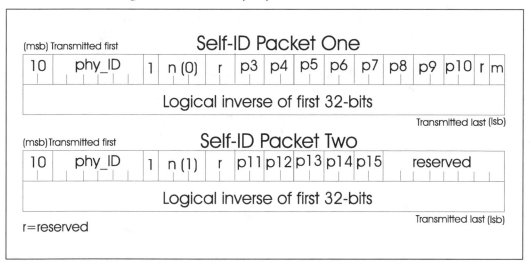

Following the transmission of the self-ID packets, data_end is signaled. When another self-ID packet must be transmitted, the previous packet ID is followed by data prefix. Only after all packets are transmitted will the sequence be ended with data_end signaling. Figure 16-14 on page 326 illustrates the protocol when transmitting one, two, and three self-ID packets.

Figure 16-14: Protocol Used to Transmit Self-ID Packets

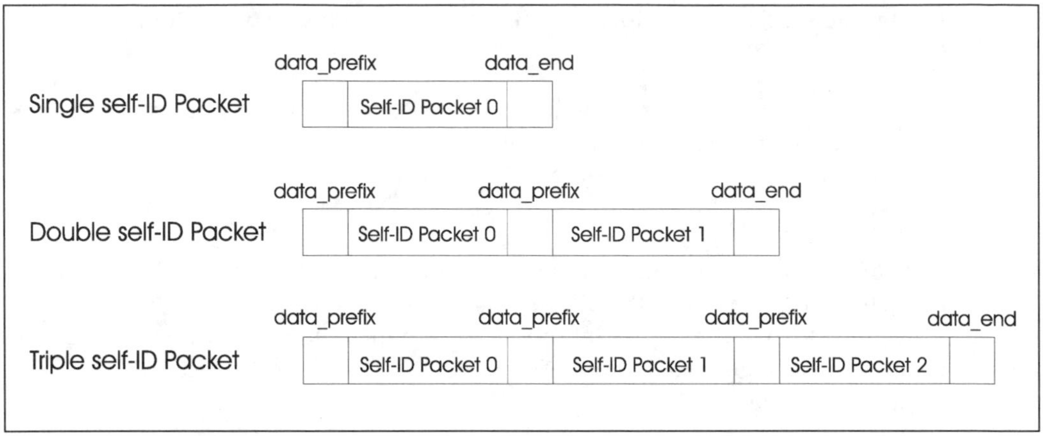

Who Uses the Self-ID Packet Information

Some nodes on the network use information provided in the self-ID packet to assist them in performing community functions that support other nodes living on the serial bus. These community functions include:

- publishing a topology map that can be accessed by other nodes
- publishing a speed map that can be read to find the maximum speed for each cable segment that is attached between two nodes.
- power management control.
- optimizing bus traffic.

These functions are performed by nodes that fulfill the roles of bus manager (Chapter 19) and isochronous resource manager (Chapter 18).

Part Four

Serial Bus Management

17 *Cycle Master*

The Previous Chapter

The previous chapter focused on the self-ID process. During self-ID all nodes are assigned addresses and specify their capabilities by broadcasting self-ID packets.

This Chapter

This chapter describes the role of the cycle master node, and defines how the cycle master is identified and enabled.

The Next Chapter

Next, the isochronous resource manager is discussed: how it is identified and enabled, and the nature of its role in the serial bus environment.

Overview

Isochronous transfers are guaranteed a constant bus bandwidth based on allocation of the number of bytes to be transferred during 125µs intervals. The root node is responsible for specifying the 125µs interval and marks the beginning of the next series of isochronous transactions by broadcasting a cycle start packet as illustrated in Figure 17-1.

Determining and Enabling the Cycle Master

A node that is cycle master capable must:

- be isochronous capable
- implement the BUS_TIME register
- be able to generate cycle start events based on an 8KHz clock that is synchronized to the CYCLE_TIME register and broadcast cycle start packets.
- set the cmc bit in the BUS_INFO_BLOCK

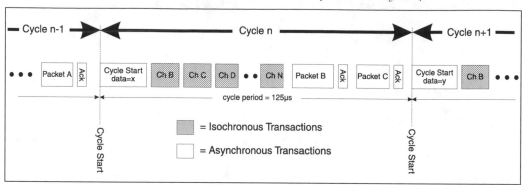

Figure 17-1: Isochronous Transactions Performed Every 125μs

The cycle master must be the root node. Following the self-ID process, the root node and the isochronous resource manager will be known. If a bus manager is present it will verify that the root node is cycle master capable and, if so, enable it; otherwise, the isochronous resource manager will perform this function. To determine if the root is cycle master capable, the cmc bit within the root node's BUS_INFO_BLOCK register will be set. If so, the root node is enabled to perform the cycle start by setting the cmstr bit in the STATE_SET register.

If the root node is not cycle master capable, other nodes are checked for cycle master capability. When a capable node is found it is selected to become the new root node. This is accomplished by broadcasting a PHY configuration packet with the force root bit "R" set to 1 and the root ID value set to the node ID of the target node. The selected node will set its root holdoff bit (RHB), while all other nodes (those not selected by the root ID value) will clear their RHB bit.

Cycle Start Packet

The cycle start packet format is illustrated in Figure 17-2 on page 331. For a description of the fields within the cycle start packet see Table 8-16 on page 196. This packet is broadcast by the cycle master at the beginning of each new cycle (nominally 125μs). The start of each cycle is synchronized to the cycle master's CYCLE_TIME register. The cycle master delivers the contents of its cycle time register in the cycle start packet. As a result, if the cycle start packet is delayed due to the previous cycle stretching beyond the nominal 125μs cycle time, the timing variation will be visible to all isochronous nodes as illustrated in Figure 17-3 on page 331.

Figure 17-2: Cycle Start Packet Contains Value of Cycle Master's CYCLE_TIME Register

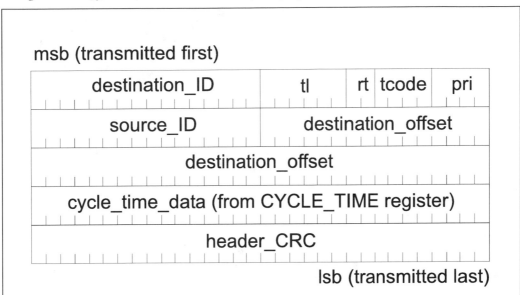

Figure 17-3: Cycle Time Variation Included in Cycle Start Packet

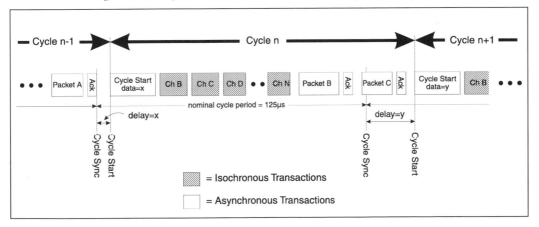

18 Isochronous Resource Manager

The Previous Chapter

The previous chapter described the role of the cycle master node, and defined how the cycle master is identified and enabled.

This Chapter

This chapter describes the role of the isochronous resource manager: how it is identified and enabled, and how other nodes interact with it.

The Next Chapter

Next, the bus manager function is described including topology map generation and access, speed map generation and access, and power management.

Overview

Following a bus reset, all traffic on the bus is terminated and all nodes perform the initialization sequence consisting of reset, tree-ID, and self-ID procedures. If this is the initial Reset due to power on, each node wishing to perform isochronous transfers must obtain an isochronous channel number and request the amount of bus bandwidth that it requires. The isochronous resource manager fulfills the role of keeping track of channel numbers and bus bandwidth that have been allocated.

If the reset occurs after isochronous traffic has started (e.g. due to attachment of new node), all bus traffic resumes as quickly as possible. Asynchronous transactions can resume immediately upon completion of the self-ID process, as well as isochronous transactions in most instances. However, isochronous transactions are delayed if the root node changes. In this case, isochronous transactions cannot start again until isochronous resources are verified and a cycle master is selected to re-initiate isochronous traffic.

Determining the Isochronous Resource Manager

Any node residing on the bus may have the ability to perform the role of isochronous resource manager (IRM). Nodes capable of becoming the isochronous resource manager must indicate their ability to fulfill this role by setting the "l" (link active) and "c" (contender) bits in packet zero of their self-ID register. This makes a given node a contender for the role of IRM. See Figure 18-1.

Figure 18-1: Contender Nodes Must Set Bits l and c in Their Self-ID Packets

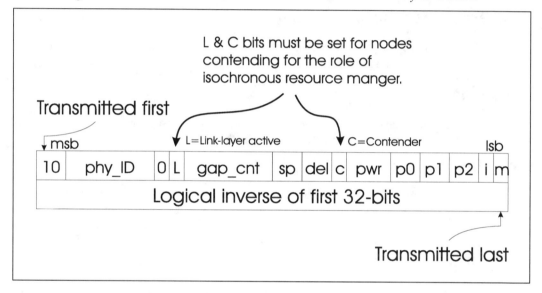

All nodes contending for the role of IRM must monitor all self-ID packets to determine if another node is also vying for the position of IRM. The competition is won by the contender having the highest value physical ID. During the self-ID process, a physical ID of zero is assigned first followed by consecutively higher IDs. Thus, a node contending for the role of IRM recognizes that it is out of the running if, after sending its own self-ID packet, it recognizes that a later self-ID packet specifies another node as a contender. Note that the highest value physical ID always belongs to the root node and its self-ID packet is always sent last. Thus, in many instances, the root node will become the IRM (i.e. when it is IRM capable).

Minimum Requirements of Isochronous Resource Managers

To be a contender for the role of IRM, a node must fulfill a set of minimum requirements:

- Support Isochronous transactions as either talker or listener.
- Link and Transaction layers must be active during configuration process.
- Implement General ROM to support Bus_Info_Block with IRMC bit set.
- Implement the Bus Manager ID register.
- Implement bus bandwidth allocation register.
- Implement channel allocation register.

The isochronous resource manager provides allocation registers whose locations are known to all nodes needing to perform isochronous transactions. Nodes wishing to perform isochronous transfers must access these registers to acquire a channel number and bus bandwidth prior to performing any isochronous transfers.

Enabling the Cycle Master

The isochronous resource manager (IRM) may also be required to enable the cycle master so that it can begin transmitting cycle start packets. Following a power reset, the "cmstr" bit within the bus_depend field of the STATE register (See Figure 21-3 on page 367) will be cleared, which disables cycle master functionality. The IRM, in the absence of the bus manager, is responsible for enabling the root to perform the cycle master functions. The IRM determines that the bus manager is absent if the value of the BUS_MANAGER_ID register remains at 3Fh for greater than 625ms after bus reset.

In the event that a bus or command reset occurs, the cycle master should keep the "cmstr" bit set so that it can automatically resume broadcast of cycle start packets. However, if the cycle master recognizes that following a bus reset and tree ID process that it is no longer the root, it must clear the "cmstr" bit. Consequently, the new root node must be enabled as the cycle master so it can start generating cycle start packets.

Resource Allocation Registers

Figure 18-2 on page 336 shows the location of the CHANNELS_AVAILABLE and BANDWIDTH_AVAILABLE register within the node space of the Isochronous Resource Manager. The BANDWIDTH_AVAILABLE register is mapped at offset 224h from the beginning of the Serial-Bus dependent address space, and the CHANNELS_AVAILABLE register is mapped beginning at offset 220h. When a node accesses these registers to obtain isochronous resources, it must perform the access using lock transactions.

Figure 18-2: Location of CHANNEL_ALLOCATION & BUS_BANDWIDTH Registers.

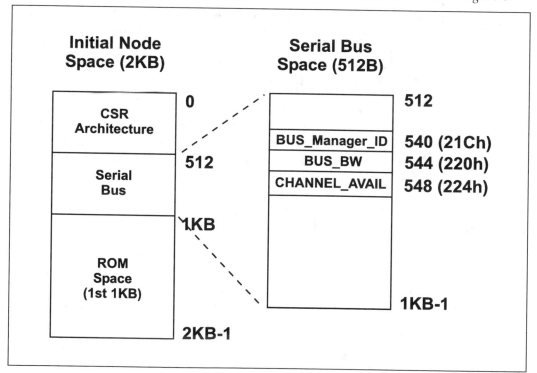

Channel Allocation

Nodes wishing to perform isochronous transfers must first obtain an isochronous channel number via the CHANNELS_AVAILABLE register.

Channels Available Register Format

This 64-bit register provides a bit map where each bit corresponds to one of the 64 possible isochronous channels supported by the serial bus as illustrated in Figure 18-3 on page 337. All bits are initialized to a value of one, thus indicating that none of the channels has been allocated.

Accessing the Channels Available Register

A node wishing to obtain an isochronous channel must first read the current register value to determine the next consecutive channel available. Note that the CHANNELS_AVAILABLE register is initialized to all ones, indicating that all channels are available. Next, the lock (compare and swap) transaction is used to request the next available channel. The lock transaction is used since more than one node may simultaneously attempt to request a channel. If no other node claims a channel number between the initial register read and the subsequent lock operation, then the lock transfer for this node will be successful; otherwise, the lock transfer will not succeed.

Figure 18-3: Format of the CHANNELS_AVAILABLE Register

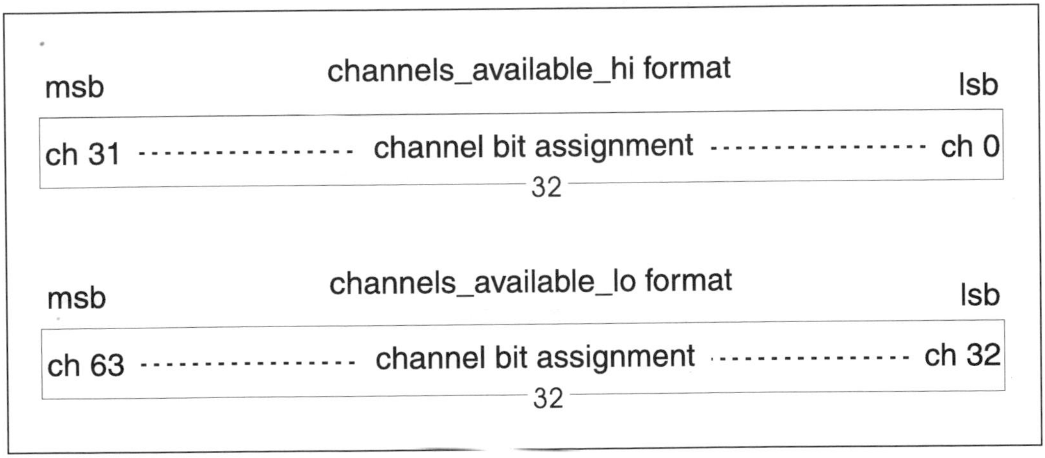

The lock compare and swap transaction contains two parameters from the requesting node that must be sent within the request packet:

- argument_value
- data_value

Figure 18-4 on page 339 illustrates the operation of the lock compare and swap transaction and assumes that previously no channels have been allocated. A node wishing to obtain a channel number will read a value of all ones from the CHANNELS_AVAILABLE register, indicating that no channels have been allocated yet. The node will then use the lock compare and swap transaction to request that channel zero be allocated to it. The value read from the channels available register is sent back to the IRM as the argument_value (FFFF FFFFh) of the lock request packet. The data_value contains the new value that will be loaded into the CHANNELS_AVAILABLE register, provided that the lock transfer is successful in allocating channel 0 to this node (FFFF FFFE). If the argument value matches the current contents of the register, then no other node has successfully obtained a channel. Thus, the data_value becomes the new value within the CHANNELS_AVAILABLE register (leaving the bit corresponding to channel 0 cleared).

Note that the data value sent back in the response packet is the contents of the register when the lock operation began, not the new register value. In this way, success of the lock compare and swap can be verified if the returned value and the argument value are the same because the register contents did not change during the time interval between the original register read and the start of the lock compare and swap operation.

Figure 18-4: Operation of Lock Compare & Swap Transaction during Channel Allocation

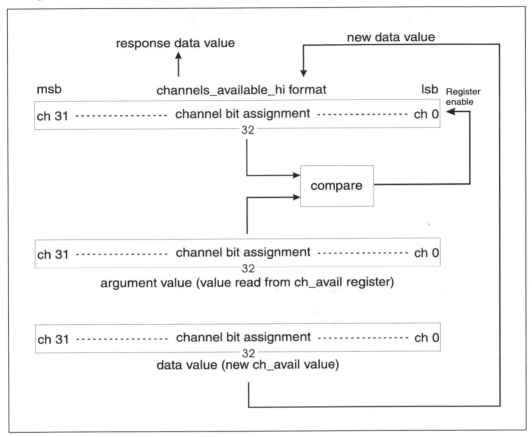

Bus Bandwidth Allocation

Isochronous nodes must access the BANDWIDTH_AVAILABLE register to request the bandwidth needed to perform their isochronous transfers. Accesses to this register support only the quadlet read and lock compare swap transaction. The bw_remaining field reflects the amount of bus bandwidth (in allocation units) that is currently available for isochronous transfers.

Bandwidth Available Register Format

Figure 18-5 illustrates the format of the BANDWIDTH_AVAILABLE register. The contents of this register represents the total bus bandwidth available for isochronous transfers.

Figure 18-5: Format of the BANDWIDTH_AVAILABLE Register

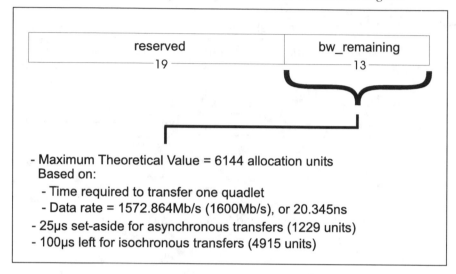

Accessing the Bandwidth Available Register

The procedure used for obtaining isochronous bus bandwidth is very similar to the process for obtaining channel numbers. The current register value is read to determine the total amount of isochronous bus bandwidth remaining. Since the value is specified in allocation units based on a transfer rate of 1600Mb/s, the requester must calculate the number of allocation units required to support the transfer size that it desires, taking into consideration the transfer speed that is supported by the requesting node. The number of allocation units required for the desired bandwidth must be subtracted from bw_remaining to determine the new bw_remaining value. The lock compare and swap transaction is then performed in an attempt to acquire the bandwidth needed. The process is illustrated in Figure 18-6.

Bandwidth requirements must include the overhead associated with transferring data.

Figure 18-6: Operation of Lock Compare & Swap Transaction during Isochronous Bandwidth Allocation

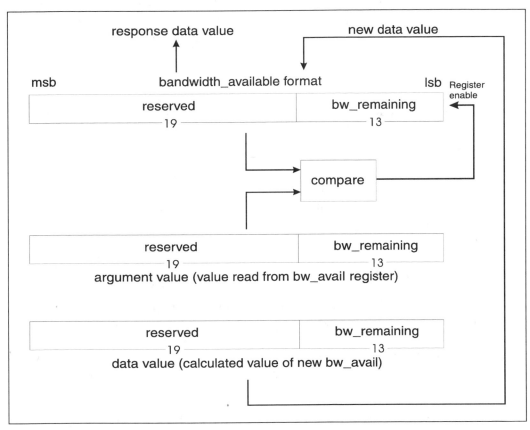

Bus Bandwidth Set-Aside for Asynchronous Transactions

The bus manager or isochronous resource manager (when the bus manger is not present) changes the bandwidth set-aside for asynchronous bandwidth by reducing the bw_remaining field using the same lock procedures described previously. This change is made when a SB_CONTROL request service is communicated to the active bus manager or isochronous resource manager. The value specified by this service defines the number of allocation units to be subtracted from the total available bus bandwidth. The serial bus specification defines a default set-aside of 25µs (1229 allocation units), leaving a 100µs of bandwidth for isochronous transfers (4915 allocation units).

Reallocation of Isochronous Resources

The attachment or detachment of a node causes a bus reset and the reallocation of resources that were assigned previously. Bus reset causes all bus traffic to cease and reconfiguration of the serial bus is performed again via the tree-ID and self-ID procedures. Following Self-ID the IRM will be known and previous owners of isochronous resources must immediately attempt to reallocate these prior resources.

Any node wishing to allocate new resources that were not allocated prior to the reset (e.g. a newly attached node), must delay any attempt to obtain the new resources for a minimum of 1000ms. This provides the opportunity for prior resources to be reallocated, thus promoting stability of the serial bus in the event of bus reset. If however, a given node fails to obtain the same prior resources, it must ensure that the corresponding talker node terminates the transfer. Note that the talker may be the prior owner of the resources or of another node.

Power Management

The isochronous resource manager in the absence of a bus manager node is also required to provide power management support. The form of power management required is restricted to applying power to nodes that do not automatically apply power to their link layer controllers during bus configuration. These nodes must receive a link-on packet to command them to apply power to the link. The isochronous resource manager must be able to perform this job. See "Power Management by IRM Node" on page 346 and Chapter 27, entitled "Power State Management," on page 459 for more information.

19 *Bus Manager*

The Previous Chapter

The previous chapter described the role of the isochronous resource manager: how it is identified and enabled, and how other nodes interact with it.

This Chapter

In this chapter, the bus manager function is described including topology map generation and access, speed map generation and access, and power management.

The Next Chapter

The next chapter discusses the bus management services that are used by the bus manager and isochronous resource manager to perform their bus management roles.

Overview

One node residing on the serial bus may be selected to provide serial bus services for the benefit of the community of all nodes residing on the bus. Whether bus management is performed and the extent to which it is performed varies depending on the capability of nodes residing on the bus. Several possibilities exist:

- Bus is fully managed — at least one node on the bus is bus manager capable, thereby providing complete bus management facilities.
- Bus is partially managed — no bus management capable node is present on the bus, but at least one node is isochronous resource manager capable. Partial bus management capability is performed by isochronous resources management capable nodes.
- Bus is unmanaged — none of the nodes residing on the bus is bus manager capable or isochronous resource manager capable.

The bus management services that may be provided include:

- publishing a topology map that can be accessed by other nodes.
- publishing a speed map that can be read to find the maximum speed for each cable segment that is attached between two nodes.
- enabling the cycle master.
- power management control.
- optimizing bus traffic.

The node that performs bus management duties may reside anywhere on the serial bus. It collects information during the self-identification sequence as each node broadcasts its self-ID packet. The bus manager node uses this information to build topology and speed maps that other nodes can access. More than one node may be a candidate for the role of bus manager and these nodes must also monitor self-ID packets in the event they are selected to handle the role of bus manager. Furthermore, any node wishing to access the topology or speed maps must also monitor the self-ID packets so it can determine which node will perform the role of bus manager, and knowing its physical ID it will be able to access the topology and speed maps.

Determining the Bus Manager

At the conclusion of the Self-ID stage of bus configuration, the isochronous resource manager will have been identified. The last node to send its self-ID packets with the "L" and "C" bits set (the last contender) wins the role of isochronous resource manager. An isochronous resource manager may optionally be bus manager capable. A bus manager capable node differentiates itself from isochronous resource manager only nodes by performing a locked compare and swap transaction to the BUS_MANAGER_ID register within the IRM. The first node that successfully updates the BUS_MANAGER_ID register with its own physical ID wins the role of bus manager.

Other nodes read the BUS_MANAGER_ID register to obtain the node ID of the bus manager. If the value in the register is 3Fh, then no bus manager has claimed the role.

Power Management

Some nodes may require bus power to operate. If bus power is available, it is supplied by one or more nodes. When nodes are attached they must have their PHY powered in order for the node to function. Other node components may also require bus power such as the link layer, node controller, and unit related hardware. Any node hardware other than the PHY and node controller must remain powered off until configuration completes. The PHY and node controller functionality must be powered so that the PHY can power up the rest of the node under direction from the bus manager or isochronous resource manager (in the absence of a bus manager node). The following discussion is based on the 1394-1995 specification. The 1394a supplement extends the definition of power management and is discussed in the next chapter.

Power Management by Bus Manager Node

The bus manager obtains power class information from each node when the PHY sends self-ID packets during bus configuration. A node may require bus power for its link and other unit hardware associated with the node. The bus manager, having monitored all self-ID packets, can calculate the total bus power sourced by nodes on the bus, as well as the total bus power required by nodes. Based on this information, the bus manager can determine if sufficient power is available to support all nodes requiring bus power. Obviously, two possibilities exist and the actions that the bus manager must take are:

- Power required exceeds power available — the bus manager must notify its application by reporting an insufficient cable power event to the link layer, which is passed to the application at the bus manager node. The actual bus manager service used is an SB_EVENT indication with the insufficient bus power parameter set. The application at the bus management node must be prepared to handle this situation. The application is responsible for determining the appropriate action. Selected nodes may be chosen to receive power (via a link-on packet), or all nodes requiring bus power may be left powered off and the user notified.
- Power required is equal to or less than power available — in this instance, all nodes that have inactive link layer are powered via the link-on packet. The application uses the SB_CONTROL service to cause the link-on packet to be transmitted.

Format of the link-on packet is shown in Figure 19-1. The two most significant bits (01b) of the packet identify it as a link-on packet. The next six bits specify the node address that this packet is targeting. When the PHY receives this packet it initiates and passes an SB_EVENT indication to the node controller, which, in turn, switches bus power to the link.

Figure 19-1: Format of the Link-On Packet Used to Apply Bus Power to a Node's Link Layer

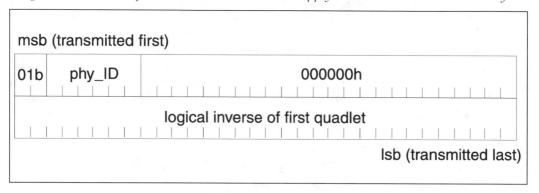

Power Management by IRM Node

The Isochronous Resource Manager (IRM) can provide a minimal level of power management by issuing link-on packets to these nodes that have an inactive link layer. The IRM recognizes those nodes that don't have their link layer powered by observing the self-ID packets that have the "L" bit cleared (0). Note that the IRM need not verify that sufficient power is available before issuing the link-on packet.

The Topology Map

Knowledge of the bus topology can be used to optimize serial bus performance. This can be accomplished by:

- Reconfiguring the topology to reduce the number of cable hops. The specification doesn't say how this should be accomplished, but user intervention is clearly required. One can envision an elaborate animated graphic to guide the user in reconfiguring the connections, or the entire issue may simply be ignored. We'll see!
- Reconfiguring the topology so that devices with the same speed capability are arranged adjacent to each other. Once again the user must assist.

All bus manager capable nodes capture self-ID packets as they are sent by each node during bus configuration. Once a node is selected as bus manager, it constructs a topology map and makes it available to all nodes. (The topology map format is shown in Figure 19-2 on page 347.) The bus manager must also perform consistency checks to ensure that the total number of ports connected to parents equals the number of ports connected to children. If the self-ID information received is inconsistent, then the length field must be cleared to zero and the topology error reported to the application via an SB_EVENT indication.

Figure 19-2: Topology Map Format

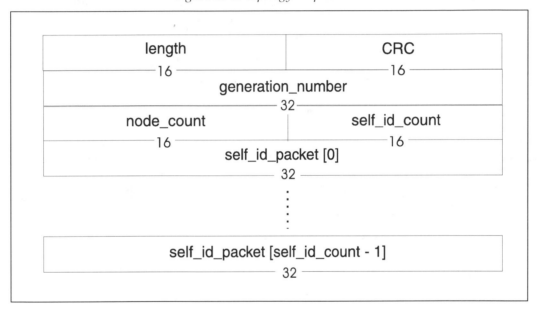

Accessing the Topology Map

An application associated with a given node that requires information from the topology map registers must perform the access using the following procedures:

1. Read the length field at offset 1000h within the initial units' address space of the bus manager node. (Location of the bus manager is found by reading the BUS_MANAGER_ID register located at the isochronous resource manager node.) If the field contains a value of zero, then the topology is invalid. Otherwise, the topology information can be read.
2. Read the quadlet entries of interest.

3. After obtaining the topology information, repeat the length field read a second time and compare it with the value read during step one. If the values are the same, then the quadlet entries read from the topology are accurate. Otherwise, the data read are invalid. In this event, the procedure may be retried.

Gap Count Optimization

Based on knowledge of the topology, the bus manager has the ability to broadcast a PHY configuration packet that sets the acknowledge gap value. The new value is based on the maximum number of cable hops that a transaction would traverse. The new gap count value is sent to all nodes via the PHY configuration packet, illustrated in Figure 19-3. When the "T" bit is set, the gap_cnt field contains a valid gap count that is used by all nodes to update their gap count.

Figure 19-3: Format of PHY Configuration Packet

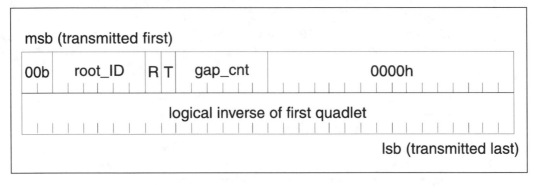

Gap count is calculated based on propagation delay across multiple cable segments. This ensures that when a transaction is being transferred between nodes, which are separated by multiple cable segments, that the round trip delay required for an acknowledge packet to be returned to the sender is shorter than the subaction gap timing. Otherwise, the node would detect the subaction gap and begin arbitration before the acknowledge packet has the opportunity to return.

Rather than calculating the gap count based on the number of cable hops, a ping packet can be sent to measure the actual propagation delay. The ping packet format is illustrated in Figure 19-4. The bus manager can transmit a ping packet and measure the amount of time that it takes for the target node to return data. The target node returns it self ID packet(s) upon receiving the ping packet.

Figure 19-4: Ping Packet Format

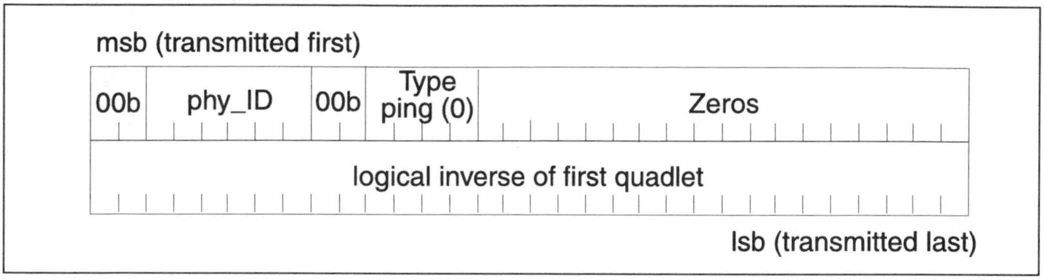

The Speed Map

Speed map information is used by nodes to determine the maximum transaction speed supported when performing transactions with a given node. Some PHYs in the path between two nodes may not support full speed packet transmission. Packets are blocked by repeaters so that nodes that do not support the transaction speed will not see the packet. Consequently, a node must know the maximum speed at which a transaction can be sent to a target node, or can use the base rate to ensure that the transaction will reach the destination. Figure 19-5 shows the speed map format.

Accessing the Speed Map

Applications wishing to access the speed map must use the following procedure:

1. Read the first quadlet of the speed map at offset 2000h within the initial units space of the bus manager node. If the length field contains zeros, the speed map is invalid. Otherwise, the entries are valid.
2. Read the speed map to obtain the speed information between two nodes. Each entry contains speed information between two nodes. The entry number (i) of interest is calculated as follows:

    $i=64 * m + n$ (where m and n are the node IDs of the two nodes of interest)

3. After reading the speed information, read the first quadlet again and compare it to the value read in step one. If they compare, the speed information is valid.

Figure 19-5: Speed Map Format

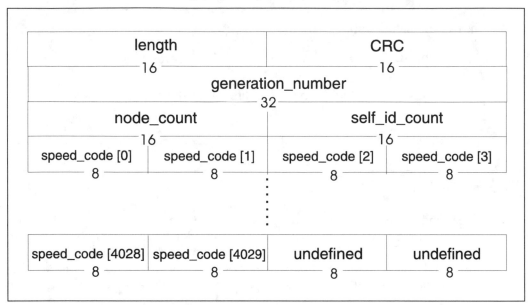

Bus Bandwidth Set-Aside

The bus manager also may update the BANDWIDTH_AVAILABLE register to reflect the 20% bus bandwidth reservation for asynchronous transactions.

20 Bus Management Services

The Previous Chapter

In the previous chapter, the bus manager function was described including topology map generation and access, speed map generation and access, and power management functions.

This Chapter

This chapter discusses the bus management services that are used by the bus manager and isochronous resource manager to perform their bus management roles.

The Next Chapter

The next chapter discusses the CSR registers defined by the ISO/IEC 13213 specification with particular focus on the registers that are required by the 1394-1995 and 1394a specifications.

Overview

A variety of bus management activities must be performed by the isochronous resource manager and the bus manager nodes as described in the two previous chapters. The local application at the node must be designed to support bus management activities if it is bus manager or isochronous manager capable. Bus management services are defined by the specification which provides the interface between the application and the bus management layer. The bus management layer passes messages and status information to the application regarding the state of the bus or management layer itself. The application also uses the interface to direct the bus management layer to take action regarding certain bus management issues. Figure 20-1 on page 352 illustrates the relationship between the bus management layer and the rest of the node.

Figure 20-1: Relationship Between Bus Management Layer and the Rest of the Node

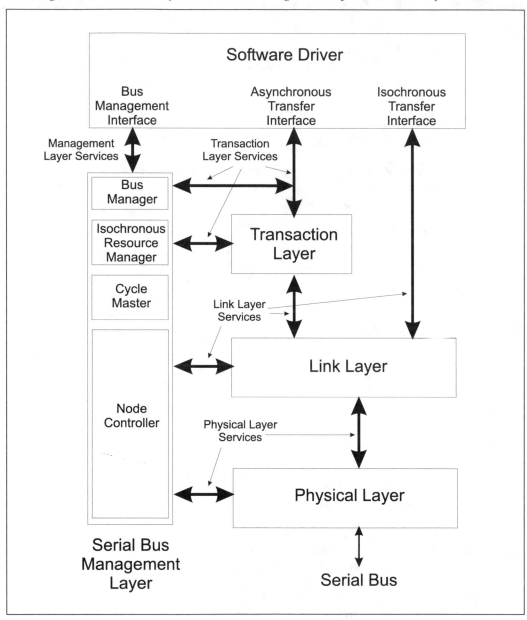

Three services are defined for the serial bus management layer:

- Serial Bus control request (SB_CONTROL.request)
- Serial Bus control confirmation (SB_CONTROL.confirmation)
- Serial Bus event indication (SB_EVENT.indication)

The Serial Bus control services are used by the application to direct the bus management layer to take some action (the request) and once the bus management layer has performed the requested operation's verification is sent back to the application (the confirmation). Status information is passed to the application by the bus management layer using the Serial Bus event indication. Each service is defined in the following sections.

Serial Bus Control Requests

The Serial Bus control request service can be used not only to specify that some action be taken related to serial bus management but also to request status information. The following list specifies the actions that can be requested by an application using the Serial Bus control request:

- Reset the bus
- Initialize the node
- Transmit a Link-on packet
- Present Status
- Transmit a PHY configuration packet

Each action is detailed below.

Bus Reset Control Request

When this request is issued by the application layer, the PHY layer is directed to signal a bus reset and initialize itself. The reset request also directs the link and transaction layer to discard all pending transactions and subactions.

The bandwidth set-aside for isochronous transactions is also passed by the bus manager application to specify the amount of bus bandwidth that should be reserved for asynchronous transactions. The bus manager application (or isochronous resource manager if no bus manager exists on the bus) specifies the number of allocation units to be subtracted from the bus BANDWIDTH_AVAILABLE register that resides within the link layer of the isochronous resource manager. The bus manager must then update the

BANDWIDTH_AVAILABLE register to reflect the bandwidth that remains for isochronous transfers. Note that this requires generation of a lock compare and swap transaction targeting the BANDWIDTH_AVAILABLE register.

Initialize Control Request

The initialize control request is used to reinitialize the node and prepare it to transmit and receive packets. Specifically, this request directs the link and transaction layers to discard all pending transactions and subactions and enable the link to receive packets and also enable the transaction layer to accept transaction requests from the application.

Link-On Control Request

This request is made only by the bus manager (required) or isochronous resource manager (optional) applications. This request directs the PHY to generate a Link-on packet to notify the target node to attempt the application of power to its link layer controller. This service also passes the physical ID of the node to whichever power is to be applied.

Present Status

This request is issued to request status information be returned to the application from the bus management layer. The SB_CONTROL.confirmation returns the status information as listed on "Serial Bus Control Confirmations" on page 356.

PHY Configuration Request

The bus manager or isochronous resource manager node are the only nodes that issue the PHY configuration request. This request causes the generation of a PHY configuration packet or one of the extended PHY packets.

Set Force Root and Set Gap Count

This broadcast packet provides the ability to change the gap count variable and to force the Root Hold Off (RHB) in the specified PHY, while forcing all other nodes to clear the RHB. The parameters passed with this request include:

- Set force root — this flag when set indicates that the "physical ID" parameter is valid and that the "R" bit in the PHY configuration packet must be set.
- Physical ID — This parameter specifies the target node that must set its force root bit, making it the root following the next bus reset. This parameter is valid if the "set force root" parameter is set.
- Set gap count — this parameter when set indicates that the gap count field contains a valid gap count value and that the "T" bit in the PHY configuration packet must be set.
- Gap count — this parameter specifies the value of the gap count field that will be sent via the PHY configuration packet. This parameter is valid when the "set gap count" parameter is set.

Extended PHY Packets

The 1394a supplement defines extended PHY packets that can be generated via the PHY configuration request. The extended packets use the PHY configuration packet format with the gap_count field specifying the extended packet type. When the PHY configuration request is issued with the "set force" and "set gap count" parameters both cleared, the gap count parameter specifies the extended packet type. Depending on the extended packet type, the physical ID parameter may define extended packet specific information. (See Chapter 10 for details regarding extended PHY packets. Parameter data are specified below for extended PHY configuration packet generation.

- Set force root — this parameter must be cleared.
- Set gap count — this parameter must be cleared.
- Gap count — this parameter defines one of the following types of extended PHY packets:
    - Ping packet
    - Remote access packet
    - Remote reply packet
    - Remote command packet
    - Remote confirmation packet
    - Resume packet
- Physical ID — physical ID of the target node.

Serial Bus Control Confirmations

This service returns a response that reports whether the previous Serial Bus control request has succeeded or failed. Additionally, this service returns a variety of status information in response to the "present status" request as listed below:

- Bandwidth set-aside — the Serial Bus control confirmation returns the actual amount of bandwidth set-aside that the bus manager was able to subtract from the BANDWIDTH_AVAILABLE register. This parameter is only valid for the bus manager or isochronous resource manager node.
- Bus manager ID — contains the 6-bit physical ID of the bus manager node. If no bus manager has been selected the physical ID value is 3Fh. This parameter is only valid for the bus manager or isochronous resource manager node.
- Cycle master ID — this parameter contains the physical ID of the node that is performing the role of cycle master. If no cycle master is active, then a value of 3Fh is returned. This parameter is only valid for the bus manager or isochronous resource manager node.
- Force Root — this parameter specifies the state of the root hold off bit (RHB) within the local PHY.
- Gap count — provides the current value of the local PHY's gap_count variable.
- Isochronous resource manager — contains the physical ID of the isochronous resource manager node. If no isochronous resource manager is active, then the value returned will be 3Fh. This parameter is only valid for the bus manager or isochronous resource manager node.
- Physical ID — this parameter contains the physical ID of this node.
- Root ID — provides the physical ID of the root node. If the root node is not capable of performing the role of cycle master or if its capable but not active, then a value of 3Fh is returned. This parameter is different from the cycle master ID parameter in that this parameter is valid for nodes other than the bus manager and isochronous resource manager.

Chapter 20: Bus Management Services

Serial Bus Event Indication

This service provides a method of reporting specific node and bus events, to the local application. The following events are reported via this service:

- Bus occupancy violation detected — the maximum bus occupancy (MAX_BUS_OCCUPANCY) timing parameter is defined by 1394-1995 but is changed to MAX_DATA_TIME by the 1394a supplement. The relevant value is used by this node to determine if a violation of the timing has occurred.
- Bus reset start — indicates that a bus reset has started.
- Bus reset complete — indicates that bus configuration has completed (i.e. all nodes have completed reset, tree ID, and self ID). This condition is detected when the first subaction gap is detected after bus reset. The following parameters are reported when this event is detected:
    - Bandwidth set-aside
    - Bus manager ID
    - Configuration time-out
    - Cycle master ID
    - Gap count
    - Gap count error
    - Insufficient cable power
    - Isochronous resource manger ID
    - Physical ID of this node
    - Root ID
    - Self ID error
    - Topology error

- Cycle too long — this parameter reports that the last isochronous transaction was too long and is reported only by the bus manager or isochronous resource manager.
- Cable power fail — this parameter indicates that cable power has failed (i.e. dropped below 7.5vdc at this node.
- Duplicate channel detected — indicates that an isochronous packet just received has the same channel number that is used by this node for transmitting isochronous packets.
- Header CRC error detected — indicates that a primary packet just received incurred a CRC error in the packet header.
- Request data error — indicates that an ack_data_error has been returned to indicate that a data error was detected within the request packet just received.

- Response acknowledge missing — this node did not receive an acknowledge packet following transmission of a response packet (i.e. an acknowledge time-out was detected).
- Response data error — indicates that an ack_data_error has been received to reflect that a data error was detected within the response packet transferred previously.
- Response format error — indicates that an ack_type_error has been received reflecting that a type error was detected within a response packet sent previously.
- Response retry failed — indicates that this node failed to successfully transfer a response prior to the retry limit interval elapsing or prior to the retry count expiring.
- Unexpected channel detected — this optional parameter is available only for the isochronous resource manager and indicates that a channel number has been used that has not been allocated via the channels_available register.
- Unknown transaction code detected — indicates that the primary packet received by this node contained a transaction code that is not supported by this node.
- Unsolicited response — indicates that this node was targeted with a response packet for which no request is pending. A valid response is verified by comparing the transaction label and destination address of the response to the label and address of a pending request.

Part Five

Registers & ROM

21 *CSR Architecture*

The Previous Chapter

The previous chapter discussed the bus management services that are used by the bus manager and isochronous resource manager to perform their bus management roles.

This Chapter

This chapter discusses the CSR registers defined by the ISO/IEC 13213 specification with particular focus on the registers that are required by the 1394 specification.

The Next Chapter

The following chapter details the contents of configuration ROM required by the ISO/IEC 13213 specification. The serial bus also defines ROM entries that are required by some nodes, depending on the capabilities.

Overview

Firewire is based on the ISO/IEC 13213 specification, commonly referred to as the Control and Status Registers (CSR) Architecture for microcomputer buses. This specification defines a common set of core features that can be implemented by a variety of buses that adhere to this standard. A group of core registers support functions common to CSR architecture buses and provide standardized offset locations within the initial register address space where these registers can be accessed. The start address location of the initial register space is at offset FFFF F000 0000h (the top 256MB block of address space) from the beginning of the node's address space as illustrated in Figure 21-1 on page 362. Note that the CSR architecture also defines configuration ROM, which is discussed in the following chapter.

FireWire System Architecture

The IEEE 1394 specification defines the subset of CSR architecture features that must be supported for serial bus compliance, and also defines specific serial bus dependent extensions to the CSRs.

Figure 21-1: Location of CSRs Within the Node's Address Space

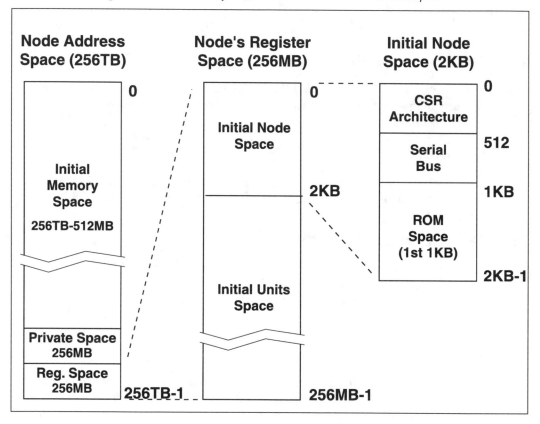

Core Registers

Table 21-1 on page 363 lists the core CSR registers defined by the CSR architecture and specifies the location of the serial bus dependent registers. The CSR architecture registers required in serial bus nodes are shaded in Table 21-1. The lighter shaded entry indicates that the register is conditionally required. The definition of each register and related register fields are specified in the following sections.

Table 21-1: Core CSR Locations and Definition

Offset (h)	Register Name	Description
000	STATE_CLEAR	State & control information
004	STATE_SET	Sets STATE_CLEAR bits
008	NODE_IDS	Specifies 16-bit node ID value
00C	RESET_START	Resets state of node
010-014	INDIRECT_ADDRESS, INDIRECT_DATA	Indirectly access ROMs > 1KB
018-01C	SPLIT_TIMEOUT_HI, SPLIT_TIMEOUT_LO	Split-request timeout
020-02C	ARGUMENT_HI, ARGUMENT_LO, TEST_START, TEST_STATUS	Optional diagnostic-test interface
030-04C	UNITS_BASE, UNITS_BOUND, MEMORY_BASE, MEMORY_BOUND	Never implemented
050-054	INTERRUPT_TARGET, INTERRUPT_MASK	Optional broadcast/nodecast interrupt
058-07C	CLOCK_VALUE, CLOCK_TICK_PERIOD, CLOCK_STROBE_ARRIVED, CLOCK_INFO	Synchronized time-of-day value and control
080-0FC	MESSAGE_REQUEST, MESSAGE_RESPONSE	Optional message passing register
100-17C	RESERVED	Reserved for CSR architecture
180-1FC	ERROR_LOG_BUFFER	Reserved for Serial Bus
200-3FC	SERIAL BUS DEPENDENT	See Table 21-5 on page 376

	Required
	Conditionally Required

Effect of Reset on the CSRs

Three types of Reset are supported by the serial bus:

- Power reset—defined by the CSR architecture, it occurs when power is applied to the link, PHY, and bus management functions. This causes all CSR registers to return to their initial values. The PHY layer is also reset and a bus reset is initiated.
- Command reset—defined by the CSR architecture and caused by a write to the RESET_START register. This reset does not result in the PHY being reset nor does it cause a bus reset.
- Bus reset—defined by the IEEE 1394 specification and caused by the addition or removal of a node or by a change in the powered state of the PHY layer of a node.
- Software initiated bus reset—a bus reset caused by the local node application writing to either the IBR (initiated bus reset) or ISBR (initiated short bus reset) bit in the PHY register space.

A power reset forces all CSR registers to the initial values. When a command or bus reset occurs, CSR registers are sometimes also returned to their initial values, while in other instances particular fields may remain unchanged as discussed in the following sections.

State Register (State_Clear & State_Set)

The STATE register is defined by the CSR architecture and provides support for status and control features. Although these registers are defined as optional within the CSR architecture specification, they are required by the serial bus specification. The STATE_CLEAR register is used to clear state bits, while the STATE_SET register provides a way to set state bits.

The STATE register format is illustrated in Figure 21-2, and the definition and usage of each field is specified in Table 21-2 on page 365. Note also that Figure 21-2 on page 365 defines the values of the individual state bits following initialization and reset, and shows the read values returned and the effects of writes on each field. The bus_dependent field is defined by the IEEE 1394 specification. Its format is illustrated in Figure 21-3 on page 367 and field definitions are listed in Table 21-3 on page 368.

State_Clear Register

Writing a value of one to a writable bit within the STATE_CLEAR register location forces that bit to be cleared to zero. Writing a zero to a bit position has no effect on the current value. This is implemented by ANDing the complement of the write-data value to the current state-bit value.

Figure 21-2: Format of the STATE Register

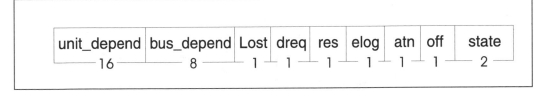

Table 21-2: Field Definitions for Register

Field Name	Description
unit_dependent	Bits within this field are intended for use by the unit architecture. Definition of these bits, if defined, are provided by a unit architecture specification.
bus_dependent	These bits are defined by the appropriate bus standard. The IEEE 1394 specification defines usage of these bits. See Figure 21-3 on page 367 and Table 21-3 on page 368 for details.
lost	This bit must be implemented by serial bus nodes. This bit is set when a power reset occurs or the node has transitioned to the dead state (due to an error). This bit is not directly affected by a bus reset. Software is expected to clear the lost bit after the node has been initialized and the I/O driver has been notified of the reset or a fatal error in the event of a node transition to the dead state.
dreq	Dreq must be implemented by serial bus nodes that are capable of initiating transaction requests. The dreq (disable request) bit is intended to be set by software to disable request generation from unreliable nodes. Nodes may provide a "back door" access to this bit so that the bit may be cleared by special-purpose processors (e.g. via a remote diagnostic interface). Nodes that cannot initiate transaction requests but can respond to such requests must have this bit permanently set (1).
res	Reserved

Table 21-2: Field Definitions for Register (Continued)

Field Name	Description
elog	Required by nodes that incorporate error logging capability. This status bit is set by node hardware when the node's error log has been updated, thereby providing a mechanism to notify software when an error has been detected. Software is expected to clear this bit after saving the contents of the error log. This bit is unaffected by bus reset.
atn	Defined as reserved by the 1394 specification.
off	Defined as reserved by the 1394 specification.
state	Required to support initializing, testing, and dead node states. This read only field reflects the state of the node as follows: 00 = Running (initialization complete, node running) 01 = Initializing (initialization reset & test in progress) 10 = Testing in progress (TEST_START invoked) 11 = Fatal error (node is inoperable)

	Required
	Conditionally Required

State_Set Register

Software can set writeable bits within the STATE register by writing a one to the corresponding bit in the STATE_SET register location.

The STATE_SET register is required to support the STATE register that must be implemented by serial bus nodes. The format of the STATE_SET register is identical to the STATE_CLEAR register. (Figure 21-2 on page 365.) Setting bits to one in the STATE_SET register cause the corresponding state bits in the STATE register to be set to 1, providing that the bit is writeable. Writing zeros to bit positions has no impact on the STATE register since the values written to the STATE_SET register are ORed with the current values in the STATE register.

Bus Depend Field

The 1394-1995 serial bus specification defines three bits with the bus_depend field of the STATE register. Figure 21-3 illustrates the format of the bus_depend field while Table 21-3 on page 368 defines the purpose and usage of the three bits. A fourth bit (abdicate) has been added by the 1394a supplement as shown in Figure 21-3 on page 367.

Figure 21-3: Format of the Bus_Dependent Field within the STATE Register

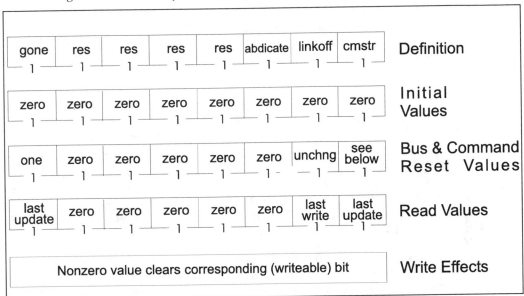

Cycle Master Enable. When a bus reset occurs all nodes participate in the bus configuration process. Following the tree ID process one node will have been designated as the root. All nodes other than the root must clear their cmstr bits to zero. The root must retain the value of cmstr that existed prior to the bus reset. In this way, when a bus reset occurs the previous root node can remain enabled across a bus reset, providing it is designed as the root node again. If this node is no longer the root following tree ID it must immediately clear its cmstr bit.

Table 21-3: Definition of the Bits within the Bus_Depend Field of the STATE Register

Field Name	Description
gone	The gone bit must be set to a one when a power, bus, or command reset occurs. A node that has its gone bit set must not transmit transaction requests. The gone bit should be cleared by software or other nodes during initialization, but only after being ready to receive requests from the node. A unit that automatically resumes operation after a bus reset may clear its own gone bit before accessing the bus. Multi-unit nodes may have individual units that either initialize other nodes or that are initialized by other nodes, resulting in the units being reactivated at different times. In such instances, the specification states that, "multi-unit nodes are expected to have unit-dependent gone bits."
linkoff	A node that draws power from the bus must implement the linkoff bit. When the linkoff bit is cleared (zero) the link layer is active and when set it is powered off. Writing a one to the STATE_SET register causes the linkoff bit to be set. The link-on packet re-applies power to the link-layer chip.
cmstr	Cycle master capable nodes must implement the cmstr bit. A value of one establishes this node as the cycle master, while a zero disables cycle master operation. This bit may only be changed by the bus manager or the isochronous resource manager if no bus manager node exists. The following rules apply: • If a node is not the root, it must ignore any attempt to set the cmstr bit to a one. • Prior to either the bus manager or isochronous resource manager setting the cmstr bit to a one, it must set the Force_Root variable to a one. Setting the Force_Root is done either via the PHY Configuration packet or via the PHY Control request (if the cycle master and bus manager roles are performed by the same node).

	Required
	Conditionally Required

Abdicate. This bit has been added to support the orderly exchange of the bus manager role between two nodes. Consequently, this bit is only required of bus manager capable nodes. The procedure to become the bus manager is as follows:

1. Another node, not currently the bus manager, may wish to be come the bus manager and must set its abdicate bit to indicate its desire.
2. The candidate bus manager initiates a bus reset .
3. Following cable configuration, bus manager capable nodes attempt to become bus manager by performing a lock compare and swap to the BUS_MANAGER_ID register as discussed under the heading "Bus_Manager_ID Register" on page 383. However, this candidate bus manager is not required to wait for 125ms (as are other candidates) before attempting the lock operation. Since it performs the lock transaction first it should win the role of bus manager.

If the candidate bus manager fails to win the role, it can then transmit a PHY configuration packet to specify itself as the root node and repeat steps 2 and 3.

Node_IDS Register

The NODE_IDS register contains the bus_ID and physical_ID values and a serial bus_dependent field. This required register is illustrated in Figure 21-4 on page 370 and Table 21-4 on page 370 defines each field.

Note that the local bus is always mapped to bus address 1023; thus, a bus_id value of all ones specifies this bus as the target as illustrated in Figure 21-5 on page 372. If the bus_id values are anything other than all ones, then another CSR bus is being targeted.

Figure 21-4: NODE_IDS Register Format

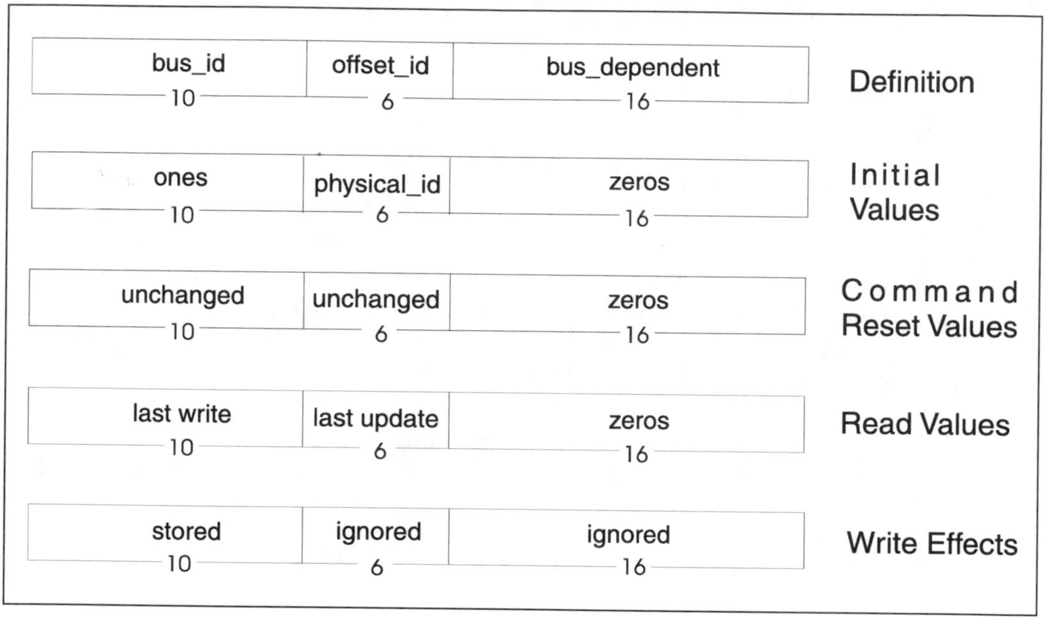

bus_id 10	offset_id 6	bus_dependent 16	Definition
ones 10	physical_id 6	zeros 16	Initial Values
unchanged 10	unchanged 6	zeros 16	Command Reset Values
last write 10	last update 6	zeros 16	Read Values
stored 10	ignored 6	ignored 16	Write Effects

Table 21-4: Definition of the Fields within the NODE_IDS Register

Field Name	Description
bus_id	The bus_id value represents the upper 10 bits of the 64-bit fixed address used by the serial bus. The bus_id field is set to all ones after a power reset, resulting in a bus address of 1023. By default a serial bus is mapped as bus 1023 as illustrated in Figure 21-5 on page 372. In a multi-bus environment the bus_id field can be updated by enumeration software to ensure unique addresses are implemented for nodes residing on different buses. This permits bridge nodes to differentiate node addresses residing on different buses in systems that implement multi-bus configurations.

Table 21-4: Definition of the Fields within the NODE_IDS Register (Continued)

Field Name	Description
offset_id	This 6-bit field is automatically updated during initialization when a unique physical ID is assigned to this node. The physical ID defines the node number that provides a unique addressable range of address space for this node. Refer to Figure 21-5 on page 372. Writes to the offset_id field are ignored.
bus_dependent	The read-only bus_dependent field is reserved, and the serial bus specification does not define its intended use.

Figure 21-5: Bus_id and Offset_id Fields Define the Address Space Allocated to a Given Serial Bus and Node.

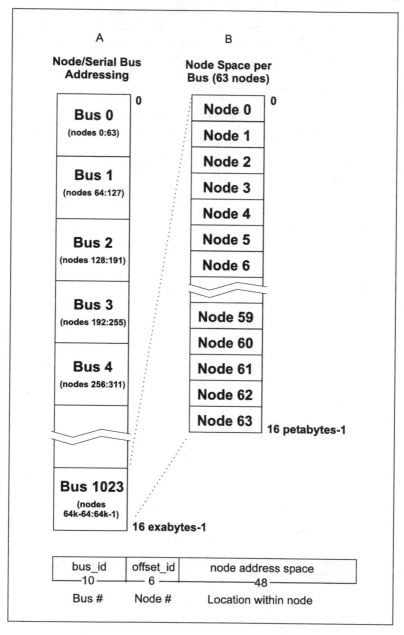

Reset_Start Register

Figure 21-6 on page 373 illustrates the format of the RESET_START register. Any write to the RESET_START register causes a command reset. Command reset initializes a node to its primary state and may optionally invoke an initialization test, depending on the state of the no test (nt) bit. The "e" value specified in the write effects of Figure 21-6 means that a write to this bit has an effect on the node (In this case, whether a test will be performed). Other CSR registers may also be affected by a command reset. The description of each register includes any effects caused by a command reset.

Figure 21-6: Format of RESET_START Register

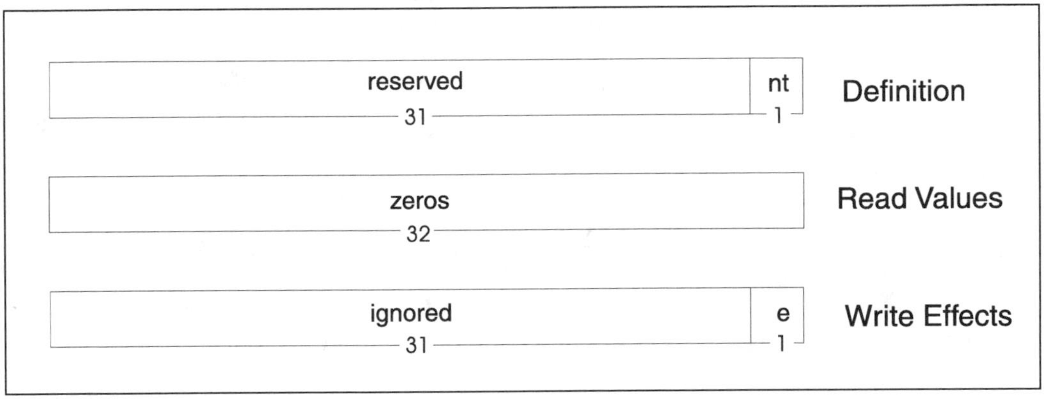

| reserved | nt | Definition |
| 31 | 1 | |

| zeros | Read Values |
| 32 | |

| ignored | e | Write Effects |
| 31 | 1 | |

Indirect_Address and Indirect_Data Registers

These registers are designated as reserved by the serial bus since the CSR-defined indirect addressing model is not used. All accesses to configuration ROM must be made by directly reading from the initial node space. Note that a ROM may require more than the 1KB of address space defined, in which case it may extend into the initial unit's address space.

Split_Timeout Register

The format of the SPLIT_TIMEOUT register is illustrated in Figure 21-7 on page 374. It must be implemented by any node that is transaction capable. A node is transaction capable if it either sends or receives transactions. Some nodes may only be capable of repeating serial bus traffic and are never the recipients of normal transaction traffic.

This register sets the default timeout value that is used to detect time-out errors during split transactions. Specifically, this register defines the maximum time that a node is given to return a response subaction. In the event of a split time-out error, the requester should terminate the transaction by reporting a response_timeout to the application.

The high portion of the register defines integers of a second; however, the serial bus specification defines only the three least-significant bits of this register, which results in a maximum of 8 second timeout. The lower portion of the register defines fractions of a second with a nominal resolution of 125µs, by using the 13 most significant bits. Note that the fractional value is in units of 1/8000 second versus the 1/8192 second defined by the CSR architecture.

Figure 21-7: Format of the SPLIT_TIMEOUT Register

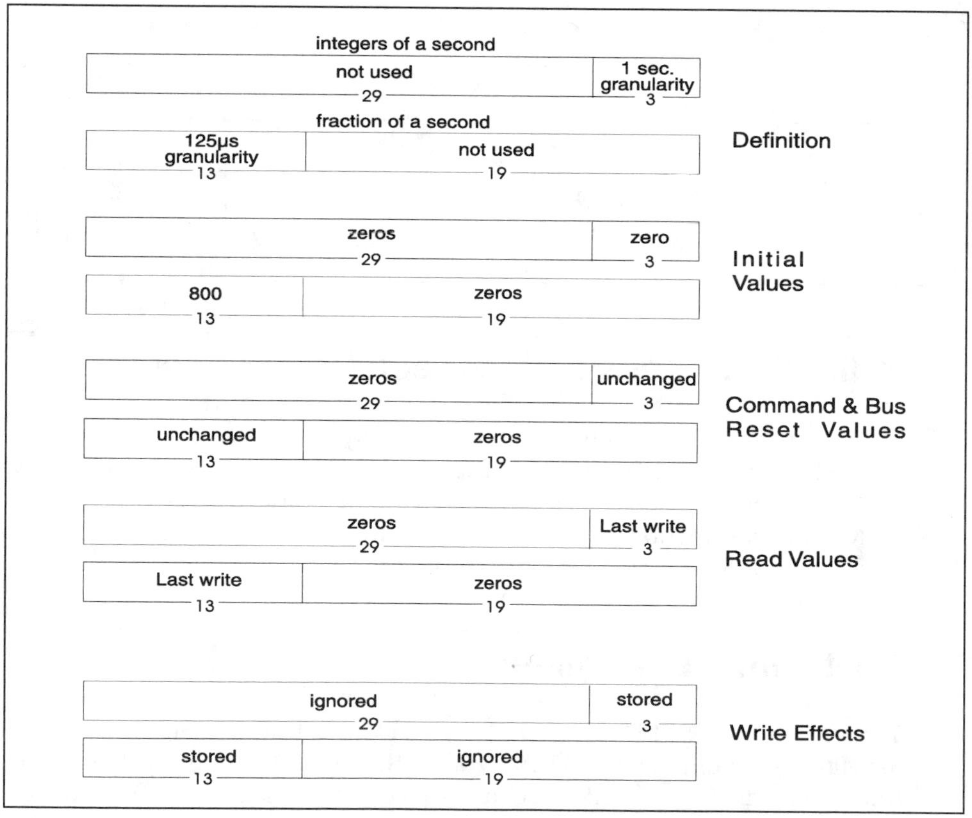

Argument, Test_Start, and Test_Status Registers

The ARGUMENT, TEST_START, and TEST_STATUS registers are optional registers used to control built-in testing capabilities. Details regarding the implementation of these registers can be found in the CSR specification.

Units_Base, Units_Bound, Memory_Base, and Memory_Bound Registers

These registers are not used by the serial bus since the addressing model is based on 64-bit fixed addressing. These registers only have meaning when performing 32- and 64-bit extended addressing.

Interrupt_Target and Interrupt_Mask Registers

These optional registers may be implemented to provide interrupt broadcast to all units implemented within a single node, referred to as a nodecast. Interrupt broadcasts are defined by the CSR architecture and can be implemented by serial bus nodes. Each bit in the INTERRUPT_TARGET register corresponds to an interrupt event, permitting up to 32 different interrupt events to be specified. The highest priority event is assigned to the most significant bit of this register and the lowest priority event to the least significant bit. If fewer than 32 interrupt events are defined, the events must correspond to the lower portion of the register with the most significant bit being the highest priority. Interrupt events are node dependent.

Particular interrupt events are broadcast to all units within the node by writing a one to the bit that corresponds to the selected event. The INTERRUPT_MASK register masks or passes the selected events by ANDing the write data being written to the INTERRUPT_TARGET register with the bits in the mask register.

Clock_Value, Clock_Tick_Period, Clock_Strobe_Arrived, and Clock_Info Registers

These clock registers are optional and typically are not implemented in a serial bus solution because the serial bus specific CYCLE_TIME register provides nearly equivalent functionality. (See page 377.)

Message_Request & Message_Response Registers

The optional MESSAGE_REQUEST and MESSAGE_RESPONSE registers provide nodes with a mechanism for broadcasting messages to all nodes on the bus or to all units within a node.

Serial Bus Dependent Registers

The CSR architecture reserves a portion of the node's initial address space for bus-dependent use. This address space is defined by the serial bus specification as defined in Table 21-5. These registers are mapped from offset 200h to 3FCh.

Table 21-5: Serial Bus Dependent CSR Register Locations and Definition

Offset (h)	Register Name	Description
200	CYCLE_TIME	Used by nodes that support isochronous transfers to maintain cycle time for isochronous transfer.
204	BUS_TIME	Required by cycle-master capable nodes to keep track of bus time.
208	POWER_FAIL_IMMINENT	Used to notify serial bus nodes that power is about to fail.
20C	POWER_SOURCE	Used in conjunction with the POWER_FAIL_IMMINENT to validate a power failure warning.
210	BUSY_TIMEOUT	Used by nodes that support transaction retry protocol.

Table 21-5: Serial Bus Dependent CSR Register Locations and Definition (Continued)

Offset (h)	Register Name	Description
214-217	Not used	Reserved
218	FAIRNESS_BUDGET	Defines the number of additional arbitration requests that can be made by a node during a single fairness interval.
21C	BUS_MANAGER_ID	Provides the physical ID of the bus manager node.
220	BANDWIDTH_AVAILABLE	Used to allocate and deallocate isochronous bus bandwidth.
224-228	CHANNELS_AVAILABLE	Used to allocate and deallocate isochronous channels.
22C	MAINT_CONTROL	Supports diagnosis and verification of error detection logic by forcing errors.
230	MAINT_UTILITY	Readable/writeable register used for debug.
234-3FC	Not used	Reserved

Cycle_Time & Bus_Time Registers

Isochronous capable nodes must implement the CYCLE_TIME and BUS_TIME registers. Writes to these registers initialize the time value using the write data value. The bus manager node or the isochronous resource manager (of bus manager is absent) is responsible for initializing the timing value. The register is then updated based on a 24.576 MHz clock. The timing value is used to track the 125µs bus timing intervals and to synchronize all isochronous nodes at the beginning of each isochronous cycle, which occurs at nominal 125µs intervals.

Figure 21-8 illustrates the format of the CYCLE_TIME and BUS_TIME registers, and the relationship between them. The CYCLE_TIME register contains three counters that are incremented by a 24.576MHz clock. Each counter is accessible as a field within the CYCLE_TIME register as follows:

- cycle_offset field (12-bits) wraps to zero after count 3071 (125µs intervals) and increments the cycle_count field.
- cycle_count field (13-bits) counts from zero to 7999d before wrapping to zero and carrying to the second_count field at 1 sec. intervals.
- second_count field (7-bits) wraps to zero after counting to all ones (127) and increments the second_count_hi field of the BUS_TIME register. Note that the CYCLE_TIME register's second_count field is aliased to the BUS_TIME register's second_count_lo field.

The BUS_TIME register is initialized via a broadcast write operation by the bus manager or, in the bus manager's absence, the isochronous resource manager. Contents of the CYCLE_TIME register are delivered at the beginning of each isochronous cycle within the cycle start packet. The cycle start packet is illustrated in Figure 21-9, with the CYCLE_TIME register contents highlighted.

Figure 21-8: Format and Relationship Between CYCLE_TIME & BUS_TIME Registers

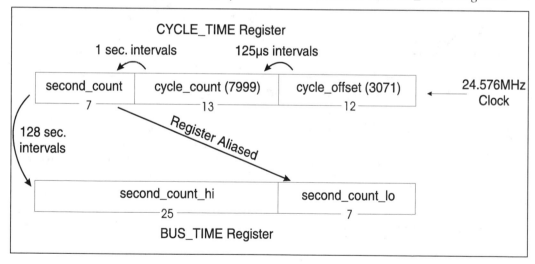

Figure 21-9: Contents of Cycle Start Packet

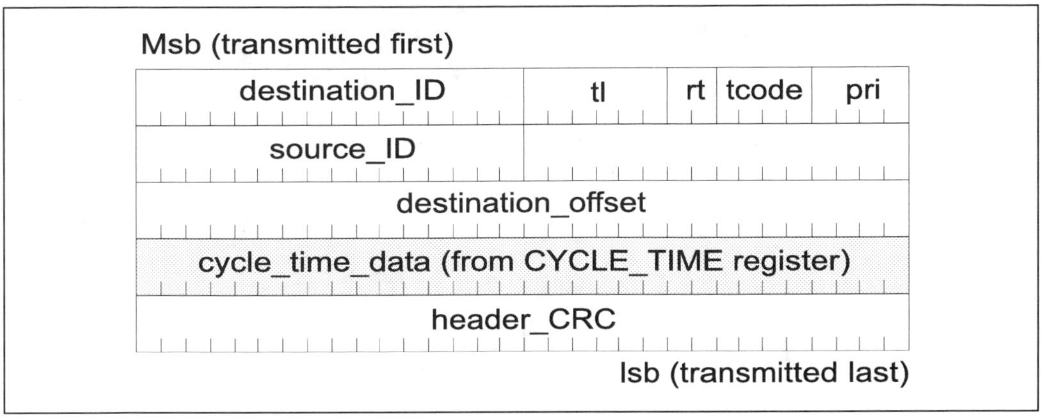

Msb (transmitted first)				
destination_ID	tl	rt	tcode	pri
source_ID				
destination_offset				
cycle_time_data (from CYCLE_TIME register)				
header_CRC				
				lsb (transmitted last)

Details regarding the initial states, effects of reset, reads, and writes are defined for both the CYCLE_TIME and BUS_TIME registers in Figure 21-10 on page 379 and Figure 21-11 on page 380, respectively. Note that these values in these registers are unaffected by any form of reset.

Figure 21-10: Actions and Their Effects on the CYCLE_TIME Register

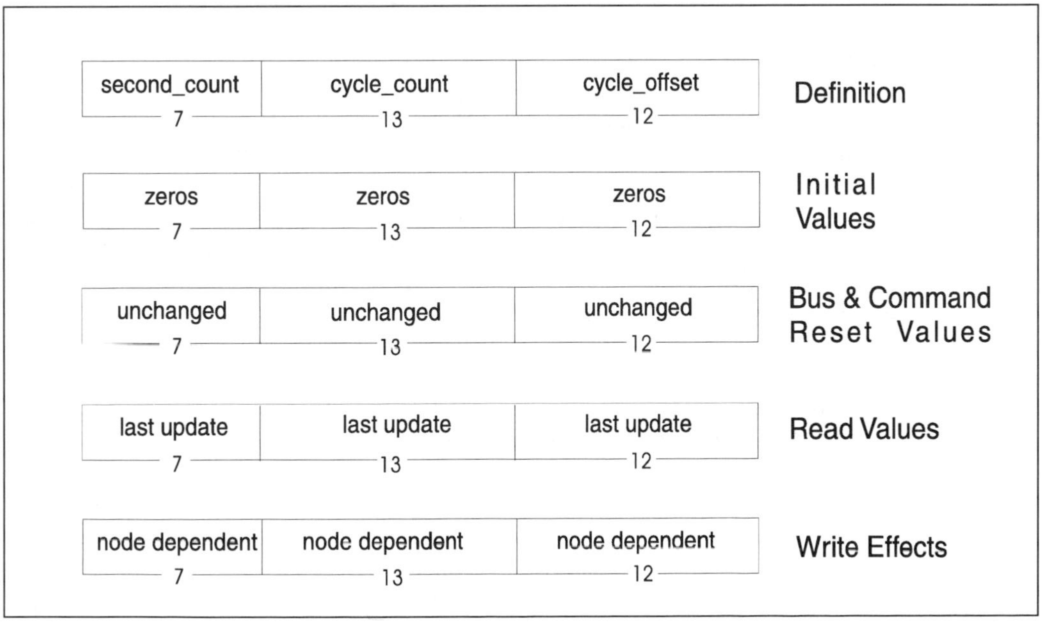

second_count 7	cycle_count 13	cycle_offset 12	Definition
zeros 7	zeros 13	zeros 12	Initial Values
unchanged 7	unchanged 13	unchanged 12	Bus & Command Reset Values
last update 7	last update 13	last update 12	Read Values
node dependent 7	node dependent 13	node dependent 12	Write Effects

Figure 21-11: Actions and Their Effects on the BUS_TIME Register

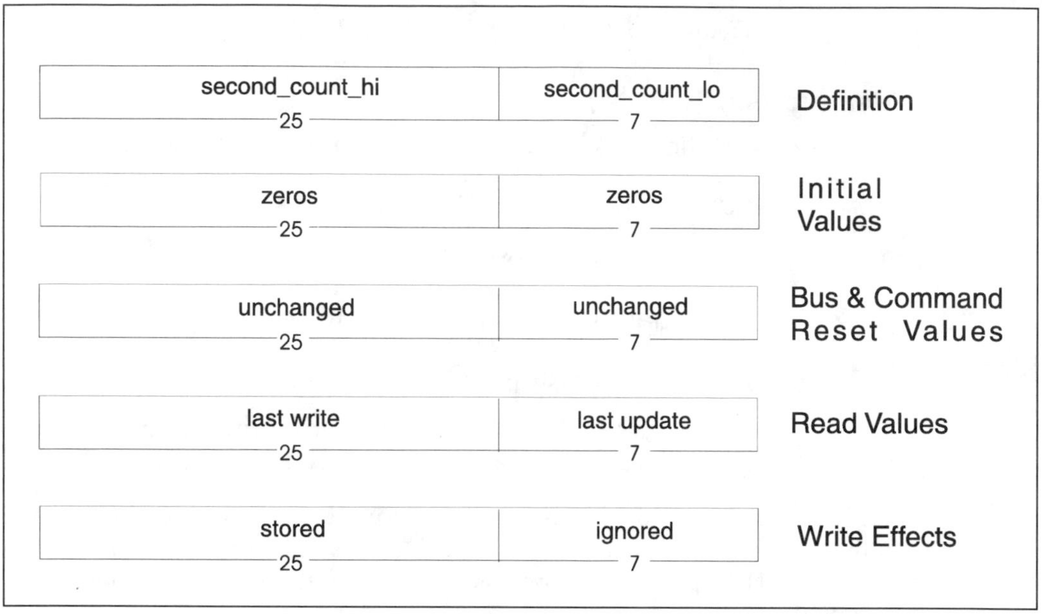

second_count_hi —— 25 ——	second_count_lo —— 7 ——	Definition
zeros —— 25 ——	zeros —— 7 ——	Initial Values
unchanged —— 25 ——	unchanged —— 7 ——	Bus & Command Reset Values
last write —— 25 ——	last update —— 7 ——	Read Values
stored —— 25 ——	ignored —— 7 ——	Write Effects

Power_Fail_Imminent & Power_Source Registers

The POWER_FAIL_IMMINENT register is optional and typically not used in the cable environment. If this register is implemented, then the POWER_SOURCE register must also be implemented. These registers provide the capability of notifying nodes that a power failure is about to occur. If this support exists, a particular node residing on the bus will have the ability to monitor the power supply and, upon detecting an imminent failure, broadcast a write to the POWER_FAIL_IMMINENT register using a node address of 3Fh (a broadcast address). Data written to the register updates the following fields (also see Figure 21-12 on page 381):

- pfi_source field — Node ID of node generating the power failure imminent (pfi) message. This value is used to verify that the write to this register originated from the power monitoring node by comparing pfi_source to the power_source field of the POWER_SOURCE register (see Figure 21-13 on page 381). If the values do not match, the write data must be ignored.
- pfi_delay field — Amount of time remaining before power is expected to go out of regulation. This value is reported in hundredths of milliseconds. Note that a value of zero indicates the minimum amount of time before

power failure (at least 100µsec.)

- pfi_flag — When set verifies that a power failure is imminent and that the values written to the other fields are valid. Writes to the register must be ignored if the pfi_flag is cleared.

Figure 21-12: Format and Behavior Summary of the POWER_FAIL_IMMINENT Register

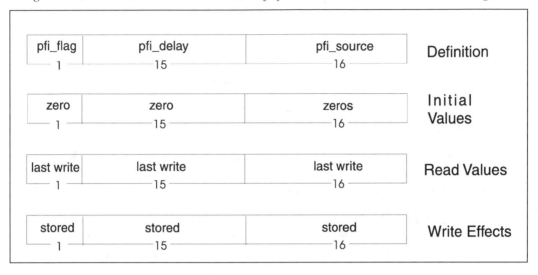

Figure 21-13: Format and Behavior Summary of the POWER_SOURCE Register

Busy_Timeout Register

The BUSY_TIMEOUT register is required for nodes that support transaction retires. This register reports transaction layer variables that specify the retry protocol supported by this node. The format of this node is specified in Figure 21-14 on page 382.

When the dual-phase retry protocol is in use, the second_limit and cycle_limit fields have non-zero values. These fields specify the amount of time that can elapse before failing a transaction. (See Chapter 21 regarding dual-phase retries and use of these fields). Nodes that do not support dual-phase retries must ignore writes to the second_limit and cycle_limit fields and reads must always return zeros.

The retry_limit field specifies the maximum number of retries that can be attempted during single-phase retries. When the retry_limit value reaches zero no more retries can occur for this transaction.

Figure 21-14: Format and Behavior Summary of BUSY_TIMEOUT Register

reserved	second_limit	cycle_limit	reserved	retry_limit	Definition
4	3	13	8	4	
zeros	zeros	200	zeros	zeros	Initial Values
4	3	13	8	4	
zeros	last write	last write	zeros	last write	Read Values
4	3	13	8	4	
ignored	stored	stored	ignored	stored	Write Effects
4	3	13	8	4	

Bus_Manager_ID Register

The BUS_MANAGER_ID register must be implemented on nodes that are iso-chronous resource manager capable. During bus configuration the node that will perform the role of bus manager is identified through the use of this regis-ter. Nodes vying for the role of bus manager use the lock compare swap transac-tions when attempting to win this role. (See "Determining the Bus Manager" on page 344 for details associated with identifying the bus manager node.) Format of the BUS_MANAGER_ID register is illustrated in Figure 21-15 on page 383. Note that the initial value of the bus manager (bus_mngr_id) field is the broad-cast address (3Fh), and thus not a valid address for the bus manager. Reads that return 3Fh indicate that the bus manager node has not yet been identified.

Figure 21-15: Format and Behavior of the BUS_MANAGER_ID Register

reserved —— 26	bus_mngr_id —— 6	Definition
zeros —— 26	3Fh —— 6	Initial Values
zeros —— 26	unchanged —— 6	Command Reset Values
zeros —— 26	last successful lock —— 6	Read Values
ignored —— 26	conditionally written —— 6	Write Effects

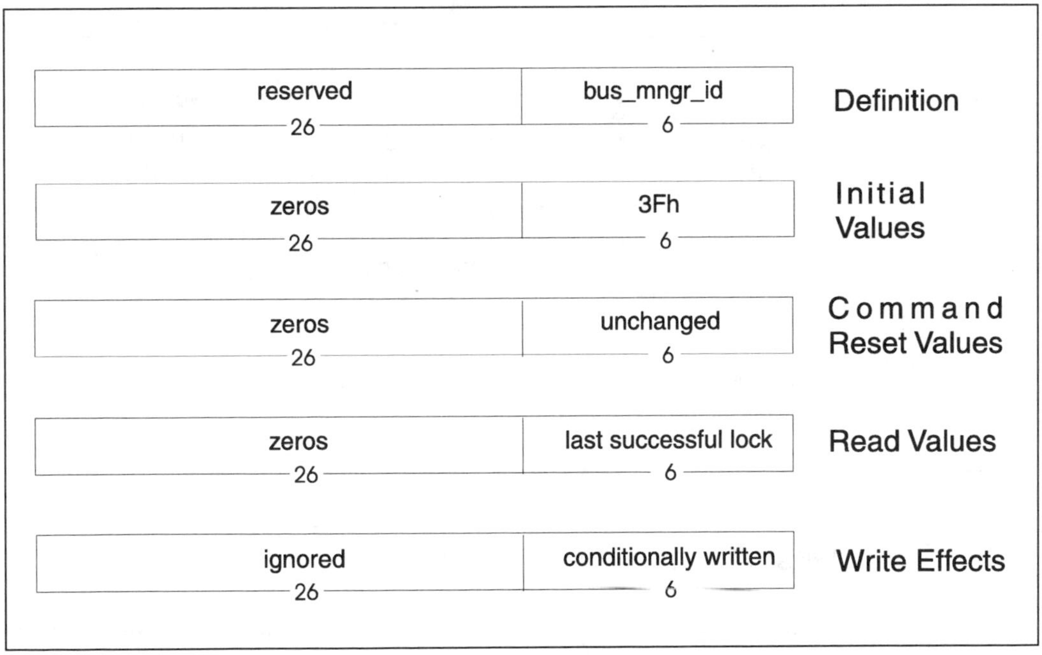

Bandwidth_Available Register

Isochronous nodes must access the BANDWIDTH_AVAILABLE register to request the bandwidth needed to perform their isochronous transfers. Accesses to this register support only the quadlet read and lock compare swap transaction. The bw_remaining field reflects the amount of bus bandwidth (in allocation units, or 20.34ns) currently available for isochronous transfers. See the section entitled "Bus Bandwidth Allocation" on page 339 for details regarding the allocation of isochronous bus bandwidth. The register format is given in Figure 21-16 on page 384.

Figure 21-16: Format and Behavior Summary of the BANDWIDTH_AVAILABLE Register

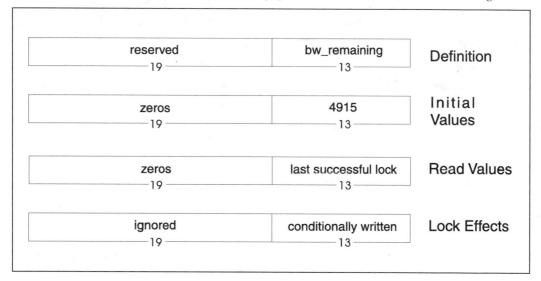

Channels_Available Register

Nodes wishing to perform isochronous transfers must first obtain an isochronous channel number via the CHANNELS_AVAILABLE register. This 64-bit register provides a bit map where each bit corresponds to one of 64 possible isochronous channels supported by the serial bus. Every bus manager and isochronous resource manager node must implement this register. However, only the node that has won the role of isochronous resource manager has valid data in its CHANNELS_AVAILABLE register. Format and behavior summary of this register is illustrated in Figure 21-17 on page 385.

Figure 21-17: Format and Behavior Summary of CHANNELS_AVAILABLE Register

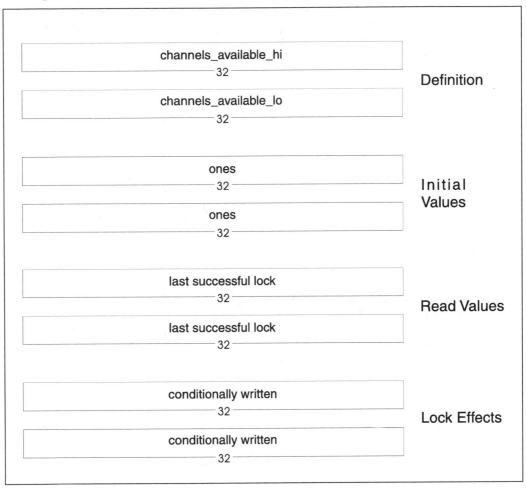

The relationship between each bit in the CHANNELS_AVAILABLE register and the 64 channel numbers is as follows:

- channels_available_hi register — channel numbers 0 (lsb) through 31 (msb).
- channels_available_lo register — channel numbers 32 (lsb) through 63 (msb).

All bits are initialized to a value of one, thus indicating that none of the channels has been allocated. A node wishing to obtain an isochronous channel must use the read and lock (compare and swap) transaction. If the channel number requested is available (i.e. the corresponding bit is set), it performs a compare and swap transaction, causing the corresponding bit in the CHANNELS_AVAILABLE register to be cleared. See the section entitled "Channel Allocation" on page 337 for more information on isochronous channel allocation and deallocation.

Maint_Control Register

Nodes may implement the optional maintenance control (MAINT_CONTROL) register to enhance error diagnosis and to verify proper operation of error detection logic within a system. This register provides the ability to simulate or force errors during the transmission of packets. Fields within the register may be set to generate various errors. Format of the MAINT_CONTROL register is illustrated in Figure 21-18 on page 387. Each field provides the following capability:

- e_hcrc (force error in header CRC value)
- e_dcrc (force error in data CRC value)
- no_pkt (discard next packet to be generated)
- f_ack (replace normal acknowledge packet with contents of ack field during next acknowledge packet)
- no_ack (discard next acknowledge packet)
- ack (contents of acknowledge packet when f_ack is set).

Maint_Utility Register

This register is optional but can be implemented for diagnostic purposes. Read or write transactions may safely target the MAINT_UTILITY register to verify successful transmission of information to and from this target node. In this way no unexpected side effects result from accessing the node. Reads return the last value written to the register, thus providing a way to verify successful reads and writes. The register's format and behavior are summarized in Figure 21-19 on page 387.

Figure 21-18: Format and Behavior of MAINT_CONTROL Register

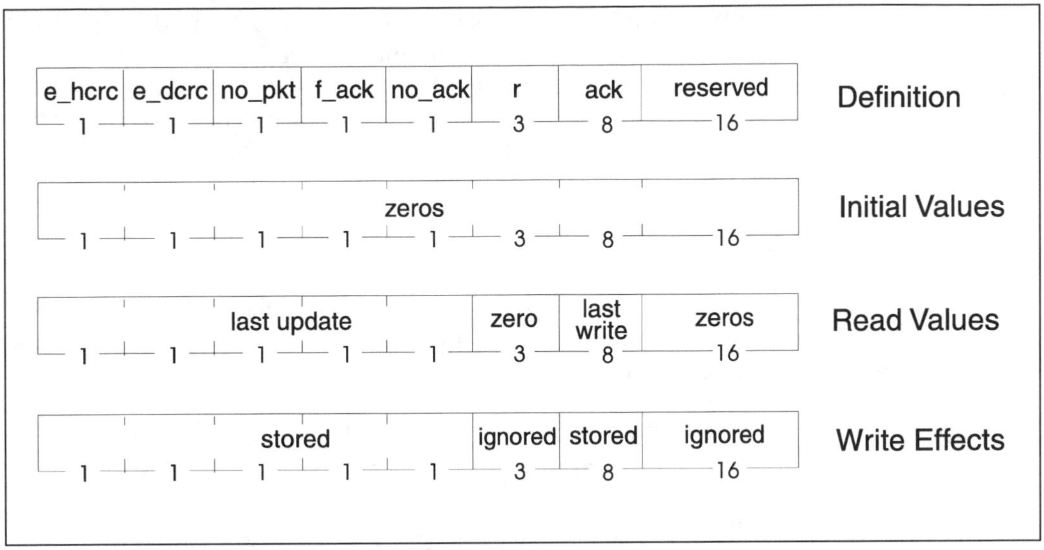

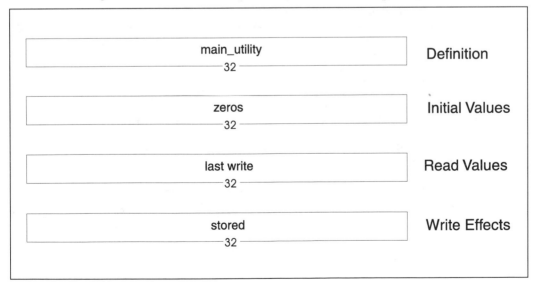

Figure 21-19: Format and Behavior of MAINT_UTILITY Register

FireWire System Architecture

Unit Registers

A portion of a node's initial unit address space is reserved for node-dependent resources by the CSR architecture and is mapped above FFFF FFF0 0800h. The 1394 specification reserves portions of this address space (FFFF FFF0 0800 - FFFF FFF0 FFFCh) for bus-dependent use. Two address ranges within this reserved space are defined for serial bus management functions:

- TOPOLOGY_MAP
- SPEED_MAP

These maps are implemented only by bus manager capable nodes, and only the active bus manager contains valid mapping information. Allocation of the node-dependent address space is listed in Table 21-6 on page 388.

Table 21-6: Addresses Allocated for the TOPOLOGY_MAP and SPEED_MAP

Offset Within Initial Units Address Space	Map Name
0800h - 08FCh	Reserved
0900h	OUTPUT_MASTER_PLUG
0904h - 097Ch	OUTPUT_PLUG
0980h	INPUT_MASTER_PLUG
0984h - 09FCh	INPUT_PLUG
0A00h - 0AFCh	Reserved
0B00h - 0CFCh	FCP command frame
0D00h - 0EFCh	FCP response frame
0F00 - 0FFCh	Reserved
1000h - 13FCh	TOPOLOGY_MAP
1400h - 1FFCh	Reserved
2000h - 2FFCh	SPEED_MAP
3000h - FFFCh	Reserved

Other address ranges (0900h - 09FCh and 0B00h - 0EFCh) are defined by the IEC 61883-1/FDIS specification.

Topology Map

Bus manager capable nodes construct a topology map that is built from the first quadlet of each self-ID packet that is broadcast during the self-ID process (including the self-ID packet delivered by the bus manager capable node itself). This topology map provides information that can be read by any node to obtain and deduce the topology of the serial bus. The topology register format is illustrated in Figure 21-20. Each field is defined below:

- length — specifies the number of quadlets in the topology map.
- CRC — covers all quadlets following the CRC and is based on the CRC-16 algorithm defined in the CSR specification.
- generation number — reflects the number of times that the bus manager has generated the topology map since the last power reset.
- node_count — specifies the number of nodes that currently reside on the serial bus. This value will be a maximum number of 63.
- self_id_count — This value specifies the total number of self-ID packets transferred. Note that this field is a sum of all self_id_packet entries.
- self_id_packets (0 ... self_id_count -1) — each 32-bit self_id_packet entry consists of the first quadlet broadcast over the serial bus during the self-ID process. Each self_id_packet is captured in order as it appears on the bus, with the first labeled as zero and each additional packet getting the next sequential number. The maximum entry is represented with a count equivalent to the final self_id_count minus one.

Figure 21-20: Format of TOPOLOGY_MAP

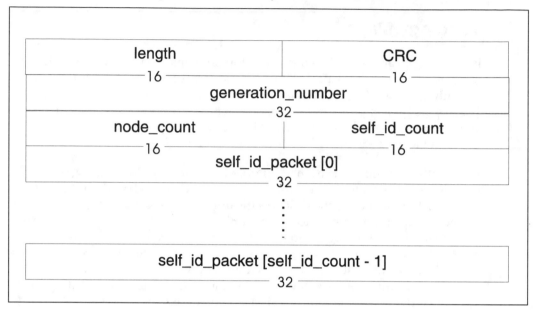

Speed Map

Bus manager capable nodes must implement the speed map register, giving other nodes the ability to determine the maximum packet speed that can be supported when transferring information between any two nodes on the serial bus. The speed information is encoded within the self-id packets and is accumulated by the bus manager to construct the speed map. Speed map data can be thought of as a matrix, where each entry specifies the maximum packet speed between any two nodes (m and n). The speed_code entry numbers 0 - 4029 are vectors that contain the maximum speed between any two nodes. These numbers are given by:

speed_code[i]=speed_code[j]; where [i]=64 · m+n & [j]=64 · n+m

Note that two entry numbers (entries speed_code[i] and speed_code[j]) give the maximum speed associated with any two nodes (m & n) and contain the same value. For example the maximum speed that can be used when transferring data between nodes 2 and 6 can be found in entries 134 and 386, with each entry specifying the same speed.

Figure 21-21 on page 391 illustrates the format of the SPEED_MAP registers. The speed map is read only and must be accessed in the proper manner. Refer to "Accessing the Speed Map" on page 349 for details regarding speed map register access. Each field is defined as follows:

- length — the number of quadlets following this quadlet. The length is fixed to a value of 3FFh.
- CRC — covers all quadlets following the CRC and is based on the CRC-16 algorithm.
- generation_number — reflects the number of times that the bus manager has generated the topology map since the last power reset.
- speed_code [0 - 4029] — vector locations that define the maximum speed that a transaction can be sent between two nodes.

Figure 21-21: Format of SPEED_MAP

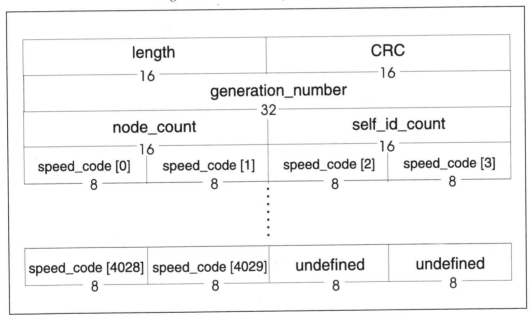

22 *PHY Registers*

The Previous Chapter

The previous chapter discussed the CSR registers defined by the ISO 13213 specification with particular focus on the registers that are required by the 1394 specification.

This Chapter

This chapter introduces PHY register maps and port registers for the 1394-1995 specification and for the 1394a supplement.

The Next Chapter

The next chapter details the contents of configuration ROM required by the ISO/IEC 13213 specification. The serial bus also defines ROM entries that are required by some nodes, depending on the capabilities.

Overview

Each 1394 PHY provides the interface to the bus and performs key functions in the communications process. These functions include:

- Bus configuration
- Arbitrating for control of the 1394 bus
- Repeating transactions to other ports
- Performing NRZ encoding/decoding
- Performing data strobe encoding/decoding
- Speed signaling and detecting transfer speed
- Detecting device attachment/detachment

The PHY registers support the functions performed by the PHY layer. These registers are mapped as offsets within the PHY and are not mapped into the 1394 node address space. The PHY registers can be read from or written to by the application residing at node and can be read by a remote node using a remote access packet. Additionally, another node can use the PHY configuration and link-on packets to change certain bits within the PHY registers of other nodes. This function is reserved for the node that performs bus management functions. These packets affect register fields related to force root, gap count, and link power features.

The section entitled, "1394-1995 PHY Register Map" details the PHY register map used by 1394-1995 compliant nodes. The 1394a supplement defines an extended PHY register map format that contains additional information needed to support new features, and is discussed in the section entitled, "1394a PHY Register Map" on page 398.

1394-1995 PHY Register Map

Figure 22-1 illustrates the PHY register map for the 1995 version of the specification. The register map contains global information that pertains to the entire node, as well as port specific registers that reflect the state and condition of each port interface. A description of each field within the PHY register map is presented in Table 22-1.

Figure 22-1: 1394-1995 PHY Register Format

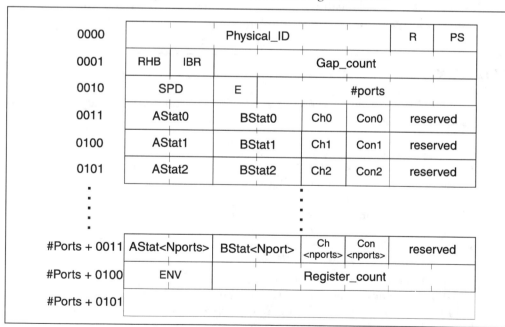

Table 22-1: Description of the PHY Register Map For 1394-1995

Name	Size (bits)	Description
Physical_ID	6	This field is updated during bus configuration (self-ID) to reflect the node ID of this device.
R	1	Root — Designates whether this node is the root node. When set to one this node is the root.
PS	1	Power status — The PHY sets this bit when it detects valid power (i.e. in the range of 7.5 33vdc).
RHB	1	Root Hold Off Bit — This field is set when the PHY detects a PHY Configuration packet whose Root_ID field matches the Physical_ID of this node and whose R bit is set. When RHB is set this node delays its participation in the tree-ID process.
IBR	1	Initiate Bus Reset — When set to one this bit causes the PHY to signal bus reset immediately. Reset is asserted for 166 microseconds after which the IBR bit is self cleared.
Gap_count	6	This register contains an initial default value of 63 following reset. This value can be updated later by the bus manager or isochronous manager nodes via the PHY configuration packet. The gap_count field value of the PHY configuration packet updates the PHY gap_count register when the "T" bit is set.
SPD	2	Indicates the top speed that this PHY can accept and transmit packets. 00=100Mb/s 01=200Mb/s 10=400Mb/s 11=Reserved
E	1	Enhanced bit: 1=enhanced register map is used (registers beyond #ports+0100 are defined.
#Ports	5	The number of ports supported by this PHY. This field determines the number of port status registers that directly follow this register field.

Table 22-1: Description of the PHY Register Map For 1394-1995

Name	Size (bits)	Description
AStat<n>	2	TPA line state on port n (0-max Port#) encoded as follows: 11=ZZ 01=1 10=0 00=invalid
BStat<n>	2	TPB line state on port n (0-max Port#) encoded as follows: 11=ZZ 01=1 10=0 00=invalid
Ch<n>	1	If Ch<n>=1, port n is a child. If Ch<n>=0, port n is a parent.
Con<n>	1	If Con<n>=1, port n is connected. If Con<n>=0, port n is disconnected.
ENV	2	Used with enhanced register. Indicates the type of environment: 00=backplane 01=cable 10 & 11=reserved
Reg_count	6	Defines number of registers that follow in the enhanced space.

Port Status Registers

The port status registers contain information regarding the connection status of each port and, if a node is attached, whether the port connects to a child or to a parent node. This information is delivered as part of the self_ID packet as port specific information.

PHY Configuration Packet

Figure 22-2 illustrates the PHY configuration packet contents. Two PHY register fields may be affected by the configuration packet:

1. Root Hold Off Bit (RHB) field
2. Gap_count field

Root Hold Off

When a PHY configuration packet is broadcast with the R bit set, then the node must compare its physical_ID to the root_ID field in the configuration packet. If the two values match, then this root must set its RHB field. If the two values do not match, then the PHY must clear the RHB. When RHB is set, this PHY will delay its participation in the tree-ID process for approximately 167µs. This ensures that this node will become the root during the next tree-ID process. Refer to "Force Root Delay" on page 299 for details regarding the tree_ID process and the force root feature.

Gap Count Optimization

The gap count field configures the gap timing employed by this PHY (e.g. when arbitrating for control of the bus and when detecting time-out conditions). The bus manager or isochronous resource manager can optimize bus performance by tuning the gap count value. The default gap count of 63 can be shortened to reduce idle time between packets. When the PHY configuration packet is delivered, all nodes check the "T" bit. If set, the "T" bit indicates that the gap_count value contained in the configuration packet should replace the current value within the PHY register's gap_count field. Since the PHY configuration packet is a broadcast packet, all nodes will update their gap_count register field to the same value.

Note that the first bus reset following the gap_count field being updated (via a PHY configuration packet) has no affect on the gap_count value. When a second bus reset occurs the gap_count field is initialized to a value of 3Fh (63d).

Figure 22-2: Format of PHY Configuration Packet

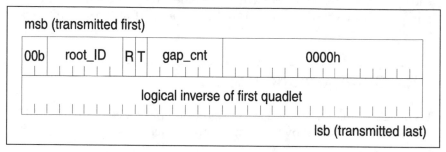

1394a PHY Register Map

An extended register map is defined by the 1394a supplement to include fields to support new features or to provide additional information missing from the 1995 version of the specification. Figure 22-3 illustrates the 1394a PHY register map and each field is described in Table 22-2 on page 399. Please note that the PHY and port register definition included here is preliminary and may change.

Figure 22-3: 1394a PHY Register Definition

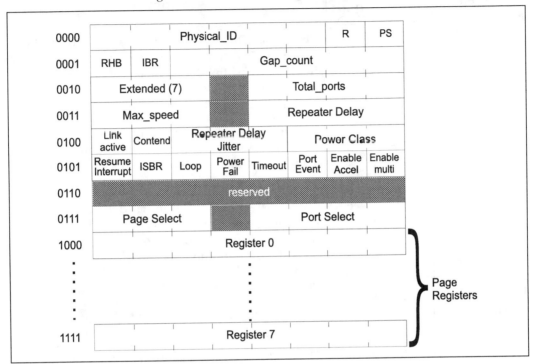

Table 22-2: Description of the PHY Register Map For 1394a

Name	Read or Write	Size (bits)	Description
Physical ID	R	6	This field is updated during bus configuration (self-ID) to reflect the node ID of this device.
R	R	1	Root — Designates whether this node is the root node. When set to one (following Tree-ID) this node is the root.
PS	R	1	Power status — The PHY sets this bit when it detects valid power (i.e. in the range of 7.5 - 33vdc).

Table 22-2: Description of the PHY Register Map For 1394a

Name	Read or Write	Size (bits)	Description
RHB	R/W	1	Root Hold Off — This field is set when the PHY detects a PHY Configuration packet whose Root_ID field matches the Physical_ID of this node and whose R bit is set. When RHB is set this node delays its participation in the tree-ID process.
IBR	R/W	1	Initiate Bus Reset — When set to one this bit causes the PHY to signal bus reset immediately. Reset is asserted for 166 microseconds after which the IBR bit is self cleared.
Gap_count	R/W	6	This register contains an initial default value of 63 following reset. This value can be updated later by the bus manager or isochronous manager nodes via the PHY configuration packet. The gap_count field value of the PHY configuration packet updates the PHY gap_count register when the "T" bit is set.
Extended	R	3	This field must have a value of 7h to indicate that the extended register map format is used.
Total_ports	R	4	This field specifies the number of ports implemented by this node.
Max_speed	R	3	Indicates the maximum transmission speed that this node supports.
Repeater Delay	R	4	Worst case repeater delay expressed as: 144 + (delay * 20) ns
Link active	R/W	1	Link enabled — This bit may be set or cleared by software and is used by the PHY when it broadcasts the "L" bit in the self-ID packet. The actual state of the self-ID "L" bit is a logical AND of this bit and the link power status (LPS) signal from the Link controller.

Table 22-2: Description of the PHY Register Map For 1394a

Name	Read or Write	Size (bits)	Description
Contend	R/W	1	Contender — Software may set or clear this bit to determine the state of the "C" bit of the self-ID packet. If no hardware dependent method is available to set this bit, it will be cleared by a power reset.
Repeater Delay Jitter	R	3	The difference between the fastest and slowest repeater delay expressed as: (jitter + 1) * 20 ns.
Power Class	R/W	3	Power class — This field contains the value that should be transferred in the "pwr" field of this node's self-ID packet.
Resume_int	R/W	1	Resume interrupt enable bit — When set (one) this PHY must set the Port_event bit if a previously suspended port returns to the resume state.
ISBR	R/W	1	Initiate short bus reset — When this bit is set, the PHY is instructed to issue a short (arbitrated) reset. This bit is self-clearing following a reset.
Loop	R/WC	1	Loop detected — This bit is set when an arbitration time-out occurs (due to a looped topology) and is cleared when a "1" is written to this bit position.
Power Fail	R/WC	1	Cable power failure detect — This bit is set when the PS bit changes from one to zero, thus indicating that power has dropped below tolerance (7.5vdc). Writing a "1" clears this bit.
Time-out	R/WC	1	Arbitration state machine time-out — This bit is set when an arbitration time-out occurs (between 200µs and 400µs). A write of one to this bit clears it.
Port_event	R/W	1	Port event detect — This bit is set by hardware when a change in the bias, connected, disabled, or fault status occurs on a given port and its Int_Enable bit is set. Also set if a resume operation starts a port and its resume_int bit is set.

Table 22-2: Description of the PHY Register Map For 1394a

Name	Read or Write	Size (bits)	Description
Enab_accel	R/W	1	Enable arbitration acceleration — When set, 1394a arbitration enhancements are enabled.
Enab_multi	R/W	1	Enable multi-speed packet concatenation — When set the link signals the speed during the data prefix of all concatenated packets transmitted.
Page_select	R/W	3	One of eight possible PHY register pages can be selected via this field. The selected register page contains up to eight registers that are accessible at offsets 1000b through 1111b. 000b = ports (port specified in Port_select field) 001b = vendor ID page 010-110b = reserved 111b = vendor-dependent information
Port_select	R/W	4	When the page_select field is zero, then the port select field specifies which port registers are accessible via offsets 1000b through 1111b. The maximum number of ports supported is 16d.

Page Select

This three-bit field can specify up to eight pages, each containing up to eight registers that are paged into the register map at offsets 1000b - 1111b. Of the possible eight pages, three values are currently defined, and are described in the following sections:

- Port Status Register Page
- Vendor Identification Register Page
- Vendor-dependent information

Port Status Register Page

Port registers are accessible via the page_select and port_select fields. When the page_select value is zero, the contents of the eight registers at offset 1000b-1111b will contain the port status registers for the port specified in the port_select field. The format of the port status registers is shown in Figure 22-4 on page 403 and the definition of each field can be found in Table 22-3 on page 404. Up to 27 ports (0-26) can be supported by a single node, thus the port_select values above 26 are reserved. When port_select values of 27-31 are used, the contents of the page registers are indeterminate.

Figure 22-4: Format of Port Registers

Offset	___							Register
0111	Page_select = 0		Res	Port_select = n				
1000	AStat		BStat	Child	Con	Bias	Disabled	Register 0
1001	Negotiated Speed		Interrupt Enable	Fault	Reserved			Register 1
1010	Reserved							Register 2
1011	Reserved							Register 3
1100	Reserved							Register 4
1101	Reserved							Register 5
1110	Reserved							Register 6
1111	Reserved							Register 7

Table 22-3: Description of the Port Status Page

Name	Size (bits)	R/W	Description
AStat<n>	2	r	TPA line state on port n (0-max Port#) encoded as follows: 11=Z 01=1 10=0 00=invalid
BStat<n>	2	r	TPB line state on port n (0-max Port#) encoded as follows: 11=Z 01=1 10=0 00=invalid
Ch<n>	1	r	If Ch<n>=1, port n is a child. If Ch<n>=0, port n is a parent.
Con<n>	1	r	If Con<n>=1, port n is connected. If Con<n>=0, port n is disconnected. This bit is set or cleared after being filtered by hysteresis logic to debounce the connect detect indication, rather than indicating a connection change for each port status change that occurs due to contact scraping when a node is attached or removed.
Bias	1	r	This bit indicates that bias voltage has been detected by the port status receiver, which indicates the possible attachment of a remote node to this port. This bit is filtered by hysteresis logic to debounce the port status output to reduce the multiple port status changes that occur due to contact scraping when a node is attached or removed.
Disabled	1	rw	Disable port. If Dis=1, then port is disabled. If Dis=0, then port is enabled. This bit gives software the ability to enable or disable the port. Figure 22-5 on page 406 illustrates the effect of the port diable feature.

Table 22-3: Description of the Port Status Page

Name	Size (bits)	R/W	Description
Negotiated Speed	3	r	This field indicates the maximum speed at which this PHY and the attached PHY can transfer packets. Note this is the same encoding as the Maximum Speed field within the 1394a register map.
Int_Enable	1	rw	Enables port event interrupts. This bit enables the PHY's Port_event field to be set by hardware when a port event of Connected, Bias, Disabled, or Fault occurs.
Fault	1	r/wc	This bit is set by hardware if an error is detected during a suspend or resume operation. A write of one clears the bit.

FireWire System Architecture

Figure 22-5: Port Disable Feature and Its Effect

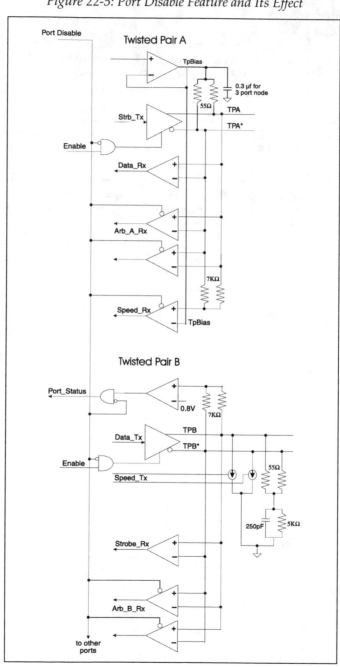

Vendor Identification Register Page

When the page_select field is loaded with a value of 001b, the vendor identification registers are accessible via offsets 1000b - 1111b. The format of these register fields is illustrated in Figure 22-6 and the description is provided in Table 22-4 on page 408.

Figure 22-6: Format of the Vendor Identification Page

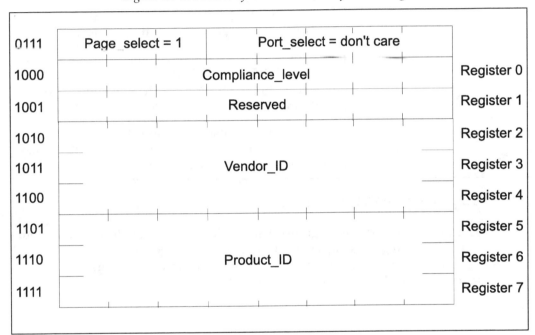

Table 22-4: Description of the Vendor Identification Page

Name	Size (bits)	Description
Compliance_level	8	Specifies which standard that this PHY complies with: 0 = not specified 1 = IEEE P1394a Other values are reserved for future versions.
Vendor_ID	24	The company ID or the Organizationally Unique Identifier (OUI) of the PHY manufacturer. The least significant byte of the Vendor_ID is mapped at offset 1010b and the most significant bit at offset 1100b.
Product_ID	24	This value is manufacturer dependent. The most significant byte of the Product_ID is at offset 1101b and the least significant byte at 1111b.

Vendor-dependent Page

This page provides eight registers that may be used for the PHY vendor's purposes. These registers are accessed by setting the page select field to 111b and using address locations 1000b - 1111b to access the individual registers. The format of these eight registers is vendor specific.

23 Configuration ROM

The Previous Chapter

The previous chapter discussed the CSR registers defined by the IEEE 1212 specification with particular focus on the registers that are required by the 1394 specification. Additional bus-specific registers are also defined by the 1394 specification and are discussed.

This Chapter

This chapter details the contents of configuration ROM required by the ISO/IEC 13213 specification. The serial bus also defines ROM entries that are required by some nodes, depending on the capabilities.

The Next Chapter

The next chapter provides a brief introduction to the power management environment introduced by the 1394a specification. The chapter introduces the three documents that further define the power management specification: Cable Power Distribution, Suspend/Resume Mechanisms, and Power State Management.

Overview

IEEE 1394 serial devices must include a ROM directory structure that provides critical information needed to configure and diagnose problems associated with the device. Information included within the ROM includes information for:

- identifying the software driver for this device
- identifying diagnostic software
- specifying bus-related capabilities of the device (e.g. whether it is bus manager capable)
- specifying optional module, node, and unit characteristics and parameters

The specification defines two ROM formats: minimal and general. The minimal format only identifies the company that manufactured the device, but it may also include vendor-defined data structures. The general ROM format defines a bus information block and root directory containing entries that may specifiy pointers to other directories and data structures.

Minimal ROM Format

Figure 23-1 illustrates the minimal ROM format that consists only of a 24-bit Vendor-ID value. The most significant 8 bits contain a value of 01h, which identifies the ROM format as minimal. Any other value will be interpreted as a general ROM format. The vendor may optionally define and implement other ROM

Figure 23-1: Minimal ROM Format

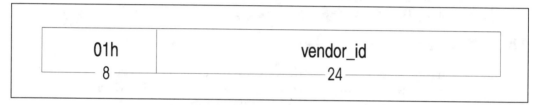

entries. These additional entries are entirely vendor-defined and not a part of the CSR architecture or the serial bus standard and can only be interpreted by vendor software.

General ROM Format

Major entries within the general ROM format consist of a bus information block and root directory. The bus information block specifies a variety of bus-related capabilities, while the root directory provides values that identify the software driver and diagnostic software along with optional pointers to other directories and data structures. Figure 23-2 illustrates the general ROM format, with the entries required by the CSR architecture shaded. Note that these shaded structures always start at the same address locations within ROM. Whether the other directories and data structures are present is bus- and vendor-dependent.

Figure 23-2: General ROM Format

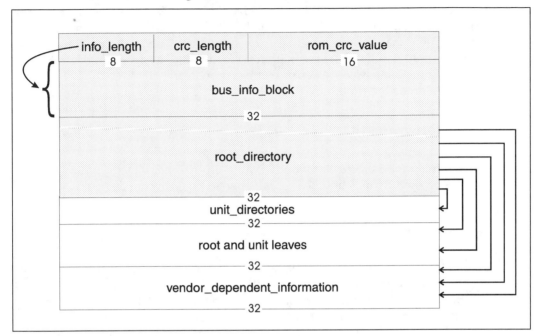

Header Information

The first quadlet of the general ROM format consists of three fields:

- info_length
- crc_length
- rom_crc_value

Info_Length

This field specifies the length of the bus_info_block field in quadlets. This value must be a value greater than 01h so that software can correctly identify the ROM format as "general" rather than "minimal."

CRC_Length

The crc_length field specifies that the total length of the general ROM quadlets are covered by the crc value. The field size of the crc_length values restricts the maximum number of quadlets that can be covered by the crc_value to 255 (1020 bytes). Note that these values cover the entire ROM up to the maximum size. However, other data structures within the general ROM also contain crc values that can be used to isolate an error that has been detected within the ROM. If the ROM is larger than the maximum size covered by the ROM_crc_value, then CRC checks should be performed on directories not covered by the ROM crc.

CRC_Value

Software performs a crc check on two byte groups that are covered by the crc. The calculated crc matches the crc_value when no errors are detected.

Bus_Info_Block (1394-1995)

The Bus_Info_Block provides critical information about bus related capabilities of this node. Only the bus_name field (the first quadlet) is specifically defined by the CSR architecture. The remainder of the Bus_Info_Block is defined by the serial bus standard. The format of the Bus_Info_Block content and format is illustrated in Figure 23-3. See page 415 for changes to the bus information block introduced by the 1394a supplement.

Figure 23-3: Format of the Bus_Info_Block

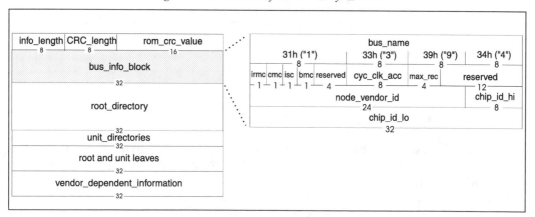

Bus_Name Field

The CSR architecture defines the bus_name field that identifies the bus that this node supports based on four ASCII characters that represent the IEEE PAR number assigned to the corresponding bus standard. The serial bus specification defines this quadlet as "1394."

Bus Characteristics Fields

A variety of bus characteristics associated with this node are defined in the second quadlet of the Bus_Info_Block. The fields illustrated in the second quadlet of Figure 23-3 define the following node characteristics:

- **irmc** (isochronous resource manager capable) — When set (1) this node is isochronous resource manager capable, otherwise the bit must be cleared (0).
- **cmc** (cycle master capable) — When set (1), this node is cycle master capable, otherwise the bit must be cleared (0).
- **isc** (isochronous capable) — When set (1), this node supports isochronous transfers, otherwise the bit must be cleared (0).
- **bmc** (bus manager capable) — When set (1), this node is bus manager capable, otherwise the bit must be cleared (0).
- **cyc_clk_acc** (cycle clock accuracy) — This 8-bit field contains a value that defines the accuracy of this node's cycle master clock in parts per million. This field is only valid for nodes that also have the **cmc** bit set. Valid values are between zero and 100d. If **cmc** is cleared, then this field must contain all ones.
- **max_rec** (maximum data record size) — This 4-bit field indirectly specifies the maximum data payload size of asynchronous write and asynchronous stream packets that this node is capable of accepting. The max_rec value is used to calculate the maximum data payload value, which is an even power of two (max packet size = 2^{max_rec+1}). The valid max_rec values and corresponding maximum data payload sizes are listed in Table 23-1. The shaded table entries reflect new max_rec values that correspond with the faster transmission speeds defined by the 1394a supplement. Note that these faster speeds and maximum payload sizes are currently not supported.

Table 23-1: max_rec values and Maximum Data Payload Sizes

max_rec Values (h)	Maximum Payload Size (bytes)
0	NA
1	4
2	8
3	16
4	32
5	64
6	128
7	256
8	512
9	1024
A	2048
B	4096
C	8192
D	16384
E & F	Reserved

Node_Vendor_ID Field

This field contains the company ID value of the manufacturer of the node. Note that this same node_vendor_id value is contained within the Node_Unique_Id leaf. See "Company ID Value Administration" on page 423 for information on obtaining a company ID.

Chip_ID Fields

Two fields comprise the chip_id value and are specified by the vendor of the node. The 8-bit chip_id_hi and 32-bit chip_id_lo values are concatenated together to form the 40-bit chip ID. Each node is uniquely identified by a 64-bit value created by concatenating the node_vendor_id, chip_id_hi, and chip_id_lo values. Note that the 64-bit node unique identifier is also contained within the Node_Unique_Id leaf.

Bus Info Block (1394a)

The 1394a supplement adds three additional fields to the bus information block and is illustrated in Chapter 23-4. The three new fields are:

- pmc (Power Management Capable) bit field
- gen (generation) field
- link_spd (link speed) field

Figure 23-4: Illustration of the Bus Information Block for 1394a Compliant Nodes

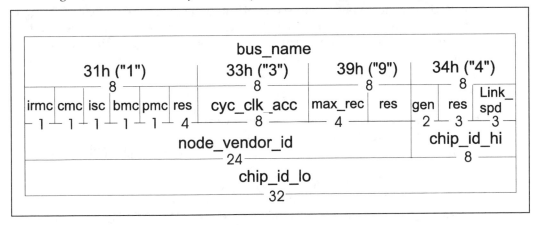

Power Management Capable

This bit specifies whether this node support the role of power manager. The power manager's function is to manage power distribution and power consumption. Power Management is discussed in Part 6 of this book.

Generation Field

Following a bus reset enumeration software must read configuration ROM to identify each node on the bus. This results in a relatively large number of asynchronous read transactions to completely characterize a device via its ROM entries. If enumeration software were able to detect that the configuration ROM contents have not changed since the last bus reset, then the number of reads could be reduced. The generation field when set indicates that a change has occurred within the configuration ROM. This includes any ROM directories or leaf entries that are mapped outside the 1KB of address space reserved for configuration ROM.

Link Speed

This field is included so that the speed capabilities of the link layer controller can be determined. It is possible that the speed of the PHY and link is different. Therefore, the maximum speed capability of the node may be limited by the link and not be consistent with speed reported by the PHY.

Root_Directory

The Root_Directory specifies the content and organization of the rest of the general ROM format. That is, entries within the root directory may include pointers to other directories or to data structures called leaves that contain various node parameters. Figure 23-5 illustrates the hierarchy of directories and leaf entries shown in the form of a tree structure. The entries contained in the hierarchy include :

- Root leaf entries — entries that define values that define some aspect of the node design (e.g. a node_vendor_id value).
- Root dependent directories — these entries point to optional directories that may specify bus-dependent, module-depend, or node-dependent information. The format of these directories and their associated entries obviously depends on the bus, module, or node implementation. Note that no bus dependent directories are defined by the serial bus standard. Module or node dependent directories are vendor-specific.
- Unit directory entries — these entries identify offsets within ROM memory where one or more unit directories are located. Each Unit_Directory entry includes an ID for the unit, thus a node may include a separate directory for each unit within the node. The serial bus standard defines only one entry that must be included within a unit directory. This entry defines additional cable power requirements for the unit specified.

- Unit dependent directories — these entries may point to optional directories that contain additional entries that define values for parameters associated with this unit.
- Unit leaf entries — these entries define parameters related to various aspects of the unit implementation.

Figure 23-5: Example Root Directory Tree

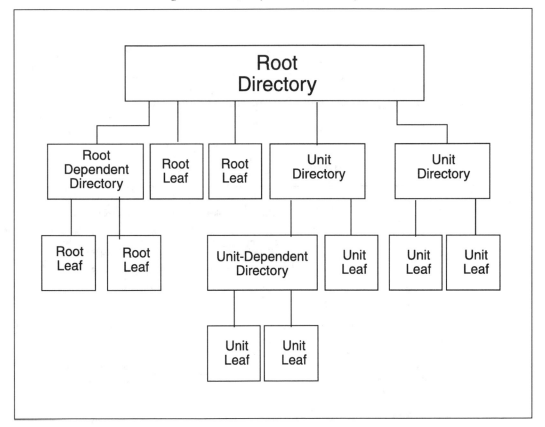

The CSR architecture defines all possible entries that can be included within the root directory. Figure 23-6 on page 418 illustrates all root directory entries that may be used in a serial bus implementation. The shaded entries in Figure 23-6 on page 418 are required by all serial bus nodes that implement the general ROM format.

All directory and leaf entries are defined by the CSR architecture as one of four types and have the generic format illustrated in Figure 23-6. Note that each entry contains a 2-bit key_type, a 6-bit key_value, and a 24-bit entry_value. The 2-bit key_type defines the nature of the entry_value as defined in Table 23-2. The key_value identifies the name and contents of each ROM directory entry.

Table 23-2: Definition of key_type and entry_values

key_type	Name	Meaning of 24-bit entry_value
0	immediate	An immediate value that specifies an ID or some parameter
1	offset	An offset value that points to a location within the initial-register-space that contains an immediate value
2	leaf	An indirect offset pointing to a leaf data entry
3	directory	An indirect offset pointing to a directory

Figure 23-6: Root Directory Entries

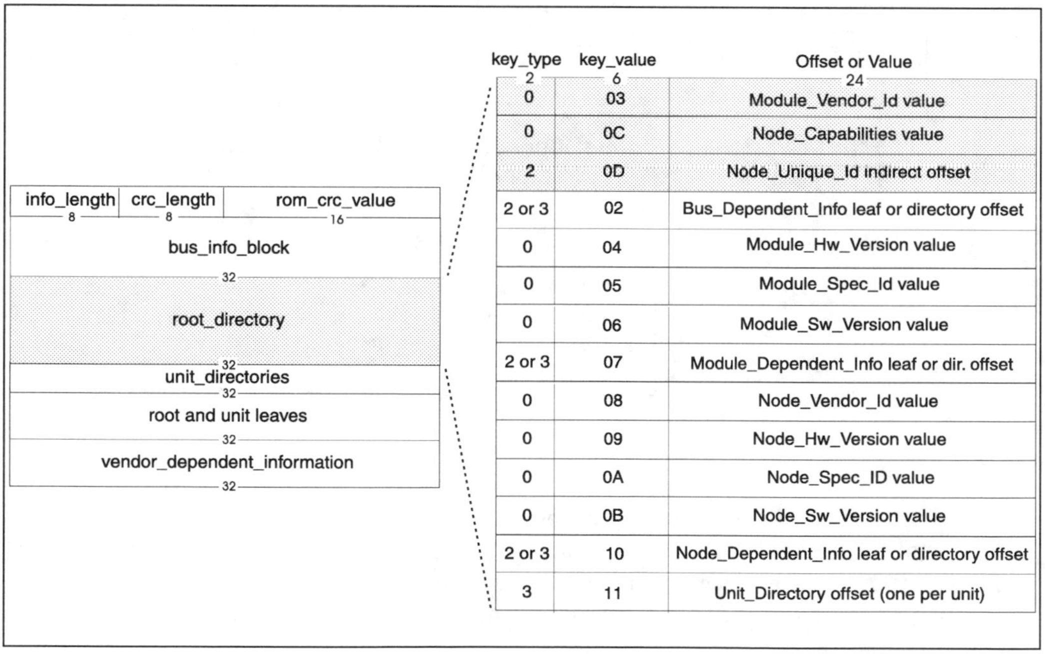

Required Root Directory Entries

The required root directory entries are listed below and are designated by shading in Figure 23-6 on page 418:

- Module_Vendor_Id
- Node_Capabilities
- Node_Unique_Id (This entry is no longer required by 1394a since it is redundant with Node_Vendor_ID and Chip_ID fields within the bus information block.)

Module_Vendor_Id. This 24-bit field is an immediate entry that contains the company ID of the manufacturer of the serial bus module. Note that this value may be the same as the node_vendor_id.

Node_Capabilities. The CSR architecture defines bit fields within the 24-bit Node_Capabilities root directory entry to identify which node options are implemented. Figure 23-7 illustrates the format of the Node_Capabilities entry and Table 23-3 decribes each field. Note that fields that must be implemented by serial bus node are shown as shaded bit fields.

Figure 23-7: Format of Node_Capabilities Root Directory Entry

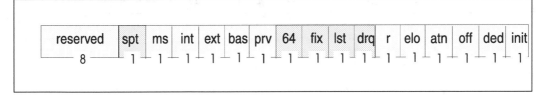

Table 23-3: Definition of Bit Fields within the Node_Capabilities Entry

Bit Field	Bit Field Description (describes meaning with bit field=1) (bit=1 feature implemented, bit=0 not implemented)
spt	Mode implements the **SPLIT_TIMEOUT** register. This bit must be set by nodes that are transaction capable. See the section entitled "Split_Timeout Register" on page 373 for definition of transaction capable.
ms	**Messaging passing** registers are implemented.
int	**INTERRUPT_TARGET** & **INTERRUPT_MASK** registers are implemented.

FireWire System Architecture

Table 23-3: Definition of Bit Fields within the Node_Capabilities Entry (Continued)

Bit Field	Bit Field Description (describes meaning with bit field=1) (bit=1 feature implemented, bit=0 not implemented)
ext	ARGUMENT registers are implemented.
bas	TEST_START & TEST_STATUS registers are implemented
prv	Node implements the **private space**.
64	Node uses **64-bit addressing** (if cleared 32-bit addressing is used). All serial bus nodes must set this bit to a one.
fix	Node uses **fixed addressing** (if cleared extended addressing used). All serial bus nodes must set this bit to a one.
lst	**Lost** bit within the STATE_CLEAR & STATE_SET is implemented.
drq	**Disable Request** bit within the STATE_CLEAR & STATE_SET is implemented.
r	**Reserved**, contains zero and is ignored when read.
elo	Node implements ERROR_LOG register and the **error log** bit in the STATE_CLEAR & STATE_SET registers is implemented.
atn	**Attention** (atn) bit within STATE_CLEAR & STATE_SET registers is implemented.
off	Node implements the **off** bit within the STATE_CLEAR & STATE_SET registers.
ded	Node supports the **dead state**.
init	Node supports the **initializing state**.

Node_Unique_Id. The Node_Unique_Id entry identifies the location of a root leaf where the node_unique_id value resides as illustrated in Figure 23-8 on page 421. Note that the 24-bit Node_Unique_Id entry is defined as an indirect offset value that specifies the location of Node_Unique_Id leaf. The contents of this leaf consists of the following fields:

- leaf_length — specifies the number of quadlets within the leaf not including the leaf_length quadlet. This leaf contains two quadlets resulting in a leaf_length value of 0002h.
- CRC16 — this value covers the following quadlets within the leaf.
- node_vendor_id — this field contains the company ID value of the manufacturer of the node.

- chip_id_hi — specifies the msb of the chip_id value, which is defined by the manufacturer of the node.
- chip_id_lo — specifies the lsb of the chip_id value.

Figure 23-8: Format and Contents of the Node_Unique_Id Entry and Leaf

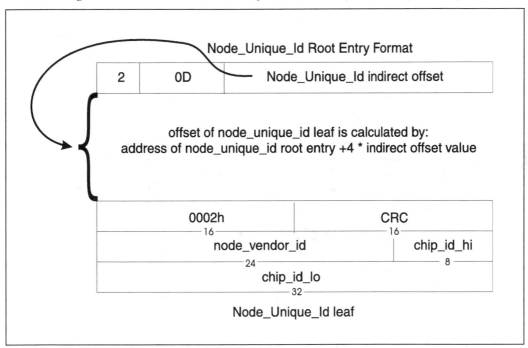

Each node is uniquely identified by a 64-bit value created by concatenating the node_vendor_id, chip_id_hi, and chip_id_lo values (Figure 23-9 on page 422). This value is termed the Extended Unique Identifier, 64-bits (EUI-64) and can be used to identify the software driver for this node. Note that the 64-bit node unique identifier is also contained within the Node_Unique_Id leaf.

Also shown in Figure 23-9, the CSR architecture is defined as an 88-bit Globally Unique Identifier (GUI) that uniquely identifies a device across all CSR-compliant buses.

Figure 23-9: CSR & Serial Bus Unique Identifiers

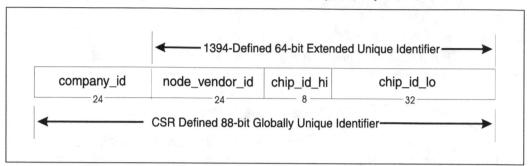

Unit_Directory & Unit_Power_Requirements. A Unit_Directory is conditionally required for each unit within the node that consumes more bus power than is specified by the "pwr" field in the self-ID packet for this node. This is necessary so that the Unit_Power_Requirements entry can be included within the Unit_Directory in ROM. Note that if the unit is self-powered these entries are not required.

Optional Root Directory Entries

Optional root directory entries are defined by the CSR architecture that can be implemented by serial bus nodes. These entries are not required by the serial bus, but can be defined by the node or module manufacturer. Following is a brief description of the optional entries.

Bus_Dependent_Info. No bus dependent information is specified by the serial bus standard.

Module_Hw_Version. The vendor that manufactured the module may choose to define a hardware version number.

Module_Spec_Id. The module specifier id may also be defined by the module vendor.

Module_Sw_Version. A module manufacturer can define a software version number that is required by this module implementation.

Company ID Value Administration

A variety of ID values are defined by the IEEE 1394 and ISO/IEC 13213 specifications, such as:

- Module_Vendor_ID
- Node_Vendor_ID
- Module_Spec_ID
- Node_Spec_ID
- Unit_Spec_ID

Each of these IDs is a 24-bit value that identifies the company that manufactured the module or node, or in the case of a "specifier" (spec) ID, the company that defined the corresponding architectural interface. These values are all based on the company_ID value, which is also commonly referred to as an Organizationally Unique Identifier, or OUI. This identifier is assigned by the IEEE Registration Authority:

Registration Authority Committee (RAC)
The Institute of Electrical and Electronic Engineers, Inc.
445 Hoes Lane
Piscataway, NJ 08855-1331

(908) 562-3812

Part Six

Power Management

24 *Introduction to Power Management*

The Previous Chapter

The previous chapter detailed the contents of configuration ROM required by the ISO/IEC 13213 specification. The serial bus also defines ROM entries that are required by some nodes, depending on the capabilities.

This Chapter

This chapter provides a brief introduction to the power management environment introduced by the 1394a specification. The chapter introduces the three documents that further define the power management specification: Cable Power Distribution, Suspend/Resume Mechanisms, and Power State Management.

The Next Chapter

The next chapter discusses power distribution in the cable environment. It discusses the four power type designations for nodes: power providers, alternate power providers, power consumers, and self-powered devices. Details regarding the power implementation of nodes are also included.

Overview

The 1394-1995 specification defines a variety of power-related issues that have been discussed in previous chapters. The 1394a supplement provides additional definition and capability regarding generation, distribution, and management of power in the 1394 environment. These additions are the focus of this chapter. Regrettably, the 1394a supplement and the associated Power Specification were still in development at the time of this writing. The reader is strongly cautioned that some of the information contained in this chapter will likely change before final approval by the 1394 Trade Association and additional information may be added. Subsequent editions of the book will include information from the final specification.

Review of 1394-1995 Power-Related Issues

The 1394-1995 specification includes a variety of features related to powering 1394 devices. In general, the specification allows nodes to be powered either by their own local power supply or from the cable. However, it also requires that the physical layer of each node must be capable of repeating serial bus traffic whether or not local power is available. This means that all nodes must be able to power their PHY layer interface with cable power, in the event that local power is off. Additionally, the specification requires that there is sufficient cable power available to power all nodes.

Other power-related requirements include:

- A single connector type is defined that includes VP and VG pins.
- Nodes may (not required) supply unregulated power to the bus. (from 8vdc - 40vdc).
- Nodes must isolate cable power from local power.
- Nodes may consume no more than 1 w of power from the bus after reset. Additional power may be consumed if sufficient bus power is available. This is under the control of the node that provides power management support.
- All nodes must report their power class in the self-ID packet during bus configuration. If the total power required by the node (including power required by internal units) exceeds the amount that can be reported in the self-ID packet (10W total), it must report the additional power that it requires in configuration ROM.
- The bus manager node must calculate the total power available on the bus and determine if sufficient power is available to power all nodes that need cable power. If sufficient power is available, the bus manager must generate a link-on packet for each device that requires cable power.
- In the absence of a bus manager node, the isochronous resource manager node is responsible for issuing the link-on packets to apply power to nodes that require bus power. Note that the isochronous resource manager is not required to validate power availability prior to sending the link-on packets.

Chapter 24: Introduction to Power Management

Goals of the 1394a Power Extensions

Members of the personal computer industry involved in implementing the 1394 serial bus have concluded that the 1995 version of the specification requires additional clarification and enhancement. To this end, the 1394 Trade Association has drafted a three part specification to further define power-related issues for the 1394 serial bus. These documents contain the following information:

- Part 1 — defines power distribution on the serial bus, including the voltage levels, types of power providers, power consumers, self-powered devices, and power down behavior.
- Part 2 — defines power states, CSR registers, and configuration ROM entries used to control and manage power.
- Part 3 — defines power conservation mechanisms (suspend and resume) for implementing low power bus states. Note, however, that the suspend and resume features were still being debated when this book was published, and have not been included here. Check MindShare's web site for later information.

The state of the power management documentation at the time of writing was:

Part 1: Cable Power Distribution (Revision 0.93)

Part 2: Suspend/Resume (Revision 0.73)

Part 3: Power State Management (Revision 0.71)

25 Cable Power Distribution

The Previous Chapter

The previous chapter provided a brief introduction to the power management environment introduced by the 1394a specification. It also discussed the state of the power specifications at the time of writing: Cable Power Distribution, Suspend/Resume Mechanisms, and Power State Management.

This Chapter

This chapter discusses power distribution in the cable environment. It discusses the four power type designations for nodes: power providers, alternate power providers, power consumers, and self-powered devices. Details regarding the power implementation of nodes is also included.

The Next Chapter

Next, the suspend and resume mechanism is defined. This capability allows the PHY layer within a node to enter a low power state under software control (either local node software or from another node). The mechanisms implemented for suspend and resume are detailed including: command and confirmation packets, suspend initiator actions, suspend target actions, and related suspend and resume signaling. The impact on PHY and port register definition is also discussed.

Power Distribution

The power distribution document provides additional definition for node power classes and introduces new terminology to describe nodes that supply power to the bus. In addition it defines the power functionality of each node in terms of four power configuration groups:

1. Power Providers
2. Alternate Power Providers
3. Power Consumers
4. Self-Powered nodes

Each of these configuration groups is described in the following sections.

Power Class Codes

The power class code definition for power providers, power consumers, and self-powered nodes is listed in Table 25-1 on page 432. Note that the class code may vary depending on whether the node is a single- or multi-port implementation. The definition of each code value is stated in Table 25-2 on page 432.

Table 25-1: Node Power Class Code Assignments For Each Power Configuration

Node Power Configuration	Self-ID Packet Power Class	
	Single Port	**Multiple Ports**
Power Provider	1, 2, 3	1, 2, 3
Alternate Power Provider	4	4
Power Consumer	4, 6, 7	NA
Self-Power	0	0, 4

Table 25-2: Definition of Power Class Values Within "Pwr" Field of Self-ID Packets

POWER_CLASS Code (binary)	Power Consumption and Source Characteristics
000	Node does not require bus power nor repeat bus power.
001	Node is self-powered and provides 15W (minimum) to the bus.
010	Node is self-powered and provides 30W (minimum) to the bus.
011	Node is self-powered and provides 45W (minimum) to the bus.

Chapter 25: Cable Power Distribution

Table 25-2: Definition of Power Class Values Within "Pwr" Field of Self-ID Packets (Continued)

POWER_CLASS Code (binary)	Power Consumption and Source Characteristics
100	Node may be powered from the bus and is using up to 3W and no additional bus power is needed to enable the link.
101	Reserved for future implementations.
110	Node is powered from the bus and consumes 3W maximum. An additional 3W maximum is needed to enable the link.
111	Node is powered from the bus and consumes 3W maximum. An additional 7W maximum is needed to enable the link.

Power Providers

Nodes that source power to the bus are termed power providers. Two classes of power providers are defined by the Power specification:

- Power Providers
- Alternate Power Providers

As shown in Table 25-2 on page 432, the amount of power that a node provides to the cable can vary. A power provider may be a single- or multi-port implementation and must use the 6-pin port connectors.

The cable power requirements are specified in Table 25-3. Note that these values differ from the 1394-1995 values.

Table 25-3: Cable Power Requirements

Condition	Limit
Maximum output current per port	1.5 amps
Minimum output voltage (power class 1,2&3)	20 vdc
Minimum output voltage (all other classes)	8 vdc
Maximum output voltage	33 vdc
Maximum output ripple (1 kHz to 400 MHz)	100 mv peak-to-peak

FireWire System Architecture

Any power provider must place a diode in the output line going to each port as illustrated in Figure 25-1 on page 434, versus a single diode for all ports for the 1995 version of the specification. This prevents current from flowing from the cable to the power supply when the cable voltage is higher than the power supply's voltage.

Figure 25-1: Power Providers Must Place Diodes in Each Port VG Line

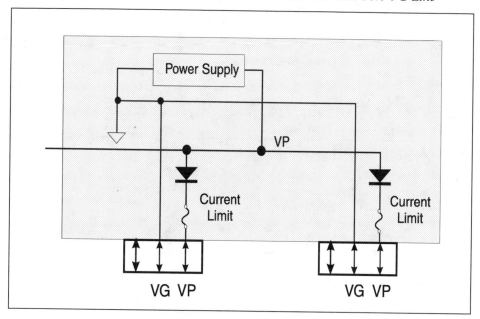

Power Provider Classes

The minimum amount of power supplied by a power provider is 15, 30, or 45W and must declare a power class of 1, 2, or 3 via its self-ID packet. The unregulated output voltage at each port must be in the range from 20vdc to 33vdc under full load conditions. Figure 25-2 on page 435 illustrates the configuration of a power provider. Power providers always deliver bus power as long as their local power source (battery or AC) remains enabled. The bus power output is not disrupted due to any action on the bus.

Chapter 25: Cable Power Distribution

A power provider should not use bus power for its PHY in the event that local power is off. When the primary system power is lost a power provide may trickle power its PHY from another power source provided by the system. In this event, multi-port power providers must continue to repeat serial bus traffic to preserve the bus topology. A power provider whose PHY is not powered cannot repeat bus traffic, and consequently will have the effect of segmenting the bus. When trickle powering its PHY, a power provider must report its power class as 000b.

Since the power provider must have diodes on each port, it is also unable to pass power. The diodes provide a means of creating power domains. Domains provide a low-cost solution for adding power incrementally to the cable.

Current limiting must also be employed by all power providers to meet regulatory requirements and must not exceed 1.5A.

Figure 25-2: Configuration of Power Provider

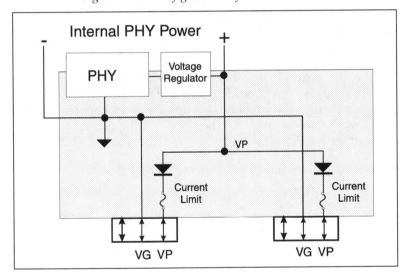

Alternate Power Providers

Alternate power providers are a subclass of power providers that supply less power than standard power providers. These power providers must specify a power class of 4 and must have one or more ports; however, two ports are recommended. An alternate power source must use only 6-pin connectors (4-pin connectors are not permitted). Alternate power providers can consume bus power in the event that its local supply is powered off. This is permitted so that the power provider can keep its PHY powered and can continue repeating serial bus traffic between ports.

An alternate provider can discontinue its bus power output dynamically, either under software control or when a particular event occurs (e.g. after a bus reset).

Maximum Voltage <20vdc. The output voltage of an alternate power provider nodes may be <20vdc (less than the minimum voltage allowed by providers). The actual power delivery capability of a alternate power provider can be found in configuration ROM (i.e. the Cable_Power_Source_Level entry). If the alternate power providers detects voltage on the cable that is greater than the voltage it provides, then it should stop providing power.

Figure 25-3 on page 437 illustrates the configuration of a alternate power provider with more than one port. The power class of this type of power provider is 4. Note that diode isolation must be implemented to prevent this power source from drawing current from another power provider on the cable that has a higher voltage than this one.

An alternate power source may also implement diodes at each port as is done with a primary power source (power class of 1,2, or 3). If this implementation is chosen this node will not be able to pass power.

Maximum Voltage >20vdc. If the launch voltage of an alternate power provider is equivalent to the levels of a power provider (>20vdc), then isolation diodes must be placed at each node (the same as power providers as illustrated in Figure 25-2 on page 435). Alternate power providers configured in this fashion must self-power their PHY.

Chapter 25: Cable Power Distribution

Figure 25-3: Alternate Power Provider with Bus Powered PHY (Power Class 4)

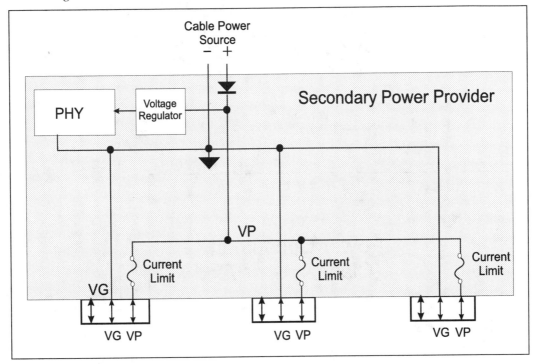

Power Consumer

Power consumers report power class values of 4, 6, or 7 via their self-ID packets. These nodes may have only one 6-pin connector and can only sink bus power.

Following reset, the node must not consume greater than 3W of power until it receives a link-on packet from the power manager. The power consumer node must be able to participate in bus configuration with a cable voltage as low as 7.5vdc. If the power consumer requires more current than can be reported in the self-ID packets, it must implement configuration ROM entries that describe the additional power required by the individual units within the node.

Figure 25-4: Power Consumer Node Implementation

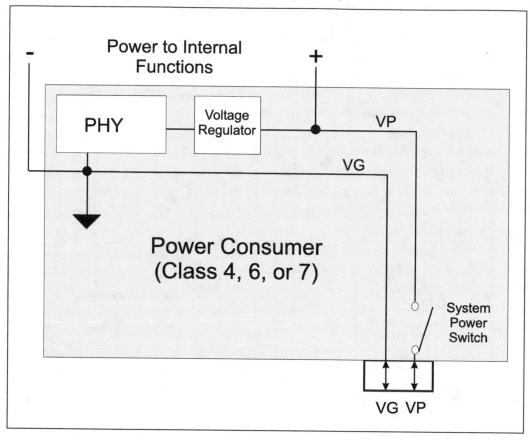

Self-Powered Nodes (Non Power Providers)

A self-powered node reports a power class of either 0 (single port) or 4 (multi-port) via its self-ID packet. When a self-powered node is powered and active it consumes no power from the bus. A self-powered single port node can never sink current from the cable, whereas, a self-powered multi-port node can sink cable power for its PHY in the event that local power is removed, and thus repeat serial bus transactions between ports.

Note that a wall powered node is required to implement at least two ports, and three are recommended. All ports must be the same type with 6-pin connectors.

This type of node is not required to be a power provider, but it is required to pass cable power between ports. (Note that power pass-through is also required by a multi-port alternate power provider when cable power is off.) In multi-port implementations, current limiting must be provided for each port connection. Note that the voltage pass-through illustrations are conceptual only, additional circuitry may be implemented. Note also that voltage pass-through must be disabled in the event that the PHY is powered off.

Self-Powered Class Zero Nodes

Class zero self-powered nodes may not source or sink cable power. Class zero self-powered nodes can have one or more ports. The connectors can be either 4-pin or 6-pin, and all connectors on the same node must be of the same type. Figure 25-5 is a conceptual illustration of the power connections in a class zero node. Note that power is not passed in multiple port implementations.

Figure 25-5: Example of Self-Powered Node (Class 0)

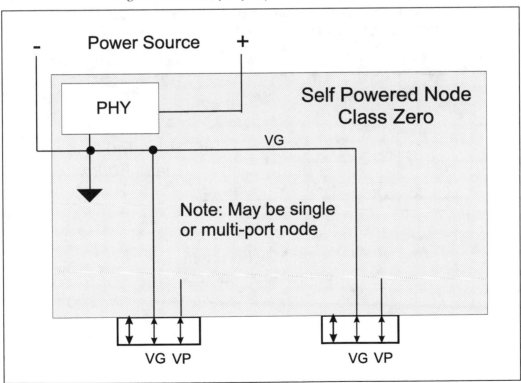

Self-Powered Class Four Nodes

Class four nodes are characterized by their ability to consume up to 3W of power for their PHY, but may not consume any cable power. All ports on class four nodes must use 6-pin connectors and must pass power. No additional cable power can be consumed in order for the link layer to be enabled. Other requirements of class four nodes vary depending on the actual number of ports and configurations. The following class-four variations are discussed:

- Two port node — no cable power used
- Three ports or more — no cable power used
- Two ports or more — PHY powered by cable if system power is lost
- Two ports or more — cable-powered PHY

Two port node — no cable power used. Figure 25-6 illustrates power passing required of a two-port node. Note that in the event that node power is lost, the PHY would not be powered and would not be able to repeat packet traffic causing the bus to be segmented. Another power source within the system must be provided to power the PHY in the event that main power is lost.

Figure 25-6: Example of Two-Port Node that Does Not Use Cable Power (Class 4).

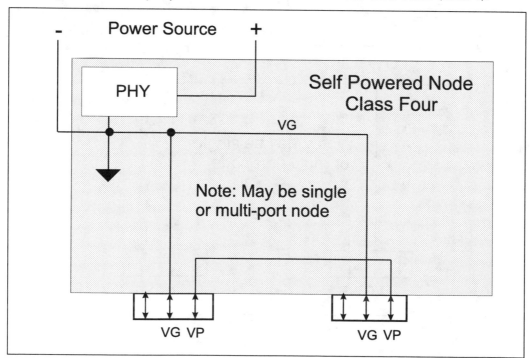

Three ports or more — no cable power used. In this example (illustrated in Figure 25-7), three or more ports are implemented. In this case, the specification requires that current limiting must be provided at each port and power must also be passed. As in the previous example, no power is consumed by the node, therefore the PHY must be trickle powered by an alternative power source within the system.

Figure 25-7: Example of Node with 3 Ports that Does Not Use Cable Power (Class 4).

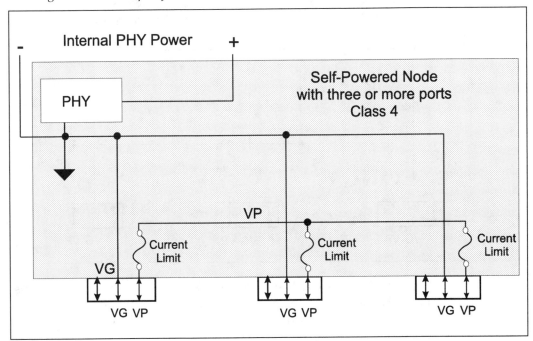

Two ports or more — cable power used when power is lost. The example illustrated in Figure 25-8 shows the PHY being powered by the cable in the event that main power is lost. Once again current limiting is required per port, along with power pass-through. Diode isolation is also needed to prevent current being drawn from the local supply in the event that higher voltage is present on the cable and vice versa.

Figure 25-8: Example of Self-Powered Node that Uses Cable Power if Main Power is Lost

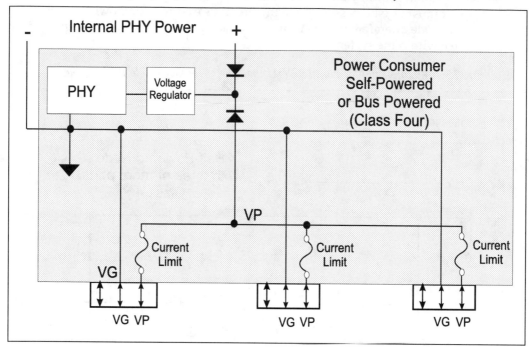

Two ports or more — cable-powered PHY. The final example illustrates a node that uses cable power for its PHY, whether or not main power is available. Power must be passed and current limiting employed. See Figure 25-9 on page 443.

Figure 25-9: Example Self-Powered Node with PHY Powered by Cable

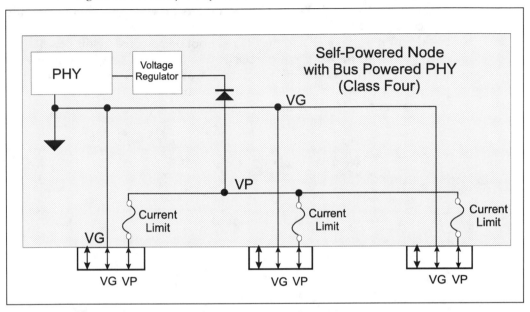

Local Power Down Summary

As mentioned in the previous sections, any self-powered device that implements two or more ports normally powers its PHY from the local supply. However, if the local supply is powered off, then the PHY must remain powered (using bus power if necessary) to maintain continuity of bus traffic across all cable segments. If the PHY power is removed, it is no longer capable of repeating serial bus transactions, resulting in segmentation of the serial bus.

Self-powered multi-port nodes must behave in one of the following ways in the event that local power is turned off. The recommended methods are presented in priority order with method one being the best solution, two second best, and three allowed but not recommended. Note also that references to power pass-through pertains to all self-powered nodes except power providers, which are unable to pass power (due to diode isolation).

1. Even though local power has been switched off, the PHY remains powered by local power. In other words, power to all internal units and the link layer has been removed, but power to the PHY remains active. Power pass-

through also remains active.

2. Local power is completely removed from all internal devices including the PHY, but the PHY can be powered using serial bus power. Power pass-through is active so that devices needing bus power downstream continue to receive power.

3. Local power is removed and the PHY cannot be powered by the bus. Power pass-through is disabled and the bus is fragmented. If power pass-through remained active with the PHY powered down, no serial bus transactions would reach nodes residing on downstream ports. They would remain powered, but could not be managed by the power manager node.

26 *Suspend & Resume*

The Previous Chapter

The previous chapter discussed power distribution in the cable environment. It discussed the four power type designations for nodes: power providers, alternate power providers, power consumers, and self-powered devices. Details regarding the power implementation of nodes was also included.

This Chapter

This chapter introduces the suspend and resume mechanisms. This capability allows the PHY layer within a node to enter a low power state under software control (either local node software or from another node). The mechanisms implemented for suspend and resume are detailed including: command and confirmation packets, suspend initiator actions, suspend target actions, and related suspend and resume signaling. The impact on PHY and port register definition is also discussed.

The Next Chapter

The next chapter describes the CSR registers and ROM entries that define power management capabilities and provide the mechanisms for controlling the power states of a node and of local units within a node.

Overview

Due to the incomplete status of the suspend/resume documentation, this chapter provides only an overview of the suspend and resume capabilities and does not attempt to detail specific consideration and corner conditions that exist.

The goal of suspend and resume is to allow a pair of attached PHY ports to enter a low power state in which recovery to full power and operation is possible. In this way, a segment of the bus may be placed into a low power state. When a port is suspended it is no longer able to receive or transmit packets. However, suspended ports can detect whether a node is attached or detached.

To help understand the suspend capabilities consider the following example. Figure 26-1 on page 446 illustrates a 1394a only topology (i.e. all nodes are 1394a compliant) that interfaces to a PCI bus. Note that the node at the PCI bus has transferred a suspend command packet that target port 2 within the VCR node. In response, the VCR transmits a confirmation packet to confirm that the suspend command has been accepted. The command packet identifies the suspend initiator (the port responsible for signaling suspend).

Figure 26-1: PCI to 1394 Bridge Node Sends Suspend Command to VCR Node, Port 2

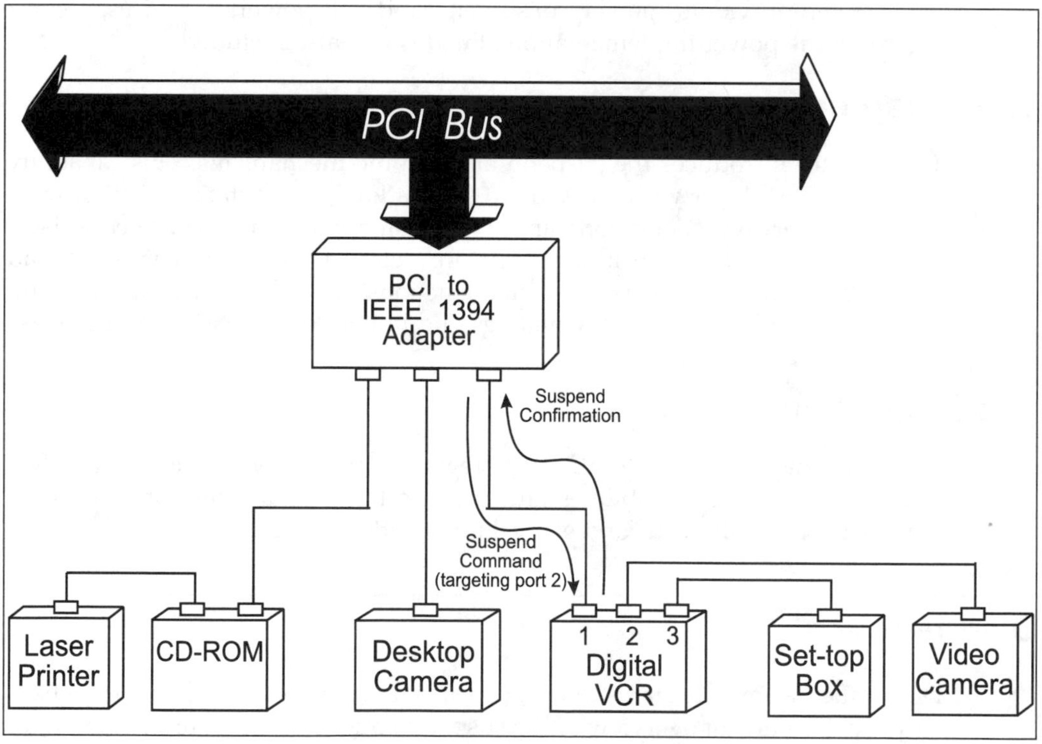

Refer to Figure 26-2. Immediately following the confirmation packet (after detecting the acknowledge gap), the suspend initiator (port 2 of the VCR node) signals suspend (TX_SUSPEND=00) to the node connected to port 2 (video camera), which detects the suspend (RX_SUSPEND=00). The video camera is referred to as the suspend target. The node containing the suspend initiator also signals data prefix to its other ports followed by a short bus reset. Bus reset is then repeated to all nodes in the system except the node or nodes attached to the suspend initiator port.

The suspend initiator and suspend target perform a handshake and both enter a low power, or suspended state. When the tree ID process is performed following the short bus reset, the VCR node will report its port 2 as inactive, making all nodes attached to the inactive port invisible to the rest of the network.

Figure 26-2: Actions Taken by the Suspend Initiator

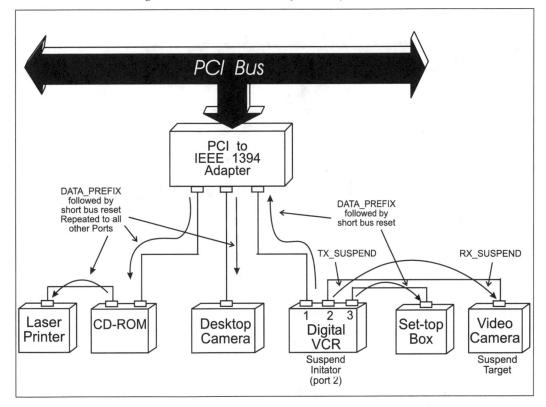

Once the bus is reset and the suspended port handshake completes, the new topology eliminates the video camera. No packets are transferred to the suspended ports and they are unable to transmit packets. (See Figure 26-3 on page 448).

If the video camera is activated by the user, it can signal resume causing a port event indication that can serve to notify the link and application. Further the video camera can signal the VCR of the event. The bus can again be reset to cause bus reconfiguration with the VCR and video camera ports once again active. Similarly, the PCI node may cause a resume operation by sending a resume command packet to the VCR. This would cause the VCR and video camera port to transition to the active state. Reset would be signaled and the bus reconfigured.

Figure 26-3: State of Network Following Bus Reset

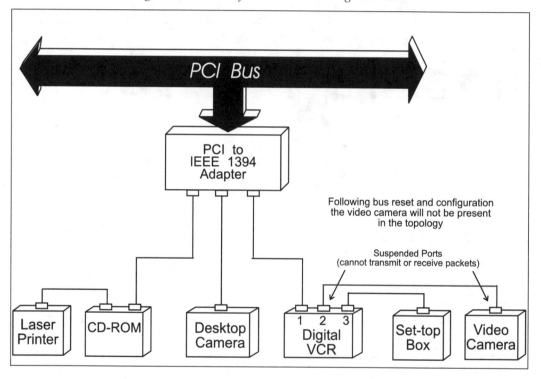

Suspending a Port

An active port may enter a suspended state under a variety of conditions:

- When a suspend command packet is received. The port number is specified in the address field of a suspend command packet. The command may be issued by another node or by the local link layer.
- When the port detects suspend signaling (RX_SUSPEND) via its arbitration

comparators.
- When the port resides within the same node as another port that has detected RX_SUSPEND.
- When the port receives disable notify (RX_DISABLE_NOTIFY).
- When TpBias is no longer detected.

Suspending via the Suspend Command Packet

Figure 26-4 on page 449 illustrates the format of the command packet that specifies "initiate suspend." The port number field specifies the specific port within the target PHY that will become the suspend initiator. The target node responds to the command packet with a confirmation packet, illustrated in Figure 26-5. This packet contains the initiate suspend command to tie this confirmation to the previous command. The phy_ID field contains the phy ID of the confirming node.

Figure 26-4: "Initiate Suspend" Command Packet Format

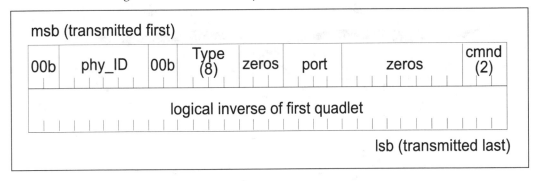

Figure 26-5: Suspend Confirmation Packet Format

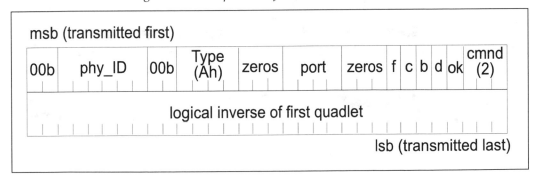

FireWire System Architecture

Once the confirmation packet has been received and the transmitting node (the suspend initiator) detects an acknowledge gap, it signals TX_SUSPEND to the suspend target and DATA_PREFIX followed by short bus reset over all other ports. See Figure 26-6 for the suspend initiator node actions at the suspended port and at other active ports. Note that all active ports at the node containing the suspend initiator will remain active and be part of the active domain. The suspend initiator port and all other ports connected become part of the inactive domain.

Figure 26-6: Action Taken by Suspend Initiator and Suspend Target Following Confirmation Packet

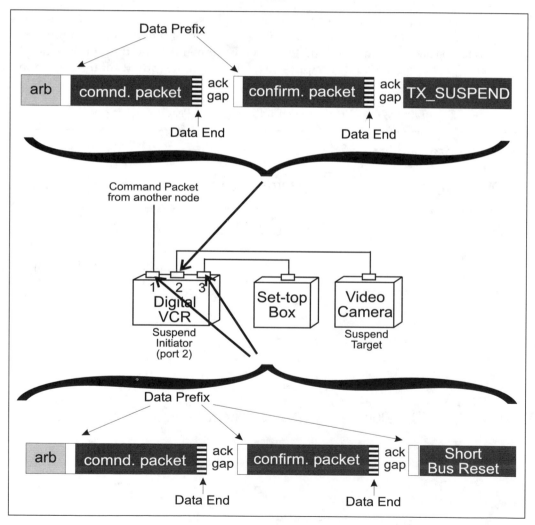

Suspending via RX_SUSPEND

When a suspend target port detects RX_SUSPEND, the target node must signal TX_SUSPEND to all of its other active ports. This action is necessary because the suspended port will isolate all branches from the network. The result is that the suspend target and all other ports within the same node along with all other ports connected to those ports will be suspended and isolated from the operation bus, thus becoming part of the inactive domain.

The BIAS Handshake

When one port signals TX_SUSPEND and the other detects RX_SUSPEND, a handshake takes place between the two nodes. The suspend target confirms receipt of RX_SUSPEND by driving TpBias low. When the suspend initiator detects TpBias low, it in turn drives its TpBias low. The suspend target continues to drive TpBias low until it detects removal of TpBias at its port status receiver, but must not drive TpBias low for greater than $BIAS\_HANDSHAKE_{MAX}$. Additionally, when the suspend target detects TpBias removed by the suspend initiator it disables its TpBias driver, thereby placing the driver into a high impedance state. The suspend initiator continues to drive its TpBias output low until the connection detect circuitry has stabilized (i.e. connect_detect becomes true), at which time it disables its TpBias driver.

Once the suspend initiator and suspend target have completed the bias handshake they will be in the low power state. The only circuitry required to remain powered is the connect detection circuitry.

Suspending via Port Disable

A port can be disabled in one of three ways:

- When it receives a disable port command packet from its local link.
- When it receives a disable port command packet from a remote node.
- When the link writes directly to a port register and sets the port disable bit.

Disable via Disable Port Command Packet (local or remote)

Figure 26-7 illustrates the format of the command packet with the command field indicating "disable port." The effect of a port disable is that only the port targeted will enter the suspended state while all other ports remain unaffected.

Figure 26-7: Format of "Disable Port" Command Packet

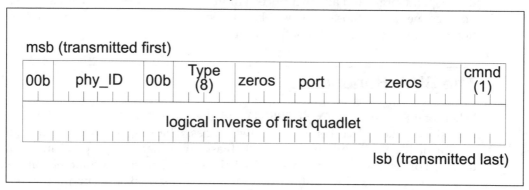

When the PHY receives this packet it must return a confirmation packet to all ports except the port target by the command field. After delivering the command it then must initiate a short bus reset to all ports except the disabled port. The port targeted by the disable port command must signal disable notify (TX_DISABLE_NOTIFY=Z1) to the attached node. Once disable notify signaling is complete, the target port is then disabled, at which time it will drive its TpBias output low until connect_detect becomes valid. It then disables its TpBias generator and the output goes to a high impedance state. Figure 26-8 on page 453 illustrates the bus actions.

Upon detecting RX_DISABLE_NOTIFY, the respondent node asserts Data_Prefix followed by reset on all of its active ports. The port on which it received the RX_DISABLE_NOTIFY will not be driven with DATA_PREFIX. The result of the disable action is that only the port being disabled is placed into a suspended state, while all other ports that were previously active remain active. Note that port disable may also result in two separate active domains being created with the nodes connected to the disabled port being isolated the rest of the network.

Figure 26-8: Illustration of Actions Taken By Target Node When Port Disable Command is
Issued

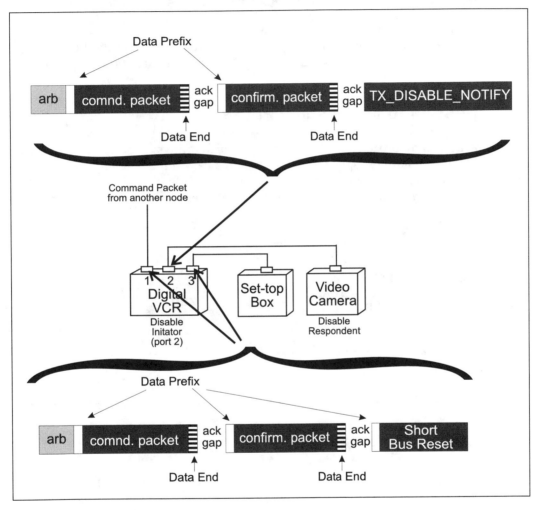

Port Suspend via Unexpected Loss of Bias

If a port suddenly detects the loss of TpBias being driven by an attached node, it
must generate reset on all active ports and drive TpBias low on the port that lost
bias. Once the connect circuitry stabilizes (connect_detect is true), the port disables its TpBias driver and enters a suspended state.

Resuming Full Operation

A port can resume to normal operation in three primary ways:

- A resume packet can be broadcast to all nodes.
- A command packet can be sent to resume a suspended or disabled port.
- A port event can cause the local application to initiate port resumption.

Resuming via Resume Packet

A node may broadcast a resume packet which targets all nodes. The causes all PHYs containing suspended port to commence resume operations for all ports that are connected and suspended. This packet is identified by a type field of Fh making it a resume broadcast packet that receives no reply. See Figure 26-9.

Figure 26-9: Format of a Resume Packet

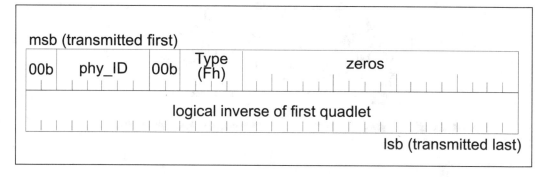

Resuming via Resume Port Command Packet

A previous suspended port can be awakened via a resume port command packet just as it was suspended. For example, if an active PHY has previously received a suspend port command packet targeting one of several ports, it will continue to operate normally and repeat packets to all other active ports except the suspended port. If a port resume packet targets the suspended port, the PHY will cause the port to drive its TpBias high to signal resume to the attached node, which in turn will drive TpBias high to all of its suspended ports, thereby waking the suspended domain. Figure 26-10 illustrates the contents of a resume port command packet.

Figure 26-10: Format of a Command Packet Defined as a Resume Port Packet

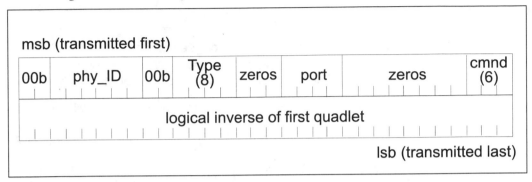

Resuming via Port Events

A port and PHY can be configured to notify the link of particular events that can be used to wake a suspended port and other nodes attached to the port that are also suspended. The individual events that can generate a port event are enabled via software within the port registers. Figure 26-11 on page 456 illustrates the port registers. The shaded bit fields within the port registers must be set to enable generation of the particular port event that can initiate a resume operation. These events are:

- Connect change
- Bias change
- Disabled change
- Fault

Figure 26-11: Port Registers and Port Event Enable Bits

0111	Page_select = 0		Res	Port_select = n			
1000	AStat	BStat		Child	Con	Bias	Disabled	Register 0
1001	Negotiated Speed		Interrupt Enable	Fault	Reserved			Register 1
1010	Reserved							Register 2
1011	Reserved							Register 3
1100	Reserved							Register 4
1101	Reserved							Register 5
1110	Reserved							Register 6
1111	Reserved							Register 7

When the "interrupt enable" bit in the port register 1 and the bit field for a given event is set, the corresponding event will cause the "port event" field in the PHY register to be set (See Figure 26-12 on page 457). The PHY will notify the link that port event has occurred. Two possibilities exist:

1. The link is powered (Link Power Status is active) — The link will be notified of the event via delivery of 4 bits of status information.
2. The link is not powered (Link Power Status is inactive) — The PHY will deliver a "linkOn" signal that causes power to be applied to the link, thus waking it up.

Once the link is notified, local software can initiate resumption of normal operation.

Figure 26-12: PHY Registers

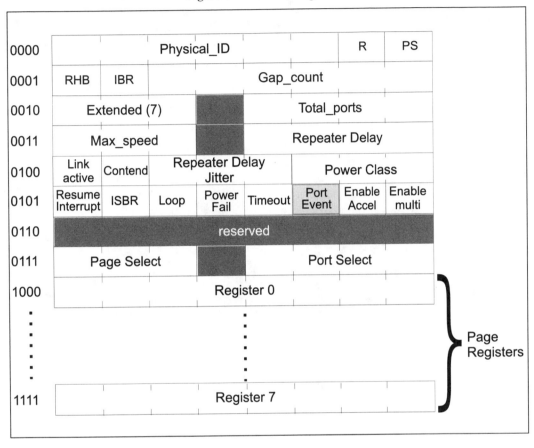

27 *Power State Management*

The Previous Chapter

The previous chapter introduced the suspend and resume mechanisms. This capability allows the PHY layer within a node to enter a low power state under software control (either local node software or from another node). The mechanisms implemented for suspend and resume were detailed including: command and confirmation packets, suspend initiator actions, suspend target actions, and related suspend and resume signaling. The impact on PHY and port register definition were also discussed.

This Chapter

This chapter describes the CSR registers and ROM entries that define power management capabilities and provide the mechanisms for controlling the power states of a node and of local units within a node.

Power Management

Power management involves the control of the power states of individual nodes or units within nodes. Four power states are defined that permit control over the node and individual units. To support power management, additional CSR registers and ROM entries are also defined.

The goal of power management is to enable applications to control transitions in the power states, so that power can be managed efficiently. This capability includes the following:

- A mechanism to allow applications at one node to determine the power-related abilities of a remote node or functional units within a node, and to determine its current power state.
- A mechanism to permit a remote application to enable a power feature and control the power state.

- A mechanism to allow a remote node to notify the power manager node of changes in its power state that affect bus operation.
- A mechanism to notify a node that has entered a low power state that a remote event has occurred that should wake the node up.
- Ability of the power manager node to facilitate the actions and capabilities required by the power management model, to determine the abilities of a power provider node, and to control the level of power that a power provider supplies to the bus.

Note that some of the power management features are controlled directly by the power manager node (i.e. the bus manager node), while other management features at the functional unit level are implementation specific and are intended to be controlled by the related application.

Power States

Four power states provide the ability to control power within each node and a functional unit within nodes. The definition of the node power states are defined for global power management control, while unit power states are specific to a given functional unit.

Node Power States

Node power states provide the operational states of the PHY and link. Table 27-1 lists the node power states. New CSR registers are defined that control the transition between states. Each state is summarized below.

Table 27-1: Node Power States

Node Power State	Link Power	PHY Power	Node Context
N0	On (or standby)	On	Preserved
N1	Off	On	Unspecified
N2	Off	Suspend	Unspecified
N3	Off	Off	Lost

Node Power State Zero (N0). This state represents the full-on power state in which the PHY and link (via a link-on packet) are both powered.

Note that N0 may include an optional standby feature, in which the link may be partially suspended and the transaction and higher layers may be in a fully suspended state, thus reducing power consumption. If a transaction targets a node that is in standby, the link must be able to decode the address and return an ACK_TARDY acknowledge code (See Table 8-15 on page 192). The link must also return to its fully functional state and initiate a wake up to the higher layers. Once the node has recovered from the standby condition, it can service the request when it is retried by the requesting node.

The amount of power consumed by the node in the N0 state is required to be less than the value reported in the self-ID packet. Actual power consumption may be reported in a new configuration ROM entry called the Node_Power_Level entry. There may exist multiple Node_Power_Level entries, one for each state.

Node Power State One (N1). The N1 state reflects the condition of the node prior to receiving the link-on packet. This state exists between bus reset and receipt of the link-on packet.

Node Power State Two (N2). N2 is the suspend state during which the link has been powered off and the PHY is in a low power condition. Consequently, the PHY is unable to perform any of its normal functions (i.e. it cannot repeat, receive, or transmit packets). The only action supported by the PHY in the N2 state is that it can detect a remote wakeup signal, causing it to return to the N0 state.

Node Power State Three (N3). N3 represents the full off condition in which the link and PHY are not powered. In this condition the node context is lost.

Unit Power States

Four power states are also defined for functional units within the node. These states are defined in Table 27-2. The unit power states have an implied relationship with an application or software driver that utilizes the functional unit.

The relationship between the node and unit power states must also be maintained to ensure sufficient power is available to support the level of power required by the unit. The node power state must always provide equal (same state value) or greater (lower state value) capability than the unit. For example, if one or more units within the node are currently running at a power state of D1, it is the responsibility of the node to not place the node into a power state lower than N1 (i.e. any request to place the node into the N2 or N3 power state would only result in a transition to N1).

Table 27-2: Unit Power States

Node Power State	Operational Condition	Description
D0 (required)	Fully operational	All unit context is maintained and full functionality is available. This state is required by all units.
D1 (optional)	Unit dependent	Power consumption is this state is less than D0. The time required to transition from D1 to D0 is less than the time to transition from D0 to D2. Unit context is preserved, but some functionality may be lost.
D2 (optional)	Unit dependent	Power consumption is this state is less than D1. The time required to transition from D2 to D0 or D1 is less than the time required to transition from D3 to either D0 or D1. Unit context may not be preserved.
D3 (optional	Not operational	No power is consumed by the unit and external power may be removed.

New CSRs

A variety of new CSR registers are required to support the power management functions. Nodes that support the new power management capability must implement some of the power-related CSRs; these nodes include:

- Power management capable nodes
- Nodes that support power management or implement one or more units that support power management.
- Nodes that implement batteries
- Units that support power management
- Power providers

The power-related CSRs are mapped within a node's initial units address space at location FFFF F001 0000h or higher. Two groups of registers are defined:

- node-specific CSRs — the start address of this register block is specified by the Node_Power_Management entry within configuration ROM. Each power-related CSR occupies a specific offset within the block as illustrated in Table 27-3.
- unit-specific CSRs — the location of the base address is specified by the node's Unit_Power_Management entry within configuration ROM. Each power-related unit CSR occupies a specific offset, illustrated in Table 27-4.

Table 27-3: Node-Specific Power-Related CSRs

Relative Offset	Name	Required	Description
00h	NODE_POWER_STATE	Mandatory	Reports the node's power state.
04h	NODE_POWER_CONTROL	Mandatory	Permits the node's power state to be managed.
08h	NOTIFICATION_ADDRESS	Optional	Destination address for power status change notification or request.
Ch	CABLE_POWER_SOURCE_STATE	Optional	Reports the node's current power provider status.
10h	CABLE_POWER_SOURCE_CONTROL	Optional	Permits the node's power provider status to change.

Table 27-3: Node-Specific Power-Related CSRs (Continued)

Relative Offset	Name	Required	Description
14h	POWER_CHANGE	Power Manager Nodes Only	Allows applications to request a change in the power state of a unit or node.

Table 27-4: Unit-Specific Power-Related CSRs

Relative Offset	Name	Required	Description
00h	UNIT_POWER_STATE	Mandatory	Reports the unit's power state
04h	UNIT_POWER_CONTROL	Mandatory	Allows unit power state to be changed.
08h	NA		Reserved
Ch	NA		Reserved
10h	NA		Reserved
18h	NA		Reserved

Node Power Control Register

This write only register gives the power manager or another application the ability to change the node's power status. Writes to this register specifies power-related actions. Note that when the node is powered from the serial bus, only the power manager is permitted to write to this register.

The NODE_POWER_CONTROL register contains a single field (named "function." The format of the register is illustrated in Figure 27-1 and the values specified for the function field are listed in Table 27-5.

Figure 27-1: Format of the NODE_POWER_CONTROL Register

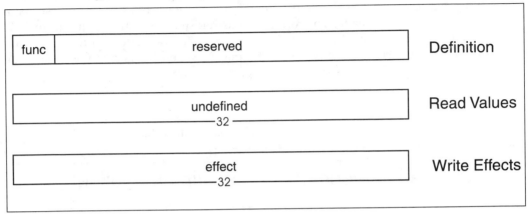

Table 27-5: Definition of Function Field Within the NODE_POWER_CONTROL Register

Field Value	Name	Description
0	NA	Reserved
1	Grant	Node may change power state to last state requested.
2	Deny	Node must not change power state, unless forced by external event (e.g. battery power depleted).
3	Wait	Node must wait 5 seconds for further power manager response before making the requested power state change.
4	Set Level 0	Change the NODE_POWER_STATE register's "lvl" field to zero.
5	Set Level 1	Change the NODE_POWER_STATE register's "lvl" field to one.
6	Set Level 2	Change the NODE_POWER_STATE register's "lvl" field to two.
7	Set Level 3	Change the NODE_POWER_STATE register's "lvl" field to three.

Notification Address Register

This register contains the 64-bit address location (quadlet aligned) that must be written to in order to signal a change in node power status or to request that a status change be made. The format of this register is illustrated in Figure 27-2. Note that the enable bit "e" defines whether the node is currently generating power status change notifications or requests. When "e" is set to one, the node generates quadlet write requests to report status and issue requests.

Figure 27-2: Format of the Notification Address Register

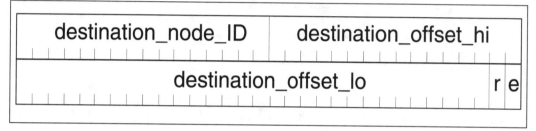

Cable Power Source State Register

This register is a read-only register used by power providers to report the node's current power sourcing status. This register contains six fields described in the bulleted list below. Format of the CABLE_POWER_SOURCE_STATE register is illustrated in Figure 27-3.

- power — the power field specifies the maximum amount of power that the node can currently provide.
- voltage — the voltage field defines the minimum voltage level in decivolts.
- rlvl — (requested level) this field defines the requested power sourcing level (0-3).
- src — (power source) this register indicates the source of power provided by this node.
  0 = node is powered from serial bus cable
  1 = node is battery powered
  2 = node is powered from electric mains
  3 = reserved
- v — (valid) indicates whether the power and voltage fields contain valid values.

- lvl — (level) this field specifies the current power sourcing level (0-3).

Figure 27-3: Format of the CABLE_POWER_SOURCE_STATE Register

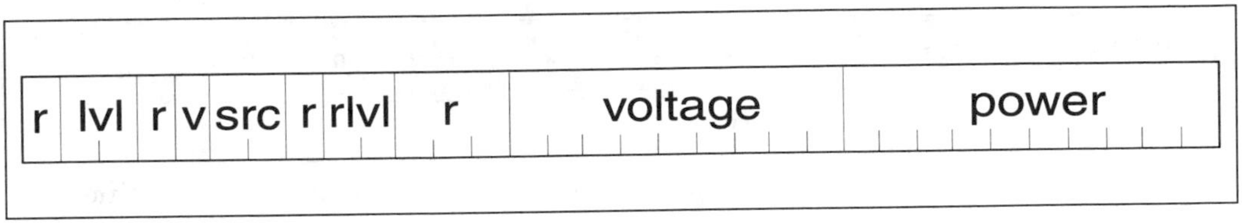

r	lvl	r	v	src	r	rlvl	r	voltage	power

Cable Power Source Control Register

This register is a write-only register that allows the power manager to change the power providers power status. This register contains a single "function" field that defines the power management function to be performed by the node. Format of this register is illustrated in Figure 27-4 and the values and definitions of the function field are defined in Table 27-6.

Figure 27-4: Format of the CABLE_POWER_SOURCE_CONTROL Register

func	reserved	Definition
undefined —— 32 ——		Read Values
effect —— 32 ——		Write Effects

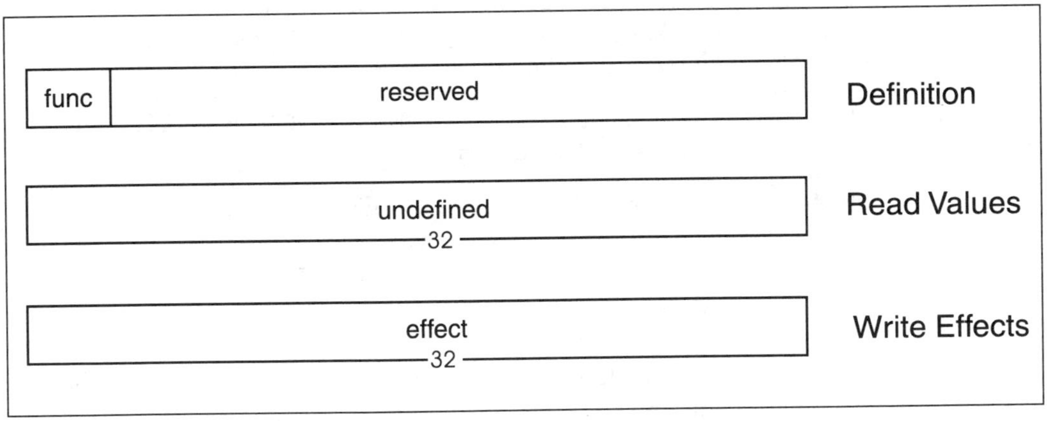

Table 27-6: Definition of Function Field Within the NODE_POWER_CONTROL Register

Field Value	Name	Description
0	NA	Reserved
1	Grant	Node may change power sourcing level to last value requested.
2	Deny	Node must not change power sourcing, unless forced by external event (e.g. battery power depleted).
3	Wait	Node must wait 5 seconds for further power manager response before making the requested power sourcing change.
4	Set Level 0	Change the CABLE_POWER_SOURCE_STATE register's "lvl" field to zero.
5	Set Level 1	Change the CABLE_POWER_SOURCE_STATE register's "lvl" field to one.
6	Set Level 2	Change the CABLE_POWER_SOURCE_STATE register's "lvl" field to two.
7	Set Level 3	Change the CABLE_POWER_SOURCE_STATE register's "lvl" field to three.

Power Change Register

A power manager node is defined as a bus manager capable node that has the "power management" bit set in the bus info block within configuration ROM. This indicates that the bus manager implements the POWER_CHANGE register and supports the new power management features. This register is used by an application to request a change in the power state of a unit within a node.

This register is mapped into the power management block at offset 14h. The register format is illustrated in Figure 27-5.

Figure 27-5: Format of the POWER_CHANGE Register

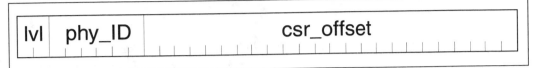

lvl	phy_ID	csr_offset

Definition of each field is described in the bulleted list below:

- lvl — this field specifies the desired power level for the unit or node.
- phy_ID — specifies the physical ID of the target node.
- csr_offset — identifies the unit or node whose power state is to be changed.

If the requested power state change fails, a RES_CONFLICT_ERROR must be returned to the requesting node. If the write request is successful, then the node must respond with RESP_COMPLETE status.

Unit Power State Register

This read-only register provides a way of changing the unit's power state. This register is only implemented if the unit architecture does not provide a mechanism for controlling the power state of the unit. If the unit architecture defines a method of controlling the unit's power state, then that method is preferred and the UNIT_POWER_STATE register will not be implemented.

The fields within the UNIT_POWER_STATE register are defined in the bulleted list below and the register format is illustrated in Figure 27-6.

- power — the power field specifies the maximum amount of power (in deciwatts) that the unit is using or can currently provide.
- voltage — the voltage field defines the minimum voltage level in decivolts.
- k — (wake_source) a value of one indicates that this unit was the source of the wake-up event.
- rlvl — (requested level) this field defines the requested power sourcing level (0-3) for the unit.
- src — (power source) this register indicates the source of power provided by this node.
  0 = unit is powered from node's power source
  1 = unit is powered from its own battery
  2 = unit is powered from electric mains
  3 = unit provides power for the node.

FireWire System Architecture

- v — (valid) indicates whether the src, wake_source, power and voltage fields contain valid values.
- lvl — (level) this field specifies the unit's current power level (0-3).

Figure 27-6: Format of UNIT_POWER_STATE Register

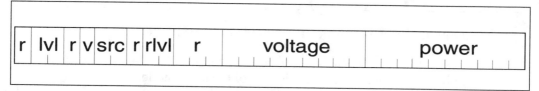

Unit Power Control Register

This write-only register allows the power manager or another application to change the unit's power status. The register contains a single "function" field whose values are specified in Table 27-7 on page 471. The format of this register is the same as Figure 27-7.

Figure 27-7: Format of UNIT_POWER_CONTROL Register

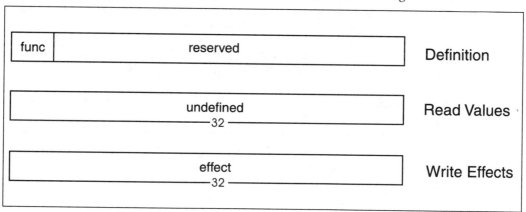

Table 27-7: Definition of Function Field Within the UNIT_POWER_CONTROL Register

Field Value	Name	Description
0	NA	Reserved
1	NA	Reserved
2	NA	Reserved
3	NA	Reserved
4	Set Level 0	Change the UNIT_POWER_STATE register's "lvl" field to zero.
5	Set Level 1	Change the UNIT_POWER_STATE register's "lvl" field to one.
6	Set Level 2	Change the UNIT_POWER_STATE register's "lvl" field to two.
7	Set Level 3	Change the UNIT_POWER_STATE register's "lvl" field to three.

Battery State Register

This read-only register provides information about the current condition of an individual battery. Format of the BATTERY_STATE register is illustrated in Figure 27-8. The register contains four fields that are defined in the following bulleted list:

- capacity — specifies the maximum battery capacity in watt-hours, when the battery is fully charged.
- available — specifies the remaining capacity of the battery as a percentage of the total capacity.
- voltage — indicates in decivolts the peak voltage of the battery.
- st — (status) specifies the current state of the battery:
  0 = battery not present
  1 = reserved
  2 = the battery installed is providing power to the unit
  3 = the battery installed is being charged

Figure 27-8: Format of the BATTERY_STATE Register

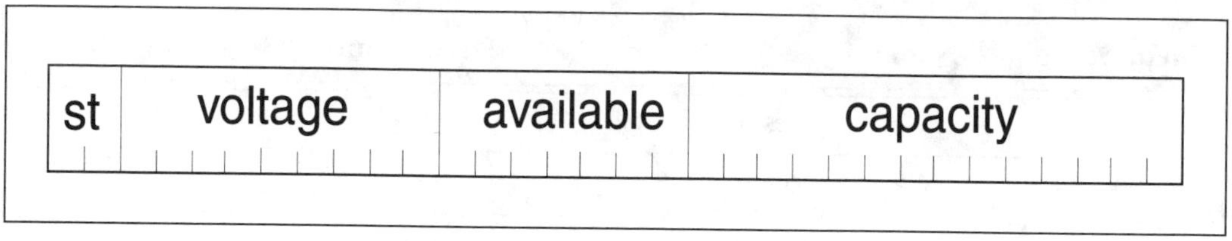

st	voltage	available	capacity

New ROM Entries

A variety of new configuration ROM entries have been defined to support the extended power management functions. For example, power manager capable nodes must include the bus info block with the "p" (power manager capable) bit set to one. Nodes and units that support power management must implement power directories where the power management-related entry resides. These directories are illustrated in Figure 27-9 on page 473.

Figure 27-9: ROM Power Directories

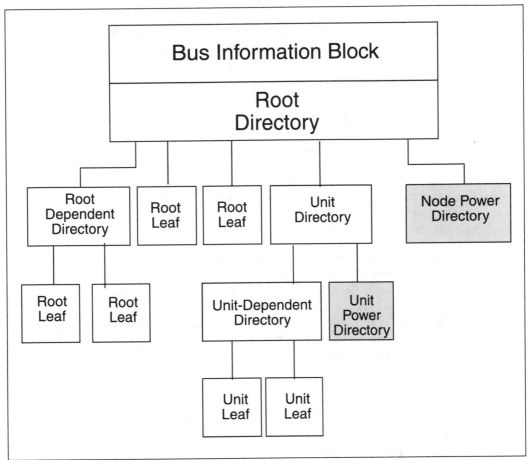

Node Power Directory Entry

This entry is located in the root directory and specifies the location of the node's power directory within configuration ROM. Only one Node_Power_Directory entry is permitted in the root node. Figure 27-10 on page 474 illustrates the format of this entry.

Figure 27-10: Format of the Node_Power_Directory Entry

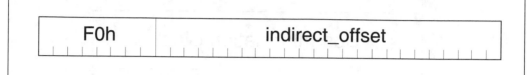

F0h	indirect_offset

Node Power Level Entry

This immediate entry is located within the node power directory and describes the amount of power consumed by a node for the specified power level. Figure 27-11 illustrates the format of this entry. The "lvl" field specifies the power level this entry pertains to. A separate Node_Power_Level entry is required for each power level supported by the node. A brief description of each field within the entry is included in the following bulleted list.

- Power_requirements — this field specifies the amount of power that the node consumes when operating at the specified level.
- Voltage — this field specifies the voltage level of the power that must be supplied to the node. The values are as follows:
  0 = power is supplied within the limits of the 1394-1995 specification.
  1 = power must be supplied at 3.3vdc.
  2 = power must be supplied at 5.0vdc.
  3 = power must be supplied at 12.0vdc.
  4-Fh = reserved
- lvl — (power level) this field indicates the power level that this entry specifies.
- w — (wakeup) this bit, when set, indicates whether this node supports the standby link mode and is only valid when the lvl field is zero.
- 30h is the concatenated values for the key-type and key_value fields.

Figure 27-11: Format of the Node_Power_Level Entry

30h	v	w	lvl	voltage	reserved	power_requirements

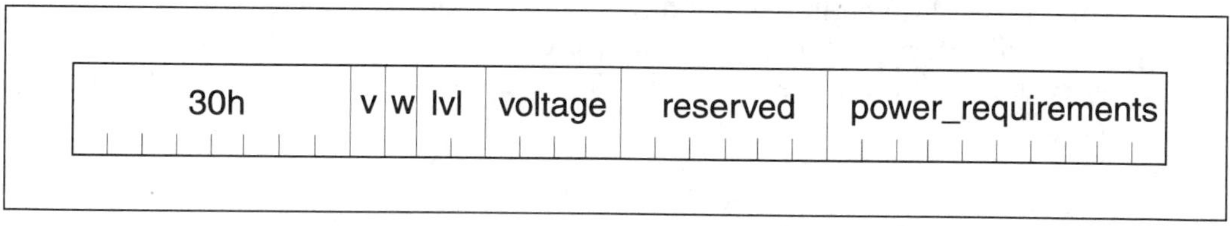

Cable Power Source Level Entry

This immediate entry specifies the amount of cable power supplied by this power provider source at the indicated power source level. Figure 27-12 illustrates the format of the Cable_Power_Source_Level entry. Each field within the entry is defined in the following bulleted list.

- Power_requirements — this field specifies in deciwatts the amount of power that this node sources to the cable while operating at the specified power level.
- Voltage — this field specifies the voltage level at which power is supplied to the cable. The possible values include:
  0 = power is supplied at 1394-1995 defined voltage levels.
  1 = power is supplied at 12vdc.
  2-Fh = reserved
- lvl — (level) specifies the power level that this entry pertains to.
- v — (valid) indicates whether or not the power information contained within this entry is valid.

Figure 27-12: Format of the Cable_Power_Source_Level Entry

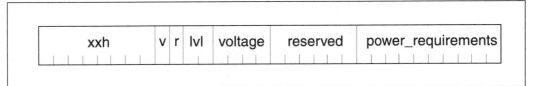

Node Power Management Entry

This immediate entry specifies the base address of the target's power management registers. Figure 27-13 illustrates the format of this entry.

Figure 27-13: Format of the Node_Power_Management Entry

FireWire System Architecture

Battery Group Entry (Node)

Nodes that implement one or more batteries must contain one or more battery group directories. The Battery_Group entry defines the location within configuration ROM of the battery group directory. Figure 27-14 illustrates the format of the Battery_Group entry. These directories must specify the characteristics and relationships between batteries.

Batteries may be installed or removed in an independent manner; thus, the battery group information defines which batteries are inserted and removed together as a single power source.

Figure 27-14: Format of Battery_Group Entry

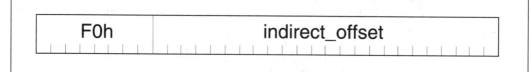

Battery State Entry

Each battery implemented within a group must have its own battery state entry within its battery group directory. This entry defines the csr register location that specifies the characteristics of where characteristic information can be found. Format of the Battery_State entry is illustrated in Figure 27-15.

Figure 27-15: Format of the Battery_State Entry

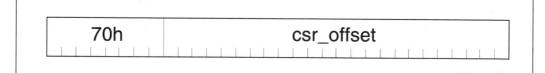

Unit Power Directory Entry

This entry is contained within a unit directory and provides an indirect offset that points to the location of a unit's power directory within configuration ROM. The format of this register is illustrated in Figure 27-16.

Figure 27-16: Format of the Unit_Power_Directory Entry within the Unit Directory

F0h	indirect_offset

Unit Power Level Entry

This entry is an immediate entry within the unit power directory. This entry specifies the power characteristics of this unit at the various power levels. Note that the "lvl" field indicates which power level that this entry pertains to; thus, each unit power directory must contain a separate Power_Level entry for each power level supported. Figure 27-17 illustrates the format of the Power_Level entry.

Figure 27-17: Format of the Unit_Power_Level Entry

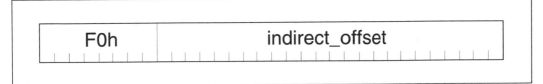

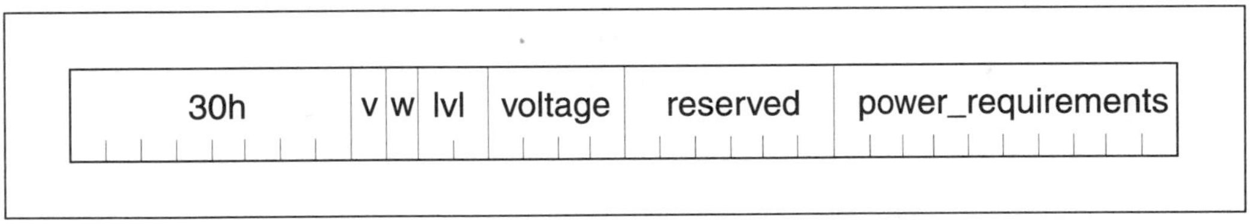

30h	v	w	lvl	voltage	reserved	power_requirements

Unit Power Management Entry

This entry is an immediate entry also located within a unit power directory. This entry specifies the base address location of the associated power management registers. The format of the Unit_Power_Management entry is illustrated in Figure 27-18.

Figure 27-18: Format of the Unit_Power_Management Entry

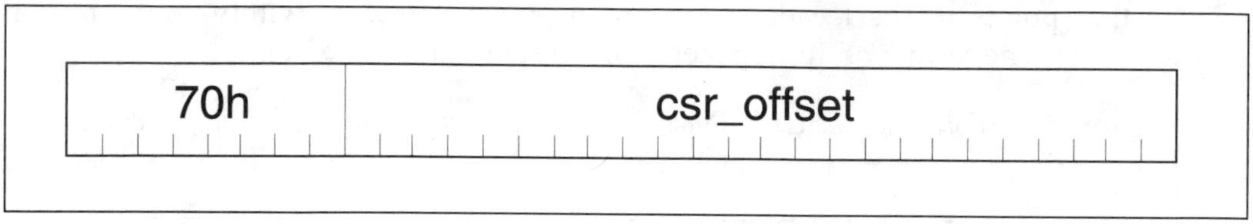

70h	csr_offset

Battery Group Entry (Unit)

This entry specifies the unit power sources when the unit is powered by batteries. A single unit may have multiple battery groups that can supply power. In this event, a unit must include separate battery group entries within the unit.

Appendix: Example 1394 Chip Solutions

Overview

Below you will see two of the most popular 1394 applications today; a 1394 enabled PC and a 1394 Digital camera. Texas Instrument's extensive 1394 portfolio includes all the silicon necessary to implement both applications. For more detailed information regarding TI's 1394 solutions, please visit our website at http://www.ti.com/sc/1394.

In this Appendix we will explain 1394 in the PC environment and in a TI 1394 camera by showing you a detailed block diagram and providing you an overview of the 1394 silicon used in each.

1394 in the PC

TI has many Link and Physical Layer Controllers necessary to implement 1394 in a PC environment; however, in this Appendix we will focus on TI's newest Link Layer TSB12LV22 and Physical Layer TSB41LV03.

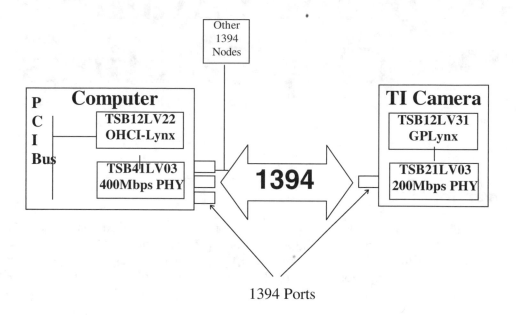

1394 Ports

TSB12LV22 / OHCI-Lynx

The industry's first Open Host Controller Interface (OHCI) Link Layer controller will revolutionize the way we use our computers. The OHCI specification provides the host PC a way to communicate with high-speed peripherals via a single OHCI driver. With an OHCI link layer device, the system software will not require a separate driver. This will enable add-in cards in the host OS as well as boot support in the PC BIOS with one Driver.

FEATURES

- Designed to IEEE1394 Open Host Controller Interface Specification
- IEEE1394-1995 Compliant, and Compatible with 1394A
- Compliant To Latest PCI Specification, Revision 2.1 and is PCI 2.2 ready
- PCI Power Management Compliant
- 3.3 Volt Core Logic with Universal PCI Interface Compatible with 3.3 Volt and 5 Volt PCI Signaling Environments

- Supports Serial Bus Data Rates of 100, 200, and 400Mbit/s
- Provides Bus Hold Buffers on Physical I/F for Low Cost Single Capacitor Isolation
- Supports Physical Write Posting of up to Three Outstanding Transactions
- Serial ROM Interface Supports 2-Wire Devices
- Supports External Cycle Timer Control for Customized Synchronization
- Implements PCI Burst Transfers and Deep FIFOs To Tolerate Large Host Latency
- Provides Four General Purpose I/Os
- Fabricated in Advanced Low-Power CMOS Process
- Packaged in 100 TQFP

OVERVIEW

The Texas Instruments OHCI-Lynx is a PCI-to-1394 host controller compatible with the latest PCI, IEEE1394, and 1394 OHCI Specifications. The chip provides the IEEE1394 link function, and is compatible with serial bus data rates of 100, 200, and 400 Mbits per second.

As required by the 1394 Open Host Controller Interface Specification, internal control registers are memory mapped and non-prefetchable. The PCI configuration header is accessed through configuration cycles specified by PCI, and provides Plug and Play compatibility. Furthermore, the OHCI-Lynx is compliant with the PCI Power Management Specification, per Microsoft's PC '98 requirements.

The OHCI-Lynx design provides PCI bus master bursting, and is capable of transferring a cacheline of data at 132Mbytes/sec after connection to the memory controller. Since PCI latency can be rather large even on a PCI Revision 2.1 system, deep FIFOs are provided to buffer 1394 data.

Physical write posting buffers are provided to enhance serial bus performance, and multiple isochronous channels are provided for simultaneous operation of real-time applications. The OHCI-Lynx also provides bus holding buffers on the phy/link interface for simple and cost effective single capacitor isolation.

BLOCK DIAGRAM

A simplified block diagram of the OHCI-Lynx is provided below.

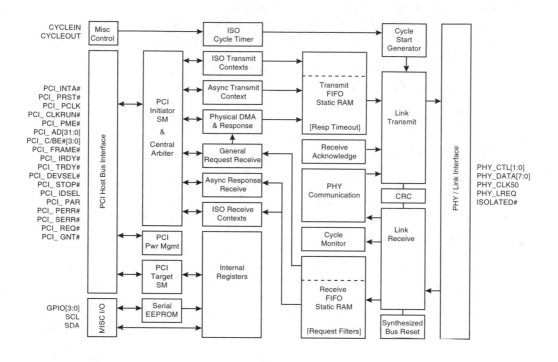

TSB41LV03

TI's newest Physical Layer is the first of many 400Mbps Physical Layers from Texas Instruments. The TSB41LV03 provides the bandwidth necessary to power the most demanding applications such as hard disk drives, hosts and multimedia peripherals. The TSB41LV03 has three 1394 ports, with the complete family supporting 2, 3, 4, and 6 port versions.

Appendix: Example 1394 Chip Solutions

FEATURES

- Supports IEEE 1394-1995 Standard for High Performance Serial Bus and 1394.A
- Provides Three Fully Compliant Cable Ports at 100/200/400 Megabits per Second (Mbit/s)
- Cable Ports Monitor Line Conditions for Active Connection to Remote Nodes
- Device Power-down Feature to Conserve Energy in Battery Powered Applications
- Inactive Ports Disabled to Save Power
- Logic Performs System Initialization and Arbitration Functions
- Encode and Decode Functions Included for Data-Strobe Bit Level Encoding
- Incoming Data Resynchronized to Local Clock
- Single 3.3 Volt Supply Operation
- Interface to Link Layer Controller Supports Optional Annex J Electrical Isolation and TIₜₘBus-Holder Isolation
- Data Interface to Link-Layer Controller Provided Through 2/4/8 Parallel Lines at 50 MHz
- 25-MHz Crystal Oscillator and PLL Provide Transmit, Receive Data at 100/200/400 Megabits per Second, and Link-Layer Controller Clock at 50 MHz
- Interoperable with 1394 Link-Layer Controllers Using 5-V Supplies
- Interoperable Across 1394 Cable with Physical Layers (PHY) Using 5-V Supplies
- Mode Power Class Information Signaling for System Power Management
- Cable Power Presence Monitoring
- Separate Cable Bias and Driver Termination Voltage Supply for Each Port
- Multiple Separate Package Terminals Provided for Analog and Digital Supplies and Grounds
- High Performance 80 Pin TQFP (PFP) Thermally Enhanced Package
- Register bits give software control of contender bits, power class bits, and 1394.A features

TSB41LV03 OVERVIEW

The TSB41LV03 provides the analog transceiver functions needed to implement a three port node in a cable-based IEEE 1394-1995 or IEEE-1394.A network. Each cable port incorporates two differential line transceivers. The transceivers include circuitry to monitor the line conditions as needed for determining connection status, for initialization and arbitration, and for packet reception and transmission. The TSB41LV03 is designed to interface with a Link Layer Controller (LLC), such as the TSB12LV22, TSB12LV21A, TSB12LV31, or TSB12C01A.

The TSB41LV03 requires an external 24.576 MHz crystal or crystal oscillator. The crystal oscillator drives an internal phase-locked loop (PLL), which generates the required 393.216 MHz reference signal. This reference signal is internally divided to provide the clock signals used to control transmission of the outbound encoded Strobe and Data information. A 49.152 MHz clock signal is supplied to the associated LLC for synchronization of the two chips and is used for resynchronization of the received data. The power-down (PD) function, when enabled by asserting the PD terminal high, stops operation of the PLL.

The TSB41LV03 supports an optional isolation barrier between itself and its LLC. When the /ISO input terminal is tied high, the LLC interface outputs behave normally. When the /ISO terminal is tied low, internal differentiating logic is enabled, and the outputs are driven such that they can be coupled through a capacitive or transformer galvanic isolation barrier as described in IEEE 1394-1995 Annex J. To operate with TI Bus Holder isolation the /ISO terminal must be tied high.

Data bits to be transmitted through the cable ports are received from the LLC on two, four or eight parallel paths (depending on the requested transmission speed) and are latched internally in the TSB41LV03 in synchronization with the 49.152 MHz system clock. These bits are combined serially, encoded, and transmitted at 98.304/196.608/392.216 Mbit/s as the outbound data-strobe information stream. During transmission, the encoded data information is transmitted differentially on the TPB cable pair(s), and the encoded strobe information is transmitted differentially on the TPA cable pair(s).

During packet reception the TPA and TPB transmitters of the receiving cable port are disabled, and the receivers for that port are enabled. The encoded data information is received on the TPA cable pair, and the encoded strobe information is received on the TPB cable pair. The received data-strobe information is decoded to recover the receive clock signal and the serial data bits. The serial data bits are split into two, four or eight bit parallel streams (depending upon the indicated receive speed), resynchronized to the local 49.152 MHz system clock and sent to the associated LLC. The received data is also transmitted (repeated) on the other active (connected) cable ports.

Both the TPA and TPB cable interfaces incorporate differential comparators to monitor the line states during initialization and arbitration. The outputs of these comparators are used by the internal logic to determine the arbitration status. The TPA channel monitors the incoming cable common-mode voltage. The value of this common-mode voltage is used during arbitration to set the speed of the next packet transmission. In addition, the TPB channel monitors the incoming cable common-mode voltage on the TPB pair for the presence of the remotely supplied twisted-pair bias voltage. The presence or absence of this common-mode voltage is used as an indication of cable connection status. The cable connection status signal is internally debounced in the TSB41LV03 and is used to initiate a bus-reset.

The TSB41LV03 provides a 1.86 Volt nominal bias voltage at the TPBIAS terminal for driver load termination. This bias voltage, when seen through a cable by a remote receiver, indicates the presence of an active connection. The value of this bias voltage has been chosen to allow interoperability between transceiver chips operating from either 5 volt nominal supplies or 3 volt nominal supplies. This bias voltage source must be stabilized by an external filter capacitor of approximately 1.0 mF.

The line drivers in the TSB41LV03 operate in a high-impedance current mode, and are designed to work with external 110W line-termination resistor networks. One network is provided at each end of a twisted-pair cable. Each network is composed of a pair of series-connected 55W resistors. The midpoint of the pair of resistors that is directly connected to the twisted pair A terminals is connected to the TPBIAS voltage terminal. The midpoint of the pair of resistors that is directly connected to the twisted-pair B terminals is coupled to ground through a parallel R-C network with recommended values of 5 KW and 250 pf. The values of the external line termination resistors are designed to meet the standard specifications when connected in parallel with the internal receiver circuits.

The driver output current, along with other internal operating currents, is set by an external resistor connected between the R0 and R1 terminals. This current setting resistor has a value of 6.3 KW, 0.5%.

The port transmitter and receiver circuitry is disabled during power-down (when the PD input terminal is asserted high), during reset (when the /RESET input terminal is asserted low), when no active cable is connected to the port, or as controlled by the internal arbitration logic. The port twisted pair bias voltage circuitry is disabled during power-down, during reset, or when the port is disabled as commanded by the LLC.

If the power supply of the TSB41LV03 is removed while the twisted pair cables are connected, then the TSB41LV03 transmitter and receiver circuitry will present a high impedance to the cable and will not load the TPBIAS voltage at the other end of the cable.

If the TSB41LV03 is being used with one or more of the ports not being brought out to a connector, the twisted pair terminals must be terminated for reliable operation. For each unused port, the TPB+ and TPB- terminals must be pulled to ground through the 5 KW resistor of the normal termination network, thus disabling the port. The TPA+, TPA-, and TPBIAS terminals of an unused port may be left unconnected.

The TESTM, SE, and SM terminals are used to set up various manufacturing test conditions. For normal operation, the TESTM terminal should be connected to Vcc, and the SE and SM terminals should be connected to ground.

Four package terminals are used as inputs to set the default value for four configuration status bits in the self-identification packet. These terminals are hard-wired high or low as a function of the equipment design. The PC[0:2] terminals are used to indicate the power-class status for the node (the need for power from the cable or the ability to supply power to the cable). The C/LKON terminal is used as an input to indicate whether the node is a contender for bus manager. The C input corresponds to the "c" field (bit 20) in the self-id packet, and PC[0:2] inputs correspond to the "pwr" field (bits 21, 22, and 23, respectively).

The PD (power-down) terminal is provided to allow a low power mode where most of the TSB41LV03 circuits are disabled to conserve energy in battery-powered applications. When the device is powered-down it does not act as a repeater.

The CNA (cable-not-active) terminal provides a high output when all twisted pair cable ports are disconnected, and can be used to determine when to power-down the TSB41LV03. The CNA output is not debounced. In power-down mode, the CNA detection circuitry remains enabled.

The LPS (link power status) terminal works with the C/LKON terminal to manage the power usage in the node. The LPS signal from the LLC indicates to the PHY that the LLC is powered up and active. During LLC power-down mode, as indicated by the LPS input being low for more than 2.56 ms, the TSB41LV03 deactivates the PHY-LLC interface to save power. The TSB41LV03 will continue the necessary repeater function required for network operation during this powered-down state.

If the PHY receives a link-on packet from another node, the C/LKON terminal is activated to output a 6.15MHz signal. The LLC recognizes this signal and reactivates the powered-down portions of the LLC. After power-up of the LLC, the LLC notifies the PHY of the power-on status via the LPS terminal. The PHY confirms notification by deactivating the 6.114 MHz signal on the C/LKON terminal, then enables the PHY-link interface.

Block Diagram

A simplified block diagram of the TSB41LV03 is shown below.

block diagram

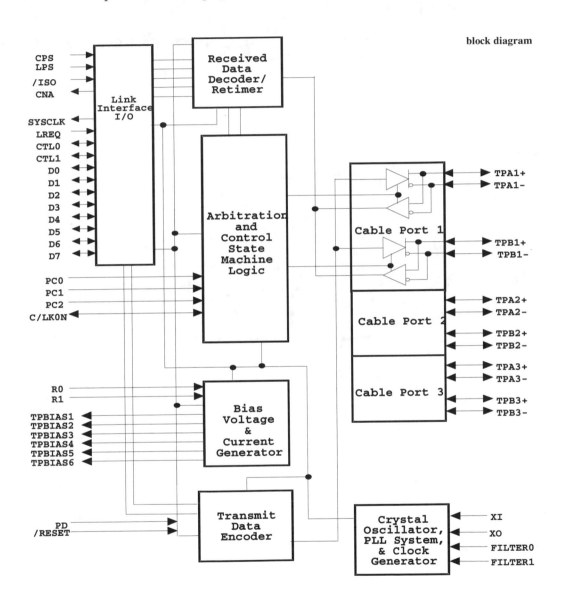

Putting it all Together

Below is a detailed block diagram of using the TSB12LV22/OHCI-Lynx and
TSB41LV03 together to provide a 1394 interface for a PC.

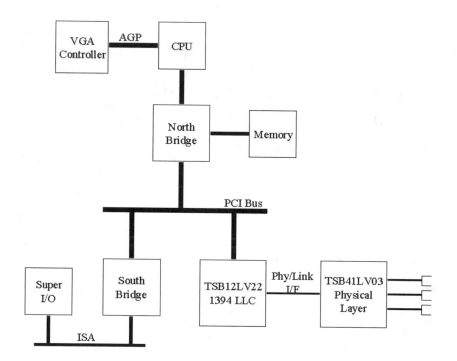

1394 in the Digital Camera

TI also provides all the 1394 silicon necessary to build a 1394 Digital Camera. TI even offers a 1394 Digital Camera design featuring the TSB12LV31 Link Layer and TSB21LV03A Physical Layer devices. The next section will provide you information on the Link and Physical layers included in this design and we will finish up with a detailed block diagram of the camera itself.

TSB12LV31 – GPLynx

The industry's first general purpose link layer controller was produced to provide a flexible, low cost way for designers of consumer electronics and computer peripheral equipment to implement 1394 in their designs. Consumer electronics vendors in digital cameras, televisions, CD players, tape decks and more are using the TSB12LV31 in their designs.

Features

- Supports IEEE 1394-1995 Standard for High-Performance Serial Bus
- Fully Interoperable with FireWire Implementation of 1394
- Compatible with Texas Instruments TSB11LV01 and TSB21LV03 Physical Layer Controllers (Phys)
- Single 3.3-V supply operation with 5-V Tolerant Capabilities using 5-V Bias Terminals
- High-performance 100-Pin PZ (S–PQFP–G100) package.
- Programmable Microcontroller Interface with 8-Bit or 16-Bit Data Bus, Three Modes of Operation, and Clock Frequency to 50 Mhz
- 50-quadlet (200-Byte) FIFO Accessed Through Microcontroller Interface Supports Asynchronous and Isochronous Operations
- Programmable FIFO Size For Asynchronous Transmit FIFO and General-Receive FIFO
- Single-Channel Support for Isochronous Transmit from Unbuffered 8-Bit Isochronous Port (IsoPort)
- Isochronous Receive to FIFO or to Unbuffered 8-Bit IsoPort
- Isochronous Header Synchronous-Bit Detection on Receive
- Automatically Reports IRM NODE_ID and Verifies Automatic 1394 Self-ID
- Supports Transfer Rates of 100 Mbits/s and 200 Mbits/s
- Asynchronous Packet Reception to Internal FIFO (Accessed Through the Microcontroller Interface)
- Asynchronous Packet Transmission from Internal FIFO (Accessed Through

the Microcontroller Interface)
- Generation of External Microcontroller Clock from SCLK (SCLK/4)
- Generation of 32-Bit Cyclic Redundancy Check (CRC) for Transmission of 1394 Packets
- 32-Bit CRC Checking on Reception of 1394 Packets

Overview

The TSB12LV31 performs bidirectional asynchronous/isochronous data transfers to and from an IEEE 1394-1995 serial bus physical layer (phy) device. The TSB12LV31 is tailored and optimized for use as a peripheral link-layer controller (LLC). TSB12LV31 asynchronous and isochronous operations are summarized as follows:

TSB12LV31 asynchronous transmit: From asynchronous transmit FIFO (ATF)

TSB12LV31 asynchronous receive: To general receive FIFO (GRF)

TSB12LV31 isochronous transmit: From 8-bit IsoPort

TSB12LV31 isochronous receive: To 8 bit IsoPort, To GRF, or To 8-bit IsoPort and To GRF

Appendix: Example 1394 Chip Solutions

Block Diagram

A simplified block diagram of the TSB12LV31 is provided below.

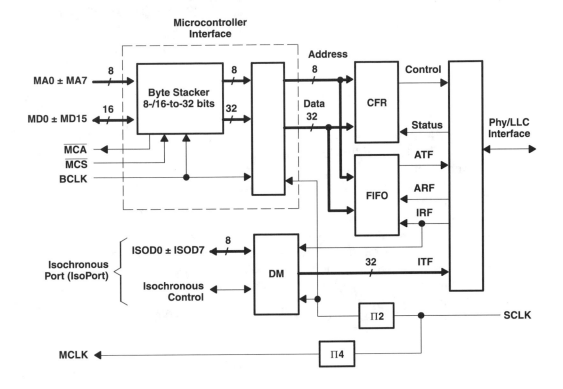

TSB21LV03A

The TSB21LV03A is a 200M/bps, 3-port device capable of sending and receiving data at 100 and 200Mbps. A few applications that the TSB21LV03A targets include host adapters, motherboards, and computer peripherals, and digital cameras and camcorders.

FEATURES

- Supports Provisions of IEEE 1394-1995 Standard for High Performance Serial Bus
- Fully Interoperable with FireWire Implementation of IEEE 1394-1995
- Provides Three Fully Compliant Cable Ports at 100/200 Megabits per Second (Mbits/s)
- Cable Ports Monitor Line Conditions for Active Connection to Remote Node Device Power-Down Feature to Conserve Energy in Battery-Powered Applications
- Inactive Ports Disabled to Save Power
- Logic Performs System Initialization and Arbitration Functions
- Encode and Decode Functions Included for Data-Strobe Bit-Level Encoding
- Incoming Data Resynchronized to Local Clock
- Single 3.3-V Supply Operation
- Interface to Link-Layer Controller Supports TI Bus-Holder Isolation
- Data Interface to Link-Layer Controller Provided Through 2/4 Parallel Lines at 50 MHz
- 25-MHz Crystal Oscillator and PLL Provide Transmit/Receive Data at 100/200 Mbits/s, and Link-Layer Controller Clock at 50 MHz
- Interoperable with 1394 Link-Layer Controllers Using 5-V Supplies
- Interoperable Across 1394 Cable with 1394 Physical Layers (Phy) Using 5-V Supplies
- Node Power-Class Information Signaling for System Power Management
- Cable Power Presence Monitoring
- Separate Cable Bias and Driver Termination Voltage Supply for Each Port
- High Performance 64-Pin TQFP (PM) Package

Appendix: Example 1394 Chip Solutions

BLOCK DIAGRAM

A simplified block diagram of the TSB21LV03A is shown below.

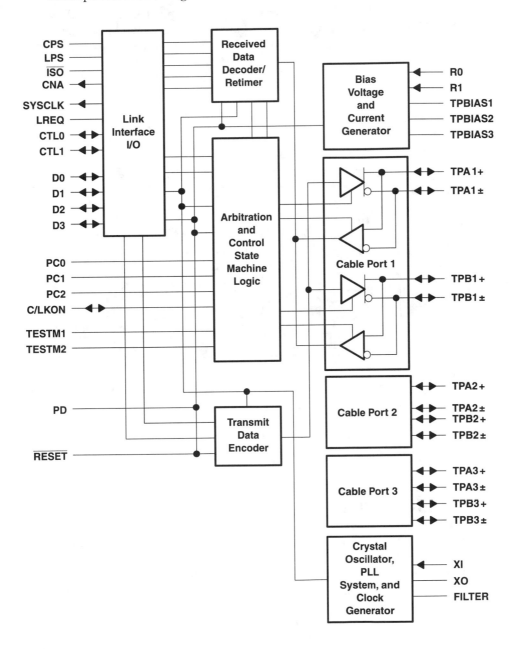

Putting it all Together

Below is a detailed block diagram of using the TSB12LV31-GPLynx and TSB21LV03A together in a 1394 digital camera application. Please note the 1394 Cable connecting to a PC, which we discussed previously.

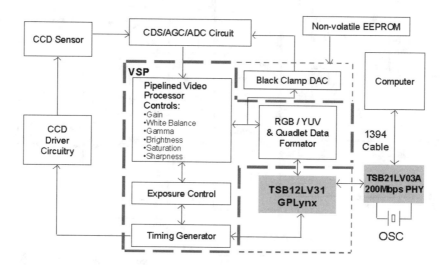

For More Information

To receive information on the full line of Texas Instruments 1394 Silicon, please visit our website at http://www.ti.com/sc/1394. You can download the latest datasheets, browse our FAQ section, and even subscribe to our newsletter.

Appendix: Glossary

acknowledge accelerated arbitration — an arbitration technique that permits a node that is returning an acknowledge packet to concatenate a new subaction to the acknowledge packet, without having to wait for the next subaction gap prior to sending a fair request.

acknowledge gap — the period of serial bus idle time during an asynchronous subaction between the request or response packet transmission and the return of the acknowledge packet. This is a short gap.

acknowledge packet — the packet returned by a target node to verify receipt of either a request or response packet during an asynchronous transaction.

arbitration — the process of determining which node will be granted ownership of the serial bus and transmit the next packet.

arbitration comparators — part of the bus interface used to detect the state of the twisted pair signals. The possible line states are Z, 0, and 1.

arbitration reset gap — a period of bus idle time that identifies the boundary between two fairness intervals. The arbitration reset gap re-enables all nodes to resume fair arbitration.

arbitration signaling — a signaling environment that permits identification of the line states of twisted pair A (TPA) and twisted pair B (TPB). The encoding of these two line states defines a particular event during serial bus arbitration time.

asynchronous packet — a packet used during asynchronous transaction time.

asynchronous transaction — a transaction performed during the fairness interval that is used by the application that does not require guaranteed bus bandwidth and can tolerate long latencies between data transfers.

base rate — the slowest transmission rate supported by the serial bus cable environment (100Mb/s).

broadcast address — the highest node ID (3Fh) that specifies that the corresponding transaction is a broadcast address.

bus management layer — the protocol layer and associated services that are employed to control the other serial bus layers (PHY, link, and transactions layers). The bus management layer also provides support for the isochronous resource manager and bus management nodes that monitor and control serial bus resources (e.g. bus power, bus optimization, and allocation of resources).

cable environment — an IEEE 1394 environment that employs cables to connect serial bus nodes versus the backplane implementation.

channel number — a number obtained by isochronous capable nodes that is used as a simplified form of addressing. This permits an isochronous transaction to be multicast to a collection of nodes (isochronous listeners) wishing to obtain isochronous data from a given serial bus talker.

concatenated transactions — two sequential packets delivered across the serial bus that have no idle time or gap between them, thereby allowing the second packet to be sent without requiring bus arbitration. This increased overall bus bandwidth is due to elimination of idle and arbitration time.

CSR architecture — the common term used to identify the bus architecture defined by the ISO/IEC 13213 specification.

cycle master — a root node responsible for initiating each isochronous interval (~125µs) by transmitting a cycle start packet.

cycle start — the beginning of an isochronous interval (initiated by the cycle master node), which notifies all isochronous capable nodes that they may begin arbitration to transmit their isochronous transactions.

cycle synchronization — a clock event that occurs at regular 125µs intervals and signals time to begin the next isochronous interval. During an isochronous interval each pending isochronous transaction is performed one time.

doublet — two bytes.

dribble bits — bits added to the end of packet transmission to ensure that packet contents get clocked through the receive circuitry. This is necessary because the receive clock is derived from the incoming data/strobe signals, and the end of packet terminates receive clock generation, otherwise leaving data in the receive circuitry. Dribble bits (just used to generate receive clocks) are added to ensure that actual packet data is flushed through the receive circuitry.

fairness interval — a non-specific period of serial bus time required for all nodes to arbitrate and complete one asynchronous subaction. Once a node has completed one subaction it disables all further fair arbitration until the next fairness interval begins (following the next arbitration reset gap).

fly-by arbitration — an arbitration technique that allows a repeating node to concatenate a subaction to either an isochronous packet or acknowledge packet that is heading toward the root node, without having to wait for the next subaction gap or isochronous gap.

force root bit — a bit within each node that forces it to delay participation in the tree ID process, which is designed to force this node to become the root.

gap — a period of bus idle time between packets. (see acknowledge gap, isochronous gap, and arbitration reset gap).

initial register space — a range of node address space defined and reserved for use immediately following a bus reset. This space contains registers and configuration ROM entries needed to configure and enable a serial bus node.

initialization phase — the phase entered by all PHY during a bus reset. This phase initializes each node in preparation for bus reconfiguration. See also tree ID and self ID.

IRM — see isochronous resource manager

isochronous arbitration — arbitration that begins following the cycle start packet for all nodes that have pending isochronous transactions to perform. This arbitration begins following isochronous gap timing.

isochronous gap — the period of bus idle prior to isochronous arbitration (e.g. time between isochronous transactions). This is a short gap.

isochronous interval — the bus interval during which isochronous transactions are performed (~125μs).

isochronous listener — a node wishing to accept isochronous data for a given channel number.

isochronous resource manager — a single node residing on the IEEE 1394 bus that provides services for all isochronous capable nodes, including isochronous channel allocation and bus bandwidth allocation.

isochronous talker — a node that transmits isochronous transactions using a given channel number and guaranteed bus bandwidth.

isochronous transaction — transmission of an isochronous packet. Unlike asynchronous transactions there is no accompanying acknowledgment or response from the target.

link — short for link layer.

link layer — the protocol layer responsible for the interface between the transaction and physical layers for asynchronous transactions and between the application and physical layer for isochronous transactions. The link layer builds packets during transmission and generates CRC, and during packet reception it decodes packets and performs data checking.

lock request packet — initiates a lock transaction by passing argument and data values to the target node.

lock response packet — sent by the target node to report completion status of the lock operation and to return the old data value from the target location. Note that the old data value equals the current data value if the lock fails.

lock transaction — a transaction consisting of a lock request and lock response that ensures that only one node be granted access to the addressed node locations while an atomic (indivisible) operation is being performed.

module — a physical package that implements one or more 1394 nodes. A module represents a replaceable unit on the serial bus.

node — as addressable device attached to the serial bus that fulfills the minimum set of requirements needed for configuration and control. Up to 63 nodes are allowed on a single serial bus.

node controller — an element within each node used to coordinate node management activities. See bus management.

node ID — a unique 16-bit number (10-bit bus number and 6-bit node address) that identifies each node in a system. Node IDs with the upper 10-bits matching the bus number field targets a node on this local bus. (Note that all nodes on a single bus must have their bus number set to the same value.) The node address target one of 63 possible nodes residing on the target bus.

non return to zero — abbreviated NRZ, this encoding technique converts bi-polar data into a digital form where positive and negative transitions stay high or low respectively, and do not return to zero until a transition occurs in the other direction.

NRZ — abbreviation for non return to zero.

octlet — eight bytes of data.

PHY — abbreviation for physical layer.

PHY configuration packet — a packet broadcast to all PHYs on the bus to adjust gap timing and to set or clear a node's force root bit.

physical layer — abbreviated PHY, the protocol layer that provides the physical interface to the serial bus. This layer provides the interface between the link layer and serial bus cable. The physical layer converts the commands and digital data received from the link layer and converts them into electrical signals used by the serial bus during transmission, and vice versa during packet reception.

port — the point of physical connection between a PHY and the serial bus cable.

priority arbitration — a form of asynchronous arbitration that permits a node to initiate a subaction even though it has already completed one subaction during this fairness interval. Used only by the cycle master (per 1995 version of the specification), but allowed by other nodes in the 1394a supplement.

protocol layers — an abstraction of the functions required to pass data between two IEEE 1394 applications. Each layer describes functionality needed by the 1394 protocol and includes the transaction layer, link layer, and physical layer.

quadlet — an aligned four bytes of data.

repeater — PHY function required to pass serial bus traffic between ports on multi-port nodes.

request — a subaction used to initiate a transaction.

request subaction — the portion of a transaction used to initiate a transaction that targets a given node. The request subaction defines the type of transaction (read, write, or lock) if it is an asynchronous transfer. Compare response subaction.

response — a subaction used to report completion status to the requesting node.

response subaction — a subaction sent by a node, which has been targeted by a previous request, to deliver completion status that includes a response code and data for read and lock requests. Compare request subaction.

self identification (ID) — part of the bus configuration process. Each PHY enters the self ID state following tree ID during bus configuration. During this state all PHYs assign themselves a physical node ID and transmit their self-ID packets.

self ID packet — a packet send by each node as part of the self-ID process that occurs during bus configuration. Self-ID packets contain information characterizing certain serial bus parameters and requirements associated with each node.

short gap — a period of idle time that is detected after 0.04 - 0.05µs. This gap timing is defined for both isochronous gaps and acknowledge gaps.

speed code — a code included in the self-ID packet that defines the maximum speed capabilities of a PHY.

speed signaling — the mechanism used by repeating nodes to report the transmission speed of the upcoming packet.

split transaction — a transaction that consists of separate request and response subactions. Compare isochronous and unified transaction.

subaction gap — a period of bus idle time prior to asynchronous arbitration (e.g. between asynchronous subactions).

subaction — a request or response packet and the corresponding acknowledge packet.

transaction — a complete transfer of information from one application to another across the serial bus. Transactions consist of single packets for isochronous transactions and two or four packets for asynchronous packets.

transaction layer — the protocol layer that provides the interface between an asynchronous application and the link layer. This layer provides the request/response protocol used by the serial bus. Note that the transaction layer is not used for isochronous transactions.

tree identification (ID) — part of the bus configuration process that is used to identify the root node and the corresponding bus topology.

unified transaction — an asynchronous write request that integrates the response into the acknowledge packet, thereby eliminating the need for a separate response subaction.

unit architecture — a document that describes a software protocol for a particular type of application. These documents define registers, ROM entries, data formats, and software functions for a given application. For example, Serial Bus Protocol 2 (SBP2) is defined for mass storage devices.

Index

Index

Index

isochronous resource manager, power management 342
isochronous resource manager, requirements 335
isochronous resources, reallocation of 342
isochronous stream packet 199
isochronous transaction layer services 80
isochronous transaction summary 202
isochronous transaction, example 63
isochronous transactions 39, 44
isochronous transfers 15, 32, 38, 41, 78

K

key_type 418
key_value 418

L

line state decode 108
line states 105
link layer 42, 47
Link/PHY interface 222
Link/PHY interface, PHY reg access 241
Link/PHY interface, PHY status 238
Link/PHY interface, receiving packets 236
linkoff 368
link-on packet 205, 212, 346, 354
lock packet 183
lock request packet 184
lock response packet 189
lock transactions 183
lock types 186
lock, compare and swap 338
locked transaction 30, 31
long reset 279
looped topology 304
looped topology detection 304
lost 365

M

MAINT_CONTROL register 386
MAINT_UTILITY register 386
make first/break last pins 87
MAX_ARB_STATE_TIME 274, 283
MAX_DATA_TIME 357

max_rec 413
maximum packet size 40
message broadcasts 34
minimal ROM format 33
module 25
Module_Vendor_Id entry 419
multiple buses 17
multi-speed concatenation 159

N

node 25
node attachment detect 97
node attachment/detachment 275
node state 366
Node_Capabilities entry 419
NODE_IDS register 369
NODE_POWER_CONTROL register 464
Node_Power_Directory entry 473
Node_Power_Level entry 474
Node_Power_Management Entry 475
Node_Unique_Id 414
Node_Unique_Id entry 419, 420
node_vendor_id 414
nodecast 375
non-return to zero 56, 123
NOTIFICATION_ADDRESS register 466
NRZ 56, 123
null isochronous packet 201

O

OHCI specification 20
Organizationally Unique Identifier (OUI) 423

P

packet acknowledgment 52
packet error handling 259
packet errors 259
packet size 40
packet transmission errors 259
Parent_Notify 286
partially managed bus 343
peer-to-peer transactions 17, 24
PHY configuration packet 205, 213, 354, 397

Index